C000235896

LEWIS FOREMAN DAY
(1845 - 1910)

UNITY IN DESIGN AND INDUSTRY

LEWIS FOREMAN DAY
(1845 - 1910)

UNITY IN DESIGN AND INDUSTRY

Joan Maria Hansen

ANTIQUE COLLECTORS' CLUB

ISBN: 978-1-85149-534-4

British Library Cataloguing-in-Publication Data
A catalogue record for this book is available from the British Library

Frontispiece. Lewis F. Day. 'Indian', 1909. Made by Turnbull & Stockdale for Liberty & Co. Contemporary reproduction, renamed 'Dante', made by Liberty & Co. © Liberty PLC. With permission

Title page. Lewis F. Day. 'Iris' tile. Made by Pilkington's Tile & Pottery Co. Shown at the Paris Exposition Universelle 1900 and at the Glasgow Exhibition 1901, where it was described as a "cloisonné tile in coloured glazes" (*Pilkington Catalogue 1900*: 23, 25, 34; *Pilkington Catalogue 1901*: 36-7)
Pilkington's Lancastrian Pottery Society

Endpapers. Lewis F. Day. 'Mortimer' wallpaper, 1896. Made by Jeffrey & Co.
Southwark Art Collection, London, PT0792

Origination by the Antique Collectors' Club Ltd., Woodbridge, Suffolk, England
Printed and bound in China

Lewis F. Day. Clock, oak case with painted dial and tiles. Retailed by Howell & James. Shown at the Paris Exposition Universelle in 1878
Private Collection. Photography, Peter Hughes

ACKNOWLEDGEMENTS

My passion for Lewis F. Day and his work has been sustained over the long haul by the support of others who have had an unshakeable belief in this project. Friends and colleagues have generously given of their time and knowledge, reviewed parts of the manuscript or images, or in other ways have kept me on track: Ralph Adron, Lesley Hoskins, Marianne Houle, Nina Koziol, Martin Levy, Barbara Morris, Pat Murphy, Nancy Owen, Linda Parry, Peter Rose, Marianne Ruggiero, Ruth Ann Saul, Susan T. Swannell, and Ron Woollacott. This book has benefited greatly from their suggestions and insights. Any errors or omissions are, of course, my own. My family has been unstinting in their love and support: My parents Charles and Leona Malin; my son Eric; and my sisters and their families: Marianne, Paul and Charlie Houle; Nancy and Jack Nicolosi, and Jack, Jr. My deep thanks to all of you for helping to make this book happen.

Piecing together Day's story has been an adventure requiring the prolonged and laborious ferreting out of primary source information. Detective work has taken me to many organisations and institutions that have provided valuable clues: Akzo Nobel Decorative Coatings Ltd.; Art Institute, Chicago; Art Workers' Guild; Arthur Sanderson Ltd.; Berkshire Record Office; H. Blairman & Sons Ltd.; Bridgeman Art Library; Brintons Ltd.; British Library; British Newspaper Library, Colindale; British Museum; Bury Art Gallery and Museum; Camden Local Studies and Archives Centre; Central Library, Bury; Cheltenham Art Gallery and Museums; Christ Church, Streatham; Church of St. Mary the Virgin, Great Dunmow, Essex; The Albert Dawson Trust; The Decorative Arts Society; Essex Record Office; Family Division of the Royal Courts of Justice; Family Records Centre, Islington; The Fine Art Society; Friends House Library; Geffrye Museum; Guildhall Library; Hanley Reference Library, Staffordshire County Council; Haslam & Whiteway Ltd.; Holborn Library, Camden; Ironbridge Gorge Museum Trust; Liberty PLC; London Metropolitan Archives; Manchester Central Library; Manchester City Galleries, Gallery of Costume and Manchester Art Gallery; Manchester Metropolitan University, Sir Kenneth Green Library, All Saints; Merchant Taylors' School, Northwood, Middlesex; National Archives, Kew; National Library of Scotland; Newberry Library, Chicago; Nordiska Museet, Stockholm; Old Merchant Taylors' Society; Pilkington's Lancastrian Pottery Society; Pilkington's Tiles Ltd.; Potteries Museum and Art Gallery, Stoke-on-Trent; PRD Photography; Paul Reeves; Religious Society of Friends in Britain; Royal College of Art Library; Royal Commission on Historical Manuscripts; Royal Pavilion Art Gallery and Museums; Ryerson and Burnham Libraries, Art Institute of Chicago; The John Rylands Library; Shropshire Records and Research Centre; W.B. Simpson & Sons Ltd.; Society of Antiquaries of London; South London Gallery; Southwark Local Studies Library; Tiles & Architectural Ceramics Society; Turnbull & Stockdale; University of Manchester; Victoria and Albert Museum (Archive of Art and Design; Museum Archive and Registry; National Art Library; V&A Images; and the following V&A departments: Ceramics and Glass; Furniture, Textiles and Fashion; Metalwork, Silver and Jewellery; Research; and Word and Image); Victorian Society; Watts of Westminster; Westminster Archives; Westminster Reference Library; Whitworth Art Gallery, University of Manchester; and Woodward Grosvenor. To all, I express my hearty thanks.

Along the way many people have generously given assistance and advice, among them: Rev. Canon and Mrs. David Ainge; Stella Beddoe; Jeremy W. Birch; Chris Blanchett; Geoffrey K. Brandwood; Virginia Brisco; Richard Bryers; Richard Burns; John

R. Burrows; Anthony Burton; Lawrence Burton; Anna Buruma; Sylvia Carlyle; Simon Carter; Michael Clark; Max Clendinning; Frances Collard; Angela and Barry Corbett; Anthony J. Cross; Judith Crouch; Gwynn and Vera Davies; John Davis; Paulo R. De Andrea; David Dewing; Max Donnelly; Ian Dungavell; Helen Dunstan; Bjorn Edlund; Berit Eldvik; Virginia Ennor; Louise Falcini; Fiona Flint; Aiden Flood; Peter Foden; Arlene Furlong; the late Albert Gallichan; Chris Giles; Alun Graves; Mary Greensted; Terry Griffiths; Janice Hack; Nick Harling; Colin Harris; Jennifer Harris; Penny Haworth; Roger Hensman; Tony Herbert; Malcolm Holmes; Kathryn Huggins; Peter Hughes; Peter Inch; Anthea Jarvis; Paul Johnson; Christopher Jordan; Bonnie Martinez Keating; Sue Kerry; Frederika Launert; Hans van Lemmen; Nancy Loader; Terence Lockett; Louise McCarron; Elaine Morris; Gillian Naylor; Bernard Nurse; Andrew McIntosh Patrick; John Powell; Frances Pritchard; Paul Reeves; Judith Rogerson; Judy Rudoe; Sheri Sandler; Ruth Shrigley; Susan M. Smee; Deborah Skinner; Gaye Smith; Joanne Smith; Yvonne Smith; Elisabet Stavenow-Hidemark; Page Talbott; David Thompson; Edward Turnbull; John Uriell; Stan Valler; Jane Wainwright; Tracey Walker; Kit Wedd; Eva White; Michael Whiteway; Christine Woods and Paul Yeowell. If I have accidentally failed to mention someone, I apologise and extend my sincere appreciation. For materials that may still be in copyright, every effort has been made to secure permissions for reproduction. If we have failed to trace a copyright holder, we ask that the publisher be notified.

Finally, my deep appreciation goes to Diana Steel and Mark Eastment for believing in this project and making it a reality, and to the superb team at Antique Collectors' Club, especially Susannah Hecht, Craig Holden, Tom Conway, Stephen Mackinlay and Richard Weale.

Thank you all.

Dedication

To Eric,
who has taught me more than he will ever know

CONTENTS

FOREWORD

To any admirer of nineteenth century British design, the name of Lewis F. Day is already familiar. As an author, journalist, art educator, design reformer and critic he had few equals. As a designer there was no one more versatile in the range of objects to which he turned his attention, and few who could match his ability to produce worthwhile designs. Lucie Armstrong, writing in the *Art Journal* in 1891, described this particularly well, when she wrote: "Mr. Lewis Day does not rush to meet every new fashion but tries to produce designs of intrinsic merit."

Day's success as a designer was greatly helped by his close involvement in, and knowledge of, British industry and an awareness of the benefits and restrictions of particular techniques. He was also an astute observer of the artistic needs of his own time and chided manufacturers who followed fashion for its own sake. With the fervour of a religious zealot he claimed that good design could not be compromised by passing fancies, but should be based on a sound knowledge of what had gone before. Yet it was his battle, alongside a number of his contemporaries, to raise the status of the designer within the world of art and manufacture at the end of the nineteenth century that is probably his lasting monument. As a leading member of the Society of Arts, the Society of Illustrators, a significant founder member of The Fifteen, the Art Workers' Guild and the Arts and Crafts Exhibition Society, he helped change attitudes towards the decorative arts in Britain, raising them to a level of influence not seen before and one that has endured almost intact to this day.

So, with such a string of achievements to his name and a high level of recognition within his own time, how is it that little is known about Day in the present century? Why is he no longer as greatly valued as such contemporaries as William Morris, Christopher Dresser, Walter Crane or C.F.A. Voysey? This has much to do with the fashion for judging the past by the criteria of the present. Unlike contemporaries, Day was neither eccentric nor bohemian in the manner in which he worked and, by all accounts, had a happy and conventional personal life. In retrospect, all this has worked against him and he is not as widely recognised as he deserves.

Furthermore, his abiding interest in industrial art, in an age that has returned to admire hand craftsmanship above all else, has also meant that his legacy is not fully appreciated. In truth he was an uncompromising perfectionist in all things, believing that hard work provided the route to success. Serious and business-like, it is no wonder that he was unpopular with many fellow designers, many of whom are celebrated now more for their lifestyles than their work. By contrast, how many of them can boast of affecting major changes in art education and, through his teaching and own studio practice, of influencing generations of young students and designers?

After an extended period of neglect, the importance of Victorian design has at last been reinstated with names such as Morris and Mackintosh, for instance, now used to describe popular and widely recognised furnishing styles. However, recounting the development of design and manufacture in Britain is, of course, more complex and infinitely more interesting than any room setting. This book, the first comprehensive biography of Day, helps redress the balance by describing the life and career of one of the artistic giants of the age, placing him firmly at the centre of one of the most internationally influential periods of design and manufacture of modern times.

Linda Parry

PREFACE

"It is so long since, and the years fall like rain. Drop by drop they blur and wipe out every trace of the steps by which it might once have been possible to track the secrets of the past."
[Lewis F. Day, 1893]

I never set out to write a book on Lewis Foreman Day. I wanted to *buy* one. In preparation for teaching a seminar on 19th-century interior design at the Newberry Library in Chicago, I searched for a book on Day and – to my utter disbelief – found none. It seemed incomprehensible that while the life and work of his colleagues and friends William Morris, Walter Crane, C.F. A. Voysey and others had been documented, Day's story had not yet been told. While sympathetic to my vociferous complaints about the lack of a book on him, colleagues retorted: "Write one".

I kept 'bumping into' Day unexpectedly: in his wallpaper in a suburban hotel, in the fabric pattern of a tote bag carried by a fellow bus traveller, in copies of his books, sent unannounced by a book dealer friend who thought I "just might want to read them"... The beauty of Day's furnishings, his clear, practical writing, and his deep convictions about the rôle of the designer for industry resonated with me. I was moved by his poignant observation that the achievements of those who have preceded us are often washed away by time. Day deserved a better fate.

So this book is the offspring of Necessity and Serendipity, born after ten years of gestation. A book is sometimes regarded as the culmination of a scholar's work on a particular subject, and in one sense that is accurate. For me, however, this book is one milestone in my continuing exploration of Day's life and work. Hopefully, it marks the beginning of the reader's own adventure with Day, for more of his tiles, furniture, textiles and other furnishings are yet to be discovered. The thrill of the chase goes on.

LEWIS . F. DAY. MASTER.A.W.G.1897.

E.R Hughes Del: 1900.

CHAPTER ONE: THE LIFE OF LEWIS FOREMAN DAY (1845-1910)

"You can trace in a man's work the influence of his travel, of his reading, of any great experience through which he has passed." [Lewis F. Day, 1908]

One of Lewis Foreman Day's earliest and most vivid memories was a visit to the Great Exhibition of 1851 in London when he was about six years old.[1] As he gazed at the wonders of manufacture, he could not have imagined that years later his own designs for textiles, wallpaper, ceramics and furniture would be shown at virtually all the major trade and industrial exhibitions of the late 19th and early 20th centuries. This child, filled "with the glow of that enthusiasm which the first world's fair excited", grew up to be a major figure in 19th-century design, with a passionate commitment to the marriage of design and industry.[2] His friendships with colleagues William Morris, Walter Crane and others situated him in the vortex of developments in the history of design. He was significantly involved in the major design movements of the day: the Aesthetic Movement, the Arts and Crafts Movement and Art Nouveau. A writer and critic, his magazine articles were read by professionals and the public alike, and his textbooks on design influenced students around the world. How all this happened can only be understood in light of his family circumstances, philosophical and religious influences on his upbringing, and his education – all of which helped form his personality and influenced his professional practice.

1.1 (opposite) Edward Robert Hughes. Lewis Foreman Day (1845-1910), Master of the Art Workers' Guild in 1897. Portrait, 1900. Red chalk on paper
© The Art Workers' Guild Trustees Limited, London/ Bridgeman Art Library

1.2 'Scene in the Interior of the Great Exhibition'. From *The Crystal Palace and Its Contents: Being an Illustrated Cyclopaedia of the Great Exhibition of the Industry of All Nations* (London: W. M. Clark, 1851-2): 41
Newberry Library, Chicago

1.3 'The Medieval Court'. From *The Crystal Palace and Its Contents: Being an Illustrated Cyclopaedia of the Great Exhibition of the Industry of All Nations* (London: W. M. Clark, 1851-2): 217
Newberry Library, Chicago

PART 1: BEGINNINGS (1845-1873)

Family background and early formative influences

December of 1844 was the culmination of a tumultuous year for Samuel Hulme Day. In the previous twelve months he had relocated his large family from Essex to London, established himself in a new business, and with his wife Mary Ann awaited the arrival of their ninth child. In a rare idle moment he may well have shaken his head in wonder at the seismic shift that had taken place in his life.

Samuel Hulme Day (1805-1876), of Stansted Mountfitchet, Essex, had married Mary Ann Lewis (1812-1895) on 25 September, 1834 at St. Clement Danes Church, London.[3] She was the daughter of Lewis Lewis, a wine merchant in the City of London and of Welsh ancestry. The couple settled near Braintree, Essex, where Samuel was a banker and later a magistrate of the County of Essex. Their family circle expanded rapidly, with six daughters and two sons arriving at almost yearly intervals: Mary Louisa (1835-1841), Isabela Ann (b.1836), Emily de Mountenay (b.1838), Barclay Lewis (b.1839), Agnes Kate (b.1840), Clara (b.1841), Mary Louisa (b.1842) and Sydney Townshend (b.1844).

In early 1844 the Days moved to London and, like his father-in-law, Samuel Hulme Day became a wine merchant in the City of London. He established his business at 21 Pudding Lane, Eastcheap, from where he would conduct his trade with the Continent for over thirty years,

1.4 St. Clement Danes Church, Strand, London. From *Magazine of Art* 3 (1880): 447

first as Claridge & Day, then, from 1847, as Samuel Hulme Day & Co. The family settled at No. 12 Rye Terrace in Peckham Rye, near Mary Ann's father, who lived at No. 4.[4] Peckham Rye, then in Surrey, was on the southeast outskirts of London. The terrace houses, which had been built in 1827, overlooked the wide expanse of Rye Common.[5] In addition to its pleasant surroundings and proximity to his wife's family, Peckham had the advantage of being within an hour's carriage ride from Samuel's business.

Born on 29 January, 1845, Lewis Foreman Day – Samuel and Mary Ann's ninth child and third son – had the double distinction of being the first of their children to be born in London and the offspring who would become the most famous in environs far beyond Peckham Rye. Lewis Foreman was named after his maternal grandfather and great-grandfather, both of whom bore the name Lewis Lewis; the reason for his middle name of Foreman is unclear. Several of the Day children had middle names that do not appear elsewhere in family records, and it is possible that they were named after friends or business associates of Samuel Hulme Day.

In late 1851 the family moved down the street to a detached house on a larger plot of land. Beaufort House, as it came to be known, provided more room for their expanding family as well as accommodating three or four servants.[6] By this time Mary Ann had given birth to four more children: Alice Mary (b.1846), Augustus Taylor (b.1847), Florence Edith (b.1849, d.1849) and Arthur Beaumont (b.1850).

When the Days settled in Peckham Rye, part of the parish of Camberwell, it was largely rural, with its ancient common, pastures and market gardens. During their childhood, Lewis and his siblings witnessed advances in transportation and speculative building that dramatically altered the bucolic landscape. The development of the Grand Surrey Canal in 1826 had encouraged settlement, and the pace of residential and business growth accelerated from the 1850s.

1.5 Rye Common, c.1840
Southwark Art Collection, London, GA0314

1.6 Peckham Rye, 2006. Formerly called Rye Terrace, the southern end of the terrace included No. 12, in which Day was born

Photography: Ron Woollacott

An omnibus service – horse-drawn vehicles operating on set schedules with standardised fares – began running between Peckham and the West End in 1851; and by 1862 the railways had come. Despite rapid changes in the larger world around them, the Day children grew up in a family that, while not wealthy, was very stable. Both their father's steady self-employment in his wine business and the residence at Beaufort House anchored the family for over thirty years. This stable home life and self-employment as modelled by his father were to be mirrored in Lewis Day's adult life.

Economic, philosophical and religious influences

Faced with the financial pressures and practical challenges of raising thirteen children – eleven of whom survived early childhood – Samuel Hulme and Mary Ann Day must have set limits on acquisition of material goods and imposed some firm rules regarding their children's daily life. The Days took their parental and religious responsibilities seriously, and as observant Anglicans, had all their children baptised within a few months of their births. The ethos of the mid-Victorian era was one of sobriety and self-help, and the Day children would have heard the virtues of moral rectitude, personal responsibility and hard work energetically promoted from the pulpit and in best-selling books such as Samuel Smiles' *Self-Help*.[7] In the case of Lewis Foreman Day, such admonitions influenced the development of what seems to have been a naturally serious personality. Day later acknowledged that a particular moral force helped shape his strict attitudes and behaviour: the Quaker influence.

On his father's side, the family claimed descent from John Day (1522-1584), the Elizabethan printer, and Samuel Cater, a notable pioneer of Quakerism in East Anglia.[8] For many generations the Day family had lived in Essex, an area in which many Quakers, more formally known as the Religious Society of Friends, had settled.[9] Lewis Day's great-grandfather, Samuel Day, was a Quaker minister and business partner of the prominent Quaker elder William Grover, of Stansted, Essex and Brighton.[10] Lewis's grandfather, Samuel Tayspill Day, severed his formal ties with the Society of Friends by marrying Ann Felsted in the Church of England in 1804 and their children were baptised into that faith. Nevertheless, he remained attached to his Quaker roots, employing Friends as

assistants in the family grocery business at Stansted, founded in 1687.[11] While it is not known to what extent the family may have retained some aspects of Quaker beliefs and practices by the time Lewis was born, Samuel Hulme Day maintained family and business ties to the Essex area after moving to London in 1844 and the family's servants usually came from Essex.

As a strict branch of the 17th-century English Puritan movement, Quakers were particularly characterised by the high value accorded to order and wise use of resources, absence of superfluity in lifestyle and manners, and independence of thought. Order was founded on directing one's resources – time, energy and money – to what one judged to be important in life. There was "no time to squander upon trifles", and even leisure and travel time abroad should be used for "allowable recreation and mental improvement", such as reading and study.[12] Order also dictated that one should manage one's finances prudently, pay just debts promptly, and live within one's financial means.[13] Quaker prohibitions against superfluity in lifestyle and manners included warnings about being seduced by changing fashions, a costly habit that "bespeaks a mind engaged with trifles, and a fondness for show".[14] Quaker independence of thought was reflected in reliance on inner direction, "the inner light" or "guidance of the enlightened conscience".[15] The plainness and directness of speech advocated by Quakers and the absence of "superfluous words" gave them "a reputation for bluntness".[16]

In whatever ways these moral precepts were inculcated in Lewis Day during his childhood and youth, they contributed to the development of an adult with a strict code of conduct – one who highly valued hard work, exhibited orderly and methodical work habits, and managed his time, energy and money well. He used travel for study, disdained fashion and the superfluous, and had a habit of 'plain speaking', or bluntness. Day's contemporaries frequently cited his independence of thought and spirit.[17] Day himself acknowledged the 'Puritan tendencies' in his personality.[18] Barclay Day noted that his brother Lewis "was proud of the Puritan strain in his blood, as he called his Quaker descent".[19] Lewis Day also had a sense of humour about his stringent attitudes and was not above poking some fun at himself publicly. When his friend Walter Crane commented: "There must be a touch of the Puritan about you", Day good-naturedly replied: "Have you only just discovered that taint in me?"[20]

Education in England and abroad

Lewis Day's first educational experiences may have been acquired in small group instruction in private homes, a common practice for families in the Camberwell area.[21] At the age of seven-and-a-half he was sent to a school in France for two years, and probably lived with relatives or friends during this time.[22] Several of the Day children were educated abroad, a practice undoubtedly facilitated by Samuel Hulme Day's connections on the Continent through his wine business. Lewis then spent three years at a private school in Brighton, where his family also had connections.[23] While it was certainly not uncommon for families to send their children away to school, the fact that his first five

1.7 Merchant Taylors' School, exterior. From *Merchant Taylors' School: Its Origin, History and Present Surroundings* (1929): pl. opp. 8
Merchant Taylors' School, Northwood

years of formal schooling were acquired away from home undoubtedly fostered independence in him from an early age.

Day's next educational experiences were acquired closer to home. Having returned to London, he entered Merchant Taylors' School on 19 January, 1858, just ten days short of his thirteenth birthday.[24] Merchant Taylors' offered practical advantages. The school was located on Suffolk Lane in the City of London, near Samuel Day's wine business; as was the case for most of the other students, Lewis lived at home with his parents.[25] His parents must have sacrificed financially to send him there, for he entered too late to win a scholarship to help pay his school fees, which, in addition to the cost of books, amounted to over £35.[26]

This major public school was established in 1561 by the Merchant Taylors' Company, one of the ancient Guilds. Located in a noisy, congested area surrounded by offices, warehouses, a brewery, and a printing works, the building was inadequate for the number of students.[27] Since a mid-day meal was not provided, most students bought food from street vendors and then amused themselves by exploring the city over the lunch hour, thereby gaining quite a vicarious knowledge of urban life.[28] Lewis must have vastly enjoyed this part of the day that further whetted his independent spirit.

The classics and mathematics formed the foundation of the curriculum, which also included Christian doctrine and Scripture studies, writing, French, drawing and modern history.[29] As was the case with most schools of the time, students were taught through memorising and translating, with little original composition.[30] This method of teaching left Lewis with an aversion to rote learning, to mindless copying from historical models, and to the imposition of a set teaching method for everyone. He later commented: "Latin verses which absorbed so much of our time at school" were "a sort of mental gymnastics, calculated to develop and strengthen the fibre of the brain", but "our time might have been very much better spent than in writing doggerel in a dead language".[31]

During his three years at the school, Lewis excelled at French and mathematics, winning prizes for his proficiency.[32] His prior schooling in France certainly gave him an advantage in foreign language study, and his skill with numbers could have led him to a career as a mathematician.[33] His high performance in these areas was not matched in his Greek studies, however, and he joked about it years later: "My own

slight acquaintance with Homer ceased when I left school, and it must be confessed that the *Iliad* was always Greek indeed to me."[34]

Lewis Day began to show an interest in design and colour during his school years.[35] His fascination with the design of things and the desire to learn on his own were revealed in an incident he recounted many years later: "When I was a boy, I remember, I thought there were so or so many alphabets; I had no notion as to how many, but I had no doubt about there being a fixed number; and I have a very distinct recollection of hesitating to buy a book of alphabets (which I coveted) hoping to find one which would include them *all*."[36] This early impulse to ferret things out for himself became a drive for self-education, one of the dominating characteristics of his life and a recurring theme in his writing.

Day left Merchant Taylors' School at the end of 1860. He then spent about a year-and-a-half in Germany, mastering the German language, and probably spent some time in France, as well.[37] Through this mix of private and public school education acquired in England and on the Continent, Day developed solid analytical, mathematical and writing skills and became fluent in French and German. He acquired a broad cultural education and developed a love of travel as a means of self-education. This education and experience would serve him well in his professional life.

1.8 Merchant Taylors' School, interior. From *Merchant Taylors' School: Its Origin, History and Present Surroundings* (1929): pl. opp. 24 Merchant Taylors' School, Northwood

The young designer and writer (1862-1872)

By the time Lewis Day returned to England in 1862, he had chosen to become a designer. It is highly likely that his career choice would have been reinforced by a visit to the London International Exhibition that year, where he would have seen the display of Japanese art that would so influence his early designs. However, his family could not afford to send him to design school.[38] Then almost eighteen years old, he lived with his parents, though he had to be self-supporting.[39] Unable to find employment in arts-related firms, he took a job as a clerk, a short-lived position as the business soon failed.[40]

Around 1865 he answered an advertisement from the stained glass firm Lavers & Barraud and was hired for office work.[41] He soon transferred into their studio and worked for the firm for two to three years.[42] The high demand for stained glass for churches, secular buildings and private houses provided opportunities for this young designer. Stained glass, which fed into Day's interest in history and his love of colour and pattern, fascinated him for the rest of his life. During his time at Lavers & Barraud, Day first learned about William Morris and his firm Morris, Marshall, Faulkner & Company. "It was in 1866, I remember, that the name of the firm first came to my ears, and I asked an old hand at design who they were. The answer was: 'A set of amateurs who are going to teach us our trade'."[43] About 1867 Day moved on to the larger stained glass firm of Clayton & Bell; he stayed for two to three years overseeing the large scale drawings used in stained glass production and possibly designing some windows, as well.[44]

1.9 South Kensington Museum, the South Court, from *Art Journal* (1887): 224

During these early work years, Day continued to educate himself by going to the South Kensington Museum in the evenings to study and sketch the collections, which resulted in an intimate knowledge of the treasures there.[45] He also would have become aware of the work of design reformers including A.W.N. Pugin, Owen Jones and others, who sought to improve the quality of design and manufacture of goods, and would have begun to consider his own response to these issues. This use of his leisure time for self-improvement was a pattern that continued throughout his life, and he later described himself as a lifelong student.[46] Day also had strong social tendencies that balanced his independence. In the 1860s he attended meetings of the Architectural Association and was a member of the Quibblers, a society of young artists and designers that included Walter Crane, R. Phené Spiers and others who would become lifelong friends and colleagues. He began writing about decorative art; the first mention of him in the professional press was in connection with an essay he had written, an early indicator of how important writing would be in his life.[47]

By late 1869 Day had decided to become a freelance designer. Self-employment, a natural development for someone so independent, was a turning point in Day's life that reflected both his practical nature

1.10 Eaton Hall, from the south west. Rebuilt 1870-82 by Alfred Waterhouse for the Duke of Westminster
Michael Whiteway

and his wide-ranging aesthetic interests. Although the details of his thinking are not known, clearly he had made an objective assessment of his situation. He had gained five years of solid workshop experience with major stained glass firms, but he had no formal training in figure work, an important component in ecclesiastical stained glass design. So he channelled his love for stained glass into designing primarily domestic windows and into scholarship of the subject. With strong interest in many types of decorative art and a high need for variety in his work, he broadened his repertoire, which also helped an independent designer financially weather the ups and downs of particular industries.

Late 1869-72 was a transitional period during which Day secured his first clients and expanded his design range. Initially he designed mostly book covers, but a major project soon came his way. Heaton, Butler & Bayne had secured a commission for decoration and stained glass as part of Alfred Waterhouse's rebuilding of Eaton Hall in Cheshire for the Duke of Westminster; in early 1870 Day went there to work on this project.[48] He must have been excited to work on such a prestigious project so soon after starting his independent practice. He maintained a working relationship with the firm after the end of the project, occasionally designing windows for them, most of them domestic.[49]

During this transition, Day continued to reside with his parents at Beaufort House. He worked out of temporary studios, advertising himself in 1872 as an "artist in ornamental design, specialty stained glass", at 4 & 5 Agar Street, Strand and in 1873 as an "artist in ornamental design", at 6 & 7 Adelphi Chambers, John St., where he shared office space with architects and surveyors. From stained glass, he moved into designing wallpaper, tiles and other domestic furnishings for manufacture. The expansion of his work into various areas of decorative art coincided with the emergence of the Aesthetic Movement, which, in its focus on the domestic interior, stressed the art value of furniture, ceramics, stained glass and other furnishings, and gloried in surface ornamentation. Despite the demands of securing design work, Day was clearly adept at time management, for he continued to write and lecture.[50] Working out of temporary studios was coming to an end, however, for he was ready to take the next big steps in his professional and personal life.

A home and studio of his own (1873)
Day's hard work paid off, for within three years of becoming a freelance designer he was financially established and able to set up his own studio. In early 1873 Day leased as his home and studio a large terrace house at 13 Mecklenburgh Square, Bloomsbury. Part of the Foundling Hospital Estate, Mecklenburgh Square was tucked in between Coram's Fields and the Hospital on the west and Gray's Inn Road on the east. The area was long associated with intellectual life, with the British Museum, University of London and publishing houses nearby. The terrace houses on the east side of the square, where No. 13 was situated, had a pleasing ambiance. Designed by Joseph Kay in 1810, their white stucco façades, neo-classical columns, fanlights and iron railings on the upper-storey windows embodied decorative restraint.[51] The middle-class residences on this quiet, leafy square were traditionally occupied by merchants and professional men.

It was to this house that the twenty-eight-year-old Day brought his bride, Ruth Emma Morrish (1850-1929), whom he had married on 3 June, 1873 at Christ Church, Streatham, Surrey. Five years his junior, Temma, as she was known, was the daughter of the late James Morrish, a Lancashire linen draper. They may have become acquainted through her brother Thomas Buxton Morrish, who was a director of Howell & James of Regent St., the prestigious department store with which Day had begun doing business. Of a warm and sociable disposition, Temma shared her husband's interest in the applied arts and was accomplished at needlework.[52]

1.11 a and b (above and top right) Terrace houses on east side of Mecklenburgh Square and the garden viewed from the east side, 1996

1.12 (right) 13 Mecklenburgh Square, Bloomsbury, London, 1996. This was Lewis F. Day's residence from 1873 to 1904

1.13 (opposite, top) Christ Church, Streatham
PCC, Christ Church, Streatham, London

1.14 (opposite, bottom) The door of 13 Mecklenburgh Square, London, 1996

Lewis and Temma Day's only daughter Ruth was born 15 April, 1874.[53] Although Day's heavy workload designing and writing would suggest that he spent most of his waking hours working, with his studio in his home he would have been present during Ruth's childhood and youth. Judging from the closeness of their relationship in later years, he must have given her considerable attention. It is fair to assume that when, in the early 1880s, Day wrote the children's book, *The Nodding Mandarin: A Tragedy in China*, he wrote it with the nine-year-old Ruth in mind.[54]

The home in Mecklenburgh Square was the centre of Day's domestic and professional life for more than thirty years. The household was rounded out by two servants, a cook and a nursemaid, who stayed with the family for decades. Both Day and Temma maintained close relationships with their families, who were always welcome at Mecklenburgh Square, as were Day's artist friends.[55] "A most genial and home-loving man", his home provided a firm anchor in his busy life.[56]

Day's lifestyle was a focused and disciplined one, organised around his independent design practice and writing. While he contended that some degree of Bohemianism – "a direction somewhat apart from the current of accepted conventions" – could be tolerated in the artist, his personal interpretation of that seemed to consist in avoiding spending money on things that meant nothing to him and habits that would be incompatible with his work.[57] He claimed that designers would better spend their resources on those things "which, luxuries though they may be to others, are necessities to them; in books, for example, travel, rest, recreation, and all manner of what may seem extravagance but is really not merely helpful but essential to their craft".[58]

Day's energy, business-like practicality and blunt manner of speaking sometimes grated on his colleagues. With his intense focus on his work and the need to manage his time productively to serve an increasing number of clients, he could be quite impatient at what he perceived to be a lack of purpose

in others, frivolous pursuits, or wasting time.[59] He recognised the trait of impatience in himself and obliquely referred to it in one of his lectures on stained glass: "There is a good window, too, at St. George's, Hanover-square, which might be studied with advantage by impatient wedding guests pending the arrival of the bride."[60]

Day's only major leisure activity was travel, which he considered absolutely essential for his work.[61] For more than forty years he travelled abroad once or twice a year, staying for about a month each time, feeding his insatiable desire to learn more about the decorative arts of other countries and periods, a source of inspiration for his designs and writing.[62] The cosmopolitan attitude seen in his extensive travelling to most countries on the Continent contrasts with the domesticity of his daily life. Rooted in his childhood, the values of a stable home life, a disciplined lifestyle, and education through travel were thus reflected in Day's adult life and made possible his prolific career as a designer and writer.

Part 2: The Designer for Industry, the Writer and Critic (1873-1899)

Building his reputation (1873-1884)

In the early 1870s Day directed his energies to securing new clients and building up his design practice. Two business relationships during this early period were long-lasting and particularly significant. They gave him the opportunity to design a wide variety of furnishings and a means of exhibiting his work at major international exhibitions. They also involved him in the promotion and marketing of their goods and provided him with additional business contacts.

The prominent department store Howell & James, located at 5-9 Regent St., retailed fabrics, millinery, women's accessories, and jewellery. The most important side of the business was that of home furnishings, including furniture, glass and ceramics, and the store also retailed the goods of several prominent art potteries. The firm commissioned design work from well-known figures, including architects Sir Matthew Digby Wyatt and Thomas Harris. Day's brother-in-law, Thomas Buxton Morrish, was a director of the firm from the early 1870s until 1884, and may have been the entrée to Day's work there.[63]

In 1872 Howell & James exhibited a gold and enamelled bridesmaid's locket designed by Day at the London International Exhibition; this was the first major exhibition at which Day's work had been shown.[64] The *Art Journal's* report on the Vienna International Exhibition of 1873 included an illustration of a clock with painted tiles, designed by "Messrs. Henry and Lewis Day" and retailed by Howell & James.[65] During the 1870s and 1880s, the store marketed a series of small clocks, many with ebonized wood cases and blue and white porcelain faces, which became a speciality of theirs. Day designed a number of clocks that fitted in well with the fashion for blue and white china at the time and the ebonized Anglo-Japanese furniture then in vogue.

From 1876 through to the early 1880s, Howell & James held annual china painting exhibitions at their galleries in Regent St., drawing large crowds and significant attention in the art press. These exhibitions included the work of both amateurs and professionals, and in 1878 Day exhibited a vase and several plates featuring figural and pictorial designs popular during this period.[66]

Shortly after going into business for himself, Day also began a working relationship with W.B. Simpson & Sons, the pre-eminent housepainters and decorators located at 456 West Strand and 100 St. Martin's Lane, whose wallpapers were block-printed by hand by Jeffrey & Co. Day secured an agreement to design wallpaper and church decoration exclusively for Simpson's.[67] His designs for dados, fillings and friezes included geometric designs and conventionalised floral and foliate patterns, some of which showed Japanese influence in their asymmetry and motifs. By this time he was beginning to achieve a reputation as a practical designer who took pains to ensure the successful end-use of the furnishings he designed. In 1883 W.B. Simpson & Sons issued a pattern book of his wallpapers that was favourably received by architects and decorators alike, both for the originality of the designs and because the patterns repeated well when installed.[68]

1.15 Lewis F. Day. Advertisement for W.B. Simpson & Sons. From *Architect* 17 (1877), Supplement: 7

Day also branched into tile design for Simpson's and encouraged the firm to develop its line of ecclesiastical and domestic stained glass. He made an agreement to design stained glass exclusively for them, an arrangement that lasted until at least mid-1886.[69] It is likely that much of the domestic stained glass (mostly geometric and floral designs) produced by the firm at their workshops in St. Martin's Lane was designed by Day.[70] He also made himself useful to his clients in the marketing of their goods. Some advertisements he designed for Simpson's mosaic tile flooring, wallpapers and stained glass ran in the *Architect* in the 1870s and 1880s.

Day's design work shown at the Paris Exposition Universelle in 1878 provided him with critical international exposure and established him in the ranks of major designers of home furnishings. A wide variety of his furnishings were exhibited, among them wallpapers for Simpson's and furniture for Gregory & Co. Day designed Howell & James's exhibit area, which included his furniture, clock cases and ceramics. The store retailed the wares of the Torquay Terra Cotta Pottery, including Day's 'Sunlight' and 'Moonlight' vases, which were illustrated in the *Art Journal's* report on the exhibition.[71]

Day also collaborated on the design and display area of the 'Princess Cabinet', a major piece exhibited by furniture manufacturer and retailer H. & J. Cooper.[72] This exhibition furniture showcased Day's talents in a dramatic way, and his reputation was greatly enhanced by the illustrated reports in the press, which were very positive.[73] In addition to raising his stature as a designer, the Paris Exposition enabled Day to make a name for himself as a journalist and critic, through his fifteen 'Notes on English Decorative Art in Paris' for the *British Architect*.

Seeking inspiration for design

Day's designs and writings reveal his conception of decorative art and the sources of inspiration that remained so consistent throughout his career. He was committed to the basic aims of design reform: improving the quality of design, raising standards of manufacture, and elevating public taste. He believed that the ultimate aim of the designer was beauty, and that decoration, or ornament, was an accessory art that fulfilled its purpose when it harmonised with the architecture or object on which it was used.[74] On the principle that ornament should reinforce the overall construction of an object and extraneous ornament should be eliminated, he was fundamentally in accord with A.W.N. Pugin, John Ruskin, and William Morris.

Of the three main sources of inspiration for Day's designs – nature, historic ornament and Eastern cultures – nature was always paramount. He contended that all the qualities that gave satisfaction in ornament existed in nature before they were expressed in art.[75] While he believed that natural forms needed some modification to suit their purpose as ornament, he cautioned that simplification should not be taken to an extreme that would render natural forms emasculated and lifeless.[76] Day thus took a middle ground between the naturalists such as John Ruskin, who espoused direct imitation of nature, and those who advocated a more severe reduction of natural forms to their basic

1.16 (above) Lewis F. Day. 'Detail and its Distribution: Instances of borders and panels'. From Day, *Instances of Accessory Art* (1880): pl. 17
Michael Whiteway

1.17 (opposite, top left) Lewis F. Day. Heraldic beasts, 1879. From Day, *Instances of Accessory Art* (1880): pl. 10
Michael Whiteway

1.18 (opposite, bottom right) Lewis F. Day. Detail, 'Painted tiles for fireplaces, etc'. From *Architect*, 25 (1881): near 435. Day's interest in Japanese asymmetrical arrangements of design elements and his use of Japanese mons, appleblossoms, waves and grids as background are seen in these tiles
Trustees of the National Library of Scotland, Edinburgh

geometric characteristics, such as Owen Jones. Unlike Walter Crane, Day generally refrained from using animals and human figures in repeat pattern, judging them to be too assertive and introducing a pictorial quality inappropriate to pattern.[77] He was fond of using grotesques – fanciful combinations of animal-like creatures and foliage – because they could be created to fit the purposes of the design.[78]

Historic forms were a source of inspiration, too, though Day was consistently against slavish imitation of past styles.[79] Believing that the past should suggest possibilities for the present, he stressed that historic forms should be modified by the mind and skill of the designer.[80] He was certainly aware of the pattern books then available and would have referred to them from time to time. For the most part, he sought historic inspiration through his lifelong practice of studying original sources first-hand, either on his travels or in museum collections, in particular those of the South Kensington Museum.

The decorative art of Japan, with its asymmetry, motifs and treatment of nature, fascinated professionals and the public alike. Day, too, drew inspiration from the decorative art of Japan, as well as China, India and the Middle East, and throughout his life, collected examples of their applied arts and studied how different cultures adapted nature to purpose.[81]

Day was unabashedly eclectic, defending eclecticism as the right of choice exercised by artists through the centuries.[82] He believed that any style could be useful as a starting point on the way to fulfilling the purpose of beauty and fitness.[83] A key principle to which he adhered throughout his life was that ornament had to be apt for its time, and "it must not only be fitted to its position, place, and purpose, but to us, our modern conditions and appliances."[84]

Accelerating his writing career

Having expanded his client base, by the mid-1870s, Day began devoting more energy to writing. Designing and writing about design were philosophically inseparable in his life. Writing had practical benefits as well, increasing his reputation and providing a second source of income. 'Decorative Art', Day's first signed series of articles for the *British Architect*, appeared in 1878 and consisted of a dozen brief illustrated articles on various aspects of applied art and ornament. Simultaneously, he contributed the 'Notes on English Decorative Art in Paris', which reported on the exhibits of British and continental manufacturers at the Paris Exposition Universelle of 1878. These articles were his first foray into international exhibition journalism, a

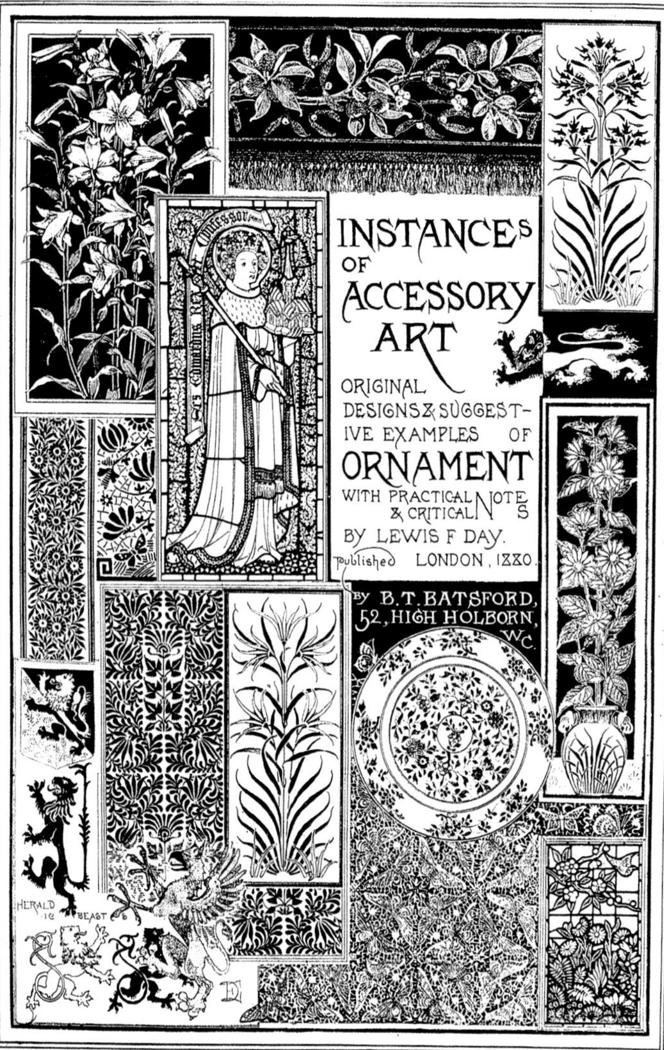

1.19 Lewis F. Day. Title page, *Instances of Accessory Art* (1880). This is the first of Day's books published by B.T. Batsford
Michael Whiteway

type of writing that would occupy him for the next thirty years.

He quickly developed a habit of making multiple uses of his work. His next series for the *British Architect* consisted of twenty-six short articles entitled 'Fortnightly Notes on Ornament' (1879), which he revised as his first book, *Instances of Accessory Art* (1880). The publication of this book launched his long and happy relationship with publisher B.T. Batsford, of 94, High Holborn. Beginning in 1877, Day also expanded his readership from professional to public audiences by writing for the *Art Journal*. Two series of articles he contributed to the *Magazine of Art* in 1880 and 1881 formed the basis for his second book, *Every-day Art* (1882).

At the height of his powers (1885-1899)

By the mid-1880s, Day was designing a wide variety of furnishings for an impressive list of clients. He had hit his stride, designing damasks for William Fry of Dublin, tapestry for the Royal Windsor Tapestry Manufactory, and curtains for Barbour, Miller & Anderson of Glasgow, McCrea of Halifax, and Cowlishaw, Nichol & Co. of Manchester. He produced patterns for impressed tiles for Wedgwood's Marsden Patent Tile line; card backs for Goodall & Co; and calendar designs for Sir J. Causton & Sons, for whom he served as art advisor.[85] His ability to turn out a prolific amount of work in a variety of styles to satisfy consumer demand made him very valuable to manufacturers. His high profile in the trade and professional press testified to his own reputation and the recognition he was able to bring to his clients, as well.

With seemingly boundless energy, he produced a huge volume of work through his disciplined lifestyle and excellent time management skills. Although he never built up a large studio, he valued highly the secretarial and administrative help of his daughter Ruth, who was known for her "knowledge, tact and patience".[86] In the 1890s he also employed a page, or messenger boy. From about 1898-1904, his assistant was designer Beatrice Waldram, whom he recruited from Clapton School of Art where she had been a pupil and teaching assistant.[87]

Day's design practice and writings revealed the general principles that undergirded his work. He identified about a half-dozen practical issues that were particularly important when designing pattern for industry:

thorough planning; working out the geometric basis of a design; dealing effectively with issues of scale and lines; dealing with the matter of emphasis; disguising repeats (a task at which he excelled but that he acknowledged was difficult); and creating patterns that would work well in a number of colour schemes.[88] Like William Morris, he stressed that the designer must bear in mind how a design would appear in the final product, for instance, the types of patterns that would hang well as curtains and those that were more suitable for a flat surface.

Day's advice was not merely theoretical, but was practical, as well. "A designer, whatever his natural gift, is of no practical use until he is at home with the conditions of manufacture," he insisted.[89] Practising what he preached, he visited manufacturing facilities, studied processes first-hand, and with his clients worked through production issues that would affect the type of design and its plan.[90] Chief among these were requirements of standardisation – the girth of the roller, the size of the woodblock, the square mesh of lines for tiles – without which manufacturers could not estimate the cost of producing goods.[91] He counselled designers to have a thorough understanding of the capacities of particular materials and the methods by which a design would be produced. He stressed that the designer should anticipate conditions that could arise during production and provide enough direction for the execution of the design by hand or machine.[92] Practising that principle, he frequently made production notes in the margins of his designs.

Rather than simply tolerating industrial and economic constraints as a necessary evil, Day relished the challenges and problems they presented. He viewed design as both art and problem-solving and derived immense satisfaction in meeting the tough challenges posed by industrial design.[93] He was adamant about the duty of the designer: "His task is to get beautiful results out of no matter what unpromising conditions. Then indeed he may claim to be an artist."[94] Day was acutely aware that while manufacturers wanted to produce artistic goods, their products also needed to be saleable and make a profit. About the desired end he had no doubt: "The best work of all cannot be arrived at until artist and manufacturer are convinced that their interest is one."[95]

The period from the mid-1880s through the 1890s witnessed Day operating at his full powers, the time in which his

1.20 (left) John Wilson's Successors Ltd. Advertisement for table linen designed by Walter Crane, Lewis F. Day and others, c.1900

1.21 (above) Beatrice Waldram. From *Arts and Crafts* 4 (1905-6): 75

Trustees of the National Library of Scotland, Edinburgh

technical skills in pattern design, facility in meeting production challenges for various types of manufacture, and his versatility in design had matured. His best work showed enormous energy and confidence, based on his continuing sources of inspiration from nature, historic sources and Eastern cultures.

The expansion of his client list from the mid-1880s on reads like a *Who's Who* of prominent firms. He designed lustre tiles for J.C. Edwards of Ruabon; tiles, art pottery and mosaic pavements for Maw & Co.; woven textiles for Alexander Morton and A.H. Lee; linen damasks for John Wilson & Sons; printed textiles for Thomas Wardle; carpets for Brinton's; and linoleum and relief wallpapers for Frederick Walton & Co. He designed a wide variety of block- and machine-printed wallpapers for Jeffrey & Co., a major client from 1885 to c.1908. He also designed schemes for domestic and public interiors. Quality stores and shops, including Howell & James, Heal's, Liberty & Co., and Dean's of Manchester retailed his designs. In addition, Day designed embroidery, lace, jewellery, fans, book covers, and other forms of graphic design. His reputation at its height, his design work was shown at virtually all major trade and industrial exhibitions, as well as the Arts and Crafts Exhibitions from the first in 1888 to 1910.

1.22 Lewis F. Day. 'Mortimer' wallpaper, 1896. Made by Jeffrey & Co.
Southwark Art Collection, London, PT0792

Influencing the growth of new firms

In his long association with Turnbull & Stockdale and Pilkington's Tile & Pottery Co., Day came close to the realisation of his dream of a marriage of design and industry. Founded in 1881, Turnbull & Stockdale printed shirt goods of other manufacturers but also developed their own line of artistic printed fabrics. Day began designing for the firm in its early days and provided the firm's first registered design, 'Victorian Renaissance', which was marketed through Howell & James.[96] The firm expanded rapidly, adding a variety of printed fabrics including indigo discharge and

duplex fabrics to their line. Day was appointed art director c.1888 and was given a seat on the firm's board of directors in 1892, a highly unusual affirmation of the importance of creative direction to corporate success.[97] His numerous connections with other designers, manufacturers, retail outlets and the trade press contributed significantly to the firm's growth in its early years. His designs for the firm represent the bulk of his work in printed textiles and were widely distributed in Britain and abroad.

Day was also very influential in the development of Pilkington's Tile & Pottery Co., (founded 1891), a late entry into the tile industry. He took great interest in the development of scientific manufacture by William and Joseph Burton, director and chemist respectively. Day was under contract from about 1895 to design tiles exclusively for Pilkington's and serve as art advisor during a critical period of the firm's growth. There is no evidence that any of the firm's other designers, who included Walter Crane and C.F.A.Voysey, had such an arrangement.[98] Day designed a wide variety of tiles for Pilkington's and influenced the shapes of the innovative Lancastrian and Lancastrian Lustre art pottery produced by the firm.

1.23 (left) Lewis F. Day. Tile with flower and swirling foliage. Made by Pilkington's Tile & Pottery Co. This pattern was shown at the Wolverhampton Exhibition, 1902 (*Pilkington Catalogue 1902*: 30) Anthony J. Cross

1.24 (above) Lewis F. Day. 'Daffodils' cretonne, c.1888. Made by Turnbull & Stockdale. From *Art Journal Supplement, Paris Exhibition 1900* (1900): 346 Angela and Barry Corbett

Maturing as a writer and critic

The period 1885-1900 was also one of great intellectual development for Day in which he worked out many of his ideas about ornament. He launched his *Textbooks of Ornamental Design: The Anatomy of Pattern* (1887), *The Planning of Ornament* (1887), *The Application of Ornament* (1888) and *Nature in Ornament* (1892). *Every-day Art*, which had been published in 1882, was revised as *Some Principles of Every-day Art* in 1890 and served as the introductory volume to the series. Day's writing style was concise and his advice practical. His key points were illustrated by his own designs, those of his contemporaries, and historic sources. The *Textbooks of Ornamental Design*, which went through numerous reprintings and editions, were approved by the Science and Art Department for design education and were often given as prizes to students.

Amazingly, Day also found time to pursue his special interests by writing *Windows: A Book about Stained Glass* (1897) and *Alphabets Old and New* (1898).[99] He expanded his relationships with major magazines including the *Magazine of Art*, for which he designed the blue and white cover used from late 1880 until 1902. He wrote about fifty pieces for the *Magazine of Art* from 1879-1902 on an encyclopedic range of topics in the applied arts. Day also designed the cover for the *Art Journal*, which was used from 1885 to 1901. He contributed articles periodically from 1877 to 1887 and, from 1893 to 1902, increased his involvement as a reviewer of contemporary developments in design. Day wrote one of the first monographs on William Morris, *William Morris and His Art*, published as an extra number of the *Art Journal* in 1899. Over the years, he also contributed to a variety of professional journals and general interest magazines, including the *Architect* as well as American publications, including the *Furnisher and Decorator* and *Architectural Record*.

Keeping good company: colleagues and students

The fierce independence seen in Day's thinking and speech was balanced by strong social tendencies, a distinguishing combination of traits recognised by his contemporaries. His activities in the wider

1.25 (left) Lewis F. Day. Cover, bound issues of *Art Journal* Paulo R. De Andrea, PRD Photography

1.26 (above) Lewis F. Day. Cover, *Textbooks of Ornamental Design*, 3rd ed., (1895)

design community reveal his friendships with fellow designers, architects, and manufacturers and indicate how enmeshed he was in major developments of the design world. He enjoyed the stimulation and benefits of a successful career, but he was also anxious to contribute to his profession and further the development of young designers.

From 1879 until his death he was a member of the Society of Arts, delivering several courses of prestigious Cantor lectures and serving for many years as Vice-President of the Applied Arts Section. He also instigated the founding of the Fifteen in 1881, a society of applied arts professionals that included Walter Crane, designer Henry Holiday and architect John D. Sedding, who met monthly at each others' houses and studios to discuss the relationship of art and design to everyday life.[100] In 1884 the group merged with students of Richard Norman Shaw to form the Art Workers' Guild, the purpose of which was to combat the increasing separation of art, architecture, design and craft by promoting unity and fellowship.[101] A very active member, Day served as Treasurer from 1884 to 1887 and as Master in 1897.

Due to its opposition to publicity, the Art Workers' Guild did not provide opportunities for publicly exhibiting members' work. A group comprised mainly of its members began organising an exhibition society in early 1886.[102] Day was one of the founders of what came to be called the Arts and Crafts Exhibition Society, which held its first exhibition in 1888.[103] Along with William Morris, Philip Webb, Heywood Sumner and Mervyn McCartney, Day served for many years on the important Selection Committee, which judged the quality of work submitted for exhibition. In the late 1880s and 1890s Day also contributed lectures and articles to the exhibition catalogues.

Though they shared concerns about the effect of industrialisation on society as well as design, those who gathered under the Arts and Crafts umbrella held a range of opinions on suitable remedies. Day agreed with Morris, Crane and others on the need to improve society as well as art, but he did not accept socialism as an answer.[104] Day did not engage in political debate in his lectures and articles, and his position on political issues of the day is unknown.[105] He channelled his energies into activities such as the Arts and Crafts Exhibition Society to improve the relationship between designers and manufacturers, to the ultimate benefit of the end-users of products.

During the 1870s and 1880s Day focused on building his career as a designer and writer, and it was not until the 1890s that he involved himself more extensively in teaching, lecturing and evaluating students' work. Although his primary influence on design education was through his textbooks, he devoted considerable energy in the 1890s and early 1900s to preparing the next generation of designers by teaching, lecturing and developing curricula. He examined and judged student work for the National Art Competition from 1890 to 1908 and evaluated schools of design for the Board of Education. He was on the committee for the School of Art Woodcarving and in 1890 gave several lectures to students on designing for high and low relief.

Day's tall and lean physique, serious and forceful manner, and energetic use of diagrams and illustrations in his lectures, must have rendered him a lively speaker.[106] Contemporary accounts refer to the generous amount of time and attention he gave to students and others who came to him for advice, noting his sound and practical suggestions, and his kind and encouraging manner.[107] Students were proud to say they had been taught by him, and among the those he mentored were designer and silversmith Omar Ramsden, designer Beatrice Waldram, and the eminent Chicago interior decorator of the late 1890s, Alice E. Neale.[108]

PART 3: DESIGNER AND WRITER EMERITUS (1900-1910)

While Day designed for a number of firms around the turn of the century, the bulk of his work was with Pilkington's Tile & Pottery Co., textile printers Turnbull & Stockdale, and wallpaper manufacturer Jeffrey & Co. His strong friendships with the principals of these firms were based on a shared goal of producing high-quality artistic goods while capitalising on advances in industrial manufacture. Through his large volume of work for these firms over a long period of time, Day was able to live out most fully his major professional preoccupation: the marriage of design and industry. The nature of his relationships with these firms was encapsulated in his work shown at the Paris Exposition Universelle in 1900. His designs and exhibition journalism for the *Art Journal*, *Manchester Guardian*, and *Magazine of Art*, revealed a designer poised at the apex of his career, thoughtfully reflecting on advances in science, changes in consumer taste, and new trends in design.

As art advisor to Pilkington's Tile & Pottery Co., Day strongly influenced the firm's exhibit in Paris. The Exposition gave the firm the opportunity to demonstrate on the international stage that modern manufacturing methods could produce tiles of high artistic merit.[109] The firm contended that its development of new glazes resulted in products of superior quality.[110] The judges evidently agreed, for Pilkington's won gold and silver medals in Paris. The firm's exhibit represented the work of well-known figures including Walter Crane, C.F.A. Voysey, and Alphonse Mucha, as well as younger designers. Over half the products exhibited by the firm were designed by Day.

Day found enormous satisfaction in working with managing director William Burton and his brother Joseph, a chemist, for they shared the vision that they were living in the age of science and that

1.27 View of the Trocadero, at the Paris Exposition Universelle 1900. From *Art Journal* (1900): 371
Trustees of the National Library of Scotland, Edinburgh

product excellence would come through the fusion of science and art.[111] Day highly regarded the Burtons's thorough knowledge of the natural properties of their material and their mastery of the processes required to bring about certain effects.[112]

Day ranked the scientific control of production processes more highly than the production of artistic effects by chance, which he termed "the happy fluke".[113] He insisted that the future of the ceramic industry lay in art wedded to control of processes, without which large-scale production of ceramics was not possible.[114] In his journalism, Day praised the science that made possible Pilkington's spectacular glazes and the wondrous colours in Louis Comfort Tiffany's favrile glass shown in Paris.[115]

By the time of the Paris Exposition, Day had been art director of Turnbull & Stockdale for a dozen years, a member of the Board for eight years, and had helped the firm become a leading manufacturer of printed textiles. He was in charge of their exhibit, which included block-printed and machine-printed cretonnes, printed velveteens, and other furnishing fabrics.[116] Many of his designs around the turn of the century reflected the general trend toward simplification in design and included airy, flowing patterns arranged in larger areas of space; flattened and stylised florals; stencil-like designs; and patterns based on 16th- and 17th-century crewelwork.

Day had begun designing wallpaper for Jeffrey & Co. in 1885, after his exclusive agreement with W.B. Simpson had expired.[117] He regarded Metford Warner – director and sole proprietor of Jeffrey & Co. from 1871 – as the Wedgwood of wallpaper manufacturers.[118] From 1885 to c.1908 Day produced scores of designs for wallpapers, many of which were featured by the firm at major international exhibitions and the Arts and Crafts Exhibitions beginning in 1888. While many of his papers were hand-block printed and were consequently expensive, he also designed less costly papers roller printed by machine. In about 1896 the firm

1.28 Photo of Lewis F. Day, early 1900s. From Turnbull & Stockdale, *Jubilee* (1931): 26

brought out Day's *Low-Price Wallpapers for Staircase Decoration Designed by Lewis F. Day*, which contained over 100 machine-printed wallpapers, dados, friezes, and borders in different colourways.

Jeffrey & Co.'s exhibit at the Paris Exposition included many printed and embossed wallpapers designed in a variety of styles by Day, Walter Crane, Heywood Sumner and Stephen Webb among others. One of Day's most masterful papers was the 'Abercorn', a sumptuous heavily embossed leather paper of intertwining fruits and leaves.[119] It was also produced in embossed copper, a costly version suitable for furniture and steamship decoration.[120]

While sumptuous and complex patterns like 'Abercorn' gave scope to Day's skills in pattern design, in his exhibition journalism, he noted the trend toward

plainer wall treatments.[121] While regretting it, he felt that if it cured excesses sometimes seen in pattern design, it would be all to the good.[122] He optimistically predicted that pattern would return to favour, because patterned papers remained the least expensive way of decorating walls.[123]

Appraising new trends in design

While Day welcomed advances in scientific manufacture that were showcased in Paris, he reacted less positively to much of Art Nouveau. He exorcised his views quite extensively in his reports on the exhibition for the *Manchester Guardian*, *Art Journal*, *Magazine of Art* and *Macmillan's*. In particular, Day criticised the French and German furniture shown in Paris for increasingly exaggerated forms and for eschewing usefulness and comfort by being "deliberately fantastic".[124] He referred to Art Nouveau as a "new artistic revolt against order" that showed symptoms of "pronounced disease", and his opinion concurred with that of Walter Crane who called it "that strange decorative disease" and C.F.A. Voysey, who criticised it as a "mad eccentricity".[125] Despite their rejection of the extremes of Art Nouveau, all three designers incorporated some of the stylistic devices associated with it that had become popular around this time, most notably the treatment of organic forms in elongated, undulating lines.

Day was firmly committed to historic precedent as a source of inspiration. Always valuing moderation highly, he thought that the total rejection of the past that characterised some Art Nouveau work was utterly ridiculous: "There is not much to choose between the folly of never looking back for direction and the foolishness of looking only behind us".[126] Day was very much a child of the mid-Victorian period, and what he judged to be a rejection of rules, restraint, and artistic discipline was anathema to his own hard-working, disciplined, 'Puritan' ethic. "Reaction is the temper of the new artist, reaction against rule of any kind," he railed, and he worried in particular about the effect of Art Nouveau on impressionable students.[127]

Day was certainly not opposed to all new developments in design. In his report

1.29 (opposite) Chief entrance to the Paris Exposition Universelle 1900, lit by electricity. From *Art Journal* (1900): 129

Trustees of the National Library of Scotland, Edinburgh

1.30 (left) Lewis F. Day. 'Abercorn' embossed imitation-leather paper, 1896. Made by Jeffrey & Co. From Day, *Ornament and Its Application* (1904): fig. 42

on the Glasgow Exhibition of 1901 for the *Art Journal*, he enthusiastically discussed the work of furniture manufacturer Wylie & Lochhead for its fine quality and designer George Walton, who he praised for creating furniture that was graceful, simple and unpretentious.[128] In Day's assessment, they achieved something new without abandoning tradition and produced the kind of furniture people could comfortably live with over the long term.[129]

Reaffirming his commitment to a marriage of design and industry

Several of the 'Friendly Disputes' between Day and Walter Crane that appeared in the *Art Journal* between 1901 and 1902 were revised and published by B.T. Batsford in 1903 as *Moot Points: Friendly Disputes on Art and Industry*, jointly authored by the two men, with humorous illustrations by Crane. In this small and neglected book, Day reiterated the core beliefs that had undergirded his professional practice and personal behaviour from his early days as a designer. While socialist Crane was disenchanted with modern manufacture and saw little hope for improvement, Day was more optimistic.[130] He was firmly grounded in the present. He acknowledged the current problems in industrial manufacture, but he believed that the supposed ideal conditions of the past were a fairy tale and that one should put energy toward improving things in the present.[131]

Day viewed design as both art and problem-solving, and he enjoyed the challenges in using design to solve practical problems.[132] He often came back to the fact that making the most of difficult situations not only developed the designer professionally, it could make the designer a better person.[133] He contended that design occurred at the nexus of art and commerce, for ancient handicraft – as well as contemporary machine manufacture of objects – involved both art and selling.[134] This being so, Day argued, the best work would be produced when the designer and manufacturer were convinced that their interest is one.

He firmly believed that design was not an autonomous activity, and he had no use for those who regarded their artistic temperament as of greater importance than working cooperatively as a member of a team.[135] He insisted that a designer could be committed to art and also be commercially competent. That required negotiating conditions that provided scope for high-quality design, but were also realistic within the economic and industrial constraints of manufacture.[136]

To promote greater interaction between designers and manufacturers, Day helped found the Design Club in 1909 and was chairman of the committee until shortly before his death.[137] By this time, he and the other well-known members – among them Walter Crane, retailer Arthur Lasenby Liberty, Metford Warner of Jeffrey & Co. and William Burton of Pilkington's – were 'emeritus' models for a generation of younger professionals. Day had lost none of his early conviction that rather than being preoccupied with past offences of machine-made art, one should look to the *future* of it.[138] Day pressed the point that if the manufacturing and artistic communities knew more about each others' work, they would find ways to bridge the gap of their differences "without going against the irresistible current of modern industry".[139]

Changing his home, studio and workload

While there were no abrupt changes in Day's life in the early 1900s, some aspects of his personal and professional circumstances began to shift. Around mid-1904 Day moved from 13 Mecklenburgh Square, which had been his home and studio for over thirty years. While it had remained relatively stable during most of the time that the Days lived there, by the turn of the century Mecklenburgh Square had begun to change, its ambience decreased by the conversion of some homes into boarding houses and increased congestion in the area. The Days' new home and studio was 15 Taviton St., Gordon Square, Bloomsbury, a quiet gated community.

There are also indications that Day suffered from bouts of illness, beginning in about 1905. During the early 1900s Day had served as tutor to the Widener Fellowship Students from the Philadelphia School of Design, whose study abroad included time at the Victoria and Albert Museum.[140] Ill health compelled him to turn these duties over to Lindsay Butterfield in 1905.[141]

Some of Day's most significant business relationships may have altered around this time, as well. His involvement with

1.31 Lewis F. Day. Detail, floral design for textile, 1908
© Liberty PLC. With permission

Pilkington's Tile & Pottery Co. was probably scaled down in about 1905, when in-house designer Gordon Forsyth became art director. How long Day held his position as art director and retained his seat on the board of directors of Turnbull & Stockdale is unclear.[142] He continued to design for both firms, as well as for Jeffrey & Co., well into the 1900s, though at a reduced level, as tastes changed and a younger generation of designers was achieving prominence.

Improving learning opportunities of designers for industry

Day pressed for further improvements in design education and opportunities for professionals to continue to learn after leaving the classroom. He lectured at major educational conferences and also evaluated schools of design, including the Royal College of Art for the Board of Education. As he had done for the past decade, he criticised two directions in design education that he felt were inappropriate for training designers for industry: an emphasis on the pictorial and fine arts or an emphasis on handicrafts, neither of which would prepare students to design for industry.[143] He advocated a blend of classroom training and practical workshop experience as the most effective way to prepare students to design under the practical conditions they would encounter when designing for manufacture. His concern was broader than just the

professional development of students, however: "The purpose of education is to fit young people for life – and for the life there is a reasonable chance and likelihood of their living – not for the ideal life beyond the reach of all but the very few".[144]

A lifelong learner himself, Day supported opportunities for designers to continue to learn and enhance their skills, in particular through museums and professional organisations. In 1908 he served with W.A.S. Benson and others on the Committee of Rearrangement of the Victoria and Albert Museum's galleries occasioned by the opening of their new buildings on Exhibition Road. At this time some museums were creating period rooms to appeal to a broader audience of visitors. The Committee recommended that the museum retain its current arrangement by materials to preserve its focus as an educational resource for designers, students and manufacturers.[145] It is not surprising that Day influenced this decision. In lectures to professional and educational groups, he continued to press for effective use of museums in teaching. In 1898 he had been awarded a silver medal by the Society of Arts for his lecture 'The Making of a Stained Glass Window', and he won a second silver medal for his lecture 'How to Make the Most of a Museum'.[146]

Day was also an energetic lecturer on current issues in professional practice to various professional and industry groups around the country, including the National Association of Master House Painters and Decorators of England and Wales (1902) and the Institute of British Decorators (1902 and 1904). An interior decorator himself, he exhorted his audiences to continue to upgrade their technical skills and try new approaches for solving decorating problems. He also continued to use his professional affiliations for his own learning. From its founding in 1894 to c.1900, he served on the committee of the Society of Illustrators, and he was elected a fellow of the Society of Antiquaries in 1904.

In the 1900s Day also continued to pursue his special interests and kept up an energetic pace of writing new books. *Art in Needlework* (1900), co-authored with Mary Buckle as technical adviser, was followed by *Lettering in Ornament* (1902), *Stained Glass* (1903), one of the Victoria and Albert Museum Art Handbooks, and *Enamelling* (1907). In his many magazine articles he reviewed his contemporaries in design, the work of younger designers who were gaining recognition, and current issues in professional practice.

He was relentless in revising previous works, refining his ideas and simplifying his language. He reworked two of his most important early works, bringing them up to date with contemporary developments and adding new illustrations. *The Anatomy of Pattern* was revised as *Pattern Design* (1903) and *The Application of Ornament* as *Ornament and Its Application* (1904). *Nature in Ornament* was revised as *Nature and Ornament* in two parts: *Nature: The Raw Material of Design* (1908) and *Nature: The Finished Product of Design* (1909). At the time of his death he was working on his third book on lettering, *Penmanship of the XVI, XVII and XVIII Centuries*, which was brought out posthumously by his daughter.

Leaving a legacy for others

Travel was a catalyst for Day's lifelong learning even in the last six months of his life. By then his forty-plus years of travel had taken him to most countries in Europe. In November 1909, he travelled to Egypt to study its art, which fascinated him and about which he intended to write a book.[147] Unfortunately, this desire remained unrealised.

In early April 1910 Day became ill from blood poisoning and died, aged sixty-five, on 18 April, 1910 at his home. His remains were cremated and interred at Highgate Cemetery. His death was widely reported in major newspapers and magazines, and mentioned most frequently were his thorough knowledge of design, methods and materials; his practical, sensible advice; his generous assistance to students; and his independence of thought and action

combined with his contribution to the major design organisations of the day.

Two years before his death Day had observed: "You can trace in a man's work the influence of his travel, of his reading, of any great experience through which he has passed".[148] His obituary in the *Glasgow Herald* referred to his international reputation, noting that his work was "familiar all the world over to those who take an interest in applied arts" and he would be "mourned by a wide circle of friends in many countries, from America to Japan".[149] Perhaps the most apt summation of his life and work was offered by Day himself: "It is his personality which gives to art its real and lasting value; not the conscious self he thrusts upon us, but the individual revealed, perhaps without his knowing it, not only in his work and in the high ideal inspiring it, but in the very way he goes about the quest for beauty".[150]

Day provided well financially for his widow and daughter, who continued to reside at Taviton St. Ruth, who had been her father's secretary, sold about 100 of his designs to the Victoria and Albert Museum and most likely destroyed any remaining business correspondence and records. She carried on some of her father's activities with the School of Art Woodcarving and the Society of Arts, and she wrote on applied art for periodicals and newspapers.[151] Never marrying, she devoted herself to religious education for the Church of England and died of influenza in 1918. Day's widow Temma survived until 1929 and made several bequests of objects designed by her late husband to museums in the north of England and the rest to family and friends.

Since Day had not established a large studio business, there was neither a firm to perpetuate his designs nor descendants to promote his work, and so his reputation was eclipsed somewhat by others. Today there is a renewed recognition of the beauty and virtuosity of Lewis F. Day's designs, which spanned the three great design movements of the day: the Aesthetic Movement, the Arts and Crafts Movement and Art Nouveau. Collectors prize his clocks, furniture, tiles and art pottery, and reproductions of his patterns for wallpapers and textiles are enjoyed by enthusiasts. Eagerly collected, Day's textbooks on design continue to influence designers, and his magazine journalism provides insightful and balanced commentary on developments in late 19th- and early 20th-century design.

1.32 Lewis F. Day. Tile with relief moulded floral design. Made by Pilkington's Tile & Pottery Co. This pattern was shown at Glasgow Exhibition 1901 as 'cloisonné tile' in coloured glazes (*Pilkington Catalogue 1901*: 36-7) Anthony J. Cross

CABINET Designed by B. J. TALBERT

FRONT ELEVATION

INSTANCES of ART in things of common use

CHAPTER TWO: THE DESIGNER FOR INDUSTRY

"A man proves himself a designer, not because he has somehow arrived at a design, but inasmuch as out of unpromising material and untoward circumstances he can shape a thing of beauty." [Lewis F. Day, 1886]

2.1 Lewis F. Day. 'Instances of art in things of common use'. From *Magazine of Art* 3 (1880): 105

Lewis Foreman Day referred to himself in various ways – as a decorative artist, as a decorator, as an artist in ornamental design, as a designer. He gave an encompassing yet succinct description of his profession in the *Manchester Guardian* in 1900 when he described his perspective as "a workman's bias towards the work in which he himself is engaged, a bias in this case toward decoration generally, towards ornament in particular, and especially towards the arts which are allied with industry."[1] Although Day designed some one-of-a-kind items – particularly furniture and ceramics – he concentrated his energies in the design of functional and beautiful objects accessible to a wider consumer market, and most of his designs were serially or mass-produced. One-off pieces were often affordable only by the wealthy, and modern manufacture was necessary to fulfil consumer demand.[2] This conviction was at the heart of his passionate commitment to a marriage of design and industry.

Day was notable among his contemporaries for the extent to which he talked about the nature of his life work and the way he went about it. As he alluded to in his comment in the *Manchester Guardian*, his approach to designing for industry can be considered in terms of the **content** (the sum of his ideas and beliefs about decorative art), **process** (practical issues involved in designing low-relief ornament and repeat pattern for industry), and the **person** (the rôle of the designer for industry).

CONTENT: DAY'S CONCEPTION OF DECORATIVE ART

An inherited mission

Day was six years old at the time of the Great Exhibition in London in 1851. At the age of 42, he noted that while the first world's fair had engendered a sense of wonderment and enthusiasm, in hindsight the "florid and debased" forms of many of the objects in the *Art Journal's Illustrated Catalogue of the Great Exhibition* rendered it "not a cheerful work."[3] There had been attempts from the 1830s on to improve design and manufacture, to advance British competitiveness, and to elevate public taste. Notable among these efforts was the opening in 1837 of the School of Design to train designers for industry. The 1851 Exhibition gave new impetus to design reform, and one significant measure was the founding of the Museum of Ornamental Art at Marlborough House (precursor to the South Kensington Museum) to house exemplary objects for the benefit of designers, manufacturers and the public. Among the leaders who

2.2 Lewis F. Day. Adaptation of the oak to ornament. From Day, *Some Principles of Every-day Art* (1890): 69

spearheaded new design reform efforts from the 1850s on were architect, designer and theorist Owen Jones, art advisor and educational administrator Richard Redgrave and civil servant Henry Cole.[4] Although a youth when these developments were underway, Day inherited the mission of design reform and remained committed to it for the rest of his life.

The nature and purpose of decorative art

Day believed that beauty was the ultimate aesthetic aim of decorative art, and while the conception of beauty might change over time and place, it was always the pursuit of the designer.[5] He stated that "difficult as it may be to define it, there is such a thing as beauty, and that all ornament should make for it – not beauty as the Greeks or Italians understood it (the conception of beauty changes with the times and with the individual), but as the designer feels it."[6] He referred to beauty in fairly general terms, identifying as its major attributes underlying order, the outcome of which is harmony, symmetry, proportion, and rhythm.[7]

In line with other 19th-century critics and designers including A.W.N. Pugin, John Ruskin, and William Morris, Day was grounded in the belief that decorative art was a significant aspect of everyday life and, consequently, deserved more than casual attention. Buildings, furnishings, clothing, books and a myriad of other objects were embellished with ornament, and, consequently, one could not escape its influence.[8] In Day's estimation, that influence was great: "I believe, even, that decorative art may have still more influence on men's lives than picture painting."[9] The ubiquitous nature of ornament in the environment affected everyone, whether they claimed any interest in it or not, so it was worth thinking about and cultivating.[10] Any discussion of it was always context-bound, he contended, for while, theoretically, ornament could be discussed independently, in practice it was "inseparable from the thing ornamented."[11]

From his early writings on, Day fixated on the *purpose* of ornament, and this consideration dominated all others, for "the most essential truth is truth to your purpose, to the end in view."[12] As an accessory art, decoration fulfilled its purpose when it enhanced and harmonised with the architecture or object on which it was used.[13] He minced no words on this point, saying that "the tyranny of the main purpose is absolute."[14]

The very first consideration in the design of decoration was its purpose.[15] The second was the place where it would be used, and congruence with both purpose and place was required for ornament to be fit.[16] Day was in accord with Pugin, Ruskin and Morris on the principle that ornament should reinforce the overall construction of an object and that extraneous ornament should be eliminated. The proportions and shape of an object had to be compatible with how it would be used, and the decoration should faithfully reinforce that through appropriate placement.[17] Since it was a part of the object itself, ornament should not be tacked on, as an afterthought.[18] The designer needed to select materials, tools and processes that would help achieve the intended result, constantly keeping the purpose in view and eliminating whatever was contrary to it.[19]

On the issue of symbolism in decorative art, Day believed that "the beauty of ornament consists in its decorative, not in any symbolic or pictorial, quality. It is perfect only when it fulfills its purpose perfectly."[20] While acknowledging that "in the design of a thoughtful man there will, as a rule, be something more than art or craft, something you may call meaning if you like", he felt that it was not required.[21] Incorporating symbolism into a design was done for personal satisfaction and should not interfere "with the essentially ornamental character of the design".[22] Symbolism would neither

2.3 Lewis F. Day. 'Studies of Apple, and Inlaid Panel Founded Upon Them'. From *Magazine of Art* 3 (1880): 192

2.4 Lewis F. Day. Book cover ornamented with marguerites, a symbol associated with Marguerite d'Angouleme, Queen of Navarre (1492-1549), who had a library of devotional books. From Day, *Nature in Ornament* (1892): pl. 123

satisfy the decorative requirements of ornament nor justify that which was poorly designed.[23] He pointed out that knowing the meaning of an ornamental form may or may not increase the artistic enjoyment of it, for the meaning of symbols can change over time, and one can enjoy the ornament of other times and cultures without ever knowing its symbolic significance.[24] "The part played by symbolism in the evolution of ornament does not affect its present use and purpose."[25] It is not surprising, then, that Day rarely referred to the use of symbolism in his work.

Sources of inspiration

Of the three main sources of inspiration for Day's designs – nature, historic ornament, and Eastern cultures – nature was always accorded primacy of place.[26] "Symmetry and contrast, variety and nicety, strength, grace, growth, and life – all the qualities that give satisfaction in ornament existed in nature before they were thought of in art," he explained, and it was from this primal source that he drew the elements that contributed to beauty in ornament and pattern.[27]

Day joined in the vociferous debate that raged during the 19th century about the relationship of nature to the design of man-made objects. He described two extremes as "strict fidelity to fact", practised by those who advocated direct imitation of nature, and the "bondage of a narrow conventionality" espoused by those who reduced natural forms to their most basic characteristics.[28] While admitting the superiority of natural beauty over that which was man-made, Day disagreed with Ruskin and the naturalists that an artist's chief responsibility was the truthful imitation of nature. The designer's loyalty is "to his purpose, which is not truth, but beauty, and beauty of a kind which does not always allow the close following of nature."[29] Ornament that was fit for its purpose stopped short of imitation because unnecessary detail was rejected in the interests of form and overall harmony with the place it was used.[30]

Day thought the use of the word "conventional" to describe some ornament created confusion, because the term could refer to a wide range of treatments: from those that were intelligent and restrained to those that were "outworn and lifeless."[31] "For my part I see nothing for it but to accept the term 'conventional' to express the kind of treatment adapted both to the use and purpose of ornament and to the material, tools, and methods of work employed upon."[32] In the argument between naturalism and conventionalism,

2.5 a, b and c (above and right) Lewis F. Day. Door panels featuring square spiral and brushwork motifs. From Day, *The Planning of Ornament*, 3rd ed. (1893): pl. 23

2.6 Lewis F. Day. 'Decorative panel of medlars'. From *Magazine of Art* 3 (1880): 271

Day stated that "the truth lies midway between."[33] Natural forms had to be modified, adapted to the purpose, place and conditions for which they were intended, for "there is little in nature which is ready made to the hand of the artist".[34]

2.7 a, b and c (above, from left to right) Lewis F. Day. Panels of strawberries, magnolia plants, and wild clematis. From *Magazine of Art 3* (1880): 356, 357

2.8 (left) Lewis F. Day. 'Comparatively natural lily panel', 1879. From Day, *Nature in Ornament* (1892): pl. 75

2.9 (left) Lewis F. Day. Door panels featuring brushwork. From *Magazine of Art* 3 (1880): 273

2.10 (above) Lewis F. Day. Door panels featuring stencilling. From Day, *The Planning of Ornament*, 3rd ed. (1893): pl. 31

Day devoted considerable attention to this issue in his writings and defined several processes the designer could use in order to appropriately adapt nature to design. First, the designer should study nature throughout the year, noting how natural forms sprouted, grew and decayed in order to identify decorative possibilities.[35] The designer mined the forms, colour and growth of nature to see possibilities for ornament, but, rather than replicating them, "uses not so much these as memories of them".[36] Lyrically, he observed: "What we think we imagine, we more than half remember."[37]

Secondly, the designer should choose forms suitable to the purpose and reject the rest.[38] The task of the designer was primarily an issue of selection, which was no easy feat: "It is as difficult to make ornament natural enough to satisfy the public as to modify nature sufficiently to please the ornamentist."[39]

2.11 Lewis F. Day. Examples of nature adapted to borders. From Day, *Instances of Accessory Art* (1880): pl. 18
Michael Whiteway

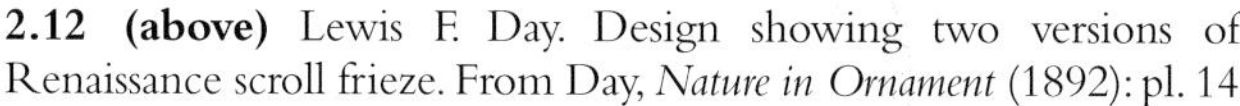

2.12 (above) Lewis F. Day. Design showing two versions of Renaissance scroll frieze. From Day, *Nature in Ornament* (1892): pl. 14

2.13 (right) Lewis F. Day. Design for back of playing cards. From Day, *Every-day Art* (1882): 76

2.14 a, b, c and d (below left) Lewis F. Day. Designs showing acanthus leaves reduced to brushwork. From Day, *Nature in Ornament* (1892): pl. 13

2.15 (below right) Lewis F. Day. Design for painted panel. From Day, *Every-day Art* (1882): 121

2.16 Lewis F. Day. Pattern showing natural forms reduced to brushwork. From Day, *Instances of Accessory Art* (1880): pl. 19
Michael Whiteway

2.17 (above) Lewis F. Day. Tile panel, oak and oak galls. From Day, *Nature in Ornament* (1892): pl. 9

2.18 (right) Lewis F. Day. The dandelion reduced to ornament, 1890. From Day, *Nature in Ornament* (1892): pl. 90

After this preliminary work, several techniques could be used to modify the natural form in a manner and to the degree that achieved the intended purpose. One could *simplify* the natural form.[40] However, simplification had to be done judiciously, since "to emasculate a natural form is not to fit it for ornamental use, and to distribute detail according to a diagram is not to design".[41] Simplification carried too far would render natural forms lifeless and, Day added, "excepting in purely geometric pattern, something in the nature of growth is to be desired in ornament, even the most abstract."[42]

An emphatic natural form like an acorn, sunflower, dandelion or thistle was particularly amenable to conventionalisation because it could be simplified without losing its particular identity.[43] He singled out pattern designer Lindsay P. Butterfield, whom he had known as a student, for his ability to simplify nature's forms, retaining their character and freshness in "the beautiful precision of his line".[44]

2.19 (left) Lindsay P. Butterfield. Pattern of lilies and poppies "which at once disguise the stems and diversify the background". From Day, *Nature and Ornament* 2 (1909): fig. 158; 139-41

2.20 (opposite) Lewis F. Day. 'Scroll and Foliage' pattern. From Day, *Nature in Ornament* (1892): pl. 48; 102. One floral form is the undergrowth of the other, providing contrast of bold forms with delicate details

Natural forms could also be *combined*, as in the case of making one form the undergrowth of another; Day used this technique in his 'Scroll and Foliage' textile design.[45] He cautioned that the combined elements should be treated in a coherent and orderly manner.[46]

Despite its inherent difficulties, the *elaboration* of natural forms also provided opportunities for the designer.[47] Day studied 15th- and 16th-century Gothic work, which featured the turning and curling of the edges and ends of various types of foliage, and he frequently used this technique himself, particularly in his wallpaper and textile designs.[48] Hi. 'Elvas' fabric and wallpaper design, which features "leaves enriched with pattern that takes the place of veining" illustrates his use of this technique.[49]

Morris was unquestionably the designer whose work most influenced Day's own designs. "The name of William Morris is identified with the most determined effort of modern times towards beauty of design," Day said, and one who "richly deserves his great reputation".[50] Among the many things that Day admired about Morris's work, one attribute stood out in particular: he was a master at the adaptation of nature to purpose. Day described Morris as "the foremost pattern-designer of his day", a "genius", and "a master of his craft who, while he used nature as his starting point, his end was ornament".[51] The influence of Morris on Day's work is seen in particular in the swirling foliage and disguised repeats of many of Day's textile and wallpaper designs of the 1880s and 1890s.

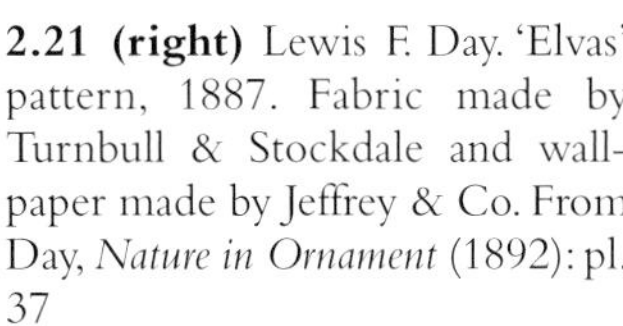

2.21 (right) Lewis F. Day. 'Elvas' pattern, 1887. Fabric made by Turnbull & Stockdale and wallpaper made by Jeffrey & Co. From Day, *Nature in Ornament* (1892): pl. 37

2.22 (below) Lewis F. Day. Pattern from paper cover of box of Elvas plums, which served as inspiration for his Elvas textile and wallpaper pattern. From Day, *Every-day Art* (1882): 4

2.23 (left) Lewis F. Day. Wallpaper pattern showing elaboration of natural forms. From Day, *Pattern Design* (1903): illus. 192

2.24 (below left) William Morris. Working drawing for 'African Marigold' textile, 1876. From Day, 'William Morris and His Art', Easter Art Annual, *Art Journal* (1899): pl. ff. 24

2.25 (below right) Frederick Hollyer. Photograph of William Morris. From Day, 'William Morris and His Art', Easter Art Annual, *Art Journal* (1899): 32

2.26 (top left) Lewis F. Day. Seaweed pattern, 1890. From Day, *Nature in Ornament* (1892): pl. 112

2.27 (top right) Lewis F. Day. Wallpaper design "in which the lines of the scroll are quite evenly balanced". From Day, *Pattern Design* (1903): illus. 4

2.28 (bottom right) Lewis F. Day. Printed cretonne. From 'Cretonnes, Printed Velvets and Linings', Turnbull & Stockdale sample book, c.1892-5

Nordiska Museet, Stockholm.
Erik Folcker Collection, 313.052

2.29 (above) Lewis F. Day. Design for 'Two Colour Scroll', 1890. Signed by Day with the notation "8 blocks". Made as both a cretonne and a printed velveteen by Turnbull & Stockdale, and possibly as a carpet by Brinton's

© Brintons Ltd. With permission

2.30 (left) Lewis F. Day. 'Two Colour Scroll' cretonne, c.1890. Made as both a cretonne and a printed velveteen by Turnbull & Stockdale

Nordiska Museet, Stockholm. Erik Folcker Collection, 317.519

Day had a rich understanding of the value of studying old work; a designer could learn how design had been adapted to the purposes and conditions of particular times and places. Day judged that there was "more benefit from *the study of ancient processes* than from the *worship of antique forms*".[52] Throughout history there was always development, growth, and modification to meet the demands of changing circumstances and, by fixating too tightly on the details of a past style, Day believed one would "inevitably lose its spirit".[53] "When a style is no longer elastic it is proof that it is dead", and tradition was not to be worshipped, but adapted and passed on, he observed.[54]

Day opposed the slavish reproduction of medieval, classical or other historic forms, which only resulted in common and dreary work.[55] Copying, he believed, also stifled the designer's own invention: "Whenever we repeat the forms invented by them there is all the difference between invention and memory, between reality and affectation, between life and galvanism."[56] The study of the past should suggest new possibilities for the present, and Day remarked that "it is as bad to be blind to all precedent as to follow a precedent blindly".[57]

To develop his selective faculty, the designer should choose examples that mean something to him.[58] Though Day found inspiration in the design of many eras, he looked in particular to the Gothic and the Renaissance

2.31 (opposite, left) Lewis F. Day. Floral tile. Made by Pilkington's Tile & Pottery Co. The pattern was shown at the Glasgow International Exhibition and described as a cloisonné tile in coloured glazes (*Pilkington Catalogue 1902*: 36-7) (The top tile has been repeated twice to show its use in a pattern) Anthony J. Cross

2.32 (opposite, right) Lewis F. Day. 'Chrysanthemum' pattern, 1889. From Day, *Nature in Ornament* (1892): pl. 40

2.33 (top left) Lewis F. Day. Wallpaper based on Renaissance inspiration, 1887. Probably made by Jeffrey & Co. From Day, 'Victorian Progress in Applied Design', *Art Journal* (1887): 195

2.34 (top right) Lewis F. Day. 'Renaissance' design, 1909. Monogrammed 'LFD'. Possibly made as a carpet by Brinton's

© Brintons Ltd. With permission

2.35 (left) Silk damask in French style. Made by Warner & Ramm, 1887. From Day, 'Victorian Progress in Applied Design', *Art Journal* (1887): 202

periods for examples of how natural forms were adapted to purpose while retaining the life in them.[59] He summarily dismissed much of the decorative art of 17th- and 18th-century France, condemning "the rockwork and the broken scrolls, the garlands and the trellises, the bows and the ribbons, and all such frivolities of the later French monarchy" for their artificiality and lack of restraint.[60] Regardless of the period from which a designer drew inspiration, for Day the task was always to adapt historic forms to the purpose and conditions of the present. Day contended that the designer does not simply "take his bucket to the well either of nature or of art", for originality and style result from adaptation, not imitation.[61]

There were several designers who Day frequently singled out for their skill in using historic forms as inspiration while creating designs that were truly their own. He respected William Burges for his eclectic use of historic sources, in particular the 13th century, and said that he was "an artist and an originator" who "did not let his learning overgrow his art or sap his invention".[62] Day noted that although Burges sometimes used rather heavy and stunted forms, and that his archaic style was not one to be widely popular, "he was a genuine artist, and a strong one, expressing himself, moreover, in all he did".[63] He also regarded sculptor Alfred Stevens as "the man of the period who came nearest to the great Italians of the Renaissance," but whose style, as exemplified in the Wellington Monument, was "too dignified to be popular".[64]

2.36 Bruce J. Talbert. Cabinet. From Day, 'Instances of art in things of common use', *Magazine of Art* 3 (1880): 105

2.37 Lewis F. Day. 'Trellis' dado, 1874. Made by Jeffrey & Co. for W.B. Simpson & Sons. Block-printed
National Archives, United Kingdom, BT43/101 Part 1 No. 282676

He admired in particular Bruce J. Talbert, and he praised his *Gothic Forms Applied to Furniture, Metal Work, and Decoration for Domestic Purposes* (1867), "a kind of pattern-book, not so much addressed to the public as to the furniture trades," for its vigorous and original designs.[65] Day thought it particularly significant that Talbert used historic inspiration to produce designs that influenced manufacture, as seen in his 'Sunflower' wallpaper produced by Jeffrey & Co.; silk and tapestry curtains for Cowlishaw, Nichol & Co., and Templeton's; and furniture for Jackson & Graham, and Marsh, Jones & Cribb.[66] With the exception of Morris, the influence of these other designers on Day was philosophical rather than stylistic: he valued what they did and their example reinforced his beliefs about how the designer should approach design.

Day also drew inspiration throughout his life from the decorative art of Japan, China, India and the Middle East. It is highly likely that Day saw the collections of Japanese applied arts exhibited at the International Exhibition of 1862 when he returned to London after finishing his studies on the Continent. Although specific Japanese sources that Day may have consulted are not known, Japanese books of prints, such as Hokusai's *Manga* (1816) were in circulation. The Oriental Warehouse of Farmer and Rogers' Great Shawl and Cloak Emporium on Regent St. opened in 1862, followed by Arthur Lasenby Liberty's East India House (later renamed Liberty & Co.) in 1875. Day would have frequented these shops, along with the likes of Edward W. Godwin, William Morris and Christopher Dresser, in order to see and acquire Japanese objects. In addition, some firms, including Minton's, began producing Japanese-inspired wares from the 1860s. Day had ample resources to feed what became a lifelong habit of studying the decorative arts of the East.

Day was very intrigued by the way different cultures adapted nature to purpose.[67] While he found the asymmetry and inventive diapering patterns of Japanese decorative art commendable, it was the Japanese treatment of nature with fitness for purpose that drew his highest praise. In acknowledging the craze for things Japanese in the late 1860s and 1870s, he commented: "The fact is, Japanese art took us by surprise, and we went fairly mad about it. But in sober

2.38 Lewis F. Day. Designs for blue and white ceramics, showing Chinese influence, 1879. From Day, *Instances of Accessory Art* (1880): pl. 25
Michael Whiteway

earnest we shall have to confess that it has taught us just the lesson that we wanted, in teaching us how to adapt natural forms without taking the nature out of them. Gothic art showed us something of this; but it did not show us so clearly, nor in so many ways, as Japanese. The study of these two styles and of nature, should enable us to master at least the difficulty of rendering natural forms aptly."[68]

Day noted the impact of Japanese art on the work of two designers he particularly admired. He highly regarded Thomas Jeckyll, whose Japanese-inspired wrought and cast-iron work for Barnard, Bishop & Barnard of Norwich had "a character of its own" and showed originality and workmanship that justified its popularity.[69] He also singled out architect and designer Edward W. Godwin, an "artist of yet higher powers," and one "who did many things more than well," as seen in the lasting influence of his Anglo-Japanese furniture on furniture design.[70] In contrast, Day was silent on the work of Christopher Dresser, a major convert to Japanese forms, and made few references to his designs.

Day collected many examples of the textiles, prints, embroideries, and ceramics of other lands, finding in them suggestions for some of his work. He found the Chinese use of colour "superlatively fine" and particularly admired the "even balance between form and colour" in Indian, Arabian, Moorish and Persian ornament.[71] In commenting on William De Morgan's wares shown at the Royal Jubilee Exhibition in 1887, Day praised "his lustre ware, which is so characteristic of him and so indicative of his influence upon current design and recent progress".[72] What impressed Day about De Morgan's use of Hispano-Moresque models was that he did not copy them but produced pottery that had "a character all the artist's own".[73] Day's fascination with the decorative arts of the Middle and Far East persisted through his life. About six months before he died, he journeyed to Egypt and planned to write a book about Egyptian decorative art, which he praised: "It is chiefly the restraint and dignity of the ornamental design that is so much to be admired in Egyptian work."[74] However, his death cut short this plan.

Much of Day's education had been acquired on the Continent, and from his early years he had been exposed to a wide range of historic ornament. As an

2.39 Lewis F. Day. Persian-inspired velveteen, 1888. Made by Thomas Wardle & Co.

V&A Images/Victoria and Albert Museum, London ,T.77-1953

adult he spent a month or two each year travelling abroad and studying first-hand the decorative art of other periods and countries, which never failed to inspire him.[75] His lectures and writings, replete with references to historic sites and museums of other countries, revealed his great appreciation for travel as a means of self-education. Since his twenties it had become his habit to use his spare time to study and sketch collections at the South Kensington Museum, which he also used as a teaching method with his students.[76]

Day was familiar with the many pattern books that were in circulation, and he would have consulted them from time to time. Two he singled out in particular were the *Analysis of Ornament*, by critic and analyst Ralph N. Wornum, and *The Grammar of Ornament*, by Owen Jones, which represented "a turning point in the history of English ornament".[77] While Day thought his "principles" were really more like "tips," and did not accept "the poor opinion he had of the natural element in design", he recognised that Jones's influence was "immense".[78] Day added that "no man did more than he towards clearing the ground for us, and so making possible the new departures which we have made since his time".[79] He noted that Pugin and Ruskin had also influenced design reform, but he attributed "even more weight to the teaching of Owen Jones, because he appealed to and touched the manufacturers, whom he somehow succeeded in persuading to believe in him, much to the improvement of their productions".[80]

In defence of eclecticism

The use of multiple sources of inspiration reveals Day's eclecticism. He acknowledged that the term eclecticism sometimes conjured up "a senseless jumbling together of different styles" and "acts on some people like a red rag on a bull".[81] However, in his estimation, eclecticism was simply the exercise of choice.[82] He was dismissive of those who derided eclecticism, noting that they would make a choice themselves and then impose their choice on others.[83] The public then was persuaded to adopt a particular style without having any real attachment to it.

Day appealed to history in his defense of eclecticism: "Art has always been eclectic."[84] Citing the examples of the Italians of the Renaissance who incorporated Arabic detail into their ornament and William Morris who worked Persian as well as Gothic influences into his designs, Day queried: "If something from Japan or Timbuctoo comes appropriate to my design, what is to hinder me from adopting it?"[85] He argued that any style could serve as a departure point for the designer, whose task was to weld the choices into a harmonious whole so that the result would be "not the confusion of styles but their fusion".[86]

A designer's choices, he reasoned, would reveal his originality, if he had any; over time he would build up his own traditions, and develop his own style.[87] A designer's style would be evidenced in the choices of inspiration, materials and methods of workmanship.[88] The designer had to be sensitive to the hints given by particular materials, tools, and methods and get out of them what they gave best.[89] For Day, the challenge always came back to considering "the use and purpose of his ornament, from the place it is to occupy, the materials it is to be in, the tools or implements with which it is to be carried out".[90]

Day firmly believed that all design was evolutionary and that "style rightly understood is the character which comes of accommodating design to its use and purpose, to the time and place to which it belongs."[91] He mused: "Perhaps in the future the more modern quality of personal individuality will take the place of one common style."[92] He reflected that the spirit of the age was "progressive", as well as "eminently sceptic and selective".[93] The term eclectic fits both his own work and the late 19th century: "It is, in fact, only the name for the selective, independent, scientific spirit which belongs very specially to modern times".[94]

Process: designing for industry

Day thought that it was impossible to state the general principles of design as a set of formal propositions, because to gain general acceptance, they would have to be so vague that they would not be of much practical help.[95] What were commonly called 'principles' were usually working rules that the designer had found useful in practice; and Day told readers of his articles and *Textbooks of Ornamental Design* to regard his comments in the same light.[96] "I offer my experience for what it is – that of one among many."[97] He was well aware of his own forceful and blunt manner of speaking, and he cautioned readers that "in the end it is your own conviction that you have to follow, not mine or any other man's".[98]

Most of Day's output as a designer was in flat or low-relief ornament, and he particularly excelled in pattern design. While his advice about purpose, process and materials was applicable to various types of design work, much of it was directed specifically to designing pattern for industry. Day's working rules were primarily centred on two issues: challenges inherent in pattern design, and the demands of designing for commercial production.[99]

2.40 Lewis F. Day. 'Construction of German Gothic Tracery Patterns', 1886. From Day, *The Anatomy of Pattern*, 4th ed. (1895): pl. 1

Challenges inherent in pattern design

Day pointed out that as "ornament in repetition", pattern resembled music, wherein a unit was repeated at regular intervals, resulting in rhythm or cadence.[100] For a pattern to flow harmoniously, the designer had to look beyond the construction of a single unit: "The balance which in a single composition satisfies the eye is not enough when it comes to repetition."[101] Designing pattern demanded analytical as well as creative skills, for as Day wryly observed: "The artist's hand does not crawl aimlessly over the paper and trail behind it flowers of the imagination."[102] The single most important component was a plan, helping the designer to identify the geometric basis of the design, to handle scale and lines, to adjust emphasis, and to use colour effectively.

Without a system or plan, the designer was subject to the perils of the unforeseen, and these loomed large in Day's mind.[103] The benefits accruing from a plan far outweighed any inconvenience in terms of time and effort required at the outset. Day advised that, while there were different methods for tackling a design problem, it was generally safer to begin with an orderly system that would predetermine the arrangement of prominent features of a design.[104] How that planning played out depended upon the type of pattern and the purpose for which it was intended.[105] "The one thing needful in design is to 'Know what you mean to do and do it' –

WIDTH OF PAPER - 21 ins

2.41 (opposite, top left) Lewis F. Day. Diagram showing construction of wallpaper pattern. From Day, *The Anatomy of Pattern*, 4th ed. (1895): pl. 27

2.42 (opposite, top right) Lewis F. Day. Completed drop pattern wallpaper design shown on pl. 27. From Day, *The Anatomy of Pattern*, 4th ed. (1895): pl. 28

2.43 (opposite, bottom left) Lewis F. Day. 'Turnover pattern revealing the vertical line on which it is reversed'. From Day, *Pattern Design* (1903): illus. 124

2.44 (opposite, bottom right) Lewis F. Day. 'Mortimer' wallpaper pattern "in which marked governing lines steady the effect", 1896. Made by Jeffrey & Co. From Day, *Pattern Design* (1903): illus. 181

2.45 (top left) Lewis F. Day. Stencil-like wallpaper pattern 10½ inches (26.7cm.) wide (half the width of the wallpaper block). Made by Jeffrey & Co. From Day, *Pattern Design* (1903): 161

2.46 (top right) Lewis F. Day. Stencil-like wallpaper pattern. From Jeffrey & Co., *Selected Hand-Printed Wall Papers* (1894-5)
Nordiska Museet, Stockholm,
Erik Folcker Collection, 310.405

2.47 (left) Lewis F. Day. Textile pattern designed on the lines of the square. From Day, *The Anatomy of Pattern*, 4th ed. (1895): pl. 18

and whatever keeps you to the point is helpful," he counselled.[106] It was critically important to bear in mind the end product for a pattern – for curtains that would hang in folds, for wallpaper that would be hung flat on a wall, and so on – and whether the pattern was meant to be a prominent feature of decoration or a restful background.[107]

Day insisted that pattern always had a geometric basis.[108] Working according to the basic geometry of repeat patterns was not a straightjacket for the designer, however: "It is in planning that originality has scope. New forms are only once in awhile to be evolved, but infinite variety is possible in arrangement of forms free to us but not our personal property."[109] After mapping out the essential elements of the geometric construction, the designer could either reveal or disguise that construction, as appropriate.[110]

Planning the basic structure of a pattern would, he maintained, give it a sense of scale and help ensure that lines fell out satisfactorily.[111] In repeat patterns, lines asserted themselves, and if they were not planned for, would be "in all probability as inelegant as they were unexpected".[112] If lines in one direction were too prominent, they could be compensated for by features that directed attention away from them.[113] Another value of a system was that it made "an obvious repeat less obvious".[114] Day was particularly masterful in his disguising of repeats, which is quite a difficult task.[115] He urged the designer to test the pattern and make sure it repeated satisfactorily before "he lets it out of his hands".[116]

2.48 (left) Lewis F. Day. "Wallpaper pattern in which the lines of recurrence are purposely lost", 1889. This paper, 'Corinthian Scroll', was made by Jeffrey & Co. Block-printed. From Day, *Pattern Design* (1903):illus. 182

2.49 (above) Diagram showing "how to prove a design". From *The Anatomy of Pattern*, 4th ed. (1895): pl. 35. Day also showed a variation of this in *Pattern Design* (1903): illus. 209

2.50 a, b and c Lewis F. Day. Designs from *The Anatomy of Pattern,* 4th ed. (1895). **(Top left)** pl. 37 (1886) "exemplifying the intentional confusion of forms"; **(bottom left)** pl. 47 "Outline which defines the form"; and **(top right)** pl. 48 "Outline which softens the form"

A plan would also help the designer handle emphatic features that otherwise could come out awkwardly.[117] For example, although stems were often necessary in a floral design, one did not want them too strongly marked.[118] Through careful planning of the pattern, the designer would determine how to emphasise certain features, subdue others, modify form, and omit distracting details.[119] The weight of mass, flow of line, and sharpness of contour all needed to be factored into the plan.[120]

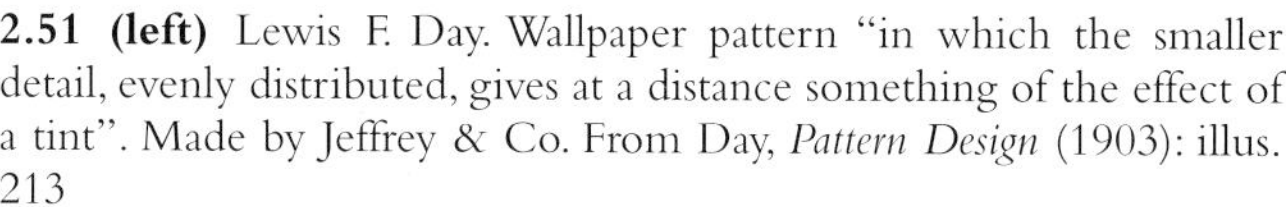

2.51 (left) Lewis F. Day. Wallpaper pattern "in which the smaller detail, evenly distributed, gives at a distance something of the effect of a tint". Made by Jeffrey & Co. From Day, *Pattern Design* (1903): illus. 213

2.52 (below left) Lewis F. Day. "Inlay pattern in which severity of line would be softened by colour of woods". From Day, *The Anatomy of Pattern*, 4th ed. (1895): pl. 39

2.53 a, b, c and d (right) Lewis F. Day. "Diagram showing effect of different colour treatments of identically the same forms". From Day, *Pattern Design* (1903): illus. 218.

Early in the planning process, the designer also needed to determine the colour scheme, which could provide liveliness, lightness, steadiness, and emphasis as needed.[121] This required the designer to calculate "the value and function of each particular colour rather than its hue" and decide which colours would be prominent and which would recede.[122] Colour could emphasise form, as in the case of drawing attention to a flower by using a bright colour. Stalks or stems could be made less obtrusive by reducing them to a colour close to that of the background, and in the case of two growths intermingled, one could be strengthened by colour and the other neutralised.[123] In one of Day's wallpaper patterns, the smaller brush strokes in the wallpaper merge at a distance with the background colour, producing an intermediate tint that helps define the cusped shapes.[124]

Animals and human figures in pattern design

Though Day acknowledged that animals and human figures could be used effectively in ornament that was not repeated, he objected to their use in repeated pattern.[125] Much of repeat pattern was meant to serve as background rather than attracting attention.[126] Day humorously remarked that "a strong personality writes, so to speak, always under its own signature; but I am not sure that I want anyone's personality to call out to me from the walls and floors of my room".[127] Animals expressed movement, which interfered with the steadiness and restfulness that a background should provide.[128] They could be visually startling in a repeat pattern, and a parade of realistic-looking animals could become very tiresome.[129] Moreover, animals used in a carpet design would appear upside down from particular vantage points in a room; and, in line with a number of contemporaries, Day was against directional designs for carpets.[130]

Animal and human figures also introduced a pictorial quality into a pattern, and the "pictorial ideal of art" was not the purpose of the designer.[131] Day also contended that in most cases, animals did not add anything to the design and usually detracted from it.[132] If, however, they were to be used, then, in order to render them fit for pattern, the life and movement characteristics of the animals should be removed through rigorous conventionalisation, thereby reducing them to ornamental forms.[133]

37. Heraldic lion.

2.54 (above) Lewis F. Day. Panel with heraldic dragon. From *Magazine of Art* 3 (1880): 375

2.55 (top right) Lewis F. Day. "Balance of ornament enough for a panel but not for a repeating pattern". From Day, *Pattern Design* (1903): illus. 3

2.56 (centre right) Lewis F. Day. Heraldic lion. From Day, *Some Principles of Every-day Art*, 2nd ed. (1894): illus. 37

2.57 (bottom right) Lewis F. Day. Panel with fish-like creatures metamorphosing into foliage, 1887. From Day, *The Planning of Ornament*, 3rd ed. (1893): pl.8

Walter Crane, with whom Day carried on a "Friendly Dispute" on the subject, agreed with Day that animals and human figures were difficult elements to use and required some degree of conventionalisation to suit the purpose of the design and the materials used.[134] Crane, however, felt that the justification, ultimately, was in the artist's treatment and argued that animals could give line and mass not achievable in other ways, provide life and movement, as well as convey meaning and allegory.[135] Crane's views were undoubtedly influenced by his early work in book illustration, and some of his wallpaper patterns exhibit his strong talents as an illustrator.

Day credited Crane with being able "to bend the human shape to ornamental purposes".[136] He thought highly of Crane's 'Wood Notes' wallpaper, which he deemed particularly suitable for dining rooms, halls and staircases.[137] The woodland creatures were subdued, half-hidden by rich leafage, and conveyed a charming sense of mystery that gradually revealed itself to the viewer.[138] He also enjoyed Crane's nursery-papers, such as 'The House that Jack Built', because they preserved the sense of fun seen in his picture books.[139]

In light of his strict views on the subject, it is not surprising that Day's own use of animal forms in repeat pattern was rare. He employed birds ornamentally in his 'Indian' textile pattern, which derived its inspiration from 18th-century Indian chintz. Their colourful plumage intermingling with flowers and leaves, the birds barely alight on the meandering stems. The birds in his wallpaper design for Jeffrey & Co. are even more rigorously conventionalised.

2.58 (left) Walter Crane. Illustration in which Crane teased Day about the latter's aversion to using animals in repeat pattern. From Crane and Day, *Moot Points* (1903): 94

2.59 (right) Walter Crane. 'Woodnotes' wallpaper, 1886. Made by Jeffrey & Co. Block-printed. From Sugden and Edmondson, *A History of English Wallpaper* (1926): pl. 130

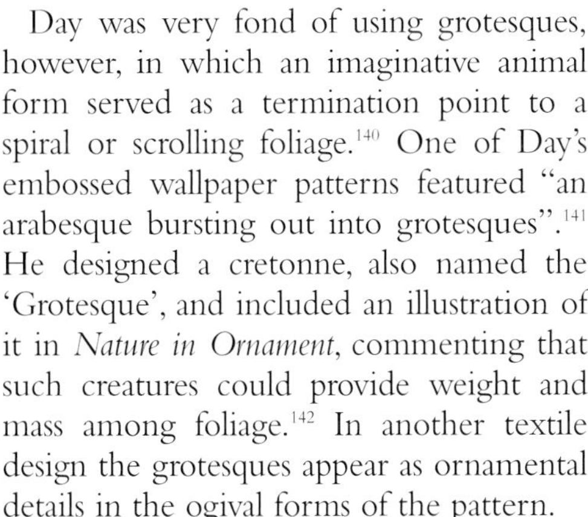

Day was very fond of using grotesques, however, in which an imaginative animal form served as a termination point to a spiral or scrolling foliage.[140] One of Day's embossed wallpaper patterns featured "an arabesque bursting out into grotesques".[141] He designed a cretonne, also named the 'Grotesque', and included an illustration of it in *Nature in Ornament*, commenting that such creatures could provide weight and mass among foliage.[142] In another textile design the grotesques appear as ornamental details in the ogival forms of the pattern.

2.60 (top left) Lewis F. Day. Wallpaper pattern for Jeffrey & Co., 1886. From Day, *The Anatomy of Pattern*, 4th ed. (1895): pl. 38

2.61 (top right) Lewis F. Day. 'Indian', 1909. Made by Turnbull & Stockdale for Liberty & Co. Contemporary reproduction, renamed 'Dante', made by Liberty & Co. © Liberty PLC. With permission

2.62 (bottom right) Lewis F. Day. Textile pattern "with grotesques, the creatures themselves reduced to ornament", 1885. Made by Turnbull & Stockdale. From Day, *The Application of Ornament*, 3rd. ed. (1895): pl. 7; ix

2.63 (top left) Lewis F. Day. 'Grotesque' embossed wallpaper, c.1890. Made by Jeffrey & Co. From Day, *Pattern Design* (1903): illus.206

2.64 (bottom left) Lewis F. Day. 'Grotesque' printed cretonne, 1886. Made by Turnbull & Stockdale. From Day, *Nature in Ornament* (1892): pl. 106

2.65 (right) Lewis F. Day. Grotesque in figured damask. From Day, *Every-day Art* (1882): 139

Grotesques lent themselves to ornament because the designer could create them to fit the purposes of his design.[143] Day particularly looked to Renaissance examples for inspiration because it was during that period in particular that "the ornamental capacities of grotesquerie have been most fully developed".[144] Day cautioned that grotesques should not look too much like a particular animal, for the most successful ones were those that derived from the imagination of the artist.[145] Nevertheless, grotesques should be consistent in their formulation and not absurdities.[146]

Demands of designing for commercial production

"A designer, whatever his natural gift, is of no practical use until he is at home with the conditions of manufacture," Day insisted.[147] Industrial and economic considerations set parameters within which the designer must work. These realities could limit the designer's choices and he had to accept this from the outset or he would simply be wasting time.[148] Thorough planning would help the designer deal with these challenges and use resources and time efficiently.[149] Production requirements affected both the character of the design and its plan.[150] Chief among these requirements was that of standardisation; without uniformity in the width of

chintzes and carpets, or without stock sizes of tiles, for example, it would be extremely difficult for manufacturers to estimate beforehand the cost of producing goods.[151]

Both the dimension and the proportions of a pattern were largely determined by the material in which it would be produced.[152] Length and width of stuffs was determined by mechanism, such as the girth of the roller for printed textiles: 30in. (76.2cm.) wide, 15in. (38.1cm.) deep; the size of the block for block-printed wallpapers: 21in. by 21in. (53.3cm. x 53.3cm.); or a square mesh of lines 6in. (15.2cm.) or 8in. (20.3cm.) apart for tiles.[153] Generally speaking, a designer was only free to work within those limits. Even if technical adjustments could be made, economics often prohibited it. As a case in point, although certain extensions beyond the dimensions of the standard wallpaper block might sometimes be made – for a repeat of 42in. (106.7cm.), for example – patterns spread over a larger area required more blocks, resulting in higher production costs than were feasible.[154] The designer also had to realise that his pattern would be viewed in two situations: in the pattern book and in the actual decorative scheme.[155]

2.66 (top left) Lewis F. Day. Drop pattern giving a diagonal line. From Day, *The Anatomy of Pattern*, 4th ed. (1895): pl. 32; xi

2.67 (bottom left) Lewis F. Day. Drop pattern giving a zigzag cross line. From Day, *The Anatomy of Pattern*, 4th ed. (1895): pl. 33; xi

2.68 (top right) Lewis F. Day. Design for 6-inch square (15.2cm.^{2}) tile. Day used this design to show how a unit of design can be turned to create a pattern four times that size. From Day, *The Anatomy of Pattern*, 4th ed. (1895): pl. 29; 40

The capacities of particular materials used and the type of manufacturing process also affected the designer's plan.[156] For example, designing a pattern with a great deal of intricacy of detail for execution in a material difficult to handle was gross misjudgment.[157] Certain types of dyes were amenable to particular processes (as is seen in indigo discharge printing of textiles), and the affinity of a material to a particular dye also had to be taken into account.[158]

Day remarked that the designer also had to create patterns that would work well "in maybe a half-dozen colour schemes", since a pattern that could be produced in only one was generally not worth producing.[159] The colour scheme was also affected by production considerations including whether the design would be block-printed by hand or machine-printed by roller. Block printing by hand produced a softer line, while roller printing by machine provided greater accuracy in the fitting of the joints of a pattern and ensured continuity of line through long production runs.[160] In planning out the colour scheme, the designer also had to think about whether there would be time for one colour to dry before the next was printed over it.[161]

The designer also needed to foresee conditions that could arise during later stages of the design and manufacturing processes.[162]

2.69 a, b and c (left and above) Lewis F. Day. 'Tudor' tiles, c.1900. Made by Pilkington's Tile & Pottery Co. Shown at the Paris Exposition 1900 and Glasgow Exhibition 1901 as "cloisonné tile in coloured glazes" (*Pilkington Catalogue 1900*: 24, 34, 27; *Pilkington Catalogue 1901*: 36-7)

(2.69 a and b, left): Roger Hensman

(2.69 c, above): Pilkington's Lancastrian Pottery Society

Sufficient direction and information needed to be given for production of the design by hand or machine.[163] Day castigated designers who, viewing their rôle as one of simply supplying designs, left it up to the manufacturer to work out the details of execution: "It is quite a common occurrence to hear artists who have fallen short of fulfilling their part of the undertaking throw blame on the workman for not satisfactorily doing what they themselves ought never to have left undone".[164] Day was not simply theorising in the pristine environment of the studio; he practised what he preached. The principals of the firms for which he designed relayed his visits to their manufacturing facilities and how he thrashed out with them the industrial and economic constraints that would affect the type of design and its plan.[165] Based on what he learned about the particular capacities of materials and manufacturing methods, he frequently made production notes in the margins of his designs.

2.70 (above) Lewis F. Day. 'Indian', 1909. Made by Turnbull & Stockdale for Liberty & Co. Contemporary reproduction in three colourways, renamed 'Dante', made by Liberty & Co.

PERSON: THE RÔLE OF THE DESIGNER FOR INDUSTRY

The high level of external activity generated by Day's relationships with clients, colleagues, students and the press, was balanced by his strong reflective tendency, which led him to think deeply about the rôle of the designer in contemporary manufacture and commerce. This was also true of many of his contemporaries. Guided by their deep convictions, many made accommodations with the realities of designing for industry, albeit in different ways. What distinguished Day, was that while facing squarely the very real problems inherent in contemporary manufacture, he never lost his faith in the possibility of a marriage of design and industry. Designing for industry was his passion and his joy, a rôle that was not second best to picture-painting, as with Crane, or designing for hand-manufacture, as with Morris.

As a lecturer, writer and critic, Day addressed many different aspects of designing for manufacture in the late 19th and early 20th centuries. Nevertheless, certain themes emerged consistently and characterised his very independent, personal response to industrialisation and the rôle of the designer. Several core

2.71 Walter Crane. Cover, *Moot Points: Friendly Disputes on Art and Industry*, Walter Crane and Lewis F. Day (1903)

beliefs structured his energies, underpinned his practice as a designer, and distinguished his business and professional relationships. These convictions ran as refrains from his early journal articles of the 1870s, through his *Textbooks of Ornamental Design* in the 1880s and 1890s, and were reiterated in *Moot Points: Friendly Disputes on Art and Industry*, co-authored with his friend and colleague Walter Crane in 1903. The two men were almost exact contemporaries, both born in 1845 and Crane outliving Day by only five years. They were friends from their early years as designers, belonged to many of the same organisations, and designed for some of the same companies, yet they had very different views.

Grounded in the present

Day admitted that designers of his day did not live under the happiest working conditions, though he added: "Past or future, ideal conditions of work are something of a fairy tale."[166] He also said that he was not ashamed of the century in which he lived and that the only course of action was to look forward, not back.[167] He recommended that a designer deal with present realities rather than trying to revert to ways of working that the world has outgrown, such as "the 'red hot pincers' and the grosing iron of the Middle Ages".[168] "What use is setting back the clock when time is all the while running on?" he queried; and he welcomed advances in science that improved manufacture and praised the futuristic perspective seen in W.A.S. Benson's electric light fittings.[169]

One of the realities of the day was the machine, and Day sharply differed from Ruskin and Morris on issues of handcraftsmanship, machine production and subdivision of labour. Since the machine provided opportunities for designers in both the saving of labour and the stimulation of demand for design work, Day perceived it to be a powerful force that should be harnessed.[170] He pointed out that the 'expedients of design' came out of handwork and that craftsmen have used aids to manufacture down through the ages.[171] Morris was not, in fact, anti-machine, but Day accepted with greater equanimity the necessity of machine-made work to fulfill consumer demand.[172]

Nevertheless, Day readily acknowledged that all outcomes of industrial manufacture were not necessarily happy ones. The availability of more goods for more people was positive, but, admittedly, some goods were poorly designed and cheaply made.[173] Day, however, pointed out that all machine manufacture was not bad, any more than all handwork was good.[174] Handwork could also be fumbling, inaccurate and incompetently produced.[175] Machinery had "practical and pecuniary value" and Day believed that if used properly, it could have artistic value, as well.[176] He stated: "Mr. Morris's theory, 'Art *for* the people *by* the people,' is a splendid dream. Perhaps it is to be more nearly realised by the aid of machinery than by any attempt to suppress it."[177]

2.72 Walter Crane. Illustration. From Crane and Day, *Moot Points* (1903): 39

Unlike Ruskin, Morris and Crane, Day accepted the necessity of subdivision of labour: "Progress has been in the direction of saving labour," he noted without regret.[178] "Much of artist-craftsmanship, so called, *is* inefficient. And the delusion that there should be no subdivision of labour goes to account for the inefficiency."[179] He did not accept the notion that anything made by the hand of man was morally superior and intrinsically better than that produced by machine. "We should not trust to the machine for what man's hand can do better, nor to man's hand for what can be better done by machine," he insisted.[180]

In referring to the diversity of views held by those who espoused the Arts and Crafts movement, he commented: "Some of us who have worked for it have no belief in reversing the current of industrial progress" and "going back to hand-labour and production on a scale which makes it prohibitively costly".[181] Day was concerned, as were other members of the movement, about the potential of well-made goods to improve people's lives. He thought it "a strange inconsistency", however, that some of them "should be so largely engaged in art which is essentially, and always must be, for the very few who have the taste to appreciate it and the purse to pay for it".[182] Day designed for high-end manufacturers including Jeffrey & Co. and Turnbull & Stockdale, and although their furnishings were not inexpensive, they were affordable to more people than hand-made products. He commended firms such as Liberty & Co. for marketing goods that were both tasteful and less expensive.[183]

While agreeing with Morris, Crane, C.R. Ashbee and others on the need to improve design and society, and being sympathetic with the sincerity of their intentions, Day did not accept socialism as the solution to the problems in contemporary manufacture and society. "Many of us recognise, of course, the intimate relationship of art to life, without arguing from that the necessity of socialism," he commented.[184] Although some of his contemporaries engaged in political debate about ways to effect societal change, others did not, and Day was in their number. Aside from a few remarks about socialism not providing an answer to societal problems, Day tended to keep his political views private.[185]

While he was "no blind admirer of the present", Day observed that negative conditions in contemporary manufacture were exacerbated partly by designers themselves.[186] "We have yet to try what seems the obvious way out of the difficulty in which a sudden change of industrial conditions has landed us – the experiment, not of returning to the rude or leisurely manner of old days, but of devoting ourselves to the solution of the artistic and industrial problem of the moment."[187] Despite present problems, Day remained optimistic: "Not the best of all possible worlds, perhaps, but not so black as pessimists paint it".[188]

While Day agreed that a designer's work was personal, it was, he said, "still the outcome of conditions, the solution of a problem set by circumstances outside himself".[189] Although his views might conjure up the image of 'keeping a stiff upper lip', Day derived immense satisfaction – even a sense of exhilaration – in meeting the challenges posed by industrial design. He always came back to the point that making the best of them proved the person.[190] "To the making of a practical designer there goes an element of pugnacity – he enjoys tackling a tough problem."[191]

In response to Crane's complaint that some patterns were dull because they were produced without joy, Day retorted that while neither of them wanted "stodgy, spiritless ornament", he found joy in working through a problem in design and satisfaction when he arrived at a solution.[192] He prosaically questioned: "Who wants poetry in a carpet or 'joy' in a wall-paper? The purpose of either is fulfilled if it

2.73 (top right) and 2.74 (bottom right) Walter Crane. Illustrations. From Crane and Day, *Moot Points*, (1903): 85 and 12 respectively

forms a plainly broken background of restful colour."[193] While Crane believed that the designer added poetry to his work for his own pleasure and that of the beholder, Day found the human quality in art did not require poetry, but rather was reflected in how the designer solved a practical design problem.[194] He felt that the workman who took pleasure in his work "has a fair chance of pleasing".[195]

Design at the nexus of art and commerce

Since applied art involved the embellishment of everyday objects that were made available through selling and buying, trade was not simply the end result of designing useful objects but rather was the reason they were made in the first place.[196] Between the act of creating objects and trading, there was "the whole range of industry more or less artistic", and Day found it difficult to divorce art from commerce. "If (as we both believe) in the best of handicraft there is art; and if (as you cannot deny) handicraft is associated with commerce, how can it be that an artist ceases to be an artist when he touches commerce?" he questioned.[197] While "manufacture" and "industry" might be prosaic, they were necessary in modern society and, Day believed, only harm would result from separating them.[198]

Unlike Crane, who detested the constraints that working for industry imposed on him, Day took them in his stride: "You hate commerce because you feel yourself tied to it. I can think kindly of it because I don't feel that it hurts me or anybody much – rightly conducted."[199] While he acknowledged that some machine-made goods were poorly designed and made, and that there were few manufacturers "of considerable taste", he held that both manufacturers and designers were to blame.[200] "You talk of trade. If it is artistically in a bad way, that is perhaps because artists abuse it instead of trying to help it," Day observed, adding that some are impelled not only "to leave it to its devices, but to lavish their best abuse upon it".[201]

Manufacturers and designers looked at industrial production from their own vantage points, and that sometimes hurt their working relationship.[202] Manufacturers knew too little about design, and if designers knew more about production methods, they would find ways to bridge the gap "without going against the irresistible current of modern industry".[203]

Day contended that rather than being preoccupied with past offences of machine-made art, one should look to the *future* of it.[204] A good working relationship between designers and manufacturers was critical to success in the production of quality goods. The best patron was the producer or trader who had both some knowledge of design and the conviction of its monetary value in the marketplace.[205] Art and commerce were inextricably connected, Day insisted, and cooperation was key: "The best work of all cannot be arrived at until artist and manufacturer are convinced that their interest is one."[206]

For the designer in industry, design was not simply an act of creative expression that set the designer apart in a lofty realm above other workers.[207] Day criticised the attitude of designers who regarded the artistic temperament as more important than the world around them and who isolated themselves from the wider community.[208] "Artists generally are too much disposed to think the world ought to treat them with special consideration," he observed.[209] "It is no exceptional experience to come upon artists who claim more consideration from the world than they have any right to ask."[210] Day's greatest scorn, however, was reserved for those who refused work they deemed beneath their creative talents even if accepting it would enable them to meet financial obligations: "Have you never known an artist who will not do the work offered him, though he is in arrears with whoever will trust him? I have. And I don't pity him."[211]

While Day rejoiced in the creative basis of design work, he felt "we make too much of the professional artist", who "carries on a trade like any other workman".[212] Day's comments reflected his own strict upbringing: "I think the man is of more account than the artist, and that the great mistake we make is in putting the artist first."[213] He added that the designer should "gain his status by his work, not talk about his due".[214] The manufacturing process through which designs were turned into wallpaper, textiles and other furnishings was inherently a social process, involving people with various rôles and skills. Day believed that instead of being impressed by his own importance, the designer would be a more meaningful contributor by working cooperatively as a member of a team.[215] Through the Arts and Crafts Exhibition Society and the Design Club, both of which he helped found, Day worked with colleagues to promote more interaction between designers, manufacturers, and retailers.

2.75 (left) and 2.76 (above) Walter Crane. Illustrations. From Crane and Day, *Moot Points* (1903): 72 and 62 respectively

Crane decried the "sacrifice of his individual ideas (which alone give a character and point to his work) for what is more or less of a compromise".[216] In contrast, there was no doubt in Day's mind that a designer could be true to his or her creative talent and also be commercially competent.[217] While manufacturers worked first for a profit and also to produce a good product, the designer worked "first for the satisfaction of expressing himself, but also for a profit. In so far as an artist sells his work he is what you call commercial".[218] Day disagreed that a designer faced a binary choice.[219] "I deny that a designer must degrade his art or starve. He must in a sense 'meet the demands of trade'; but he may do it in a way which makes a better man of him, and no worse artist."[220] He insisted that it was only the *excessive* concern with money that hurt the artist: "I maintain that the necessity of earning our living is no misfortune, but a good thing for us."[221]

Day observed that while a person was free to choose a profession, freedom did not extend to rebelling "against conditions to which, by implication, he agreed in choosing it".[222] The designer had no right to expect sympathy from a manufacturer, but only the opportunity to do good work.[223] Some designers expected "more than fair conditions", and while a situation might be less than ideal, a competent and willing designer could negotiate terms that would allow use of creative skills.[224] The challenge was to accept the conditions of the situation, figure out what needed to be done, and make the challenges work in one's favour.[225] Day pragmatically contended that if his designs worked out well, work would likely flow to him.[226]

The economic and commercial restrictions of the present might not be the ones the designer would have chosen, but they should be considered an opportunity rather than an obstacle.[227] Competence in designing for industry demanded hard work, technical skills and compromise. Working within the conditions of industry and negotiating terms under which he could work while still meeting business demands could make the designer a better artist and a better person.[228] Day added that the way a designer worked through these challenges revealed the person: "A man proves himself a designer, not because he has somehow arrived at a design, but inasmuch as out of unpromising material and untoward circumstances he can shape a thing of beauty."[229]

2.77 (left) and 2.78 (above) Walter Crane. Illustrations. From Crane and Day, *Moot Points* (1903): 53 and 23 respectively

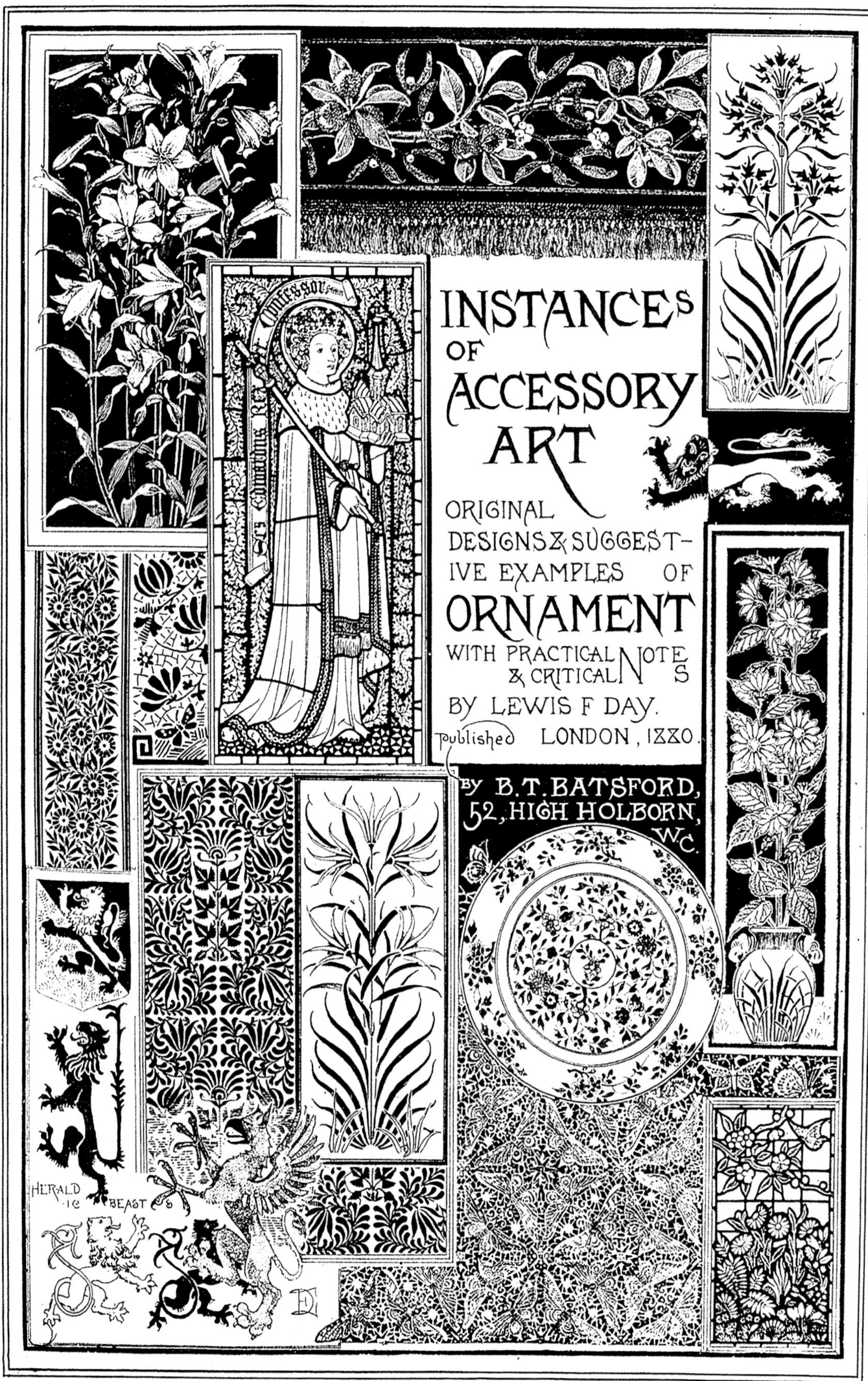
INSTANCES OF ACCESSORY ART
ORIGINAL DESIGNS & SUGGESTIVE EXAMPLES OF ORNAMENT
WITH PRACTICAL & CRITICAL NOTES
BY LEWIS F DAY.
Published LONDON, 1880.
BY B.T. BATSFORD, 52, HIGH HOLBORN, W.C.
HERALDIC BEAST

CHAPTER THREE: THE WRITER AND CRITIC

"One cannot work day after day, and year after year, at anything in which one is deeply interested, without having something to say about it." [Lewis F. Day, 1904]

3.1 Lewis F. Day. Title page, *Instances of Accessory Art* (1880). This neatly encapsulates how Day found inspiration for his designs in nature, historic ornament, and the Far East
Michael Whiteway

Lewis Foreman Day was first mentioned in the professional press in late 1868, when he was still employed by the stained glass firm Clayton & Bell. He was cited for winning a best essay prize from the Architectural Association for his paper 'The History and Application of Stained Glass'.[1] This event was an early indication of the inseparable nature of designing and writing in Day's life. It was also an omen of the prolific output of books and articles for professional, trade and general publications that would follow over the next forty years.

Day was certainly not the only designer of his generation to achieve recognition as a writer: William Morris penned art and social criticism, as well as prose romances and poetry; in addition to his books and articles on design, Walter Crane ventured into socialist commentary; and William De Morgan became a prolific novelist in later life. In contrast to these colleagues, Day confined his writing solely to the applied arts. His range within that field was encyclopedic, with topics clustered into a half-dozen areas: the design of ornament and pattern; interior decoration; trade and industrial exhibitions; professional issues; the rôle of the designer for industry; and scholarly work on special areas of interest, including stained glass, lettering, and needlework.

Day's articles and books not only provide valuable commentary on the design milieu of the period, they also help fill in the gaps in the absence of much personal information, correspondence and business records. His careers as designer and writer occurred in tandem and mutually reinforced each other, for both gave scope to the creative and analytical sides of his personality. Day's passion for talking about design was wedded to a thorough command of written language. This skill enabled him to express his ideas effectively to both professionals in the decorative arts as well as to the general public. His growth and development as a writer can be traced through three main phases: his writings for professional journals and general interest publications in the 1870s to early 1880s; his emergence as a major critic and author of textbooks on design from the mid-1880s onward; and his steadfast commitment to communicating, even in his last years.

THE 1870S TO MID-1880S: ESTABLISHING HIMSELF AS A WRITER

The importance of writing in Day's life

Designing and writing were indivisible in Day's life. In his mind they were two aspects of a unified process that involved both creating graphic images and verbally expressing them. In his first series of articles on 'Decorative Art' for the *British Architect* in 1878, he explained the philosophical congruence of his dual career as designer and writer: "It is my trade or profession, and one cannot work day after day, and year after year, at anything in which one is deeply interested, without having something to say about it."[2] Rather than being prompted to write by an external force or circumstance, the impulse came from within. He indicated this in his unvarnished words in the preface to his second book *Every-day Art*: "Some there may be to whom these essays will not be the less interesting from the fact, that they originated in my having something to say about my art, instead of having to say something."[3] Day refused to choose one activity over the other: "I am a decorative artist who has found time to write on most subjects connected with ornament to promote the educational purpose I have had in view."[4]

Practical and financial benefits also accrued from writing. Describing alternation between types of tasks as "essential to the well-being of the artist", Day observed: "The one kind of work is a relief from the other. He can no more be perpetually working his brains, or pumping his emotions, than he can keep up perpetual motion of his limbs. It is with us as with the weather-clock, when the little old man and the little old woman each have their turn; when the one is out, the other is in."[5] Although specific details of his income are unknown, it would seem from the number of articles he wrote and the many editions of his books, that he earned a significant income from writing. In Day's spoof article 'Another Moot Point: An Imaginary Debate, Lewis F. Day v. Hansard', the interviewer Hansard asks whether he can inquire of Day which pays better – designing or writing – and Day simply replies "No".[6] Aware that people may have wondered about it, Day chose to address the question in a humorous and non-committal way. Writing also bolstered Day's reputation, for he observed that the public was more likely to remember the name of an author than who designed their wallpaper.[7]

Making a name for himself with major periodicals

Day had set up his independent design practice by the beginning of 1870, and for the first few years he directed his energies to securing new clients. He soon established connections with the professional press, as well. His first major publishing relationship was with the *British Architect*, and his extensive writing for that journal made his reputation as a decorative arts writer with professional audiences. His first signed series, 'Decorative Art', ran monthly from January to December 1878 and consisted of brief articles on various aspects of applied art and ornament, accompanied by one or more illustrations by him.[8]

Day simultaneously broadened his rôle with the *British Architect* by becoming a critic of contemporary events. From June through to December of 1878, he contributed 'Notes on English Decorative Art in Paris', fifteen illustrated reports on the exhibits of British and continental manufacturers at the Paris Exposition Universelle in 1878. The Paris exhibition was particularly significant for Day in two respects: it gave him his first opportunity to report on international exhibitions, events that he would review for various magazines and newspapers into the early 20th century. The Paris exhibition bolstered his international reputation as a versatile designer through the many examples of his work exhibited there, including the 'Princess Cabinet' for H.&J. Cooper, wallpapers for W.B. Simpson, and ceramics for Howell & James, for whom he also designed the exhibit area. Although he mentioned some of his own work in his exhibition reports for the *British Architect*, these references were relatively few and quite reticent in comparison with his extended discussion of other designers and manufacturers. Day developed a practice in these early years of alerting readers to his connection with particular firms, so they could take that into account.

Day's monthly contributions to the journal continued the following year, with twenty-six short illustrated articles entitled 'Fortnightly Notes on Ornament' appearing from January through to December 1879. When, in 1881, the *British Architect* initiated its weekly series 'Friends in Council', Day, along with prominent architects and designers – including George Gilbert Scott, John P. Seddon, Edward W. Godwin, and Bruce J. Talbert – contributed short informal essays "intended to embody the practical ideas of practical men".[9] Most of Day's contributions, which appeared between 1881 and 1884, focused on professional practice issues, among them copyright, eclecticism, and the relationship of the decorator to the architect. Although his regular contributions ceased in early 1884, the *British Architect* continued to report on Day's design work; regularly reviewed his books; and occasionally reprinted or paraphrased his lectures and articles written for other publications.

From professional to public audiences

Day was clearly interested in expanding his readership beyond his professional peers, and in the late 1870s to early 1880s he wrote articles for art and design periodicals directed at the educated public. His first signed article for the *Art Journal*, 'An Apology for the Conventional', appeared in early 1877; he subsequently contributed several additional articles, which ran from 1881 to 1882.

During this period he also had a more extensive relationship with the *Magazine of Art*, published by Cassell, Petter, Galpin & Co. The catalyst for the founding of the magazine was the Paris Exposition Universelle in 1878, which had heightened public interest in British designers and manufacturers. From its inception, the publication was defined as "a serious magazine to be devoted to Art, which should cater for the mass of the public at least as effectively as the 'Art Journal' was at that time catering for a much wealthier class".[10] Included in this wide audience were art lovers, collectors, students and "the man in the street", all of whom were appealed to by the price of the *Magazine of Art*, which was considerably less expensive than that of its competitor.[11] Among the early contributors to the publication were designers Alan Cole and Henry Holiday, painter Sir John Millais, and illustrator Randolph Caldecott.[12]

3.2 Lewis F. Day. Cover, *Magazine of Art* 4 (1881)
Paulo R. DeAndrea, PRD Photography

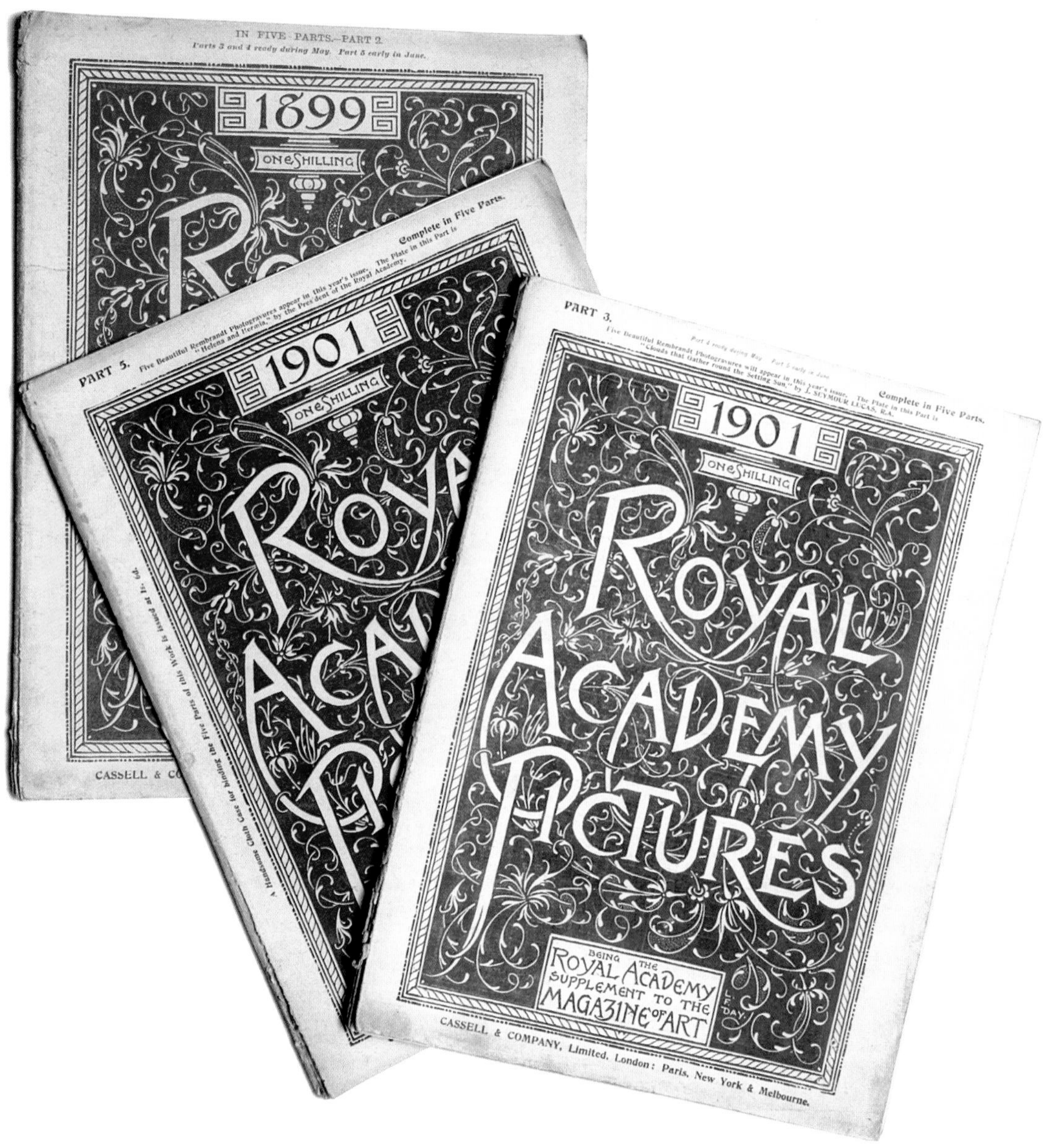

3.3 Lewis F. Day. Cover, *Royal Academy Pictures* (1889-1901) Paulo R. DeAndrea, PRD Photography

Day's first series in 1879 – running under the banner 'Decorative Art' – consisted of four articles, which discussed ornament, principles of taste and considerations about home furnishing. A second series followed in 1881 and dealt with more specific aspects of domestic interior decoration and the woman's rôle in that process. His contributions to the *Magazine of Art* became more frequent from the early 1880s. Day's abiding love for the history and practice of stained glass were reflected in the series of three articles he contributed in 1882, some of the material being adapted from his Society of Arts lecture of that year. In these articles he traced the developments from the earliest examples of stained glass through to late Gothic examples. In 1885 a second series of three articles covered historical developments and technical advances from Gothic stained glass to that of the late 16th century.

Day also designed the blue and white *Magazine of Art* cover that was used from late 1880 until 1902. It was lauded in the magazine's 1899 retrospective as "one of the most beautiful, elegant, and graceful that enshrines any magazine in the world".[13] Day also designed the cover for *Royal Academy Pictures*, a supplement published by the *Magazine of Art* beginning in 1888.

In addition to the *British Architect*, *Magazine of Art*, and *Art Journal*, Day contributed articles to other major trade and consumer publications including the *Architect* from 1884 to 1885. He also became known in America as one of the influential figures of the English decorative arts movement alongside William Morris and Walter Crane. Along with architect Robert Edis, design critics F. Edward Hulme and Gilbert R. Redgrave, and advice-giver Mary Eliza Haweis, Day was a London contributor to the New York publication *Decorator and Furnisher*. He wrote a lengthy illustrated article, 'The Obsolete Teachings of Owen Jones', for the premier issue in October 1882, and this was followed by his article 'Door Decoration' in 1883. Thereafter he seems not to have contributed further, although his name remained on the list of contributors until June 1886, when the publication was redesigned. Day's ideas and those of his contemporaries reached a wide audience because publications frequently discussed or paraphrased articles that had been originally written for their competitors.

3.4 Lewis F. Day. Title page, *Instances of Accessory Art* (1880) Michael Whiteway

Day's relationship with B.T. Batsford

Adaptable and efficient, Day often made multiple uses of his articles and lectures, through which he developed his ideas and got feedback from his audiences. He then reworked them into books, providing readers with a more permanent form of reference. His first book, *Instances of Accessory Art*, published in 1880 by B.T. Batsford, was a revision of the text and illustrations of 'Fortnightly Notes on Ornament', which had appeared in the *British Architect* the preceding year.

His second book, *Every-day Art*, was published by Batsford in 1882, and was based on the two series of articles he had contributed to the *Magazine of Art* in 1879 and 1881. "In style it aims at a happy mean between the technical and the popular, and it has fairly well hit the mark," one review commented, commending the book for its apt illustrations and practical advice.[14] Both the *Architect* and the *Journal of Decorative Art* also noted its usefulness to professionals and amateurs alike and approved of its modest price of 7s. 6d, which put it in the middle range for books of this type.[15]

Day's relationship with his publisher B.T.

3.5 (left) Lewis F. Day. Cover, *Every-day Art* (1882)
Paulo R. DeAndrea, PRD Photography

3.6 (below) Randolph Schwabe. Reconstruction of the premises of B.T. Batsford at 94 High Holborn in 1893 (since demolished). From Hector Bolitho, (ed.), *A Batsford Century: The Record of a Hundred Years of Publishing and Bookselling 1843-1943* (1944): frontispiece

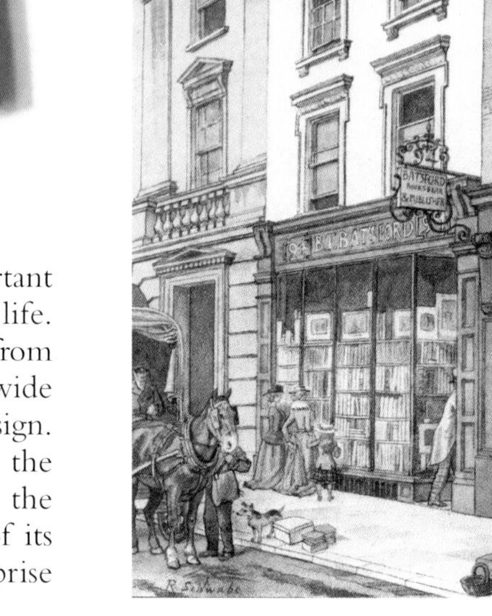

Batsford was one of the most important relationships of his professional life. Located at 94 High Holborn, not far from where Day lived, Batsford produced a wide range of books on architecture and design. The firm was highly regarded by the professional and trade press, both for the high quality of content and design of its books, as well as for its business enterprise and promotion.[16]

Herbert Batsford, youngest son of founder B.T. Batsford, remarked on the level of trust between his family and Lewis F. Day, the author of so many of their successful books. The formal agreements between the parties were of the simplest type; both sides preferred to operate on the level of mutual trust and collaboration "rather than be bound by long, elaborate legal documents".[17] He also observed that, in an age in which many authors moved from one publisher to another, Day remained steadfast in his relationship with the Batsford firm.[18] Day also designed the covers and the endpapers for his books; as a symbol of the closeness of this relationship, he entwined the initials LFD and BTB in the design of the endpapers.

In the early 1880s Day also wrote two other small books that, while of lesser stature than his design books, nevertheless had significant connections to his life at that time. He was doing a great deal of design work for the up-market department store Howell & James, and in 1880 the store issued his *Tapestry Painting and Its Application*, a twenty-four-page instructional handbook on materials and methods for customers attending classes at the store. It exemplifies his effort to provide other services to clients in addition to his design work for them.

3.7 (top left) Herbert Batsford (1861-1917). From *A Batsford Century* (1944): fig. 13

3.8 (left) Interior of the Batsford shop at 94 High Holborn. From *A Batsford Century* (1944): fig. 19

3.9 (above) Bradley Thomas (B.T.) Batsford (1821-1904). Photograph from 1880s. From *A Batsford Century* (1944): fig. 12

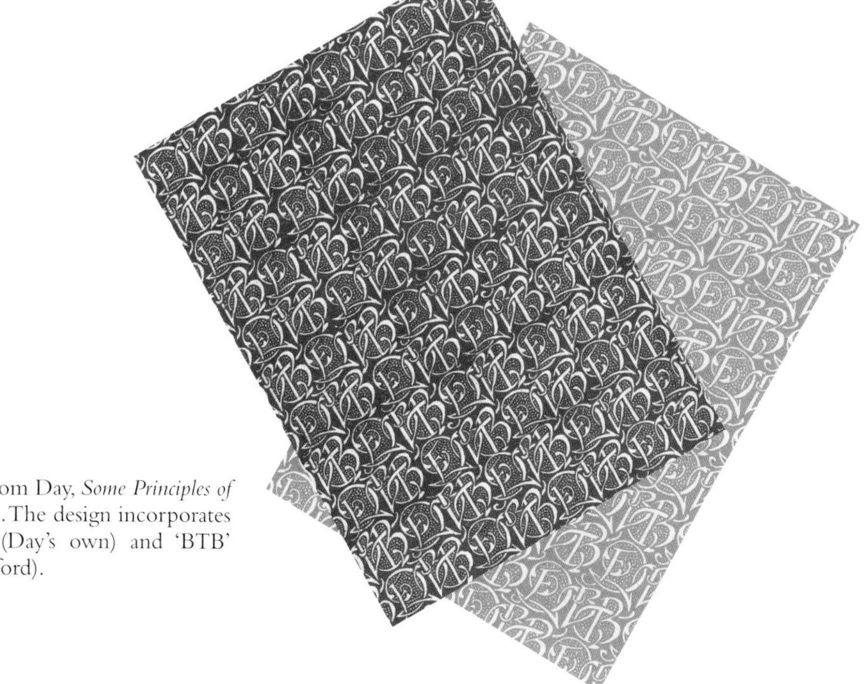

3.10 Lewis F. Day. Endpapers. From Day, *Some Principles of Every-day Art*, 2nd ed. rev. (1898). The design incorporates the intertwined initials 'LFD' (Day's own) and 'BTB' (those of his publisher B.T. Batsford).

In a very different vein, Day wrote and illustrated a children's book, *The Nodding Mandarin: A Tragedy in China*, published by Marshall, Simpkin in 1883. He identified himself as editor of the text rather than writer, so it is possible that the story may have been a folk tale or story in common circulation. His daughter Ruth was about nine years old at the time, and he may have undertaken this project to amuse Ruth and her friends.

Even in this little adventure of china figurines on a carved mantelpiece, Day's love of domestic design is seen in illustrative details including a clock case with blue and white china face, wallpaper with a pattern of swirling leaves, and a Persian-style rug.

3.11 a, b and c Lewis F. Day. Cover (above) and plates (top and bottom left), *The Nodding Mandarin: A Tragedy in China* (1883)
Geffrye Museum, London

THE MID-1880S TO 1900: AT THE HEIGHT OF HIS CAREER

Launching his Textbooks of Ornamental Design

The mid-1880s to the early 1900s was a period of great intellectual development for Day, one in which he worked out many of his ideas about design and launched his *Textbooks of Ornamental Design*. The first two of the *Textbooks*, *The Anatomy of Pattern* and *The Planning of Ornament*, were published by Batsford in 1887. They were followed by *The Application of Ornament* a year later. These three small illustrated books were largely based on the series of Day's prestigious Cantor Lectures for the Society of Arts in late 1886 on 'The Principles and Practice of Ornamental Design'.[19] Day greatly appreciated the opportunity given to him by his friend Henry Trueman Wood, Chair of the Applied Arts Section of the Society, to give these illustrated lectures. They gave him the chance to comprehensively work out his ideas in visual and verbal form and to gauge the response from his audience.[20] The *Textbooks of Ornamental Design* were thus both a process for him to develop his ideas and a product through which students, professionals and general readers could get practical advice.

3.12 (below left) Lewis F. Day. Cover, *The Planning of Ornament*, 3rd. ed. (1893)
Paulo R. DeAndrea, PRD Photography

3.13 (below right) Lewis F. Day. Cover, *The Anatomy of Pattern*, 4th ed. (1896)
Paulo R. DeAndrea, PRD Photography

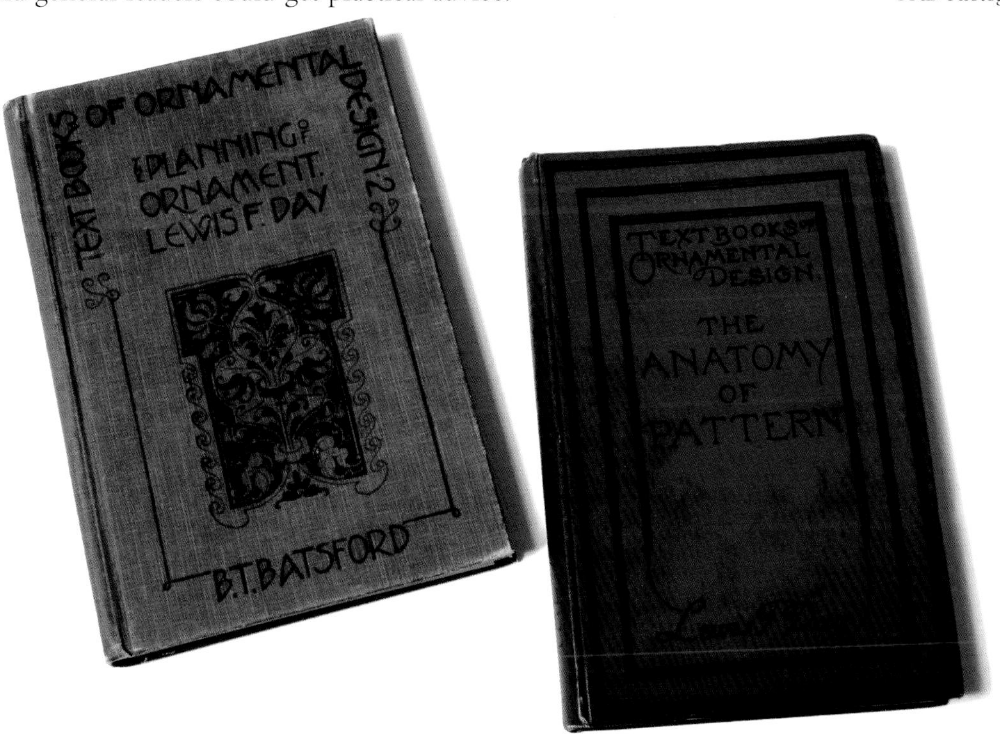

The first three *Textbooks* formed a trilogy that gave a succinct overview of applied art and ornament. Profusely illustrated with his own designs as well as those of others, Day's writing provided a glimpse into the mind of the designer as he went about his work. *The Anatomy of Pattern* discussed types of patterns, the lines on which they are constructed, and their appropriate use in various materials. *The Planning of Ornament* treated the planning and distribution of nonrepeating flat and low-relief ornament and the requirements of decorating specific items such as panels, book covers, vases, and cabinets. In *The Application of Ornament*, Day delved into issues of style, craft and the influence of materials and tools. He contended that the practice of design must be discussed in specifics: "It is only in theory, however, that ornament can be independently discussed. Practically it exists only relatively to its application. Apart from its place and purpose, and the process of its doing, there is no such thing as ornament."[21]

3.14 Lewis F. Day. Cover, *Textbooks of Ornamental Design*, 3rd. ed. (1895)

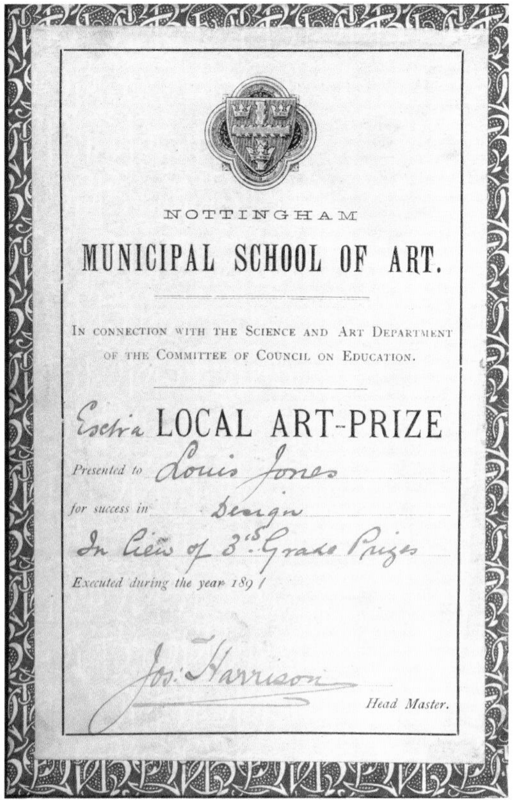

NOTTINGHAM

MUNICIPAL SCHOOL OF ART.

In connection with the Science and Art Department of the Committee of Council on Education.

Extra LOCAL ART-PRIZE

Presented to Louis Jones

for success in Design

In lieu of 3rd Grade Prizes

Executed during the year 1891

Jos. Harrison

Head Master.

3.15 Nottingham Municipal School of Art. Award plate. From Day, *Nature in Ornament* (1892): inside front cover

The strong intellectual framework of these books is evident even in the original versions. However, Day kept revising both the text and the illustrations in his books, and over the years the treatment of his subject became more cohesive and was expressed in clearer, simpler language. The individual textbooks that made up the trilogy of the *Textbooks of Ornamental Design*, which went through many editions through to the 1890s, were available singly at a price of 3s. 6d. each or bound together in one volume at a price of 10s. 6d. The *Textbooks* were approved by the Science and Art Department, which regulated the curriculum for design education throughout the country, and they were often given as prizes to students.

Reviews in the professional, trade and art press indicate that his books were highly regarded; Day was described as "a designer of a very high order, who knows his subject better than most men".[22] The qualities most often praised by reviewers were the high calibre of the illustrations; clarity and conciseness of the writing; and the books' usefulness and practicality.[23] The *Studio* was particularly effusive, referring to the "wide popularity of these super-excellent treatises".[24] The reviewer added that to try to assess their value was "as futile as to write an essay on the usefulness of Bradshaw to railway travellers".[25]

Day wanted to have an introductory volume to the *Textbooks of Ornamental Design*, so he substantially revised *Every-day Art*, which by 1890 was out of print. Feeling that much of the specific advice he had given on interior decoration was by then out of date and of little interest, he discarded the first half of the book and reworked the second half. The revised book was published as *Some Principles of Every-day Art* in 1890, selling at a price of 3s. 6d. As its revised title indicates, it dealt much less with specific directives in furnishing and relied on more general principles that could be applied in a variety of ways.

One of Day's most important works, *Nature in Ornament*, was published in 1892. Day again drew on the lectures on 'Principles and Practice of Ornamental Design' that he had given to the Society of Arts in 1886. This copiously illustrated book is particularly significant because it is the fullest exposition of Day's ideas on his major source of inspiration for design: nature. How nature should be used in decorative art – rendered naturalistically with fidelity to detail or conventionalised to capture its essence – was a topic of intense debate among contemporary artists and critics at the time. Day took a middle ground, contending that while nature was the primary source of inspiration for the designer, natural forms had to be modified, adapted to the purpose, place and conditions for which they were intended.[26]

3.16 a and b Lewis F. Day. Cover and spine, *Nature in Ornament* (1892)
Paulo R. DeAndrea, PRD Photography

A SELECTION OF
WORKS ON DECORATIVE ART
PUBLISHED BY
B. T. BATSFORD, 94, HIGH HOLBORN, LONDON.

MR. DAY'S TEXT BOOKS OF ORNAMENTAL DESIGN,
Approved by the Science and Art Department.

Some Principles of Every-Day Art; Introductory Chapters on the Arts not Fine. In great part re-written from "Every-Day Art," and containing nearly all the original Illustrations; forming a Prefatory Volume to the Series. Second Edition, revised, with further Illustrations. Crown 8vo, cloth, 3*s.* 6*d.*

The Anatomy of Pattern. Fourth Edition. With 41 full-page Illustrations, and Diagrams in the text. Crown 8vo, cloth, 3*s.* 6*d.*

The Planning of Ornament. Third Edition. With 41 full-page Illustrations. Crown 8vo, cloth, 3*s.* 6*d.*

The Application of Ornament. Third Edition. With 48 full-page Illustrations, and others in the Text. Crown 8vo, cloth, 3*s.* 6*d.*

Ornamental Design; comprising the above Three Works. Handsomely bound in one volume. Cloth gilt, gilt top, 10*s.* 6*d.*

Nature in Ornament, with 123 full-page Plates and 192 Illustrations in the Text. Second Edition (third thousand). Thick Crown 8vo, cloth richly gilt, from a Design specially prepared by the Author. Price 12*s.* 6*d.*

"A book more beautiful for its Illustrations, or one more helpful to Students of Art, can hardly be imagined."—*The Queen.*
"The Treatise should be in the hands of every Student of Ornamental Design. It is profusely and admirably illustrated, and well printed."—*The Magazine of Art.*

3.17 B.T. Batsford. Advertisement for Day's books. From Day, *Textbooks of Ornamental Design*, 3rd. ed. (1895): inserted at back of volume

The book received a very positive reception in the professional press, which recommended its use, adding: "With its combined excellence of illustrations and text, and quality of production, it is almost a model textbook".[27] The *Art Journal*, while laudatory about certain aspects of the text, criticised it for over-emphasis on vegetative form and insufficient attention to animal and human forms.[28] The *Magazine of Art* rated it as "probably the best" of Day's textbooks, achieving a balance between naturalism and conventionalism, and concluded that every student of design should read it.[29] The *Studio* judged the treatment to be exhaustive, "until you feel what he has not explained is not worth explaining".[30]

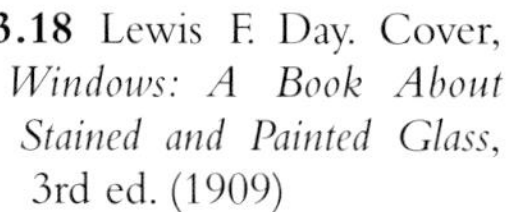

3.18 Lewis F. Day. Cover, *Windows: A Book About Stained and Painted Glass*, 3rd ed. (1909)

Day also found time to write several books on specialised subjects of long-standing interest. His masterwork, *Windows: A Book About Stained and Painted Glass*, was published in 1897. In the preface to the first edition, Day cited Goethe's parable about poems being like stained-glass windows – dark when seen from without, beautifully coloured when seen from within – and said that he hoped his book would help the reader appreciate their beauty with an insider's perspective.[31] "Early training in the workshop, long practice in design, deep interest in glass, and loving study of it – these are my excuse for writing about it."[32] Many years of travel on the Continent, "during which glass-hunting has been my recreation and delight", rendered Day a scholar, but he described his book as a "practical" and "popular" treatment of the subject.[33] He dedicated it to those who knew little about the subject, those who knew something and wanted to know more, and experts.[34] Reviews appeared in major publications, including the *Art Journal*, which accurately referred to it as a "labour of love", and the *Architect*, which recommended it to all who wanted to learn more and increase their enjoyment of stained glass windows.[35]

From his days as a schoolboy, Day had been fascinated by alphabets and lettering. *Alphabets Old and New*, published in 1898 and marketed as one of the *Textbooks of Ornamental Design*, reflected this. The text included over 170 illustrations; in the preface to the first edition, he explained his approach: the ancient forms of lettering were taken "as far as might be, from original sources, and drawing with every care to keep the spirit of the original. I have not scrupled, however, to supply the letters missing in old manuscripts or inscriptions".[36] He said he knew scholars would not be confused by this and workmen would appreciate "alphabets as complete as possible".[37] This and several other books by Day were jointly issued by B.T. Batsford and Scribner's Sons in New York for the American market.

3.19 a and b Lewis F. Day. Capitals designed for woodcarving, letters A-N and O-Z. Probably carved by students at the School of Art Woodcarving, South Kensington. From Day, *Alphabets Old and New*, 3rd ed. (1910): illus. 195

Day's magazine journalism

In addition to his prodigious output of books, during this period, Day enhanced his stature as a critic and journalist by expanding his relationships with magazines. The extent of his writing for the *Magazine of Art* is attested to by the fact that between 1879 and 1901 Day wrote almost fifty pieces for the publication, spanning an encyclopedic range of topics. He dispensed practical advice on tasks such as selection of wallpaper and hanging of pictures, traced historical developments in the decorative arts in England and continental Europe, and discussed current practices in design education. He critiqued the work of British and continental designers, reported on current exhibitions, philosophised on the rôle of the designer and craftsman in a changing milieu, and reviewed recently published books.

He also developed more extensive ties with the *Art Journal*. He had written a few articles for the *Journal* between 1877 and 1882, and between 1885 and 1887 he penned a half-dozen more. These included 'Victorian Progress in Applied Design', his comprehensive review of major developments in design from the Great Exhibition of 1851 to the Royal Jubilee Exhibition in 1887.[38] As he had done for the *Magazine of Art*, Day designed a cover for the *Art Journal*, which was used from 1885 through to 1900, and a second used from 1901. Probably no other designer of the period can be said to have designed the covers of both the major general art publications and ones that were used for so long. He also designed the cover for the *Art Annual*, which featured the work of prominent painters.

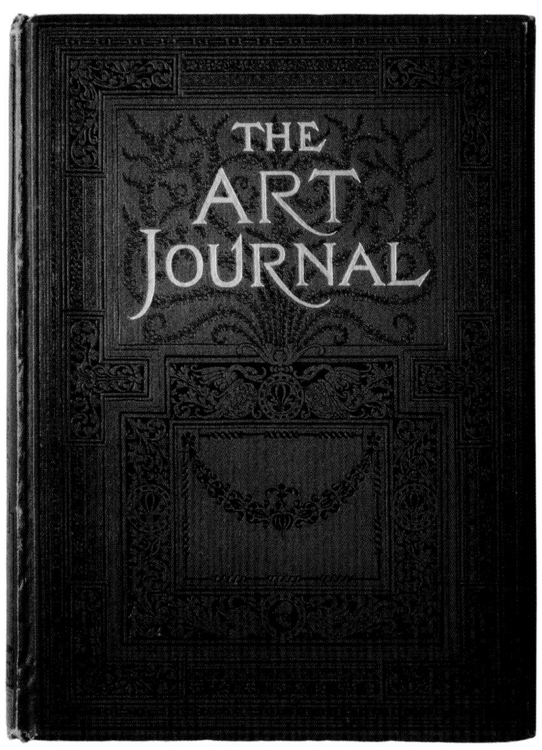

Day's heaviest involvement with the *Art Journal* was from 1893-1902, which coincided exactly with the editorship of David Croal Thomson. During this period, the *Art Journal* responded to a heightened interest in the decorative arts prompted by the Arts and Crafts Movement.[39] Day's rôle with the magazine became more formalised; his 1893 editorial statement explained that he would be regularly reviewing "work of current interest in decoration and decorative design, ornament, and industrial and applied art generally", and he invited "manufacturers, decorators, dealers, importers, and others" to send specimens of work or photographs for his review.[40] During this nine-year period, Day contributed over fifty articles to the *Art Journal*, including a report on the 1893 World's Columbian Exposition in Chicago, for which he designed the British Section catalogue cover. He also authored 'William Morris and His Art', which appeared as an extra number of the *Art Journal* in 1899 and was one of the first monographs on Morris.[41]

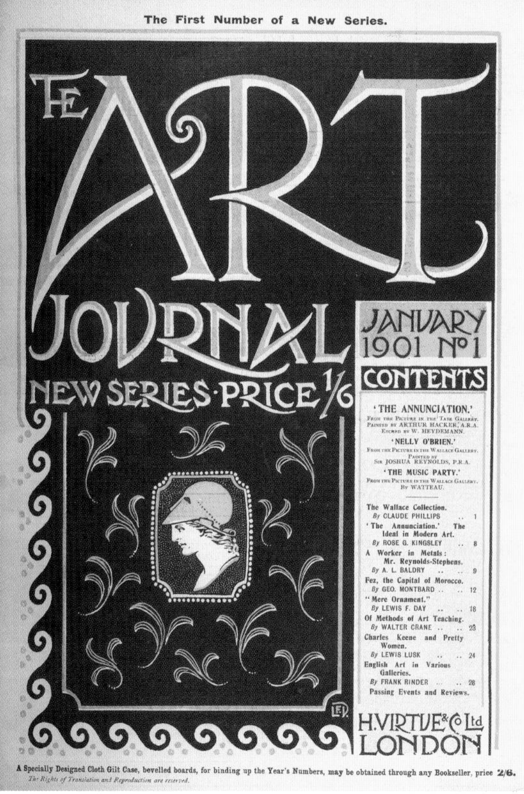

3.20 (opposite, top left) Lewis F. Day. Cover, *Art Journal* (1887) Paulo R. DeAndrea, PRD Photography

3.21 (opposite, top right) Lewis F. Day. Cover, bound issues of the *Art Journal* (1898)
Paulo R. DeAndrea, PRD Photography

3.22 (opposite, bottom right) Lewis F. Day. Cover of *Art Journal* used from January, 1901
Newberry Library, Chicago

3.23 (top left) Lewis F. Day. Cover, 'Official Catalogue of the British Section', Chicago World's Columbian Exposition, 1893. From Day, *Some Principles of Every-day Art,* 2nd ed. (1894): illus. 35

3.24 (below left) B.T. Batsford. Advertisement for Lewis F. Day's books. From *Art Journal, Easter Annual Advertiser* (1899): 5

3.25 (below right) John Henry Dearle. Cover, Easter Art Annual, *Art Journal* (1899). Although the cover title differs slightly, the title of Lewis F. Day's monograph is 'William Morris and His Art'

THE EASTER ANN

A LIST OF Mr. LEWIS F. DAY'S BOOKS.

WINDOWS: A BOOK ABOUT STAINED AND PAINTED GLASS. Containing 410 pages, with 50 full-page plates, and upwards of 200 other illustrations of Historical Examples. Large 8vo, cloth gilt, price 21s. net.

The Art Journal says:—"The book is a masterpiece in its way. . . . Amply illustrated and carefully printed, it will long remain the authority on its subject."

The Studio says:—"Mr. Day has done a worthy piece of work in more than his usual admirable manner. . . . The illustrations are all good, and some the best black-and-white drawings of stained glass yet produced. It is a book which reflects great credit on all concerned in its production, and adds new laurels even to one who is Master of the Art Workers' Guild."

ALPHABETS, OLD AND NEW. Containing over 150 complete Alphabets, 30 series of Numerals, and numerous facsimiles of Ancient Dates, &c., for the use of Craftsmen, Designers, and all Art Workers, with an Introductory Essay on "Art in the Alphabet." Crown 8vo, cloth, price 3s. 6d. net. (*Just Published.*)

The Art Journal says:—"Everyone who employs practical lettering will be grateful for 'Alphabets, Old and New.' . . . Mr. Day has written a scholarly and pithy introduction dealing with the development of the alphabet, and also contributes some beautiful alphabets of his own design, besides those given by other contemporary designers."

NATURE IN ORNAMENT. Third Edition (5th thousand), with 123 full-page plates, and 192 illustrations in the Text, and a copious index to them. Thick crown 8vo, cloth, gilt, price 12s. 6d.

The Queen says:—"A book more beautiful for its illustrations or one more helpful to Students of Art can hardly be imagined."

The Magazine of Art says:—"The Treatise should be in the hands of every Student of Ornamental design. It is profusely and admirably illustrated and well printed.

TEXT BOOKS OF ORNAMENTAL DESIGN.

Price 3s. 6d. each. Crown 8vo, bound in cloth.

SOME PRINCIPLES OF EVERY-DAY LIFE: Introductory Chapters on the Arts not Fine. Numerous illustrations. Second Edition, enlarged, with further illustrations.

The Athenæum says:—"If anybody wants a sensible book on Art as applied to everyday ornament, let him buy Mr. Day's nicely-printed little volume, and read it carefully from the beginning to the end. Easy to follow, well arranged, and extremely concise . . . Mr. Day knows what to say and how to say it."

The Pall Mall Gazette says:—"Mr. Day is an excellent teacher of 'the arts not fine,' and his small volume, which is capitally illustrated, can be thoroughly recommended as a good handbook to the appreciation of decorative art."

THE ANATOMY OF PATTERN. Fourth Edition, revised, with 41 full-page illustrations.

THE PLANNING OF ORNAMENT. Fourth Edition, further revised, with 41 full-page illustrations, many re-drawn.

THE APPLICATION OF ORNAMENT. Fourth Edition, further revised, with 48 full-page illustrations, and 7 illustrations in the Text.

ORNAMENTAL DESIGN: comprising the above Three Works, handsomely bound in one volume, cloth gilt, gilt top, price 10s. 6d.

B. T. BATSFORD, 94, High Holborn, London.

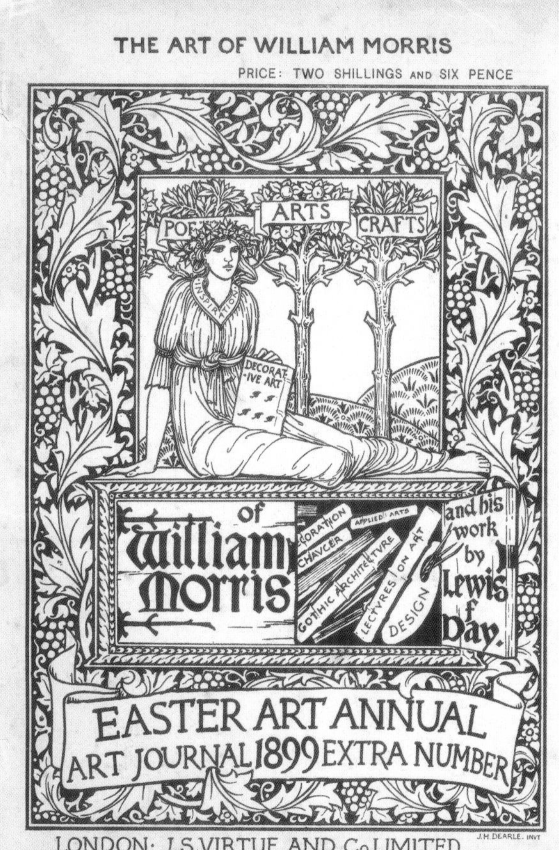

1900–1910: WRITER EMERITUS IN CHANGING TIMES

Day's magazine articles at the turn of the century

Day's reports on the Paris Exposition Universelle of 1900 and the Glasgow International Exhibition of 1901 reflect his reaction to some of the changes that were occurring in decorative art at the turn of the century. He enthusiastically embraced changes in technology that had made possible some of the wares exhibited in Paris, such as the outstanding glazes on the ceramics of Pilkington's Tiles & Pottery Co. and the spectacular glassware of Tiffany & Co.[42] Day prophesied that the future of the ceramic industry was in the marriage of art and science, without which large-scale production of ceramics was not possible.[43]

His view of Art Nouveau was less positive. In 1900 the *Art Journal* carried his article 'L'Art Nouveau', a fairly stinging indictment of what he perceived to be the worst excesses of the New Art. He found fault with the lack of restraint and rejection of all historic precedent seen in much of the Art Nouveau work shown at the Paris Exposition.[44] He was appalled in particular by the fantastic shapes of much of the French and German furniture, which he felt typified rejection of sound principles of furniture design.

Some of these same criticisms found their way into articles he wrote at around the same time for general interest publications. With his connections in the Manchester area through his work for Turnbull & Stockdale and Pilkington's Tile & Pottery Co., it is not surprising that he wrote for that city's major daily newspaper. The *Manchester Guardian* had a history of using the services of specialist writers on cultural topics, and Day was an occasional contributor.[45] Day wrote a series of four articles entitled 'Decorative Art at the Paris Exhibition' for the *Manchester Guardian* in 1900. These were followed a year later by his article 'The "New Art" at South Kensington', in which he vented his

3.26 Walter Crane. Detail of cover, *Moot Points: Friendly Disputes on Art and Industry*, Walter Crane and Lewis F. Day (1903)

worries about the possibly deleterious effects of Art Nouveau on impressionable students.[46] Over the next half-dozen years he contributed other articles, mostly on current events in the design world.

Day continued to report on the work of his contemporaries and current events for various publications. He penned another tribute to William Morris, a man who discovered "the very work he was born to do, and did it with a conscience, with a delight in doing it which contributed in no slight degree to his success and that of the artistic movement of his day".[47] His features on designers Walter Crane, Lindsay Butterfield, John Dearle, and botanical illustrator G. Woolliscroft Rhead appeared in the *Art Journal* from 1901 to 1905. His articles also appeared occasionally in American publications, and in the early 1900s the general interest magazine *Macmillan's* featured several of his articles on contemporary developments in design and professional practice.

Day and his friend Walter Crane carried on a series of 'Friendly Disputes' in the pages of the *Art Journal* between 1901 and 1902. These were reworked and published by Batsford in 1903 as *Moot Points: Friendly Disputes on Art and Industry*, co-authored by the two men. The issues they debated in this public forum – trade and industry, the designer as artist, design and the consumer – were further enlivened with humorous illustrations by Crane. The small size of the book belies the wealth of information it contains on the differing views of the two men on the rôle of the designer for industry. One reviewer commented: "Those who spend a shilling on it will be rewarded, for this kind of talk, though it is perhaps inconclusive, at all events illustrates the point of view of the craftsman, the artist, and to some extent the public," and he added: "The Arts and Crafts Society evidently numbers men of very different outlook amongst its members."[48]

Bettering his books, writing new ones

By the turn of the century, many of Day's books had gone through numerous editions and reprintings. In 1903-4 he reworked two of his early *Textbooks* and brought them up to date with contemporary developments. *The Anatomy of Pattern* was thoroughly revised as *Pattern Design*. Priced at 7s. 6d., this book became Day's fullest exposition of designing repeat patterns. One reviewer was unequivocal that *Pattern Design* was "superior in every way" to *The Anatomy of Pattern* because "we have the results of a more matured experience and of a longer and more varied practice in design".[49] The reviewer particularly recommended the chapter on pattern planning and another on proving patterns, and observed: "Mr. Day does not pose as one of those artists whose pencil is guided by an angel. He reveals some of the secrets of his studio as if he did not mind people believing that he owed his success simply to his capacity for taking pains."[50] The *Magazine of Art* praised it, saying of Day that "no one could be more catholic in his teaching or more all-embracing in his examples. If this book had been published in France it would assuredly have been 'crowned' by the Academie."[51]

Day followed suit with *The Application of Ornament*, which was revised as *Ornament and Its Application*. Published by Batsford in 1904 and selling at a price of 8s. 6d, it was also issued for the American market by Batsford and Scribner's Sons in New York. As Day alluded to in the preface, the relation of natural forms to ornament was treated in *Nature in Ornament*, and repeat pattern and its construction had been covered in *Pattern Design*; this book logically focused on "the appropriateness of pattern to the process of its execution".[52] Day thus viewed these books as intimately interrelated and, indeed, the three taken together are the best summary of Day's mature views on ornament and design. The *Studio* called it "an invaluable aid to teacher and student", praising the illustrations that were "a complete series of object lessons, bringing into prominence the chief points dealt with in the text".[53] The *Decorator* judged it to be "a complete scholarly and practical treatise" and particularly commended it for giving the source, author, date and present location for illustrations.[54]

From 1900 to 1903 the indefatigable Day also wrote three new books on his special interests. He had begun collecting embroideries from around the world before his marriage, and he and wife Temma continued to add to the collection. Needlework was a major creative outlet for women during this period, and in 1900 Batsford published *Art in Needlework*, written by Day with technical assistance from Mary Buckle, an accomplished

3.27 a and b Lewis F. Day. Covers, *Art in Needlework* (1900) and *Ornament and Its Application* (1904)

embroideress. She had executed and exhibited a number of embroideries designed by Day at the Arts and Crafts Exhibitions, and photographs of some of these were included in *Art in Needlework*. By 1907, the book had run to three editions.[55]

Lettering in Ornament was published in 1902 as a companion volume to *Alphabets Old and New*. Whereas the latter had treated alphabets exclusively, *Lettering in Ornament* dealt with the ornamental use of letters in decoration.[56] Day wrote it for both practical designers and scholars and included commentary on the history of lettering. The book contained about 180 illustrations. He was very interested in the approach of his contemporaries to lettering, and the illustrations included the work of Walter Crane, Raffles Davidson, Harry Soane, R. Anning Bell, W. Eden Nesfield and Beatrice Waldram, then an assistant to Day in his studio. One reviewer noted that, as was typically the case with Day's books, a strong feature was its clarity and conciseness of the text.[57]

At the request of the Board of Education, Day wrote *Stained Glass*, published by Chapman & Hall in 1903 as one of the Art Handbooks of the Victoria and Albert Museum. Its 155 pages provided an illustrated guide to stained glass from early Gothic to the Renaissance, with most of the examples drawn from the museum's collection. The professional press praised it for its summary of the development of stained glass art and for its usefulness as a guide to the museum's stained glass.[58]

3.28 (right) Lewis F. Day. Cover, *Lettering in Ornament*, 2nd ed. (1914)

3.29 (below) Lewis F. Day. Design for newspaper heading. From Day, *Lettering in Ornament*, 2nd ed. (1914): illus. 17

3.30 (top) Lewis F. Day. Bradford Sunday Guild logo, "lettering with ornament to soften effect". From Day, *Lettering in Ornament*, 2nd ed. (1914): illus. 187

3.31 (bottom left) W. Eden Nesfield. Title page, *Specimens of Medieval Architecture* (1862). From Day, *Lettering in Ornament*, 2nd ed. (1914): illus. 24

3.32 (right) R. Anning Bell. Poster for City of Liverpool School of Architecture and Applied Art. From Day, *Lettering in Ornament*, 2nd ed. (1914): illus. 18

A communicator to the end

The importance of writing in Day's life remained undiminished even in his last years. Despite indications that he had bouts of illness from about 1905, he kept up a daunting pace of writing. Among the relatively few magazine articles that he wrote after 1905 was 'Some Conclusions', the most succinct summary of his views on ornament and design, the "working rules" he had found useful over his forty years of practice.[59] Covering major topics, including beauty, the purpose of ornament, and the adaptation of nature to purpose, it stood as a kind of manifesto of the fundamental beliefs about design that had structured his design practice.

Most of Day's attention during his final years was on revising earlier books and writing new ones, with continuing administrative and secretarial support from his daughter Ruth. He was relentless in improving earlier works – clarifying and refining his ideas, simplifying language for the reader, and updating examples and illustrations. *Nature in Ornament* (1892), his major exposition on the relationship of nature to applied art, was substantially revised as a two-volume work, *Nature and Ornament*. The first volume, *Nature: The Raw Material of Design*, was published in 1908, with the second volume, *Nature: The Finished Product of Design*, issued the following year. The first volume was a departure from his previous work in that it contained a greater level of detail about botanical forms that could be used by the designer.[60] It included about 280 illustrations, most of which were by Miss J. Foord, "whose work reveals a fullness of observation and an intimacy with plant life that is only rendered possible by one who loves her work".[61] The two volumes were also available as one bound text at a price of 12s. 6d.

With his characteristic thoroughness, Day revised *Alphabets Old and New* in 1906 (2nd ed.) and again in 1910 (3rd ed.); the third edition (revised and enlarged) of *Art in Needlework* was published in 1907. *Windows: A Book about Stained Glass* (1897) had gone through two editions by 1909. Day's love for stained glass was so great and his fidelity to detail so strict that in preparation for the third edition, he revisited the sites along with his wife Temma to see what had happened in the intervening years to the stained glass examples he had used in the original text.[62]

However, Day also approached new topics. *Enamelling*, published in 1907, dealt with the history, technical and artistic aspects of the subject. It was written not "for the learned, but for artists, craftsmen, students, and lovers of enamelling".[63] In the preface Day admitted that he was neither an authority on the history of this craft nor an enameller himself. His aim was simply to put the information that was available on the subject into a "handy, readable and easily intelligible shape", particularly for those who would see museum collections of enamels.[64] In a review of the book, the *Builder* recommended that museum-goers read the book first and then take it along on their visit as a handy reference.[65]

In his last year, Day lost none of his intellectual aggressiveness in pursuing lifelong learning. He was engaged in two major projects at the time of his death, the first of which was another book on lettering. Although his youthful fascination with alphabets and calligraphy had already resulted in two books, he continued to mine this subject for what he could learn about developments during certain historical periods. He studied a significant collection of writing books owned by the Batsford family and, recognising their importance as a resource for writers, engravers and designers, selected examples for his book *Penmanship of the XVIth, XVIIth, & VIIIth Centuries*.[66] Day died before this project was completed, and the book was brought out by his daughter Ruth Day shortly after her father's death with assistance from the Batsfords and calligraphy scholar Percy J. Smith.

The second project stemmed from Day's love of the decorative art of the Middle and Far East, in which he had found such

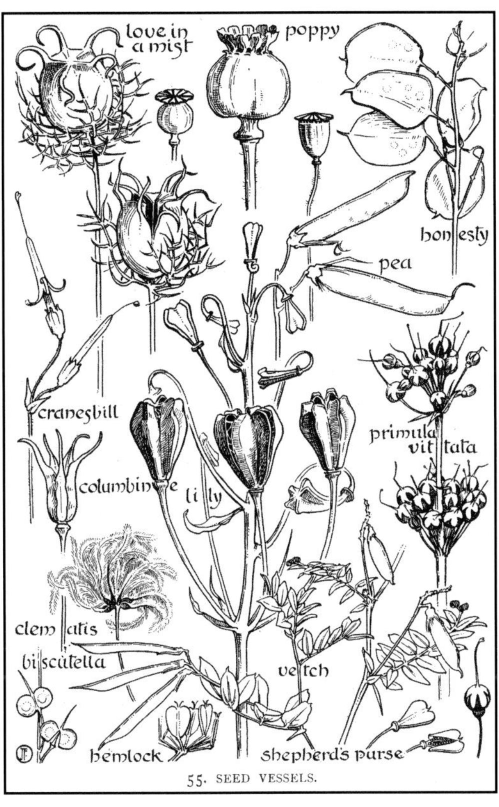

inspiration for his own work. He was intrigued by Egyptian art for its use of colour and for two other qualities he highly valued: "It is chiefly the restraint and dignity of the ornamental design that is so much to be admired in Egyptian work."[67] He had travelled to Egypt about six months before he died, and was planning to write a book about Egyptian decorative art and design.[68] To the very end, the graphic image and the written word had remained inseparable in Day's life.

3.33 (top left) Miss J. Foord. Botanical illustration, seed vessels. From Day, *Nature and Ornament 1: Nature the Raw Material of Design* (1908): illus. 55

3.34 (top right) Lewis F. Day. Cover, *Nature and Ornament 1: Nature the Raw Material of Design* (1908)

3.35 (right) Lewis F. Day. Cover, *Nature and Ornament 2: Ornament the finished Product of Design* (1909)

CHAPTER FOUR: STAINED GLASS

"I have sat for hours at a time in pure enjoyment of its magnificence – basking in its glory."
[Lewis F. Day, 1878]

4.1 Lewis F. Day. Stained glass window for Church of St. Mary the Virgin, Great Dunmow, Essex. Executed by Walter J. Pearce and installed 1906
© Great Dunmow PCC. Photography, Gwynn Davies

Lewis Foreman Day's passion for stained glass was a powerful current that ran unabated from his youth to his very last days. He lyrically described its intellectual and emotional impact: "Let me say at once that I yield to no one in the admiration of it – I have given probably more of my time and thought to it than any other object; I have sat for hours at a time in pure enjoyment of its magnificence – basking in its glory."[1] He was endlessly fascinated by its history, contemporary use and future possibilities, and he mined them with unflagging energy. "I have gone to glass to get pleasure out of it, to learn something from it, to find out the way it was done, and why it was done so, and what might yet perhaps be done."[2] Stained glass provided the entrée to his careers as designer and writer and became a major area of scholarship. While his output in stained glass design was small compared to that of textiles, wallpaper and ceramics, the subject was always of paramount interest to him.

Day's work took place during a vibrant era in the design and manufacture of stained glass. Production of stained glass windows was a major area of the decorative arts in Britain from about 1840 to World War I. Records indicate that the Church of England built over 1,700 new churches in England and Wales between 1840 and 1876 and restored over 7,000 more.[3] Even "a conservative estimate of the number of stained glass windows supplied in the Victorian period to churches in England and Wales alone would be in the region of 80,000", and the number would be even higher with the inclusion of Roman Catholic churches and those of other denominations.[4] The erection of public buildings and the boom in house-building also created demand for stained glass and resulted in significant competition within the industry. In addition to meeting demand at home, British firms also exported large numbers of stained glass windows to countries abroad, in particular America, where over 4,000 churches were under construction by the late 1880s.[5] The fine reputation of British stained glass was underscored at the large industrial exhibitions of the late 19th century; by the time of Queen Victoria's death in 1901, the British stained glass industry was in a leading position internationally.[6]

It is often difficult or impossible to definitively identify the designer of windows of this period as most windows were unsigned. Most of the archives and records of the major firms for which Day designed windows – Lavers & Barraud; Clayton & Bell; Heaton, Butler & Bayne; and W.B. Simpson & Sons – have been destroyed or disappeared. Many churches, public buildings and houses of the Victorian period have been altered or demolished – their windows along with them. In addition, Day's business records have not survived.

Fortunately, Day's work in stained glass can be explored through a few surviving windows, a small number of his original designs, as well as illustrations in his articles and books, and his many writings. From studying these, one is left in no doubt of the passion that sustained his work.

The stained glass designer

The early years: 1862-1869

Having finished his formal education on the Continent, Day returned to England in about 1862, with the intent of becoming a designer.[7] As the ninth of thirteen children, his most pressing need was to find a job so that he could be self-supporting. With no jobs immediately available in decorative arts firms, he became a clerk with a local business that closed shortly thereafter.[8] In about 1864-5, he responded to an advertisement for a position with the major stained glass firm Lavers & Barraud and was hired as an office clerk, but moved into studio work a few months later.[9]

Day, who was then about twenty years old, certainly must have been pleased and excited to have started his designing career with such a prestigious firm, which was known for its progressive approach and high-quality windows.[10] He had been exposed to a wealth of examples of fine old glass during his childhood and youth while living abroad, and the experience had fed his love of colour and pattern, as well as his fascination with history. Although no evidence survives of his work at Lavers & Barraud, he undoubtedly acquired some very good practical experience in the various processes in stained glass manufacture.

Day worked for Lavers & Barraud for two to three years and then moved on to the larger firm Clayton & Bell.[11] Founded in 1855, the firm was one of the largest and most prolific in the Victorian period and was favoured by a number of Gothic Revival architects including George Gilbert Scott and George Edmund Street.[12] It was also a training ground for a number of young designers who were later to become prominent in their fields: Charles Eamer Kempe (1834-1907), John Burlison (1843-1891) and Thomas John Grylls (1845-1913).[13] During the time that Day worked at Clayton & Bell he was "keeper of cartoons", working with the full-size drawings from which the glass windows were produced.[14] He continued to gain experience in the technical aspects of making windows and may have done some designing, as well.

From the 1860s on, Day energetically joined professional associations, which offered opportunities to meet other young designers, make business contacts with well-known figures, and pursue further learning. The Architectural Association, comprised primarily of those employed by architectural practices, held meetings fortnightly and offered classes designed to increase members' practical knowledge of their profession.[15] The Association also sponsored competitions, with prizes given for essays, figure drawing and architectural designs related to construction and practice. The earliest reference to Day in contemporary periodicals is in the autumn of 1868, when he won a best essay prize for his submission 'The History and Application of Stained Glass'.[16] Regrettably, the essay does not appear to have been published.

The turning point

Having garnered five years of solid experience with two of the most prominent stained glass firms, Day, then almost twenty-five years of age, came to a turning point in his professional life. By late 1869 he decided to become an independent designer. Despite his intense love of stained glass, that field was no longer a viable option for full-time work, for several reasons. First, he lacked formal training in drawing the human figure, an integral part of ecclesiastical stained glass.[17] The way he confronted this shortcoming – by channelling his energies primarily into design of non-figural stained glass, writing and scholarship – reveals much about the balance of the ideal and the practical sides of

his character. In addition, with his wide-ranging interests and a need for variety in his work, he could never have been satisfied by designing for only one type of applied art. On a practical level, he also realised that diversifying his design work would provide greater financial stability in the long run. Finally, with his extremely independent nature, it is inconceivable that Day would have been happy working within the confines of a firm his entire life. His departure from Clayton & Bell in late 1869 marked the end of full-time employment with stained glass firms.

4.2 Lewis F. Day. "Portion of a stained glass window, showing its adaptation to the exigencies of glazing". From Day, *Every-day Art* (1882): 93

The freelance designer: 1870–1910

Domestic glass

The housing boom of the 1870s and 1880s, and the resulting demand for stained glass for interior decoration, gave Day the opportunity to secure some prominent clients at the start of his freelance practice. The first of these was the highly respected stained glass firm of Heaton, Butler & Bayne. Day thought the firm was one of the best in this business, claiming that "in certain kinds of domestic work and certainly in heraldic glass, they are unrivalled".[18] When, in 1870, Alfred Waterhouse began rebuilding Eaton Hall in Cheshire, seat of the Duke of Westminster, Heaton, Butler & Bayne was awarded the commission for the interior decoration.[19]

4.3 and 4.4 Eaton Hall, (left) viewed from the south west, (below) the Saloon. Rebuilt, 1870-82, by Alfred Waterhouse for the Duke of Westminster Michael Whiteway

Early that year Day went to Eaton Hall where he executed special glasswork for a year or two.[20] After the Eaton Hall project, Day occasionally designed domestic stained glass windows for Heaton, Butler & Bayne, but none of these windows or their designs have been traced.[21] Working out of shared office space and temporary studios, he began to obtain commissions for other types of design as well as stained glass.

By the early 1870s Day was designing wallpaper and church decoration for the well-known interior decorating firm W.B. Simpson & Sons, located at 456 West Strand and 100 St. Martin's Lane. Day encouraged the firm to develop its line of stained glass and entered into an agreement to design stained glass exclusively for the firm. In the 1870s both ecclesiastical and domestic stained glass windows were made on the upper floor of the premises at St. Martin's Lane.[22] Day designed stained glass for Simpson's until at least the late 1880s and also designed some of their advertisements for stained glass, which ran in the trade publications.[23]

Virtually all the firm's design books and records from this period have been destroyed during the wars and in various moves.[24] Although it is unknown how many church windows he designed for Simpson's, it is likely that much of the domestic stained glass produced by the firm in the 1870s and 1880s, mainly geometric, floral and foliate designs, was Day's work.[25] W.B. Simpson & Sons registered some of their designs: between 10 July 1882 and 27 February 1883, the firm provisionally registered 14 ornamental designs that appear to be for domestic stained glass. These include motifs of

flowers, leaves, pods, foliage, fruit, ribbons, and medallions. None of these designs are signed, although based on the amount of work he was doing for the firm at that time, as well as motifs and stylistic qualities, some of them are likely to be Day's designs.

Day's stained glass designs were primarily for houses, and he included illustrations of some windows in his magazine articles and books.[26] Most of these were of flowers and foliage, often accompanied by a border of shells or geometric motifs. An early design included in his book *Every-day Art* (1882) illustrates how Day capitalized on the constraints of the material used, namely lead-lines, to create a Japanese-influenced grid with intertwining appleblossoms.[27]

4.5 (top) Lewis F. Day. Advertisement for W. B Simpson & Sons. From *Architect* 17 (1877), Supplement: 7

4.6 (bottom) Lewis F. Day. Three window glazing designs with flowers and butterflies. From Day, *Instances of Accessory Art* (1880): pl.5 Michael Whiteway

4.7 (above) Lewis F. Day. Adaptation of Tudor rose to stained glass, 1880. From Day, *Every-day Art* (1882): 63

4.8 (right) Lewis F. Day. Design for stained glass window featuring apple-blossoms. Described by Day as showing "frank acceptance of the lead-lines in window glazing" and "showing Gothic and Japanese influence". From Day, *Every-day Art* (1882): 130; *Some Principles of Every-day Art* (1890): 26

Day had quite a bit to say on the use of stained glass in the home. He read his paper 'Stained Glass: Its Application to Domestic Architecture' at a meeting of the Architectural Association in early 1872 and a summary of it appeared in the *Architect*.[28] While he would later incorporate comments on domestic glass in his articles and books, this was his only article exclusively devoted to domestic glass. Day's approach was practical, rather than antiquarian. He thought it an advantage that examples of old domestic glass were relatively rare. That forced the worker to exercise his own ideas and invention rather than adhere slavishly to tradition, as often happened in ecclesiastical glass.[29]

He observed that it was particularly important for the designer to bear in mind that the requirements of stained glass used in houses differed markedly from its use in churches. Ecclesiastical glass was often sombre in tone and monumental in design. Domestic glass was meant to be cheering and light in treatment, since it was lived with day in and day out in the home.[30] Domestic glass could also have more refined detail since it was likely to be seen at close range.[31] While ecclesiastical glass subdued light, domestic glass saved as much of it as possible while softening it and tingeing it with colour. It blocked unsightly views and preserved privacy. Rich and dark tones were suitable only in rooms that were larger than ordinary or where darker tones were desired, such as a study.[32]

4.9 Lewis F. Day. Quarry decoration in stained glass, with flowering tree branches (pyrus japonica) formally arranged. From Day, *Instances of Accessory Art* (1880): pl. 20

Michael Whiteway

Day suggested various forms of glazing suitable to domestic use: glazing in quarries (small diamond-shaped or rectangular panes of glass); alternating square and diamond quarries; alternating plain quarries with bull's eyes or painted grisaille (grayish or silvery glass); or using plain glazing (pale tints of whitish glass glazed so that the lead lines formed an ornamental pattern).[33] He stressed that whatever choices were made, the window should look compatible with its surroundings.[34] He noted that while "large unbroken sheets of glass" were inartistic, plate glass was sometimes necessary.[35] Plate glass could, he noted, be enhanced through brushwork or embossing with scrollwork or foliage, and this could be done in such a way that the result did not resemble that of a public house.[36] Using solid paints, stain, half-tints and other techniques of glass painting, with thought and skill a designer could produce interesting effects even without using coloured glass.

Stained glass for churches and public buildings

Day designed a few windows for churches and public secular buildings, but details about them are scanty. The earliest surviving original design by Day for an ecclesiastical window was for Heaton, Butler & Bayne in 1874 and was for the outer lights of a window for the Methodist Church in Belfast.[37] In the 1880s, he produced a few designs for stained glass in public secular buildings, including two for the Empire Music Hall in Leicester Square in 1887; he also collaborated with Hugh Arthur Kennedy in 1888 on a memorial window.[38] Whether any of these designs were produced is unknown.

In 1891 Day collaborated with Walter Crane on two memorial windows for Christ Church, Streatham. Designed by architect James Wild in the Italian Romanesque style, the church was constructed in 1841, and interior decoration was completed by Owen Jones in 1851. The windows were in memory of Rev. Wodehouse Raven, first Vicar of Christ Church. Day was intimately acquainted with this church as he and his wife had been married there and Rev. Raven had baptized their daughter Ruth. It is likely that the commission for these windows came through this connection.

4.10 (above) Lewis F. Day. Glazing in white glass, with the leads forming the pattern. From Day, *Ornament and Its Application* (1904): illus. 9

4.11 (right) Church of St. Mary the Virgin, Great Dunmow, Essex. Southwest entrance

One window features the figures of Christ and St. Peter, with the words "Feed My Sheep", and the second a figure of the widow of Nain kneeling before Christ, who counsels, "Weep Not". Crane designed the figures and Day the canopy of foliage, the border, and the calligraphy for both windows.[39] Although the windows were originally installed at the east ends of the north and south aisles, they were preserved during World War II and later transferred to the north wall, at which time most of the ornamental details Day had designed were omitted.[40]

The Church of St. Mary the Virgin at Great Dunmow, Essex, contains a stained glass window that stands as Day's masterpiece. The church, portions of which date to the 13th century, was largely rebuilt in the 14th and 15th centuries in the Decorated and Perpendicular styles; over the course of its history it had lost some of its windows. [41]

In the early 1900s Day designed a memorial window to Charlotte Young (died 5 December 1904), her father, mother and sister. The Youngs were painters and glaziers and it is highly likely they would have known of Day, whose own family origins were in Essex. The window was executed by Walter J. Pearce, noted Arts and Crafts designer and craftsman, whose studio was in Manchester.[42] The window was installed in the northeast corner of the nave in March 1906.[43]

4.12 Church of St. Mary the Virgin, Great Dunmow, Essex. Interior © Great Dunmow PCC Photography, Gwynn Davies

4.13 and details (opposite and left) Lewis F. Day. Stained glass window for Church of St. Mary the Virgin, Great Dunmow, Essex. Executed by Walter J. Pearce and installed 1906

© Great Dunmow PCC. Photography, Gwynn Davies

4.14 (above) Church of St. Mary the Virgin, Great Dunmow, Essex. Brass plaque beneath Day's stained glass window

© Great Dunmow PCC. Photography, Gwynn Davies

Sometimes referred to by parishioners as the 'Vine Window', it is one of Day's most successful renditions of the human figure. The design is organised around the figure of a stylised Christ standing on grapes, from which wine flows into a jug. Encircling the figure are words from the New Testament passage: "I am the vine and ye are the branches. He that abideth in me and I in him the same beareth much fruit. Abide ye in my love."[44] Some of the foliage and the vine break through the double circle and spill from the outer border. The design features painted leaves and tendrils and angel heads around Christ's halo. The window was illustrated in the *Art Journal*, along with these comments: "The window, by Mr. Lewis F. Day, was one of a group of noteworthy cartoons by him, suggesting deep glowing effects in the jewel-like medium of the completed work. By the device of the outstretched hands, the significance, human and divine, of the figure occupies the whole field of the three-lighted window."[45]

This window exemplifies Day's belief that pictorial forms must be compatible with the capacities of the material, seen here in the choice and arrangement of the full-bodied glass. The rich colours of the window are one of its most outstanding

4.15 a and b Lewis F. Day. Details, stained glass window for Church of St. Mary the Virgin, Great Dunmow, Essex. Executed by Walter J. Pearce and installed 1906

© Great Dunmow PCC
Photography, Gwynn Davies

4.16 (left) Church of St. Mary the Virgin, Great Dunmow, Essex. North side of church, over-looking graveyard
© Great Dunmow PCC. Photography, Gwynn Davies

4.17 (below) Walter J. Pearce. Advertisement. From *Studio* 23 (1901)

features. In his lecture 'Stained Glass Windows: As They Were, Are, and Should Be', given to the Society of Arts in 1882, Day had strongly stated his position on colour: "You may say that it is after all a question of individual preference, whether we like best form or colour. But remember, colour is the only excuse for stained glass. Glass affords opportunities for a brilliancy of colour which no other medium offers, whereas it does not lend itself at all to refinement of form, and if form is what is wanted, any other medium would do, not only as well, but better than glass."[46]

An unsigned account in the church diary related that the striking colour scheme prompted discussion when the window was first installed. It went on to say that parishioners had come to be fond of it, especially at the time of sunset in early summer, when the light shone through it and made the most of the rich colours.[47] The writer

noted that depending on the position of the sun, the plain glass in the southeast window opposite allowed light to flow into the church and on through Day's window, which could then be seen in full colour from the graveyard outside the church. Day, who was known for his scrupulous examination of the conditions of design and manufacture, would have been well aware that this would happen and made the most of it in his choice of palette.

The spiritual dimension of this phenomenon was revealed in the writer's observation that on a sunny winter afternoon, "at a certain point in the north churchyard, you can see the fine figure of our Lord shining out over the graves, as though he were saying to troubled souls I am the Resurrection and the Life".[48] Referring to Day's own words, the account also commended him for following his own advice, "proving his deep reverence for the great men gone before, by daring, as they dared, to be himself".[49]

Day's assessment of the stained glass industry

Recurring themes in Day's writings and lectures are the problems in contemporary stained glass manufacture and the direction in which the highly competitive industry should move. Rapidly changing tastes in decorative arts during the 19th century contributed to the demand for new windows and to the replacement of windows that were considered old-fashioned. The Gothic Revival from the late 1830s to the late 1860s spurred the demand for stained glass for the building and restoration of churches. The waning of the Gothic Revival with its ecclesiastically-inspired designs and the emergence in the late 1860s of the Queen Anne Movement in architecture and the Aesthetic Movement in the decorative arts brought into vogue lighter designs. Many of these showed Japanese influence in motifs and asymmetry. This trend in turn was supplanted by the simplified designs and emphasis on materials of the Arts and Crafts Movement in the late 1880s and the sinuous designs of Art Nouveau around the turn of the century.

Day contended that the major challenge in meeting the demand for high-quality stained glass to meet these shifts in demand was not a technical one. Scientific advances had made possible the production of high-quality glass for making new windows or restoring old ones.[50] He noted that production of large pieces of clear plate glass had been perfected by this point and added: "There is now no mystery whatever about the composition of old glass; and we can make to-day glass quite equal to any that was ever made, and do besides what the medieval man could not do."[51] Nevertheless, there were some real problems that plagued the stained glass industry, and he related these to manufacturers, designers, and the public.

Design and production challenges facing manufacturers

Demand for stained glass and frequent changes in taste put pressure on stained glass firms to produce more windows more quickly, and they responded in two main ways. The huge volume of work that accrued to larger firms forced them to make production methods more

efficient, largely through subdivision of labour. One or more artists provided the initial sketch; draughtsmen turned the sketch into a full-sized cartoon or drawing; and craftsmen then executed the drawing, which included selection of glass, painting, firing, cutting, leading, assembly and installation.[52]

Firms also responded to increased demand by offering various grades of window, a cheaper line with machine-made quarries and a more expensive line, with new cartoons commissioned from established designers.[53] Between 1850 and 1880 the cost of a memorial church window was about £200 to £300.[54] Day did not rail at stained glass studios for having to move toward mass-production techniques to meet demand for glass. He accepted this as a present-day reality of manufacture. Nor did he criticize them for producing less costly versions, for they could be well-designed.

As they competed for ecclesiastical and domestic commissions, heads of stained glass firms were well-aware of the need to accommodate various tastes in the marketplace. Indeed, the principals of the three prominent firms for which Day had designed were artists themselves: Francis Philip Barraud, of Lavers & Barraud; Alfred Bell of Clayton & Bell; and Robert Turnhill Bayne of Heaton, Butler & Bayne; and their firms also employed designers. Day also recognised that architects who commissioned windows were highly influential in their design and execution as were clergy and the patrons who paid for memorial windows.[55] Day took in his stride these influences on window design and was not wedded to one particular style in stained glass.

He did chastise manufacturers, however, for failing to invest more money in good designs, which was necessary if contemporary stained glass was to be of high quality. As long as picture painting paid better, artists would not be inclined to pursue stained glass design.[56] While old glass was designed by noted artists of the day, he observed: "The great part of ours is manufactured at a price; and if sometimes the manufacturer gets a good price for it, the draughtsman may think himself happy if he earns six pounds a week, while the average glass-painter earns much less."[57]

Demands of the medium on the designer

Day also pointed out that designers often lacked knowledge of the properties of stained glass, used inappropriate techniques, and fixated too much on the past. It was the first order of business for the designer to take into account "the inevitable conditions" of the material for which he was designing, not avoid them.[58] First and foremost this required "knowledge of the whole practical ground-work of his subject and that was really science".[59] This entailed a technical understanding of the properties of glass, how it would cut, how it might crack, lead lines that held pieces together, and the bars that supported the window in its setting.

While it was, at the time, fashionable to "over-estimate the charm of accident", Day cast his vote for advances in glass-making: "It ought to be possible by scientific means to obtain those accidents that the medieval men produced by accident."[60] A competent designer certainly was not a slave of his material, and he should know how far its capabilities could be pushed. "He guides it, as a woman does her husband, without his knowing it; but, like her, he knows how far it is safe to go, and stops discreetly short of the point at which the stubbornness innate in materials (no less than in man) asserts itself at last," he wryly observed.[61]

Day contended that by focusing primarily on figure design and pictorial effect, a designer would over-depend on paint and neglect the capacities inherent in glass itself. Seeing imperfections in the glass, the designer painted on it to achieve a "flatter, more even" surface.[62] Use of a "heavily painted shadow" and striving for "a delicacy incompatible with glass-painting" resulted in a "weakness of

4.18 Lewis F. Day. Design for stained glass window featuring growth of the vine. From Day, *Nature in Ornament* (1892): pl. 59

effect".[63] The monumental character and overall effect of a window was then "sacrificed to delicacy, and that delicacy is itself marred by the leads which hold the glass together, and the bars which support it in its place".[64] To the viewer, the effect would be similar to looking at the picture through a grille, and "the absurdity of this delicately modelled flesh-painting with a black line a quarter of an inch wide across it is too obvious to need remark".[65] He advised that painting be kept to a minimum and be used where it is really needed, such as details in a face.[66]

Day believed that the designer should study old glass "as a painter studies the old masters", but that this should not "blind him to the possibilities of the future".[67] Glass painting should be fit for the present time, Day insisted, and that required a designer to be archeologist, craftsman and artist. "We want the three fused into one – a man who is at once familiar with old work, master of his craft, and accomplished artist; a man, too well-versed in the art of the past to ignore it, too skillful to blunder, too conscious of his own power to be the slave of his knowledge; a man who is experimenting always, but basing his experiments on experience, and proving his deep reverence for the great men gone before, by daring, as they dared, to be himself".[68]

Public reception of stained glass

Day lamented that the general public had a lack of understanding of fine glass. Since they did not want to pay enough for stained glass to tempt painters of merit to do glass painting, examples of good work were scarce. The public preferred "to pay a price at which moderate merchandise can be turned out, rather than a sum which would remunerate an able artist at the rate of art".[69] Despite his scepticism of the ability of the public to properly value stained glass – or perhaps because of it – Day directed much of his writing not just to professionals but to a more general readership. A technique he used on

several occasions was to duplicate in writing the function of tour guide, walking the reader, as it were, through a church or museum and highlighting worthy examples of stained glass.[70] He seemed to enjoy this technique and believed that if readers had some knowledge and information ahead of time, they would better understand and enjoy what they saw, and, perhaps, would be better patrons of decorative art, as well.

THE SCHOLAR OF STAINED GLASS

Lectures and articles

Between 1869 and 1910, Day wrote over a dozen articles and two books on stained glass. A brief review of these illustrates how much time and attention he gave to the subject and reveals his views about the development of stained glass. Some of Day's articles were originally delivered as lectures to professional societies or special interest groups, and the *Architect*, *Builder* and *British Architect* often printed either the entire lecture or an abstract of it, thus sharing his ideas with a wider audience. As has been noted, Day's first essay, 'The History and Application of Stained Glass', was read at a meeting of the Architectural Association in January, 1869.[71] Three years later he read his paper 'Stained Glass: Its Application to Domestic Architecture' to the same group.[72] In the early 1870s, however, Day directed most of his efforts to building up his client base, and it was not until 1878 that his next article on stained glass appeared. As a journalist reporting on the Paris Exposition Universelle in 1878 for the *British Architect*, he reviewed the stained glass exhibited, finding British glass there vastly superior to that of the French.[73]

From 1881 to 1886 Day produced a large quantity of designs for textiles, wallpaper and tiles for a number of prestigious firms. He was obviously excellent at time management, for he also found time to lecture and write extensively during these years. In early 1882, he delivered his lecture 'Stained Glass Windows: As They Were, Are, and Should Be' to the Society of Arts, with which he was involved for over thirty years.[74] It was in his customary style, weaving the history, design, and technical aspects of stained glass into a cohesive presentation. A lively and engaging lecturer, Day enriched his presentations with lantern slides or illustrations of examples of English and continental glass, and his lectures drew considerable attention in the press. In 1886 Day lectured again to the Architectural Association on 'Some Lessons in Old Glass'.[75]

Day wrote on the topic of stained glass for a general readership, as well. A series of three articles covering the early history of stained glass appeared in the *Magazine of Art* between 1882 and 1883.[76] Apparently these articles, parts of which were adapted from his Society of Arts lecture of 1882, were well-received, because a second series followed in 1885. Day began where he had left off in the first series and discussed developments to the late 16th century.[77] He never tired of his subject, and he penned several additional articles in the 1890s and early 1900s.[78]

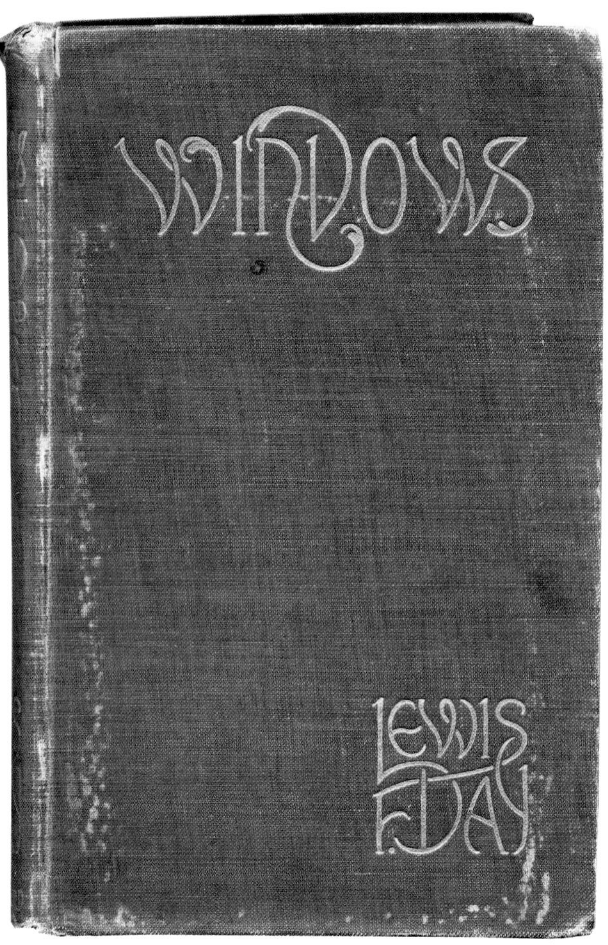

4.19 Lewis F. Day. Cover, *Windows: A Book About Stained and Painted Glass*, 3rd ed. (1909)

Day's masterwork: *Windows*

Day's lectures and writings had been a way for him to refine his ideas about the history and technique of stained glass, and they were all a preparation for his major work, *Windows: A Book About Stained and Painted Glass*, published by B.T. Batsford in 1897.[79] In the preface to the first edition, Day cited Goethe's comparison of poems to stained glass windows – dark when seen from without, beautifully coloured when seen from within – and expressed his hope that this book would help readers to view stained glass from "within".[80]

Windows was the distillation of many years of experience and study. "Early training in the workshop, long practice in design, deep interest in glass, and loving study of it – these are my excuse for writing about it."[81] For over forty years he devoted much of his leisure time to thoroughly researching stained glass on his travels throughout continental Europe and Britain. While this work was certainly scholarly, he described it as a "practical" and "popular" treatment of the history and practice of stained glass art.[82] Walter Crane later remarked that Day probably knew more about the technical aspects of the subject than anyone else.[83] The text drew positive reviews in a number of periodicals, among them the *Artist*, *Art Journal*, *Magazine of Art*, the *Studio*, and the *Architect*, which heartily recommended it to both professionals and amateurs.[84] Harry Powell of the famous glass-making firm James Powell & Sons, commented that Day's book *Windows* "would be the classic of the art of stained glass for many years to come".[85]

In 1898 Day gave his lecture 'The Making of a Stained Glass Window' to the Society of Arts.[86] He focused primarily on technical considerations of mosaic, glass, stain, painting, glazing and bars. His rationale was that "the root of all decorative design is the material in which it is done, out of which, I may say, it is to grow".[87] Walter Crane, who chaired the meeting, commended Day for giving such an interesting, practical, and admirably illustrated lecture.[88] Crane was not alone in his view, for the Society awarded Day a silver medal for this lecture.

Throughout all these works, one can trace Day's views about the origins and historical development of stained glass. Although it could be looked at from the perspective of glass or that of painting, stained glass actually traced its descent from mosaic work, rather than from painting, and in its earliest stage of development, the craftsman's vantage point prevailed.[89] Nevertheless, stained glass developed in a pictorial direction.[90] As time went on, the divergence widened between the decorative aspects (wherein pieces of glass are crafted together in keeping with the characteristics of glass and demands of the bars and leads in a window) and the pictorial aspects (the creation of pictures).[91]

The glass of the 13th century was crude in design and rude in execution. Day contended that a better balance between the requirements of the material and the desire to create pictures was achieved in the late Gothic and early Renaissance period, i.e. in the late 15th and early 16th centuries.[92] After the middle of the 16th century, stained glass art deteriorated because the picture became the priority through greater use of painted detail, and the demands of material and its setting were forgotten.[93] The pictorial had gone too far, and disregard of the issues of craftsmanship "brought the art of glass-painting to ruin," contended Day.[94] After the middle of the 17th century, stained glass "became more and more like abortive picture painting and less and less like glass", and from then on into the 18th century there were very few examples of good glass.[95] Despite his indictment of much of post-Renaissance glass, Day admitted that later styles had aspects to admire and respect.[96] At the top of his list of contemporary stained glass designers was Edward Burne-Jones, "who stands without rival as artist in glass", and whose glass "is worthy to be named with the best old glass".[97] Day gave him the highest accolade when he stated that Burne-Jones was "a master of his material as well as of colour".[98] Day believed that a masterful use of colour resulted not from theories of colour, but rather from feeling, and that this quality was evidenced in the work of Burne-Jones.[99]

Passionate to the end

Day's passion for stained glass did not wane even in the last few years of his life. He continued to write new books, revise earlier ones, and join in professional dialogue. At the request of the Board of Education, he wrote *Stained Glass*, published in 1903 as one of the Art Handbooks of the Victoria and Albert Museum.[100] Priced at 4s. and about 150 pages, it was an illustrated guide to stained glass from early Gothic to Renaissance, with most of the examples drawn from the museum's collection. The *Magazine of Art* lauded it as "a masterly little production which explains the styles and development of the art of design as applied to it", as did the *Builder*, which cited it as a "very useful inventory of the glass in the museum".[101] Day also authored the article on stained glass for the *Encyclopedia Britannica*, 11th edition.[102] Family friend Dorothy Maud Ross relayed that glassmaker Harry Powell had originally been asked to write it but had deferred to Day's expertise.[103]

In preparation for the third edition of his book *Windows*, in 1909, Day and his wife revisited the sites mentioned in the book to verify information and to see what had happened to the stained glass there in the intervening years.[104] In March 1910, several weeks before his death, Day chaired a meeting of the Society of Arts at which Noel Heaton gave his lecture on 'The Foundations of Stained Glass Work'.[105] Stained glass was the subject of Day's first paper before the Society in 1882, and somehow it seems fitting that it was also the subject of the last meeting he chaired before his death. While his design work was small in quantity and rarely mentioned in accounts of stained glass, his writings are still valuable for their historical information and perspectives on stained glass as decorative art.

CHAPTER FIVE: WALLPAPER

"We may as well adopt paper as the simplest, cheapest, and most effective means of giving interest to an expanse of wall." [Lewis F. Day, 1882]

5.1 Lewis F. Day. 'Pomegranate' wallpaper, 1874. Made by Jeffrey & Co. for W.B. Simpson & Sons. Block-printed. (Pattern has been extended to show repeat)
National Archives, United Kingdom, BT43/101 Part 1 No. 282671

Within two years of establishing his own design studio, Lewis Foreman Day had begun to achieve a reputation in professional circles as a designer of stained glass and other furnishings. The prominent Regent St. emporium Howell & James had exhibited furnishings designed by him at the international exhibitions in London in 1872 and Vienna in 1873. However, it was in his wallpaper designs – first registered in 1874 – that Day initially demonstrated his prodigious talent for pattern design. From then on, and for the next thirty-five years, Day provided wallpaper patterns for several leading decorating firms and manufacturers. Although any correspondence, diaries and ledger books Day may have kept have been lost, a substantial amount of evidence of his work is to be found in manufacturers' logs, designs registered at the Patent Office, illustrations in his books, original sketches, and surviving examples of actual wallpapers. More than 150 patterns were put into commercial production, rendering wallpaper design one of Day's most prolific activities.

Day designed wallpaper during a period that witnessed enormous demographic, economic, social and technological changes – many of which affected the wallpaper trade. The growing number of people who could count themselves as belonging to the middle classes now had not only the financial means, but also the desire to furnish their homes attractively. A wide array of books and magazines informed them about principles of "good taste" and offered advice on selection of suitable types and patterns of wallpaper for halls, drawing and dining rooms, bedrooms and nurseries. Machine production of wallpaper made a bewildering variety of papers – printed, embossed, flocked, lacquered, and gilded – available to eager buyers. Output of wallpaper increased from just over 1 million pieces in 1834 to 32 million in 1874.[1] In addressing the phenomenal growth of the industry, in 1876 the *Furniture Gazette* noted that "about three-fifths of all the paper-hangings now sold are produced by machinery".[2]

Wallpapers hand-printed from woodblocks were primarily aimed at the upper end of the market. Though many of Day's papers fell into this category, he also designed a substantial number of wallpapers that were roller printed by machine and were more affordable to those middle-class professionals or business people who wanted to have well-designed and produced papers to grace their walls. Day was intellectually stimulated and creatively energised by the practical demands and production challenges inherent in wallpaper design. His enjoyment of the interplay of the analytical and creative sides of his personality permeated his early work for W.B. Simpson & Sons. It resulted in masterful designs for Frederick Walton Co. that made the most of the capacities of new relief materials, and found its fullest expression in his varied repertoire and huge output for Jeffrey & Co.

DAY'S EARLY WORK IN WALLPAPER DESIGN

The scenario of wallpaper design

When Day began designing wallpapers, a plethora of styles was available to householders. Popular patterns featured realistic depictions of flowers, fruit and foliage, often accompanied by naturalistic details and use of perspective. Floral designs were often inspired by French styles based on historic revivals of Louis XIII through to Louis XVI. Particularly favoured by many consumers were the Rococo-inspired floral patterns incorporating trellises, ribbons and scrollwork. *Trompe l'oeil* papers imitating marble, wood and textiles were also available. Gaudy patterns printed in strong colours often found favour with the public.

It is inconceivable that Day would have looked to France for inspiration for his own work, objecting both on aesthetic and on moral grounds to the imitation of French designs. The serious-minded Day despised the Rococo for its frivolity and lack of restraint, writing on one occasion that he would not insult his readers by even discussing it.[3] Though he grudgingly admitted that the Louis XVI-style work made for monarchs in silks and painted panels was exquisite, he insisted that a happy effect was not achievable by imitating this in wallpaper: "If you really must have Louis XVI, you had better paint your walls, or hang them with silk, and not paper them."[4] He criticised the attempts by English manufacturers to follow the frivolity of French fashion and remarked: "Our safety is in doing what we can do best."[5]

5.2 James Huntington. French-influenced English wallpaper, c.1860. From Sugden and Edmonson, *A History of English Wallpaper* (1926): pl. 105

More fundamental to Day's approach to wallpaper design was his philosophical alignment with the beliefs of A.W.N. Pugin, John Ruskin, and William Morris that the quality of objects of everyday life – furniture, textiles, ceramics, wallpaper – affected those who used them and consequently should be artful. These ideas had gained greater currency with the emergence of the Aesthetic Movement in the late 1860s. Day agreed that the effect of one's surroundings was inescapable, whether people claimed any interest in furnishings or not.[6] In comparing the impact of decorative and fine art, he commented: "I believe, even, that decorative art may have still more influence on men's lives than picture painting."[7]

Day positioned himself with other designers, architects and manufacturers who sought to raise the standards of design and production of wallpaper. Chief among manufacturers as a force for change was Metford Warner, director and sole proprietor of wallpaper manufacturer Jeffrey & Co. from 1871. Warner, who printed Morris & Co.'s papers, enlisted the talents of noted architects and designers including William Burges, Charles Locke Eastlake, Edward W. Godwin, Bruce Talbert and Walter Crane to design patterns, thus raising wallpaper to the level of art. Day's close colleagueship with Metford Warner spanned his entire career in wallpaper design.

Day's entrée to wallpaper design

In about 1874, Day negotiated an agreement to design church decoration and wallpapers exclusively for W.B. Simpson & Sons.[8] Shortly thereafter, he branched into designing stained glass and tiles for the firm as well; and from then on, through to the mid-1880s, Simpson's was one of Day's major clients. Although particulars about the designs he supplied to the firm for other types of furnishings are scarce, much evidence of Day's work in wallpaper design remains.

W.B. Simpson & Sons, a London firm located at 100, St. Martin's Lane, and 456, West Strand, was founded in 1833 under the name W.B. and F. Simpson, "house-painters". Over the ensuing decades the firm achieved prominence as decorators who offered enamelled iron, art tiles, stained glass, and wallpapers, which were printed for them by Jeffrey & Co. Although most of the firm's business records from the early years were lost over the course of two world wars and relocations of the firm, fortunately Simpson's registered a number of Day's wallpaper designs in mid-1874 and periodically thereafter.[9]

It is clear from illustrations and accounts in the trade press that Day regularly supplied Simpson's with designs for wall treatments, although the total number of patterns is not known. During this early period, Day set the course that he would follow throughout his years in wallpaper design: he drew inspiration from nature, Eastern cultures and historic ornament; took a very disciplined approach to pattern design; and exhibited a decidedly practical bent. Talking about what he did was inextricably bound with the doing of it, and from the late 1870s on, Day aired his views about how wallpaper could be used effectively in interior decoration.

Sources of inspiration

It is highly likely that Day saw the collections of Japanese applied arts exhibited at the 1862 London International Exhibition when he returned home after finishing his studies on the Continent. Although specific sources Day may have consulted are not known, there were a number of opportunities for him to study the arts of Japan. Books of prints, including Hokusai's *Manga* (1816), were in circulation, and two notable shops – the Oriental Warehouse of Farmer and Rogers' Great Shawl and Cloak Emporium (opened 1862) and East India House (opened 1875 and later renamed Liberty & Co.) – carried goods from the Far East.

As did other designers, such as Godwin and Talbert, Day experimented with Japanese motifs and techniques for organising patterns. He was particularly impressed with Japan's example "in teaching us how to adapt natural forms without taking the nature out of them", and he frequently included examples of Japanese decorative art in his articles and books.[10] The influence of the Japanese treatment of nature and use of techniques such as layering of patterns, asymmetry, and incorporation of particular motifs, are seen in a cluster of Day's designs registered by Simpson's in mid-1874. The 'Trellis Dado' is a tightly constructed pattern in which highly-stylised daisies and leaves weave diagonally in and out of an underlying grid, or trellis. The 'Apple Blossom' wallpaper features branches, leaves, overlapping blossoms and buds arranged asymmetrically. The pattern was available with a plain background or superimposed against a grid of small squares.

5.3 (above) Lewis F. Day. 'Trellis' dado, 1874. Made by Jeffrey & Co. for W.B. Simpson & Sons. Block-printed
National Archives, United Kingdom, BT43/101 Part 1 No. 282676

5.4 (right) Lewis F. Day. 'Appleblossom' wallpaper, 1874. Made by Jeffrey & Co. for W.B. Simpson & Sons. Block-printed
National Archives, United Kingdom, BT43/101 Part 1 No. 282670

Day employed similar devices in his 'Pomegranate' wallpaper. The fruit, reduced to a simple circular form, overlaps in groups of twos and threes, linked by a web-like arrangement of stems and leaves that weave over and under the fruit. The background pattern is composed of finely-drawn lines suggesting a maze. The fruit is grouped more tightly in Day's pattern than in William Morris's 'Fruit' pattern (also known as the 'Pomegranate' pattern), which dates to about eight years earlier. Day's papers were hand-printed from wood blocks by Jeffrey & Co., which also printed Morris's papers.

Day was certainly influenced in these early years by the mid-century design reformers, including Owen Jones. They rejected naturalistic detail and perspective and advocated patterns in which forms from nature or historic sources were abstracted, or simplified to their basic elements. These stylised forms were sometimes combined with

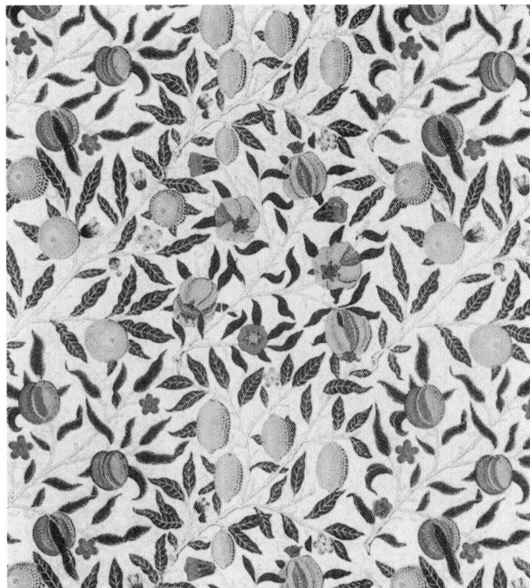

5.5 (above left) Lewis F. Day. 'Pomegranate' wallpaper, 1874. Made by Jeffrey & Co. for W.B. Simpson & Sons. Block-printed National Archives, United Kingdom, BT43/101 Part 1 No.282671

5.6 (above right) William Morris. 'Fruit' wallpaper (also known as 'Pomegranate'), c.1866. Made by Jeffrey & Co. for Morris, Marshall, Faulkner & Co. Block-printed. From Sugden and Edmondson, *A History of English Wallpaper* (1926): pl. 111

5.7 (below) Lewis F. Day. Design for 'Sprig and Scroll' wallpaper, 1876. Described by Day as a "wall pattern suggestive of painted tiles". From Day, *Every-day Art* (1882): 125

geometric shapes into patterns that were based on simple mathematical repeats. With the absence of light and shade that creates dimensionality, design reform patterns were 'flat', which was deemed in keeping with the hard, flat wall surface that they decorated, a point emphasised by Charles Locke Eastlake and other critics.[11]

While he agreed that it was necessary to reform design and ultimately public taste in wallpaper selection, like other designers Day came to his own conclusions about how natural forms should be treated. He described the two extremes in this ongoing debate as "strict fidelity to fact", practised by those who advocated direct imitation of natural forms, and the "bondage of a narrow conventionality", espoused by those who reduced natural forms to their most basic characteristics.[12] Day advocated a moderate approach, contending that natural forms had to be modified to suit the purpose and place for the designs and the materials in which they were produced.[13] Day advised that this should be done judiciously, however, for "excepting in purely geometric pattern, something in the nature of growth is to be desired in ornament, even the most abstract".[14]

Two of Day's designs registered by Simpson's in early 1876 provide an

5.8 (right) Lewis F. Day. 'Wave' dado, 1876. Made by Jeffrey & Co. for W.B. Simpson & Sons. Block-printed
National Archives, United Kingdom, BT43/101 Part 1 No. 299516

5.9 (below) Lewis F. Day. 'Peony' wallpaper, 1877. Made by Jeffrey & Co. for W.B. Simpson & Sons. Block-printed
National Archives, United Kingdom, BT43/102 No. 316484

interesting comparison of the ways he experimented with the conventionalisation of natural forms. The 'Wave' dado features elements reduced to their most geometric forms, with regularly repeating squares containing fans ornamented with C-scrolls suggesting waves. While Day designed a few dados in this manner, he never seemed as comfortable as Christopher Dresser in abstracting natural forms to this degree. Day's 'Sprig and Scroll' filling paper, with its flat foliage and flowers superimposed over a grid suggesting tiles, is more typical of his way of honouring nature while simplifying it.[15]

Around this time, Day was also experimenting with a looser composition of design elements. His 'Peony' filling paper, while retaining stylised forms from nature, exhibits a freer asymmetrical arrangement. This paper was printed in several colourways, one of which featured olive-toned leaves and peony buds layered over a cream background pattern of five-petalled flowers outlined in gold.

Simpson's registered additional designs by Day in 1876 and 1877, and some of these may be the ones that the firm featured in their display at the Paris Exposition Universelle of 1878. In his journalistic reports on the exhibition for the *British Architect*, Day detailed his designs as a staircase pattern featuring a "soft brown scroll with grayish blue rosettes or flowers on a vellum ground", a wallpaper, with a "leaf pattern in pale reds", a wallpaper with "a blossom pattern in blues on dark blue", a "deep frieze of flowing scroll work", and "a dado in browns and gold".[16]

A versatile designer with a practical bent

Day was acutely aware that colour would affect a product's marketability. Many of his wallpaper designs from this period were available in several versions, including the subdued tertiary colours favoured by apostles of Aestheticism. Olive green, khaki, muted gold and drab brown were deemed artistic and preferable to the mid-century's brighter and sometimes harsher colours. Precisely what Day thought of the vogue for drab tones is unclear. He was preoccupied with relationships between form and colour and was opposed to the imposition of rules of colour. In his later years he succinctly stated the underlying principle that had governed his designs from the beginning: "The colour scheme is part of the construction."[17] Rather than be seduced by a particular colour-scheme, he insisted, the designer had to devise a pattern that would work in several different colourways, since a pattern that was suitable only for one would not be worth manufacturing.[18]

In addition to his concern for manufacturing considerations, Day also focused on the way his designs would work when installed. In 1883 the *Architect* announced that Simpson's had "issued a new pattern-book of papers, all of which have been designed by the same artist, and are executed in his own colourings".[19] An accompanying illustration featured a treatment for a staircase and adjoining wall based on an unnamed dado with panels of leafy brushwork. It was used with his 'Shell' filling paper, a pattern of intertwining spirals and simplified ancient scallop shell motif that had been revived in the 18th and 19th centuries; his 'Festoon' frieze, composed of daisies and leafy tendrils, completed the scheme. This wall arrangement aptly illustrates the love of surface pattern so characteristic of the period.

Day used this design to illustrate the concept that in a pattern such as this, "any two opposite features should be precisely opposite", and branches or spirals must turn "on precisely the same level" because "the eye expects a level".[20] He warned: "Inaccuracy in either of these respects, though it may pass in a drawing for artistic freedom, is almost sure, in repetition on the wall, to give the impression that it is out of the straight."[21] Accuracy, he insisted, was not optional: "In what concerns the equilibrium of a pattern it is impossible to be too mechanically exact."[22] Decorators recognised Day's skill in foreseeing and forestalling installation problems. Metford Warner later noted that this pattern book was favourably received by architects and decorators, both for the originality of the patterns and because they would repeat well when hung on the wall.[23]

5.10 Lewis F. Day. 'Shell' wallpaper. From Jeffrey & Co., *Selected Hand-Printed Wall Papers* (1894-5)

Nordiska Museet, Stockholm, Erik Folcker Collection, 310.405

5.11 Lewis F. Day. 'Festoon' frieze, 'Shell' wallpaper, unnamed dado, c.1883. Made by Jeffrey & Co. for W.B. Simpson & Sons. From *Architect* 30 (1883): 69, near 69

Trustees of the National Library of Scotland, Edinburgh

Day's views on decorating walls and ceilings

Talking about what he did was always important to Day, and from the late 1870s on he straightforwardly shared his ideas about the rôle of wallpaper in interior decorating schemes. Day contended that wallpaper was "the simplest, cheapest, and most effective means of giving interest to an expanse of wall".[24] He agreed with Morris that wallpaper was really a "makeshift" that lacked the dignity of wall-painting and the substantiality of more permanent forms of decoration, such as wood-carving. However, since most people were renting their homes and, consequently, bearing the brunt of the decorating expense to the financial benefit of the landlord, wallpaper was the practical option for making one's home habitable.[25]

As is seen in his 1883 staircase decoration in the *Architect*, Day had a clear preference for the tripartite wall decoration of dado, filling and frieze that had been advocated by Eastlake. Day recommended a dado that was darker than the walls above for both practical and artistic reasons.[26] Visually, it would "help to connect the furniture and make the place compact and snug".[27] In rooms with light-coloured walls and dark furniture, a darker band around the base of the wall would hold the furniture together and prevent it from standing out too strongly as it would against a light background.[28] A dado "somewhat severe or stiff" in design would be in keeping with its function as a base and would serve as a foil or contrast to a freer pattern in the filling above.[29] A dark-coloured dado would not show dirt and would also better survive the wear and tear that this part of the wall suffered. A relief material such as Lincrusta-Walton in a simple unpretentious pattern could serve well due to its durability.[30]

Day was also undoubtedly predisposed to the tripartite wall because it gave vent to his love of pattern and offered the creative challenge of designing patterns that worked well together. He certainly was not alone in this activity, for Talbert, Crane and a number of other designers were turning out effective tripartite wall decorations during this period.

Day advised that the main factor in choice of a filling paper was whether one wanted it to be a prominent feature of the interior scheme or whether it was to serve as a background for pictures. In the latter case, a "simple all-over pattern" lighter in colour than the dado would be an appropriate and unobtrusive choice.[31] He did not favour papers that were too assertive, remarking that "a strong personality writes, so to speak, always under its own signature; but I am not sure that I want anyone's personality to call out to me from the walls and floor of my room".[32] The degree to which a pattern was assertive was ultimately left up to the buyer, because many papers of the period, including some of Day's, were in fact assertive, at least in some colourways.

The wall treatment could be finished off with a frieze to avoid the appearance of the filling disappearing behind the cornice. Day advocated the use of a frieze – "deeper or shallower according to the height of the room, very similar in tone, and in character, to the wall-paper" – that would carry the eye to the ceiling, giving the appearance of height.[33] This would be best accomplished if the frieze did not provide too great a contrast in colour or pattern from the filling. The cornice could be painted in an intermediate colour or, if the mouldings were very plain, stencilling could provide added interest.[34]

Day advised that ceilings be either distempered or papered. Since the ceiling was not a feature of a room that one could look at conveniently for any length of time, hand-painting it was not worthwhile. The colour chosen for the ceiling should be a lighter tone of one or two of the wall colours, and whether it was painted or papered, white should be avoided, since it had a tendency to make

5.12 (above) Lewis F. Day. Design for ceiling paper with all-over daisy pattern. From Day, *Pattern Design* (1903): illus. 179

5.13 (right) Lewis F. Day. Design for ceiling paper with all-over daisy pattern. From *The Planning of Ornament*, 3rd ed. (1893): pl. 20

5.14 (left) Lewis F. Day. Design for ceiling paper featuring scrollwork. From Day, *Pattern Design* (1903): illus. 156

5.15 (below) Lewis F. Day. Design for ceiling paper featuring "feathery composite foliage". From Day, *Pattern Design* (1903): 92–3; illus. 118

anything else nearby look dirty.[35] The choice of a suitable ceiling paper presented the buyer with particular difficulties, the chief one being that it was very difficult to judge from the selection in pattern books which paper would look best on a ceiling. A pattern might look very sparse in the sample book, but it would not appear that way when installed.[36] "On a ceiling the pattern can scarcely be too 'open'", Day advised.[37] He continued that a ceiling papered with a simple diaper – small repeated pattern – had the added advantage of disguising the all-too-common ceiling cracks in modern houses.[38] Day noted that relief papers could be used to good effect, provided that they resembled moulded ceilings "with interlacing geometric ribs" and were not too heavily embossed.[39] The addition of wood mouldings affixed to the wall could add breadth and boldness to the overall interior scheme.[40]

5.16 Lewis F. Day. Lincrusta-Walton frieze, c.1886. Made by Frederick Walton Co. From *Journal of Decorative Art* 6 (1886): 894

Trustees of the National Library of Scotland, Edinburgh

Day's work for Frederick Walton Co. & designs for relief materials

By the end of 1884, when his contract to design wallpapers exclusively for Simpson's had lapsed, Day had become well-known as a very versatile and practical designer. He was ready for some new challenges, and one of the ways he satisfied this need was through his work for Frederick Walton Co. He apparently began by designing linoleum, although no designs have been traced.[41] Of the firm's surviving records from this period, no references to Day's work have been located. However, the frequent discussions in the trade press in the 1880s and 1890s of his work for Frederick Walton Co. suggest that the firm carried his designs for dados, fillings, friezes, door panels and tablemats for at least a dozen years.

Day's work for the Walton firm shows a pairing of his maturing design skills with his lively interest in the development of new products. It also reveals his knowledge of the special capacities of new relief materials and his grasp of the practical installation issues they presented. Day's work took place during a period of rapid growth in the firm's manufacture and marketing of new relief materials.

In 1877, Frederick Walton, the inventor of linoleum, developed a wallcovering made from some of the same ingredients. 'Linoleum Muralis', or Lincrusta-Walton, was manufactured from linseed oil, wood pulp and other components. The surface of Lincrusta-Walton was embossed in relief by machine rollers and resembled traditional relief decorations, such as woodcarving, plasterwork and embossed leather. Strong, durable and practical, Lincrusta withstood wear and tear in areas of heavy foot traffic, was waterproof, easy to install, and could be left plain or painted and gilded. Its original stiff canvas backing was replaced with a light waterproof paper in 1887, making it even lighter to handle and easier to hang.[42]

Since it was waterproof and washable, Lincrusta was seen as a sanitary option for decorating hospitals, hotels, railway cars, and private dwellings. Suitable for dados, fillings, friezes, door and shutter panels and ceilings, it also was deemed a practical choice for halls and stairways because it had the added advantage of hiding defects in a wall. Although never an inexpensive wallcovering, Lincrusta was certainly less costly than woodcarving or plasterwork, and due to its durability, it was seen as economical in the long run. The Walton firm broadened Lincrusta's appeal by introducing a less expensive version several years after its introduction.[43] By the late 1890s the firm had close to forty patterns priced at a shilling per yard; a press report noted that "in several cases where shilling patterns have been before the trade for two or three years, the sale of them has been simply prodigious".[44]

"Solid in relief, solid in colour and solid in value", Lincrusta was touted as the "King of wall decorations", and its growing popularity was attested to by the fact that between 1879-1884 sales of Lincrusta tripled.[45] The firm aggressively developed the Lincrusta line by using the talents of leading designers including Christopher Dresser, George Haité, Owen Davis, and Day, and appealed to the eclectic tastes of the marketplace by offering patterns in a wide variety of styles and a full range of colours and tones. The artistic and functional benefits of the product, along with shrewd marketing, enabled Lincrusta to prosper despite tough competition from other relief products on the market, such as Anaglypta, Tynecastle Tapestry, and Cordelova and the rubber and cork-based materials, such as Cortecine, Calcorian and Subercorium.[46]

Day's designs: a fusion of art and problem-solving

Even in his earlier work for Simpson's, Day had demonstrated his firm belief that design was both art and problem-solving.[47] Designs that have been positively identified as Day's for Frederick Walton Co. draw from two main sources of artistic inspiration: nature and historic ornament. Some of Day's best designs for relief materials were inspired by the Renaissance. With the waning of the Gothic Revival in the 1860s, interest in Renaissance forms had grown, and Day's own interest in how nature was adapted to purpose during that period had deepened by the mid-1880s. The embossed and gilded leather wallcoverings of the 16th and 17th centuries also provided inspiration for 19th-century designers.

The *Architect* illustrated a Renaissance-style design (signed and dated 1885), praising it as a drop pattern with a repeat "wider than the width of the material, by which means a bigger and broader effect is produced than would otherwise be possible within the same space".[48] The rich, bold design features swags, dense foliage, and amorini romping among scrolling trails of leaves, berries and acorns. It is an unusual example of

5.17 (left) Lewis F. Day. Lincrusta-Walton wallpaper, 1885. From *Architect* 33 (1885): pl. near 195

Trustees of the National Library of Scotland, Edinburgh

5.18 (below) Lewis F. Day. 'Feather Leaf' Lincrusta-Walton dado, 1896. Made by Frederick Walton Co. From *Journal of Decorative Art* 16 (1896): 314

Trustees of the National Library of Scotland, Edinburgh

Day's work because it incorporates figures, a practice he generally avoided, contending that human and animal figures introduced an undesirable restlessness into a repeat pattern that was meant to serve as a background.[49] In this design Day seems to have been following his own advice that if used, figures should be treated ornamentally, to ensure "they are so lost in the general effect of surface richness as not prominently to assert themselves as figures".[50]

Day was energised by using design to solve practical decorating problems. He clearly relished such challenges and admitted: "To the making of a practical designer there goes an element of pugnacity – he enjoys tackling a tough problem."[51] Day's problem-solving approach was reflected in one of his panel designs singled out by the trade press for its "general excellence and usefulness".[52] Although the usual dimensions of Lincrusta-Walton were a width of 18in. to 19in. (45.7-48.3cm.) and a length of 12yds. (11m.) there was some variation.[53] Day's fretwork pattern with accompanying floral insets was supplied in continuous lengths that could be arranged in over a dozen combinations, all illustrated in the *Journal of Decorative Art* and accompanied by Day's directions for use. One reviewer enthused that "its adaptability as a dado, frieze, pilaster, or panel is so very marked, and its merits as a design so excellent, that it is almost unique in its usefulness in this respect, and we most heartily recommend its frequent adoption to the trade".[54] Day was evidently pleased with this design, for he included it in *The Planning of Ornament* to show how designs can be altered to fit particular circumstances.[55]

Day's embossed dado with a bold design of waving ferns in a drop repeat was marketed by Walton's in the late 1890s.[56] Identified in the firm's advertising as 'Feather Leaf', No. #829, it was 26½in. (67.3cm.) wide and priced at 3 shillings per yard.[57] The adaptability of the fern motif to relief designs apparently intrigued Day, because around the same time he designed an embossed tile pattern in a somewhat simpler arrangement of ferns for Pilkington's Tile & Pottery Co.

Frederick Walton Co. also marketed tablemats with patterns by Day and other leading designers. The firm advertised that these mats, "which are in sets of six, from 9 by 6in. [22.9 x 15.2cm.] to 14½ by 10½in. [36.8 x 26.7cm.], are sold at 2s.6d. and 3s.6d. per set".[58] Repeating its strategy of offering seemingly limitless choices, the firm proudly added that this "dainty novelty" was available in "42 Selections in Pattern and Colour".[59] Specific patterns by Day have not been traced.

Day's views on relief materials

Day thought that Lincrusta was "the material, *par excellence*" for an inexpensive dado because of its ability to withstand wear and tear.[60] He was not unequivocally in favour of the firm's accumulation of patterns, however. Some patterns continued to be carried for a number of years as new designs were introduced, resulting in an array of nearly 2,000 designs by 1893.[61] Day criticised the company for producing too many patterns that were "too finikin and fussy for use in any dignified scheme of decoration".[62] He advised that "broad and simple designs", particularly those based on historic ornament, were most appropriate to the characteristics of relief materials and he noted that the firm's pattern books had too few of these.[63] In 1898 the firm brought out its Cameoid line, a hollow-backed, high-relief, light-weight product fabricated out of pressed paper that was particularly suitable for ceilings and friezes. Although the trade press of the time referred to Lewis Day as having produced patterns for Cameoid, these designs have yet to be traced.[64]

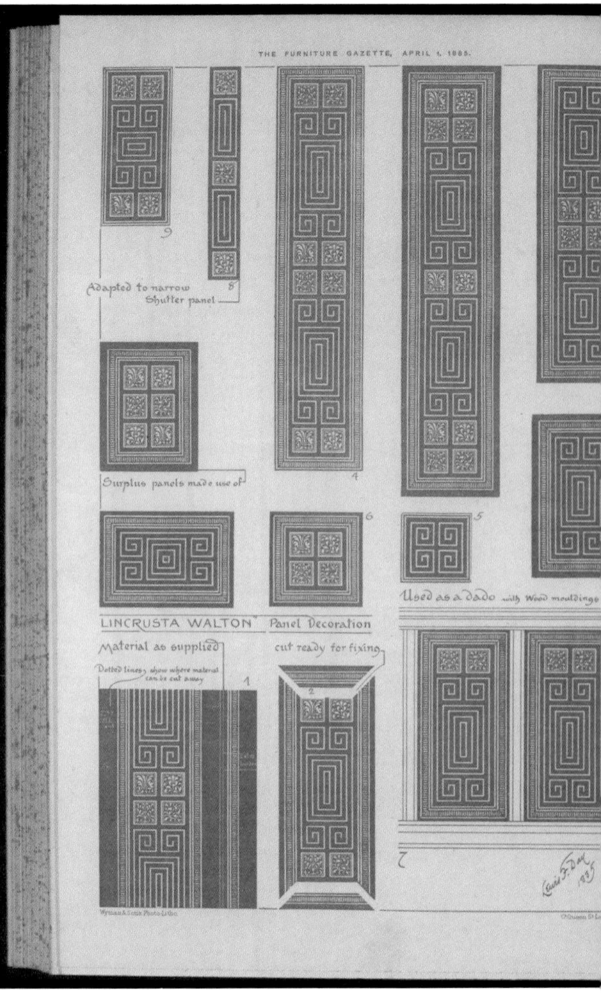

5.19 Lewis F. Day. "Lincrusta-Walton Decoration no. 436, Suitable for Panels, Friezes, Pilasters, Dados, etc.", 1885. Made by Frederick Walton Co. From *Journal of Decorative Art* 16 (1896): 187

Trustees of the National Library of Scotland, Edinburgh

A HAPPY COLLABORATION: LEWIS F. DAY AND JEFFREY & CO.

Day's relationship with Metford Warner

Day began designing for Jeffrey & Co. in 1885, by which time his agreement to design wallpapers exclusively for W.B. Simpson & Sons had expired.[65] Day and Metford Warner, managing director of Jeffrey & Co., had known each other for over a decade through their mutual involvement with Simpson's, whose papers were printed by Jeffrey. The two men travelled in the same professional circles and held each other in high mutual regard. Day referred to Warner as the Wedgwood of the wallpaper trade.[66] In turn, Warner recognised Day's mastery of line, ability to design in a variety of styles to satisfy diverse consumer tastes, and his facility in designing for production. He also greatly enjoyed discussing with Day designs for various types of papers and critiquing the finished product.[67] While both men had an extensive historical knowledge of their craft, they also believed in exploiting the manufacturing possibilities of the present.

This relationship occurred at a significant point in Day's career. By the mid-1880s he was reaching his full stature as a designer in terms of both his abilities and reputation. His work for Jeffrey & Co. spanned more than twenty years, and in his huge volume of work for the firm he operated at full vigour. His versatility was demonstrated in the design of a wide range of hand block-printed wallpapers, including flocked, lacquered, stamped, and embossed leather papers. He also produced numerous designs for less expensive machine-printed papers, which were affordable to those of more moderate means. Day worked well within the evolving taste preferences of the time, and his designs could never be described as avant-garde. Where he distinguished himself was in the variety and number of his wall-papers, which were prominently featured at trade and industrial exhibitions and carried in the firm's catalogues and sample books, some for many years. In his work for Jeffrey & Co. Day gave full play to his mature skills as a designer for industry and derived enormous satisfaction in the process.

His friendship with Metford Warner also provided Day with scope for expressing some of his most fundamental beliefs about designing for industry: that design is both art and problem-solving; that the designer is not autonomous, but is a member of a manufacturing team; and that one could be "true to one's art" and still be commercially competent. Most importantly, he was collaborating with a manufacturer who also believed in the possibility of a compatible marriage of design and industry.[68]

Day's early designs for Jeffrey & Co.
The first Jeffrey & Co. catalogue in which Day's wallpapers were included was the firm's 1885 'Patent Hygienic Wall Papers'. This catalogue featured both block-printed and machine-printed papers that were free from the dangers of arsenic and were also non-absorbent and thus 'sanitary'. They could be cleaned with soap and water with no detriment to the colour and did not

5.20 (top left) Lewis F. Day. 'Imperial' wallpaper, 1885. From Jeffrey & Co., *Patent Hygienic Wall Papers* (c.1885) Arthur Sanderson Ltd

5.21 (bottom left) Lewis F. Day. 'Imperial' wallpaper. From Jeffrey & Co., *Selected Hand-Printed Wall Papers* (1894-5) Nordiska Museet, Stockholm, Erik Folcker Collection, 310.405

5.22 (right) Lewis F. Day. 'Imperial' wallpaper with dado and border. Made by Jeffrey & Co. From Erik G. Folcker, *Engleska Papperstapeter* (Stockholm: 1893): fig. 7 Private Collection

5.23 Walter Crane. 'The House that Jack Built' nursery wallpaper, 1886. Made by Jeffrey & Co. Machine-printed. From Day, *The Application of Ornament*, 3rd ed. (1895): pl. 5

5.24 and detail Lewis F. Day. 'Pied Piper of Hamlin' nursery wallpaper, 1885. From Jeffrey & Co., *Patent Hygienic Wall Papers* (c.1885) Arthur Sanderson Ltd.

have the undesirable gloss of other sanitary papers.[69] Jeffrey & Co. exhibited papers treated by this patent process at the International Health Exhibition in 1884 and won two gold medals.

The firm promoted these papers not only as "healthful", but also as "artistic", for the designs had been provided by such prominent figures as William Burges, Charles Locke Eastlake, John D. Sedding, Bruce Talbert, Walter Crane and Day. One of Day's patterns was the 'Imperial' filling paper, which went into production in 1885. The pattern features brushwork of leaves, flowers, buds and pods in an airy, rhythmical arrangement. The washable version of the filling paper was priced from 5d./yd. and the non-washable version from 4d./yd. At the Edinburgh Exhibition in 1886, the filling paper was exhibited along with an unnamed dado and border. The *British Architect* noted that the scheme was "made up of cleverly conventionalised flower work of a most graceful type," adding that "the design is one of the best wall coverings Jeffrey has produced".[70]

Day's nursery paper 'Pied Piper of Hamlin' was also included in the catalogue. The paper was marketed at 3¼d./yd. for washable and 2½d./yd. for the non-washable version. The paper, which had an accompanying 'Rat Border', is a rarity in Day's work in two respects. It is the only nursery paper he is known to have designed, and it incorporated human

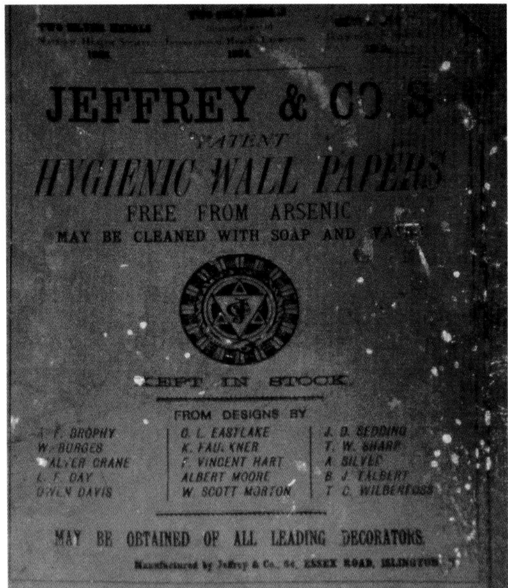

5.25 Jeffrey & Co. Cover, *Patent Hygienic Wall Papers*, c.1885 Arthur Sanderson Ltd

and animal figures into the repeated design, a practice he did not advocate. He contended that not only did they express movement and, therefore, interfered with the steadiness and restfulness that a background should provide, they were also difficult to conventionalise enough to suit the purposes of ornament without taking the character out of them.[71] In this pattern, the expressions on the children's faces are grim, and even the background foliage is stiff, lacking the flowing rhythm seen in his best work. Known for his gravitas, Day did not seem comfortable working with a child-oriented design that demanded a lighthearted playfulness, and this design lacks the charm and sense of fun that is seen in Walter Crane's nursery papers, such as 'The House that Jack Built'.

The *Victorian Series*

In late 1888 or early 1889, Jeffrey issued an important trade catalogue of wallpapers entitled *Illustrations of the Victorian Series, and Other Wall-Papers* that drew a great deal of attention in the press.[72] The *British Architect* was laudatory: "The material of which this folio is made up represents the best work of our best English designers, and that architect or decorator must be hard to please who cannot find amongst Messrs. Jeffrey's varied designs, something to fit his wants, whatever they be."[73] The *Magazine of Art* wholeheartedly agreed: "Mr. William Morris and Messrs. Jeffrey are fast educating the public up to understanding that it is far preferable, and far cheaper, to have good papers on the walls than indifferent pictures."[74] Judging it to be "a very distinct advance in the design of paper-hangings", the *Magazine of Art* added: "With these india-proof impressions before us it is easier than it would otherwise be to appreciate the skill and decorative instinct" seen in large and bold patterns such as Crane's 'Wood Notes', Sedding's 'Jacobean', and Day's 'Medici' and 'Lucca', two Renaissance-inspired patterns.[75]

"The Victorian Wall-papers are printed in ordinary colours, as well as in rich shades of varied flock, with or without gold", the catalogue explained.[76] Although

5.26 Jeffrey & Co. Cover, *Illustrations of the Victorian Series and Other Wall-Papers*, c.1889. Illustration by Walter Crane
Manchester Metropolitan University, Special Collections

the method of production was not specified, most of the papers were probably block-printed and included a wide array of types, including embossed leather-papers, staircase decorations and ceiling papers. The catalogue emphasised that while the designs were "larger in scale than the ordinary patterns," they were "not merely adapted to the decoration of mansions and staircases, but are often available also for rooms of moderate size".[77] The catalogue also pointed out that these patterns were designed to avoid both the coarseness that was sometimes evident in pattern books and "the real danger" of selecting a pattern that would prove too small for the size of a room.

The construction of the catalogue was very clever, "arranged after the fashion of a folding screen, which shuts like a book and reads both ways, so that room is obtained for a double number of examples".[78] A number of features made it a practical and useful reference album for decorators. The

5.27 (left) Lewis F. Day. 'Lucca' wallpaper, 1888. Made by Jeffrey & Co. Block-printed
Whitworth Art Gallery, University of Manchester, W.1967.767

5.28 (above) Walter Crane. 'Woodnotes' wallpaper, 1886. Made by Jeffrey & Co. Block-printed. From Sugden and Edmondson, *A History of English Wallpaper* (1926): pl.130

illustrations could be opened out to show a series, and measurements of the repeat of a pattern were given. Tables showed how to calculate the amount of wallpaper needed for rooms of various sizes. Special designs for staircases and directions for their use were included, along with guidance on the selection and installation of leather-papers and ceiling papers. The firm's shrewd marketing emphasised that the decorator – and, consequently, the consumer – was not simply buying wallpaper, but rather the solution to a problem. The catalogue also reminded the reader that a wide selection of papers could be seen in Jeffrey & Co.'s own showrooms as well as through dealers. The *Victorian Series* was apparently quite popular, and Jeffrey & Co. continued to promote it into the late 1890s.

Ten of Day's designs were included in the *Victorian Series*: three wallpapers, five ceiling papers, and two staircase papers. A number of pages in the catalogue were devoted to addressing the very real difficulties faced by consumers in decorating staircases. Day's 'Arabesque Panel', comprising a dado, frieze, filling paper and border, was cited as the simplest way of dealing with the problem of variation in the rake of the stairs and curve of the skirting. Day's 'Henri II', in production from 1887 and priced from 4d./yd., was also singled out as a way of overcoming this challenge satisfactorily. A straight-lined scheme requiring a rigid line for its base, the arrangement included a dado-band, upright strip, dividing border, filling and frieze that could be adjusted to fit varying treads of stairs and variation in heights. Jeffrey's 'Patterns of New Artistic Wall Papers for 1887' included a lithograph that showed "at a glance how easily and with what decorative effect this can be used".[79]

Although the precise number of ceiling patterns Day designed for Jeffrey & Co. is unknown, five of them were featured in the *Victorian Series* and illustrate three main types of patterns: non-directional overall patterns, geometric repeats, and interlacing scrollwork. These papers ranged in price from 3-5d./yd. for the printed versions to 16-18d./yd. for raised flock. The 'Daisy' paper, a non-directional, overall pattern of flower-heads and leafy tendrils, was the least expensive, priced from 3d./yd. in colour and at 16d./yd. in raised flock. Although sales records are scarce, information in the 1889 to 1904 order books for decorating firm Cowtan & Sons suggest that the 'Daisy' ceiling pattern was useful for various rooms.[80]

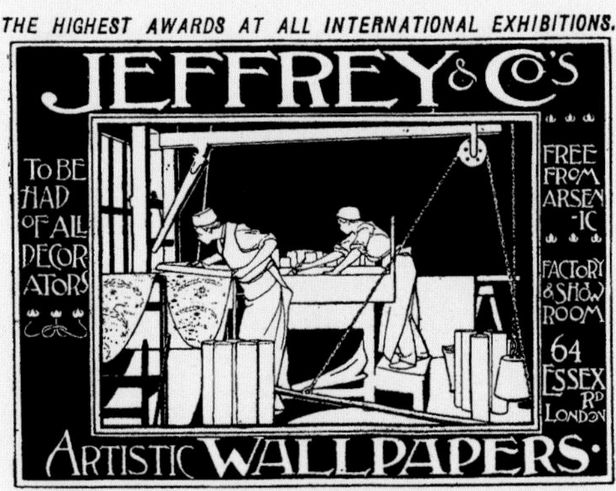

5.29 (above) Jeffrey & Co. Advertisement. From Easter Art Annual, *Art Journal* (1899): back cover

5.30 (top right) Jeffrey & Co. Advertisement. From *Studio* 14 (1898): inside front cover

5.31 Lewis F. Day. 'Henri II' wallpaper, 1887. Made by Jeffrey & Co. Machine-printed

Whitworth Art Gallery, University of Manchester, W.1967.720

5.32 (left) Lewis F. Day. 'Daisy' ceiling paper, c.1889. From Jeffrey & Co., *Illustrations of the Victorian Series and Other Wall-Papers* (c.1889)
Manchester Metropolitan University, Special Collections

5.33 (above) Lewis F. Day. 'Etruscan' ceiling paper, c.1889. From Jeffrey & Co., *Illustrations of the Victorian Series and Other Wall-Papers* (c.1889)
Manchester Metropolitan University, Special Collections

5.34 (below) Lewis F. Day. 'Wreath' ceiling paper, 1888. From Jeffrey & Co., *Illustrations of the Victorian Series and Other Wall-Papers* (c.1889)
Manchester Metropolitan University, Special Collections

Two geometric diapers, 'Wreath' and 'Ducal', are structured on regularly repeating combinations of floral and foliate forms arranged in roundels and squares. Day's most elaborate ceiling pattern was the 'Etruscan', a complicated geometric design and – priced from 5d./yd. in colour and at 18d./yd. in raised flock – the most expensive of his ceiling papers in this series. One of the large-scale geometric patterns suited to the more public rooms of the house, it was a practical design that "should centre with the centre of the room"; if any portion of the pattern met the cornice in an awkward manner, that portion could be omitted and compensated for with borders or marginal strips available from the firm.[81]

The 'Neo-Grec', singled out by the *British Architect* as among the "capital designs", incorporates leafy tendrils in airy scrollwork, illustrating Day's preference for light and open patterns for ceilings.[82] Priced in colour from 4½d./yd., it was also available in raised flock at 17d./yd. Of his three main types of ceiling patterns, those based on interlacing scrollwork seem to most successfully meet his own criterion of openness for a ceiling paper, and he included an illustration of the 'Neo-Grec' in his article 'Wall-Paper Decoration' for the *Magazine of Art* in 1892.[83]

Jeffrey & Co. promoted the raised flock versions of ceiling papers in particular. Not only were they the most durable, the raised surface added firmness, which made them easy to hang. The firm also pressed the advantage of their versatility: "The undyed flock may be painted to harmonise with the room, or it may be left its natural colour on a white or tinted, or gold ground, to be painted perhaps at some later day."[84] It is not surprising that the firm so strongly touted the benefits of their raised flocked versions: they were three to four times more expensive than the printed ones.

5.35 (top) Lewis F. Day. 'Neo-Grec' ceiling paper, 1888. From Jeffrey & Co., *Illustrations of the Victorian Series and Other Wall-Papers* (c.1889)
Manchester Metropolitan University, Special Collections

5.36 (bottom) Jeffrey & Co. Advertisement. From Easter Art Annual, *Art Journal* (1897): inside back cover

Extending the market for more affordable wallpapers

In the spring of 1896 Jeffrey & Co. advertised a special collection of *Low-price Wallpapers for Staircase Decoration Designed by Lewis F. Day*, which contained 112 machine-printed wallpapers, dados, friezes and borders in different colourways.[85] This catalogue aptly illustrates Day's efforts to extend the market for his papers beyond the more financially well-off consumer to those of more moderate means. The catalogue also provides somewhat of a review of much of his work – in a simpler, more basic form.

Many of the papers, which were suitable for various rooms of the house, had first been produced as block-printed papers. Day chose designs that would effectively translate to machine prints due to the linearity of the designs, the small areas of flat colour, and the reduced number of colours. Although the catalogue is undated, the patterns were originally designed between 1874 and the early 1890s and include designs originally produced for Simpson's as well as patterns that had appeared in the *Victorian Series*. While they continued on as painters and decorators, Simpson's had ceased manufacture of wallpaper in about 1893.[86] It is likely that this catalogue was released by Jeffrey & Co. sometime between 1893 and 1896. Sales records are scarce, and it is not possible to determine how well these less expensive papers sold. With most of them priced from 3½d./yd. to 6½d./yd., they were considerably less expensive than the hand-printed versions would have been and certainly would have extended the market for artistic furnishings to less affluent households.

5.37 (left) Lewis F. Day. 'Cactus' wallpaper, 1891. Made by Jeffrey & Co. © Manchester Art Gallery, 1934.22/12 x

5.38 (above) Lewis F. Day. Wallpaper. From Jeffrey & Co., *Selected Hand-Printed Wall Papers* (1894-5)
Nordiska Museet, Stockholm, Erik Folcker Collection, 310.405

Exhibitions and designs of the late 1880s and 1890s

Day garnered a great deal of exposure for his wallpaper designs that were shown by Jeffrey & Co. at major international trade and industrial exhibitions and at the Arts and Crafts Exhibitions beginning in 1888. Among Day's designs featured at the Paris Exposition Universelle in 1889 were the 'Corinthian Scroll', the embossed leather paper the 'Arabesque', and a frieze that surmounted the whole of Jeffrey & Co.'s exhibit in the British Section of the Industrial Court.[87] Metford Warner commented that Day's 'Corinthian Scroll' and Walter Crane's 'Peacock Garden' in flock were the chief features of Jeffrey & Co.'s exhibit.[88] 'Corinthian Scroll' is an exuberant pattern of swirling acanthus leaves against a background of delicate horizontal lines suggesting texture. The version shown in Paris was hand-printed from eight wood blocks in tones of russet, olives and yellows, enriched with gilding.[89] It was featured in the *Art Journal Supplement, Paris Exhibition 1889*, and Day used this paper in his book *Pattern Design* as an example of one in which "the lines of recurrence are purposely lost".[90]

The firm proudly announced that Day's 1889 'Trocadero' design, "printed in tones of Crimson Flocks, has been specially manufactured as a background to the Pictures throughout the Fine Art Galleries of the British Section" at the request of the committee of the Fine Art Section.[91] The paper was "coloured under the direction of Sir Frederick Leighton".[92] In *Pattern Design* (1903), Day used the 'Trocadero' as an example of a "false drop" pattern, a variation of a drop pattern that works only on square lines.[93] The original version of the paper was hand-printed using three blocks.[94] The design was also produced in a machine-printed version priced at 6d./yd. and was included in the *Low-Price Series* of Day's papers issued by Jeffrey & Co.

At the Chicago World's Columbian Exposition in 1893, Day's 'Lily' frieze ran around the top of the exhibit, and

5.39 (top) Lewis F. Day. 'Corinthian Scroll' wallpaper, 1889. Made by Jeffrey & Co. Block-printed
Southwark Art Collection, London, PT0794

5.40 (bottom) Walter Crane. 'Peacock Garden' wallpaper, 1889. Made by Jeffrey & Co. Block-printed. From Sugden and Edmondson, *A History of English Wallpaper* (1926): pl. 131

5.41 (above) Lewis F. Day. 'Trocadero' wallpaper, 1889. Made by Jeffrey & Co. Block-printed. From Day, *Pattern Design* (1903): illus.101

5.42 (below) Lewis F. Day. 'Piccolomini' wallpaper, 1893. Made by Jeffrey & Co. Block-printed. From Sugden and Edmondson, *A History of Emglish Wallpaper* (1926): pl. 154

'Piccolomini', expressly designed for this exhibition, was mounted on each side of one of the entrances. The latter was a large-scale pattern of flowers and foliage scrolling in circles that required four blocks in its basic version; for the exhibition it was produced in reds, russets, and orange enriched with gilding, and required 24 blocks.[95] It was a sumptuous rendition, and, at 21 shillings a roll of 12 yards, an expensive one. Below this paper, the wood dado featured inserted copper plates of Day's design the 'Grotesque', "burnished in such a manner that they glow with iridescent colours, varying in effect from every point of view".[96] A second colourway of the 'Piccolomini', in "a harmony of blues and olives printed in transparent colours on a talc ground, giving all the appearances of a rich silk", was hung between two of Walter Crane's embossed papers: 'Peacock Garden' on a silver ground and 'Golden Age' on a gold ground.[97]

Several of Day's other block-printed papers dating to the early 1890s show enormous energy and confidence in the use

of natural forms. The 'Como' (c.1894) is a rich pattern structured by branches arranged in ogival forms, with interweaving flowers and leaves. The 'Roman' (c.1894) is a large, double-width pattern of acanthus leaves in circular swirls. The 'Shaftesbury', a half-drop pattern of yellow poppy heads and seed cases intermingled with swirling leaves in soft greens, is enhanced by a background of horizontal gold lines. In contrast, the 'Mortimer' (1896) is a stencil-like pattern of scrolls, flowers, and leafy tendrils.

5.43 (left) Lewis F. Day. 'Grotesque' embossed wallpaper, c.1890. Made by Jeffrey & Co. From Day, *Pattern Design* (1903): illus.206

5.44 (above) Page from Jeffrey & Co., *Book of Destroyed Blocks: High Relief Embossed Patterns (Nos. 001 to 003273)* (undated), showing samples of Walter Crane's 'Cockatoo and Pomegranate' (top), Lewis F. Day's 'Grotesque' (centre), and Walter Crane's 'Golden Age' (bottom) Arthur Sanderson Ltd.

5.45 and 5.46 Lindsay P. Butterfield (above). C.F.A. Voysey (right). Wallpapers. From Jeffrey & Co., *Selected Hand-Printed Wall Papers* (1894-5)
Nordiska Museet, Stockholm, Erik Folcker Collection, 310.405

5.47 (opposite) Lewis F. Day. 'Mortimer' wallpaper, 1896. Made by Jeffrey & Co.
Southwark Art Collection, London, PT0792

5.48 (above) Lewis F. Day. 'Roman' wallpaper, 1894. Made by Jeffrey & Co. Block-printed. From Sugden and Edmondson, *A History of English Wallpaper* (1926): pl. 134

5.49 (left) Lewis F. Day. 'Como' wallpaper, 1894. Made by Jeffrey & Co. Block-printed. From Sugden and Edmondson, *A History of English Wallpaper* (1926): pl. 135

5.50 (opposite) Lewis F. Day. 'Shaftesbury' (also known as 'Poppy Head') wallpaper, 1891. Made by Jeffrey & Co. Block-printed © Manchester Art Gallery, 1934.22/35xvi

5.51 (above) Lewis F. Day. 'Abercorn' embossed imitation-leather paper, 1896. Made by Jeffrey & Co. © Manchester Art Gallery, 1934.22/12 xiv

Day noted in his journalistic reports of the 1900 Paris Exposition Universelle for the *Art Journal* that while Jeffrey & Co. had been allotted only a small space, they exhibited far more types of wallpaper than the French. Jeffrey & Co.'s exhibit included "machine as well as block-printed papers; papers printed in distemper, wash colours, flock, and lacquer; papers finished by stamping; embossed leather papers, gilt, lacquered, and painted by hand; real leather; and, finally, embossed sheet copper for wall decoration".[98] One of Day's own most masterful embossed papers was the 'Abercorn', designed in 1896 and in production from 1898.[99] The heavily embossed imitation-leather paper features stalks forming an ogival pattern with intertwining fruits and leaves. Day included an illustration of this pattern in *Ornament and Its Application* to show how the designer must make sure to keep the high relief areas of the design clear of the joints so there would be no discrepancy in the fitting of one piece to another.[100]

The paper, which had been shown at the Northern Art Workers' Guild Exhibition in 1898, was "as sumptuous as a hanging of old Spanish gilt leather", enthused the *Art Journal*.[101] It was shown in Paris in silver against a background in light blue and green lacquers.[102] Jeffrey & Co.'s *Catalogue of Embossed Copper Work for Interior Decoration* advised that the pattern was also produced in embossed copper, priced at 21 shillings for a length of 4ft. by 21in. (121.9cm. x 53.3cm.), rendering it suitable – albeit very expensive – for "furniture, yacht and steamship fitments".[103]

Day's changing views about wallpaper arrangements and later designs

As an emeritus designer around the turn of the century, Day modified some of his ideas about the design and use of wallpaper in interior schemes. He recognised that public taste in surface ornamentation had changed, and his writings and some of his designs post-1900 reflect this. Conceding that the tripartite wall arrangement had gone out of favour by the early 1890s, he agreed that a two-part wall treatment was a suitable option. The depth of the frieze would depend on whether there was an architectural feature that predetermined the depth; if it was too narrow, a band of plain colour could be painted to separate the frieze from the wall below or a wooden picture rail could be installed. Ever economical, Day noted that since a narrow frieze looked simply like a border and was not less expensive than a deeper one, it made sense to choose a frieze that was between 18in. (45.7cm.) and 3ft. deep (91.4cm.).[104] The cost of a relatively expensive frieze and a single-print paper for the rest of the wall would not be higher than the choice of one elaborate paper to cover the entire wall.[105]

5.52 (left) Metford Warner. From Sugden and Edmondson, *A History of English Wallpaper* (1926): dedication

5.53 (opposite, top) Lewis F. Day. (Left) 'Lahore,' 1903 and (right) 'Neo-Grec,' 1902. Block-printed wallpapers. Made by Jeffrey & Co. From *Art Journal* (1904): 60
Newberry Library, Chicago

5.54 (opposite, bottom) Lewis F. Day. Detail, 'Neo-Grec' wallpaper, 1902. Made by Jeffrey & Co. From Day, *Nature and Ornament 2: Ornament the Finished Product of Design* (1909): illus. 5

Day continued to design wallpapers for Jeffrey & Co. until at least 1908, and several of his later papers reflect consumer preference for the simpler interior schemes at the turn of the century. Day produced some charming and graceful designs for fillings and friezes for a two-part wall. His airy 1902 design 'Neo-Grec', produced beginning 1903, contained a frieze and filling in one piece, a type of paper Jeffrey marketed at this time. The press was complimentary, one critic commending it for its suitability for various rooms and suggesting the red colourway for billiard rooms and pale blue for a morning room.[106] The *Decorator* praised its "certain classical feeling" and the *Art Journal* included an illustration of it in shades of green, cream and gold, along with a second wall treatment, the 'Lahore'.[107]

The 1904 design 'Jacobite', is based on 16th- and 17th-century crewelwork, a popular source of inspiration for wallpaper and textile patterns in the early 1900s, including some of Day's. This pattern, printed against an oatmeal background suggesting the texture of fabric, was shown at the Franco-British Exhibition in 1908 and required 16 blocks.

A testament to the enduring popularity of more naturalistic designs, 'Delhi' (1907) is a lush pattern of Eastern inspiration. It is a symmetrical design of a multi-petalled flower surrounded by scrolling, flowering foliage. Six blocks were used in its production, and the colours were so carefully graded that the effect resembles a watercolour painting.

Day noted the trend toward plainer wall treatments in his journalistic reports on the Paris Exposition for the *Manchester Guardian*: "Pattern being for the moment out of favour, it is not surprising that the Exhibition does not contain much that is new or interesting in the way of wallpapers and the like."[108] He added: "In wall decoration repeated pattern – which, it must be allowed, has been terribly misused – has gone out of favour. We find more often plain walls with only a painted frieze, or woven wallhangings more or less reticently enriched with embroidery."[109]

With his great love for and consummate skill in designing repeat pattern, it is not surprising that Day regretted this change in consumer taste and the consequent "lull in the production of patterned materials of all kinds".[110] He saw this trend as a natural reaction to recent over-elaboration in design, and if it ultimately led to a more judicious use of pattern, that was all to the good. "The turn of pattern must soon come round again," he optimistically predicted, and while most wall coverings must be machine-made in order for them to be affordable to the vast majority of people, the patterns should reflect the "skill and judgment, taste, ingenuity and fancy" of the designer.[111]

5.55 (left) Lewis F. Day. 'Jacobite' wallpaper, 1904. Made by Jeffrey & Co. Block-printed. From *Art Journal* (1905): pl. opp. 284
Trustees of the National Library of Scotland, Edinburgh

5.56 (opposite) Lewis F. Day. 'Delhi' wallpaper, 1907. Made by Jeffrey & Co. Block-printed
Southwark Art Collection, London, PT0793

6.1 Lewis F. Day. 'Iris' tile. Made by Pilkington's Tile & Pottery Co. Shown at the Paris Exposition Universelle 1900 and at the Glasgow Exhibition 1901, where it was described as a "cloisonné tile in coloured glazes" (*Pilkington Catalogue 1900*: 23, 25, 34; *Pilkington Catalogue 1901*: 36-7) Pilkington's Lancastrian Pottery Society

CHAPTER SIX: TILES AND ART POTTERY

"It would hardly be overstating the case to say that the artists who have achieved greatness are those who, in addition to the temperament, the imagination, the genius of the artist, have also the science which enables them to make the most of it." [Lewis F. Day, 1904]

Tiles and art pottery were a major area of Lewis Foreman Day's work. His designs and writings, which span virtually the entire period from 1870-1910, capture all the energy, variety and abundance that characterised the industry as a whole during its heyday. Day's range was wide: from designs for one-of-a-kind pieces of art pottery, to those for tiles that would be executed through larger-scale production by major firms. His prolific work demonstrates his skills in designing for a wide variety of different types of manufacture and decoration. In his many articles and books Day gave a running commentary on developments in tile and art pottery manufacture and articulated particular challenges and opportunities in the industry.

By the time Day began designing tiles in the mid-1870s, British tile production had grown into a major industry, fuelled by technical developments, market demand and aesthetic influences. Geometric and encaustic floor tiles, with patterns in coloured clay impressed into the body of the tile, had been used increasingly from the 1830s. By the next decade, lighter-weight tiles for walls and other decorative uses were being produced by squeezing damp, powdery clay into dies under a screw press.[1] Technical advances in printing technology and the development of glazes (including ready-made ones) from the 1850s had increased exponentially the ways tiles could be decorated.[2] While hand-made and hand-decorated tiles could be expensive, machine-made and mechanically-decorated tiles were cheaper and simpler to make, rendering tiles available for use in settings from the palatial to the modest.

Construction of public buildings and the housing boom of the 1880s and 1890s boosted market demand for tiles. Both functional and decorative, ornamental tiles were considered ideal for public places – railway stations, churches, hospitals, town halls, museums, and shops such as dairies and butchers – because they were durable, easy to clean and hygienic. These qualities made them equally desirable for the porches, entrance halls, baths and kitchens of private houses. Their fireproof and heat-reflecting capacities rendered them an integral part of cast-iron fireplaces that were increasingly being installed in 19th-century homes.[3] Used singly or combined in panels, tiles enhanced jardinières, hall chairs, umbrella stands, cabinetwork and flower boxes.

Use of decorated tiles was also a reflection of the preference for surface decoration during the period. The emergence of the Aesthetic Movement in the late 1860s, which stressed that utilitarian objects could also have aesthetic value, blessed their use. A bevy of writers on household art, among them Charles Locke Eastlake and

Robert W. Edis, advised consumers how to incorporate tiles and art pottery into interior decoration schemes.[4] Noted designers of the period, including William Morris, Christopher Dresser, John Moyr Smith, William De Morgan, Walter Crane, and Lewis F. Day found ample scope for their talents in the design of tiles and art pottery.

The preoccupation on the part of the artistically élite and other opinion leaders about the relationship of manufactured objects and art continued throughout the rest of the century. Wanting to project an artistic image, while simultaneously accommodating frequent changes in consumer taste, firms produced aesthetically appealing tiles in a wide variety of styles and price levels. Manufacturers and retailers astutely and aggressively marketed their wares through advertisements in trade and consumer publications, catalogues, and exhibitions.

The boom in production from 1870-1910 generated work for established tile-producers such as Minton Hollins and prompted some older ceramics firms like Josiah Wedgwood & Sons to branch into tile-making. Demand for tiles also resulted in the founding of new enterprises, including J.C. Edwards (founded 1870) and Pilkington's Tile & Pottery Co. (founded 1891). British firms eventually dominated both the home and international markets for tiles during this period. Many tile-making firms expanded into making art pottery as well, although these ventures usually were small and of shorter duration than their tile business.

Day's work embodies in microcosm the aesthetic, market and technological forces that propelled the industry. His love of ceramic design is evident in the 1870s to early 1880s, when he designed hand-decorated pieces that were one-of-a-kind or produced in small batches and became known as a journalist and critic of ceramic design. That passion grew in the early 1880s to early 1890s, when he directed his energies toward designing for new manufacturing and decorating technologies used in larger-scale production. It culminated in his relationship with Pilkington's Tile & Pottery Co. from the early 1890s, through which he expressed his belief that the future of the industry lay in the marriage of science and art.

MAKING HIS REPUTATION IN TILES AND ART POTTERY

By the time Lewis F. Day set up his independent design practice in late 1869, he had already decided to design tiles and art pottery. A couple of original early watercolour sketches dating from 1869 to 1871 survive, and they reveal his early experimentation with ceramic shapes for vases and plates. They also show that in these early years he was planning out geometric ornament and natural forms such as seaweed and apple-blossoms, motifs he would later use on his art pottery and tiles. Whether any of these early designs were produced is unknown.

Day did not immediately pursue ceramic design, however. Over the next few years his main attention and energies were directed toward establishing a solid client base, and his first clients engaged him for design of stained glass and book covers.[5]

W.B. Simpson & Sons

Day's introduction to ceramic design came in the mid-1870s through two clients for whom he had designed other types of furnishings. From about 1873 Day had an agreement to design wallpaper and church decoration exclusively for the well-known interior decorating firm W.B. Simpson & Sons; within a few years he also began designing stained glass and tiles for the firm.[6] Located at 456 West Strand and 100 St. Martin's Lane, Simpson's was the London agent for the Shropshire tile manufacturing firm Maw & Co.[7] Simpson's also produced its own art tiles for walls, fireplaces and other interior decoration. Using biscuit tiles obtained primarily from Maw, Simpson's procured designs from freelancers as well as in-house artists, who hand-painted the tiles,

6.2 Lewis F. Day. Sketch for ceramics, undated (c.1869-71) Watercolour and ink on paper
Manchester Metropolitan University, Special Collections

which were then glazed and fired in the firm's kilns.

Some designs by Day may have been included in the twenty-two earthenware patterns registered by Simpson's between 1876 and 1883, though none has been firmly attributed. A number of these registered tile designs incorporated leaf and pod, daisy, and chrysanthemum motifs; though it is known that Day used these motifs, they were all in common circulation and popular among designers of the day. Archival information on Day's specific tile designs is lacking because most of the firm's records were destroyed during World War II bombings or lost during various moves.[8] Day may also have designed some encaustic and mosaic tile pavements, a major area of the firm's work. He provided Simpson's with advertisements for furnishings that he designed for them; among these is one for mosaic pavements for entrance halls, public buildings and churches. Though the amount of work Day did in tile design for the firm appears to have been small compared to that of wallpaper and stained glass, it was significant because it gave him the chance to gain experience in tile design. It also probably provided a referral to Maw, who became a major client of his in the mid-1880s.

Howell & James of Regent Street

The early client most responsible for raising Day's profile as a ceramic designer was Howell & James, the prestigious department store located at 5-9 Regent St. Howell & James offered high-quality fabrics, jewellery, silver, tapestry and furniture, and eventually sold the wares of a number of prominent art potteries, including Minton's, Doulton & Co., C.H. Brannam, Burmantofts, the Torquay Terra-Cotta Pottery and the American firm Rookwood Pottery.[9] The store also marketed furnishings under their own name, commissioning designs from freelance designers, including John Moyr Smith and architect Thomas Harris.

Day began working with the store c.1871, initially designing jewellery, but expanding quickly into furniture, tapestry, plaques and clock cases. During the 1870s and 1880s, Howell & James marketed these small clocks – many featuring blue and white china faces and dark wood or ebonized cases – which became a store speciality and one of the furnishings for which Day is best known.[10]

In the mid-1870s he was decorating art pottery on his own and, aside from pieces given to family and friends, it is possible that Howell & James retailed some of these wares. These pieces, primarily in blue and white, featured motifs *au courant* in the highly popular activity of china painting and were in keeping with the types of wares offered by the store. Mostly dishes and plaques, they featured figural subjects or motifs from nature. Whether Day painted all these pieces himself or had some assistance is open to speculation, as is where they were glazed and fired.

Day frequently signed and dated his work, and one piece – a plate dated 1876, featuring a spider's web painted over the glaze – particularly reflects his designs at this time and the current rage for blue and white china. Day later used this design for a tile. He was also experimenting with other subject matter for plates, including portrait heads and grotesque motifs. The latter was an early indicator of his interest in combining animal forms and foliage in a fanciful way to suit the purposes of design, a technique that would come to full flowering in his designs of the 1880s and 1890s.[11]

Though he was enthusiastic about the aesthetic merits of blue and white, Day was sceptical about the longevity of this fashion: "The worship of Blue and White is a *culte* which is not likely to take lasting hold of the ordinary British mind," he commented, adding rather acerbically that, in their eagerness to embrace the latest novelty on the market, "fashionable Philistines will forsake it without a regret".[12]

From early on Day had a multifaceted relationship with Howell & James that involved him not only in the design of furnishings, but also in the store's marketing and special events. Day's brother-in-law, Thomas Buxton Morrish, was a director of the firm from the early 1870s until 1884, and he may have been the point of entry for Day's work for Howell & James.[13] Morrish certainly would have been influential in Day obtaining the commission to design their exhibit for the Paris Exposition Universelle of 1878, an important venue for the store's international marketing efforts and one that gave a huge boost to Day's reputation as a designer and journalist.

The exhibit, constructed as a roofless room, had outer walls that were used to display the ceramic work of professionals and amateurs, many of whom took china-painting classes at the store.[14] The inner walls, decorated in tri-partite fashion with dado, upper wall and frieze, created a backdrop for a walnut fireplace and overmantel enhanced with tiles, display shelves, and an Aesthetic-style clock. The overall colour scheme of browns, yellows, buff, terracotta and reds was intended to produce a rich effect, but in his journalistic reports on the exhibition for the *British Architect*, Day revealed his dissatisfaction with the end result. He felt that it had fallen short of the original plan, with too many vases, plates, plaques, clocks and other decorative pieces crowded into "every available inch" of a small space.[15]

The overcrowding resulted from the last-minute inclusion of wares from the Torquay Terra-Cotta Pottery, which had not been allotted enough space of their own by the exhibition organisers.[16] Howell & James retailed the ceramics of this new firm, founded just four years earlier, which used in-house artists and freelance designers, including Day, who designed a pair of vases that were manufactured by the firm and shown by Howell & James at this exhibition.[17]

Apparently, these terracotta vases, one depicting 'Sunlight' and the other 'Moonlight', were painted by Alexander Fisher, Sr., then head of the art department at Torquay Pottery.[18] The fine-grained red earthenware provided a smooth surface for decorative detail. Featuring a figure in white enamel and "enriched with Indian ornamentation, in sepia, brown, white, and gold", the vases drew praise from the press; certainly the young firm's profile in the ceramics industry was raised by this positive press coverage.[19] The *Art Journal Illustrated Catalogue of the Paris Exhibition 1878* included images of the vases, along with a clock that Day had designed for Howell & James.[20]

Day was also involved in Howell & James's famous china painting exhibitions,

6.3 (opposite, top) Lewis F. Day. Blue and white plate with motif of crab and seaweed. From Day, *Instances of Accessory Art* (1880): pl. 27
Michael Whiteway

6.4 (opposite, centre) Lewis F. Day. Plate with spider motif, monogrammed 'LFD', 1876
The Albert Dawson Collection

6.5 (opposite, bottom) Lewis F. Day. Design for painted tile. From *Architect* 26 (1881): near 159
Trustees of the National Library of Scotland, Edinburgh

6.6 (left) Howell & James exhibit, Paris Exposition Universelle 1878, designed by Lewis F. Day. From *British Architect* 10 (1878): near 126-7

6.7 (above) Lewis F. Day. Vases depicting 'Sunlight' (right) and 'Moonlight' (left), 1878. Painted by Alexander Fisher, Sr. Made by Torquay Terra-Cotta Pottery Co. H. Blairman & Sons

Messrs. HOWELL & JAMES'
ART-POTTERY AND TAPESTRY PAINTING CLASSES FOR LADIES,
Under the direction of MISS FLORENCE JUDD
(Of Minton's late Studio),
And MR. J. STUART DONLEVY.

FULL PARTICULARS OF TERMS, &c., POST FREE ON APPLICATION.

THESE CLASSES are HELD DAILY (Saturdays excepted), in SEPARATE and SPECIALLY-ARRANGED STUDIOS at
Messrs. HOWELL & JAMES' ART-GALLERIES,
5, REGENT STREET, PALL MALL, LONDON. [5018

Messrs HOWELL & JAMES'
TAPESTRY-PAINTING
AND
ART-POTTERY CLASSES
Are held daily (Saturdays excepted)
IN THE
NEW STUDIOS AT THEIR ART-GALLERIES,
5, 7, 9, REGENT STREET, PALL MALL, LONDON.

Terms and full particulars post free on application.
[6513

6.8 (above left) Charlotte H. Spiers. China plate with "poppies and tiger lilies", exhibited at the Howell & James Fifth Annual Exhibition of Paintings on China, 1880. From *Magazine of Art* 3 (1880): 392

6.9 a and b (above) Howell & James. Advertisements for classes held at the store. From *Magazine of Art* 3 (1880): inside front cover (top); *Magazine of Art* 4 (1881): inside front cover

which were initiated by his brother-in-law in 1876.[21] Morrish astutely scheduled them to occur annually in May, at the height of London's social Season, to encourage participation by the upper classes and to secure the patronage of royalty, including H.R.H. the Prince of Wales.[22] Held annually in the store's galleries in Regent St. from 1876 to the mid-1880s, the exhibitions were judged by members of the Royal Academy and drew as many as 10,000 people.[23] Avidly reviewed by leading periodicals including the *Magazine of Art*, *British Architect*, *Art Journal*, and *The Queen*, the exhibitions showcased the work of both professional and amateur china painters and reinforced the store's cachet with well-heeled customers and artists. For the third exhibition in 1878, Day exhibited his 'Moonlight' vase again, along with a grasshopper plate and portrait heads of Raphael and Dante, typical of the pictorial designs popular during this period.[24]

As a journalist for the *British Architect*, Day also critiqued these events and the current vogue for china painting. One of the factors prompting the mostly-female amateurs to take classes at Howell & James and exhibit their china painting was the chance to earn prizes and medals and obtain remunerative work – a growing social concern for women who needed to supplement insufficient incomes. While this philanthropic aspect of Howell & James's exhibitions was regarded favourably in the press, some of the amateur work was criticised for striving for effects that were too ambitious and inappropriate for china painting.[25] Day agreed with these criticisms, and several themes ran through his critiques.

Day was not opposed to amateurs engaging in decorative art. In fact, he wrote an instructional book on tapestry painting for persons taking classes at the store, and he taught and mentored a number of women who became prominent figures in the decorative arts. He did object, however, to the lack of a sense of fitness that characterised much of the amateur work; he noted that some of the work leaned "rather obviously to the side of mere prettiness" and cautioned that "all plaques and panels used in furniture, and tiles used in decoration, must conform to decorative fitness, and take their places in the general scheme".[26] He observed that Japanese and Chinese decorative art demonstrated "a sense of the relation of means to end that is wanting among us".[27]

Another weakness of some amateur submissions, which eventually out-numbered those of professionals, was the lack of regard for the capacities of the materials used. Day stressed that it was "the highest wisdom to get the utmost out of your material", to take advantage of its strengths and "attempt nothing that will bring into prominence its limitations".[28] In the case of china painting, one should choose colours to be delighted in for their own sake rather than attempting to produce 'natural' colour, an unrealistic goal due to the limited palette that could be fired successfully in the kiln.[29] However reflective Day's comments were of general attitudes toward this amateur work, they failed to address both the realities of how difficult it was for most women to obtain the necessary and often rigourous training needed to design well and the desire of some to simply have a pleasurable hobby in a period in which they were also socially circumscribed.

Miller, Little & Co.

By about 1880, Day was producing a great many designs for art tiles on his own.[30] From c.1881 to 1884, Miller, Little, & Co., located at Devonshire St., Portman Square, London, was the sole agent for Day's tiles.[31] The history of this firm (known at various points as Messrs F. Miller & Co., Messrs. Fred. Miller, Miller & Co., and Miller, Little & Co.) is hazy, though it is known that the firm traded in the 1880s. Fred Miller was a decorative artist, writer and habitué of Howell & James's galleries, where he would undoubtedly have met Day, who by this time was quite well-known. The Miller firm – apparently catering to the artistically aware and at least moderately well-off consumer – marketed fire screens; painted and stained glass for hall and staircase windows; decorative panels for doors, cabinets, screens and friezes; tapestry paintings; and painted vases, plaques and tiles.

Day designed a wide variety of decorative tiles for use in fireplaces and on walls and furniture. The press reported that they were hand-painted underglaze, but whether Day painted them all himself or had some assistance is open to speculation.[32] They were produced, glazed and fired in London by Miller & Co.[33] Day strongly favoured the method of first painting the pottery and tiles and then glazing, because this method resulted in greater permanency and durability for the design, since the glaze protected the painting.[34] The range of colours that could be used was limited; pigments such as cobalt, iron and copper were often used because they could withstand firing under high temperatures. Underglaze was also a method in which the glazing had to be very carefully controlled, for while applying glaze to the hand-painted piece could produce a softness that enhanced the painting, it could also cause the colours to run.

Miller & Co. exhibited a substantial number of Day's hand-painted tiles at building and trade exhibitions in the early 1880s and also at the British Architect Museum in Manchester, where architects could select and purchase building materials.[35] An 1881 advertisement for the museum referred to "figure subjects, flowers, conventional ornament" by Day that were "suitable for a great variety of work".[36] Some of these were probably among the twenty-six designs for single tiles, borders and panels illustrated in the *British Architect* between August-October 1881.[37]

The extensive reports in the trade press of Day's tiles indicate the wide variety of styles in which he was working by this time. Some of his floral and leafy designs were quite conventionalised, or simplified to their basic elements. This was in keeping with design reform notions that

rather than having naturalistic detail and dimensionality, patterns for floors and walls should be 'flat', in keeping with the surface that they decorated.[38] Day advocated a moderate approach, contending that while natural forms had to be modified to suit the purpose and place for which they were intended and the materials in which they would be produced, the nature of growth should be preserved.[39] Some of Day's earliest designs for painted tiles were featured in early 1877 in the *Architect*. They included stencil-like renditions of flowers and leaves described as "essentially brush work" in which "the forms of the detail are in a measure determined by the method of execution".[40] Day saw this technique as an effective method of adapting natural forms to ornamental purpose.[41]

Much of the china painting in the 1870s and 1880s was quite pictorial, with popular motifs including portrait heads, scenes from literary works, or Japanese-inspired birds, insects, flowers, and peacock feathers. Some of Day's designs followed this general trend. He treated the tile as a mini-canvas, executing designs of popular characters from Shakespeare, putti, birds and insects, as well as motifs of seaweed, leaves, daisies, and strawberries.[42] More than a dozen of these were featured in the pages of the *Architect* in mid-1881.[43] Tiles like these could be used singly or in combination with plain tiles on walls, fireplaces and furniture.

Other designs reveal the Japanese influence on Day's tile and wallpaper designs during this period. (For a full discussion of the Japanese influence on Day's designs, see *Chapter 2: The Designer for Industry*.)

He was particularly impressed with Japan's example "in teaching us how to adapt natural forms without taking the nature out of them".[44] The influence of the Japanese treatment of nature and use of techniques – such as layering of patterns, asymmetry, and incorporation of particular Oriental motifs – are seen in a cluster of Day's designs that appeared in the *Architect* in 1877. His design for a 'Fish' tile frieze is a dense pattern of carp in raging waves, obviously influenced in its motif and arrangement of design elements by 19th-century Japanese woodcuts such as those of Hokusai. Designed for the back of a washstand, the blue and white tiles could be arranged as "either a continuous frieze, or a series of alternating square and oblong panels".[45] Believing that design was both art and problem-solving, Day delighted in contriving ways in which design elements could be made to work in various combinations to suit particular decorating challenges.[46] Also strongly Japanese in character are some fireplace tiles from about 1881 that feature overlapping mons, fractured planes, and motifs of waves, clouds, butterflies and appleblossoms.[47]

Day was obviously trying to appeal to a variety of tastes and budgets, because the trade press reported that consumers could purchase his tiles from the Miller firm in a wide selection of subjects and prices, "from a shilling to a guinea" per tile.[48] They would have appealed in type and price to those artistically aware persons with a yearly income of about £300 to £800, which would have allowed for some discretionary funds for decorative furnishings. Day signed many of his designs and hand-painted pieces, using his signature or monogram, sometimes including the date. This was not uniformly the case, however, and it is likely that many examples of his tiles and art pottery have yet to be identified.

6.10 a, b, c, d, e and f (opposite) Lewis F. Day. Tiles with conventionalised flowers and leaves. From *Architect* 17 (1877): near 196 Newberry Library, Chicago

6.11 (above) Lewis F. Day. Designs for pictorial tiles. From *Architect* 26 (1881): near 159 Trustees of the National Library of Scotland, Edinburgh

PAINTED
TILES
FOR FIRE-PLACES &C
FROM DESIGNS
BY Lewis F. Day

6.12 (opposite, top) Lewis F. Day. "Painted tiles for fireplaces, etc". From *Architect* 25 (1881): near 435

Trustees of the National Library of Scotland, Edinburgh

6.13 (opposite, bottom) Lewis F. Day. Tile frieze showing Japanese influence. From *Architect* 17 (1877): near 196

Newberry Library, Chicago

6.14 (right) Lewis F. Day. Painted tile pattern. From Day, *Every-day Art* (1882): 123

6.15 (below) Lewis F. Day. Designs for painted tiles. From *British Architect* 16 (1881): 414

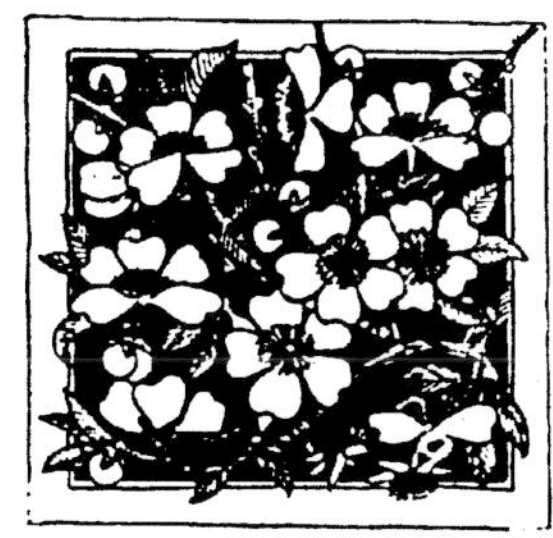

Designing for new manufacturing and decorating technologies

By the early 1880s, Day began directing his energies towards a new phase in his ceramic work. His interest had shifted from designing tiles that were to be totally decorated by hand and produced in small batches, to designing for new manufacturing and decorating technologies used in larger-scale production. An astute business person, Day used his relationships with Simpson's and Howell & James, along with his growing reputation, to secure several major manufacturers of tiles and art pottery as clients.

Josiah Wedgwood & Sons

Day's increasing interest in new tile-making techniques is seen in his work for Josiah Wedgwood & Sons, Ltd., an old established firm that began making decorative tiles in the early 1880s. In 1880 the Staffordshire firm purchased from George Anthony Marsden the patent for a tile manufacturing technique to produce low-relief, impressed patterns in coloured clay.[49] Tiles produced by this mechanical technique, registered by the firm as Wedgwood Patent Impressed, resembled those decorated by the more expensive Barbotine process of hand-painting in coloured slip (clay mixed with water) used by the French in the 1870s to 1890s.[50] Some of the tiles in the Marsden Patent line, as they were known, may have also been enhanced after manufacture by some additional hand-painting. Wedgwood manufactured these tiles from late 1881 until early 1888, and Lewis Day was among the independent designers who produced some of the early patterns.[51] Day's skill as a draughtsman was well-suited to this technique of producing pure, clean lines of relief decoration. A surviving Marsden Patent Tiles pattern book includes some leafy floral designs by Day, who also designed tile panels, including a large one for the Quinta Schools, Chirk.[52] His work seems to have been confined to the early days of production. Despite the fact that the firm won several medals for its Marsden Patent Tiles over the half-dozen years of production, the line was economically unfeasible and production ceased in early 1888.

6.16 (above) Lewis F. Day. Tiles, early 1880s. Registered as Wedgwood Patent Impressed, sometimes referred to as Marsden Patent Tiles. Made by Josiah Wedgwood & Sons — Roger Hensman

6.17 (opposite, left) Tiles. Probably designed by Lewis F. Day. Registered as Wedgwood Patent Impressed. Made by Josiah Wedgwood & Sons — Roger Hensman

6.18 (opposite, right) Lewis F. Day. Tile, c.1885. Hand-painted. Made by J.C. Edwards, Ruabon, Clwyd, North Wales — Hans van Lemmen

J.C. Edwards of Ruabon

By the mid-1880s, Day's fascination with new decorating technologies was paired with his increased confidence and brio in adapting forms from nature, as is seen in his tile designs for J.C. Edwards of Ruabon, Cywd, North Wales. Founded in 1870 as a manufacturer of architectural faïence, glazed and enamelled bricks, terracotta, and encaustic and mosaic tiles, the firm also produced decorated glazed tiles, including ruby lustre tiles. Lustre, used on medieval Islamic pottery and on Italian majolica in the early 16th century, was revived in the 19th century by William De Morgan, among others.[53] Lustre tiles became very popular in the 1880s and were often used in fireplace surrounds, where firelight glinting off the lustre created a soft, shimmering effect.

A metallic oxide was applied by hand or mechanically to the tile, which was then briefly fired in the kiln in a reducing atmosphere that removed the oxygen from the metallic oxide, leaving behind a shiny, metallic deposit on the surface of the tile. Although copper was most frequently used, a variety of colours and effects could be produced by using other oxides, such as silver. The firm was also known for its tiles painted in the popular 'Persian' colours – rich deep blues, emerald greens, purples, and coral-tinged reds – which drew their inspiration from Middle Eastern, Hispanic and Italian Renaissance pottery. Lewis Day produced designs that were used on both the lustre tiles and those decorated in 'Persian' colours. His patterns, which probably date from the late 1880s to the early 1890s, included acanthus leaves, pods and peonies. These lush designs fill most of the tile space with the distilled energy of natural forms. Used singly, in repeats, or in combinations with plain tiles, they were available in a variety of colours and effects.

Maw & Co.

Day's biggest ceramics client in the mid-1880s to early 1890s was Maw & Co., of Jackfield, Shropshire. Maw secured Day's services sometime in 1886, evidently with an eye towards preparing its exhibit for the 1887 Royal Jubilee Exhibition held in

Manchester. His name certainly would have been familiar to Maw because by that time he was well-known as a designer and writer on decorative art. He also may have been specifically recommended to the firm by W.B. Simpson & Sons, because Maw had a practice of requesting its London agent to recommend designers.[54] In securing this client, Day found ample scope for his skills, as Maw was notable for the size of its operations, the diversity of its wares, and its embrace of advances in manufacture and decoration of tiles.

Founded in 1850 as an encaustic tile-making business by George and Arthur Maw, the firm diversified over the next few decades into production of a wide variety of floor and wall tiles. By the 1890s Maw & Co. had become the largest and most prolific tile manufacturer in the world, exporting to America, Asia and Europe.[55] To meet product demand and frequent changes in consumer taste, the firm used designs from its in-house artists as well as independent designers, including A.W.N. Pugin, Charles Locke Eastlake, Owen Jones, William Burges, Walter Crane, and Day.[56] Consistent with a number of other tile firms, Maw & Co. had expanded its product line to include art pottery by the 1880s.[57]

Day's value to a firm like Maw is aptly illustrated in the number of his tiles and items of art pottery that were shown at the 1887 Royal Jubilee Exhibition in Manchester and in the extensive coverage this occasioned in the press. The firm's exhibit included several chimneypiece arrangements, at least two of which featured Day's designs. The first included an outer band of tiles in reds, with a middle band composed of four figural panels – Shepherd, Fowler, Woodman and one unidentified figure – interspersed with leafy and floral tiles.[58] Day's interest in Renaissance forms had grown by the mid 1880s, and this influence is seen in the inner band of tiles, a bold and energetic 'Arabesque' design for jambs and frieze.[59] The design, in blue, brown and yellow, incorporated candelabra forms with scrolling acanthus leaves and putti. One critic at the time complained that the figures in the outer and inner bands were not in proportion to each other; however, Day had not designed them to be used together. The figures in the outer band were originally designed c.1877, with the tiles of leaves and flowers c.1881 for Miller, Little & Co. Manufacturers would often squeeze as many of their notable wares as possible into limited exhibition space, displaying items not necessarily meant to be used together.

A second fireplace featured his 'Days of the Week' design, "a charming display", in blue and yellow on pale cream.[60] This design included portrait medallions representing the seven days, interspersed with leafy tendrils, scrolls, and festoons. In both this design and the 'Arabesque', the jambs were complete in themselves, but the frieze was adaptable to various fireplace widths through the inclusion of extra tiles, reflecting Day's practicality.[61]

Day's designs for Maw often incorporated popular motifs from nature, and some of his brushwork floral and foliate patterns are similar to those produced for Miller & Co. in the early 1880s. Others are more dense designs, displaying more of the nature of growth in the forms, a greater flowing rhythm of lines, and his mastery of the curve; these qualities are also seen in his wallpaper and textile designs from the mid-1880s. Some of his most powerful designs incorporated mythical beasts: fanciful four-legged creatures, gryphons and dragons breathing fire.

While Day generally avoided using animals in design because they were difficult to conventionalise without losing their character, he did like to use grotesques because one could fancifully alter them to suit the purpose of design.[62] In these designs, Day's sober personality gave way to a sense of playfulness. The prancing beasts and swirling foliage exhibit enormous energy and confidence and number among his finest ceramic designs of this period. While Day lacked formal training in drawing the human figure, his years of travel

6.19 (above) Lewis F. Day. 'Arabesque' chimneypiece. Made by Maw & Co. From *Journal of Decorative* Art 7 (1887): 137

Trustees of the National Library of Scotland, Edinburgh

6.20 (right) Lewis F. Day. Chimneypiece with lustre tile dragon plaque and chargers. Made by Maw & Co. From *Journal of Decorative Art* 7 (1887): 138

Trustees of the National Library of Scotland, Edinburgh

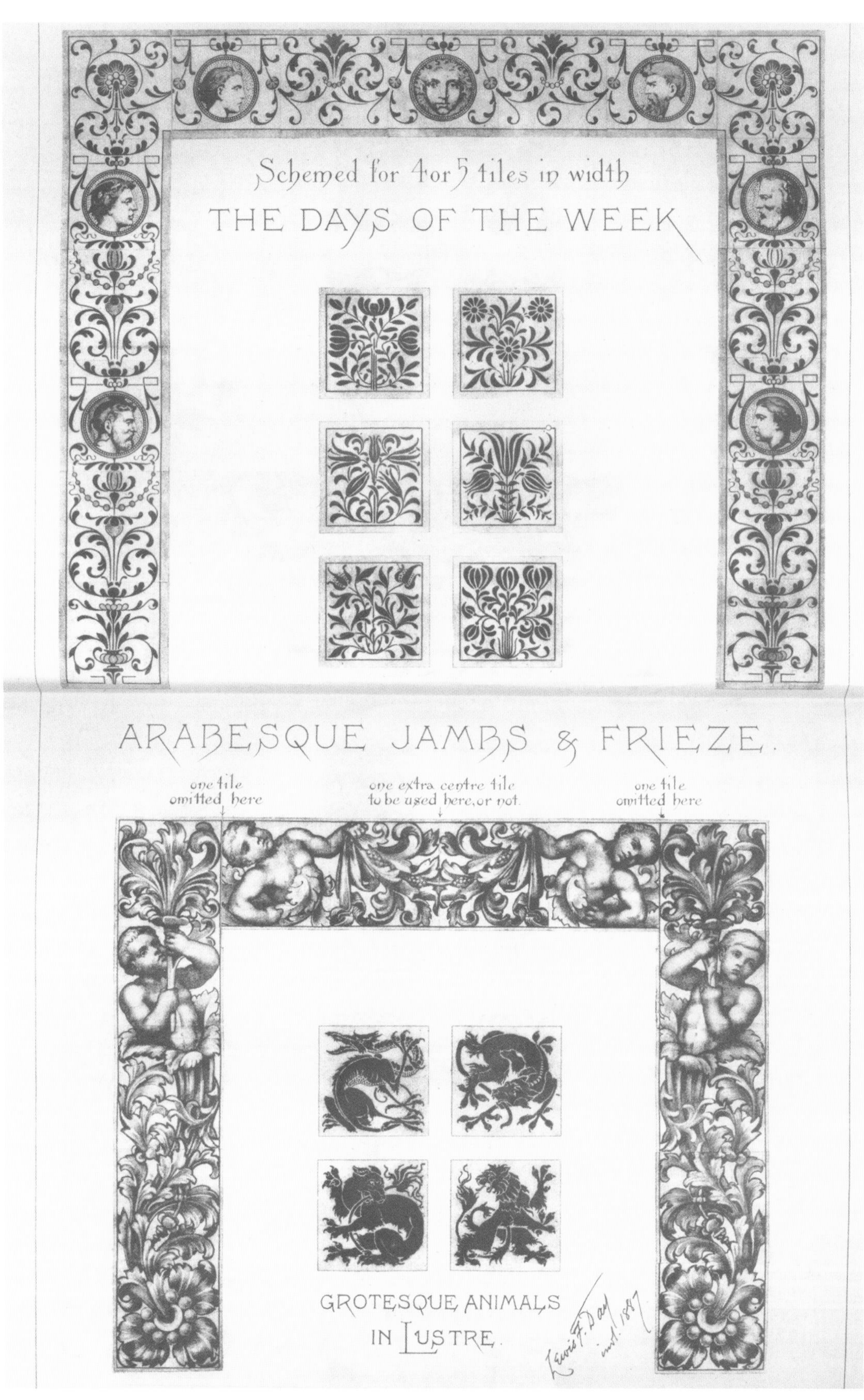
Schemed for 4 or 5 tiles in width
THE DAYS OF THE WEEK
ARABESQUE JAMBS & FRIEZE.
one tile omitted here
one extra centre tile to be used here, or not.
one tile omitted here
GROTESQUE ANIMALS IN LUSTRE.
Lewis F. Day inv. 1887

6.21 (opposite) Lewis F. Day. Fireplace tiles, including 'Arabesque' and 'Days of the Week' arrangements, floral and foliate patterns, and grotesque animals, 1887. Made by Maw & Co. From *Architect* 39 (1888): near 9

Newberry Library, Chicago

6.22 a, b, c and d (below) Lewis F. Day. Tiles with grotesque animals in lustre, 1887. Made by Maw & Co. Note that while 3 tiles are the same design as shown in the *Architect* in 1888, the bottom right tile is different.

© Copyright the Trustees of The British Museum, London. (Top left) No. 1980, -3-7, 167; K86123. (Top right) No. 1980, -3-7, 167; K86124. (Bottom left) No. 1980, -3-7, 167; K86122. (Bottom right) No. 1980, -3-7, 167; K86125[1]

6.23 (right) Lewis F. Day. Lustre plaques. Made by Maw & Co. From Day, *Nature in Ornament* (1892): pl. 102

MAW & COMPANY, LIMITED,
Benthall Works, Jackfield, Shropshire,
ENGLAND.

PLATE 2A.

No. 1.

No. 2.

Scale 1" = 1'

DECORATIVE PANELS BY LEWIS F. DAY.

6.24 (above) Lewis F. Day. Tile panels. Made by Maw & Co. From Maw & Co., *Catalogue* (undated, c.1907): pl. 2A, No. 1, No. 2 Ironbridge Gorge Museum Trust, Library and Archives, Coalbrookdale, D/MAW/7/30

6.25 (opposite) Lewis F. Day. Lily border for tile panel, 1889. Made by Maw & Co. From Day, *Nature in Ornament* (1892): pl. 39

and study of historic motifs, along with his fertile imagination and skilled draughtsmanship, resulted in fabulous creatures and vegetation that fairly leap to life.

Day designed the decoration for vases, plates, plaques, chargers, and at least one frieze for Maw & Co. He probably also designed the shapes for some of these, many of which were hand-decorated in Persian colours or lustre. Shown at the Royal Jubilee Exhibition were a tile plaque with dragon motif and two chargers, one featuring the heraldry of Queen Victoria and the other comprising a shamrock, rose and thistle representing Ireland, England and Scotland.[63]

Day had a thorough knowledge of materials and processes used in tile production, for he often visited his clients' manufacturing facilities to ensure that his designs would execute well. He greatly respected Maw's mastery of complex properties and production techniques, particularly in glazes, which had led to the firm's high reputation.[64] The contemporary press praised Maw's use of underglaze painting because it increased the durability of the tile's surface. The *Art Journal* took particular notice of this: "It may be noted that all the tiles manufactured by this firm are painted under glaze, so that the colour being covered becomes a part of the tile and is imperishable, whereas in the case of over-glaze or enamel painting, the colour being placed on the top of the glaze is liable to scratching and chipping."[65]

Day loved the "depth and richness of colour" of the firm's blue, green and purple Persian-inspired wares, adding that "one would describe it as velvety, did not that term imply something more proper to a textile than to a ceramic product, whereas it has really all the juicy quality peculiar to molten glaze".[66] The firm was also famous for its ruby and d'oro lustre tiles and pottery, "whose charm lies in their rich colouring and the 'shot' effects, varying with every change of position and every fresh light".[67] Day rhapsodised: "By the use of lustre (chiefly silver, it would seem) on cleverly chosen enamel grounds, they have

produced an astonishing variety of strangely beautiful iridescence."[68] He noted that while Maw followed De Morgan's example in producing lustreware, they had arrived at their method of lustre painting independent of De Morgan.[69]

Maw actively promoted its Persian and lustreware tiles and pottery and other wares at major trade and industrial exhibitions at home and abroad and at the Arts and Crafts Exhibitions beginning in 1888. An advertisement designed by Day for Maw in the late 1880s illustrates how vigorously the firm marketed its wide variety of floor and wall tiles in the professional press. The advertisement, signed with Day's initials, touted Maw's lustre and relief tiles "plain and ornamental, for walls, hearths, floors, etc., embossed, glazed, printed, painted, mosaic and encaustic".[70] It appeared in professional journals including the *Architect*, *Builder* and *British Architect* from the late 1880s to at

least 1910, long after he had ceased designing for the firm.

Attesting to his adeptness in designing tiles for various interior uses, Day also designed large-scale tile panels and flooring for Maw & Co. At the 1889 Arts and Crafts Exhibition the firm displayed two hand-painted decorative wall panels designed by him.[71] The first was a bold, Persian-inspired design in which trumpet-like stalks and tulip forms fill the tile space. The second featured a Renaissance-inspired arrangement in which two smaller panels of swirling foliage and putti frame a larger central panel, which contains the figure of an angel. The inspiration for the central panel was a stone carving in the Cathedral at Rimini, Italy, which Day would have seen on his many travels.[72] An undated catalogue entitled *Tiling by Maw & Company Limited* contains full-colour illustrations of these panels, which were priced at £15 to £20 for a panel about 8ft. by 4ft. (2.4m. x 1.2m.).[73] Both panels were adaptable to different architectural specifications and were offered in Maw's domestic, colonial and foreign edition catalogues for a number of years.[74]

One of the firm's specialities was its line of "Patent Mosaic Tiles" for flooring. The face of these 6-inch square (15.2cm.^{2}) tiles featured small spaces of variously coloured clay separated by indented lines depicting the joints, which were filled in with cement when the tiles were laid.[75] The effect was similar to that of a Roman mosaic pavement, with the virtue of hardness, but without the labour-intensive and, consequently, expensive process that the original entailed.[76] How many ceramic mosaic pavements Day designed for the firm is unknown, though one, incorporating a female figure, deer, rabbit and snake in an Eden-like setting, was featured in the *Architectural Record* in 1892.[77]

By the early 1890s, changes in management at Maw & Co. were being felt by the outside designers. The firm had become a limited company in 1888, and from that point on, in-house designers including Charles Henry Temple assumed a larger rôle in the firm's designs.[78] By that time, however, Day had moved on to a new relationship that was to figure prominently in his work until the last years of his life.

6.26 (above) Lewis F. Day. Advertisement for Maw & Co. tiles. From *Architect* 57 (1897): 20
Trustees of the National Library of Scotland, Edinburgh

6.27 a and b (opposite, top left and top right) Lewis F. Day. Tile with bell-shaped flower and leaves in low relief, c.1895. Made by Pilkington's Tile Co. (By 1900 the firm had changed its name to Pilkington's Tile & Pottery Co., and since many of Day's designs stayed in production for a number of years, the firm's full name is used hereafter to avoid confusion.)
(a, top left) Roger Hensman
(b, top right) Anthony J. Cross

6.28 (opposite, centre right) Lewis F. Day. Tile featuring three flowers in low relief, c.1895. Made by Pilkington's Tile & Pottery Co.
Anthony J. Cross

6.29 (opposite, bottom right) Lewis F. Day. Tile with flower and leaves in low relief, c.1895. Monogrammed 'LFD' in lower right. Made by Pilkington's Tile & Pottery Co.
Pilkington's Lancastrian Pottery Society

A SHARED VISION: DAY AND PILKINGTON'S TILE & POTTERY CO.

Day's new adventure came with Pilkington's Tile Co., founded in 1891 at Clifton Junction, near Manchester, by the Pilkington family, colliery owners and investors. Day's connection with the firm, which began in its early days, would exclusively occupy his skills in ceramic design for over a dozen years.[79] Through his relationship with Pilkington's, Day demonstrated his versatility in producing a prolific number of designs for a wide variety of production methods. He also influenced the design direction of the firm during its first dozen years and realised his belief that the future of the industry lay in the fusion of science and art.

Day's connection with the firm came through William Burton, a chemist whom the Pilkingtons hired in October 1892 as first manager. Burton may initially have become aware of Day's work in tile designs while at Wedgwood, where he was employed from 1887-1890.[80] William Burton was joined in the Pilkington's venture by his brother Joseph Burton, also a chemist.[81] The firm was a late entry into a very competitive industry populated by well-established and reputable firms.[82] Day was fascinated by the firm's scientific approach to ceramics manufacture, and he and the Burtons shared a common vision of uniting artistry with scientific advances to produce objects of excellence – in short, the marriage of art and industry.[83]

6.30 (top left) Lewis F. Day. Cloisonné tile, c.1895. Made by Pilkington's Tile & Pottery Co. The firm marketed these as the speciality 'cloisonné' tiles, since the raised earthen outline resembled the wire bands or 'cloisons' separating the colours on Chinese enamels. Anthony J. Cross

6.31 (bottom left) Lewis F. Day. Tiles, c.1895. Made by Pilkington's Tile & Pottery Co. From Day, *Ornament and Its Application* (1904): fig. 194. Day described this as a tile "in which a fine raised earthen outline separates the cells of variously coloured deep rich glaze". From Day, 'Tiles', *Art Journal* (1895): 348

Pilkington's began tile production in January 1893.[84] The firm registered some of their designs, and it would appear that Day's designs were among the earliest registered in 1895.[85] One of these, a design for a 6-inch square (15.2cm.²) tile, features bell-shaped flowers and leaves on a turquoise background, with translucent glazes.[86] The decoration was applied by tube-lining, a technique of producing designs in relief by trailing slip, a mixture of clay and water, onto the surface of the tile. His draughtsmanship lent itself well to techniques that were based on controlled yet flowing line.

By 1895 Day had designed many printed, painted and embossed tiles, and he was enthusiastic about the firm's adventurous approach to tile decoration. Several decorating techniques were sometimes combined on tiles, and various coloured glazes both enhanced the designs and added an individualised, one-of-a-kind look to tiles that were industrially manufactured. In his 1895 article 'Tiles' for the *Art Journal* he enthused: "The most striking of the firm's new departures is a kind of cloisonné enamel, in which a fine raised earthen outline separates the cells of variously coloured deep rich glaze"; the article also featured illustrations of a pair of his cloisonné tiles with stylised leaves and stems.[87] This method was so named because the raised outline resembled the wire bands or 'cloisons' separating the colours on Chinese enamels.

Artists and designers had their own marks that sometimes appeared on wares. Even tiles that were produced mechanically could have painting and glazing applied by hand. Day's monogram consisted of his three initials, though tile designs in general were rarely marked.[88]

6.32 (far left) Lewis F. Day. Tile panel with trailing flowers, leaves and butterflies. Made by Pilkington's Tile & Pottery Co.
Anthony J. Cross

6.33 (left) Lewis F. Day. Tile panel with flowers and swirling foliage. Made by Pilkington's Tile & Pottery Co. A similar design for 6-inch square (15.2cm.^{2}) tiles was shown at the Wolverhampton Exhibition, 1902
Pilkington's Lancastrian Pottery Society

Pilkington's had its own in-house artists and designers and also gave commissions to other freelance designers including Walter Crane and C.F.A. Voysey. The firm saw a clear advantage in engaging designers with different styles to satisfy various consumer tastes. While many of Crane's designs incorporated the human figure, Voysey's designs were based on flat, stylised motifs such as birds and trees. Day's were often based on historic ornament or were conventionalised floral or foliate designs. In addition to designing pictorial or emblematic tiles that could be mixed with plain tiles, all three designers were skilled in creating designs that formed repeats.

From at least January 1896 Day had a contract with Pilkington's that rendered his rôle far more formal and extensive than that of other outside designers. The contract provided that Day be paid a retainer fee of £50 for general consulting services, with the stipulation that he would not design for any of Pilkington's competitors, nor advise them, during this period. The contract also provided that he be paid according to his ordinary rate for all actual designs; that he be remunerated for site visits to the factory or their London showrooms; it guaranteed that Pilkington's would give him commissions for designs totalling at least £100; and it allowed him to submit experimental designs to them up to a charge of £20. The firm expressed its "warm appreciation" for the design and consulting services he had already rendered them, seeming to suggest that a similar arrangement may have been in place earlier.[89] Day's contract was probably renewed on an annual basis, for company documents indicate that he still had an arrangement with the same basic provisions in 1899, although the retainer had been increased to £100.[90] There is nothing in the company's records to indicate that Crane, Voysey or any other freelance designers were offered contracts similar to Day's.[91]

Day was hugely influential in the development of the firm during its first

6.34 a and b (top left and top right) Lewis F. Day. Tiles with flower and swirling foliage. Made by Pilkington's Tile & Pottery Co. Pattern was shown at the Wolverhampton Exhibition, 1902
(a, left) Pilkington's Lancastrian Pottery Society
(b, right) Anthony J. Cross

6.35 (bottom left) Lewis F. Day. Floral tile. Made by Pilkington's Tile & Pottery Co. Anthony J. Cross

6.36 (bottom right) Lewis F. Day. Floral tile. Made by Pilkington's Tile & Pottery Co. The pattern was shown at the Glasgow International Exhibition and described as a "cloisonné tile in coloured glazes" (*Pilkington Catalogue 1901*: 36-7) Anthony J. Cross

dozen years. His many magazine articles and books were a resource on design and ornament used by the artists at Pilkington's.[92] The knowledge of competitors' wares and their promotional activities gained as a journalist reporting on major exhibitions would have been very helpful to the firm in determining their marketing strategy. While William Burton and Day both studied historic decorative art and ancient processes, they were committed to exploiting the possibilities of the present. The force of this conviction was at the heart of the firm's quick development of their product line, shown at the art and trade exhibitions of the period.

Pilkington's exhibited tiles designed by Day and others at major trade exhibitions from the mid-1890s, including the 1895 Arts and Crafts Exhibition (Manchester); the 1896 Arts and Crafts Exhibition (London); the 1897 Building Trades Exhibition (London); and the 1898 Northern Art Workers' Guild Exhibition (Manchester). Exhibition catalogues reveal both the large quantity of designs he produced for the firm and his ability to design for many types of tile production and decoration, including modelling in low relief, printing, tube-lining, hand-painting underglaze, and hand-painting in coloured clays or white porcelain slip. Day also designed a panel of mosaic tesserae in sunstone glaze, hearth tiles, ceramic mosaic pavements, and encaustic tile pavements.

The firm distinguished itself for combining high-quality design with a technical virtuosity in colours and superiority in glazing.[93] Coating tiles or pottery with a glaze sealed the surface and could also alter the decoration; and advances in chemistry had increased options for producing a variety of effects through the use of clear, coloured, opaque or translucent glazes.[94] The trade press remarked that a distinctive feature setting Pilkington's apart from its competitors was the "luscious" quality of the glazes, which were outstanding for their softness, richness and liquidity.[95] Day contended that Pilkington's had produced "glazes of exceptional purity and depth of colour".[96]

Day also pointed out the difference between the quality of Pilkington's printed tiles and others on the market. An 1881 article in *The Artist and Journal of Home Culture* had quoted him as complaining that the majority of printed tiles were poorly designed, "eminently inartistic", "obviously cheap" and "proportionately nasty".[97] In contrast, Pilkington's were masters of colour printing: "They appear to have carried colour printing, if not farther than anyone else, at least as far as it has yet been carried; whether by more solid printing or by more perfectly fused glaze, they have somehow almost entirely got rid of that poverty of colour which one has come to associate with the idea of printed tiles."[98]

Major exhibitions of the early 1900s

In less than a decade, the firm, now known as Pilkington's Tile and Pottery Co. Ltd., had realised an artistic reputation and commercial success, with branch offices in Manchester, London, Paris, Capetown and Sydney. The Paris Exposition Universelle of 1900 gave the firm international exposure and a platform for publicising both its philosophy of scientific manufacture and its command of production techniques. Day's influence on the artistic direction of the firm is clearly seen in his involvement in the overall exhibit, his own designs, and his reports on the exhibition as a journalist.

In his introduction in the firm's *Catalogue* for the exhibition, William Burton asserted that the firm's exhibit demonstrated that "the absence of artistic merit is not a necessary accompaniment of modern methods of manufacture".[99] He added that designers such as Walter Crane, C.F.A. Voysey, Edgar Wood, and the younger generation represented by John Chambers, Florence Steele and J.R. Cooper had, "under the able artistic guidance of Mr. Lewis F. Day", capitalised on the possibilities of modern manufacture, producing results that "challenge comparison with the work of past times".[100] While not claiming to have solved all problems of tile production, "we have brought scientific knowledge and artistic skill to bear on the problem of workshop production in a greater degree than has ever been the case in England before in the manufacture of tiles."[101] Judges evidently agreed, for Pilkington's won gold and silver medals at the Paris Exposition.

Day relished his involvement in the firm's exhibit in Paris. In his reports on the exhibition for the *Manchester Guardian*, Day noted that other than Pilkington's and Doulton's Lambeth ware, there were few

6.37 a and b (top left and top right) Lewis F. Day. 'Peony' tiles. Made by Pilkington's Tile & Pottery Co. Shown at the Paris Exposition 1900 (*Pilkington Catalogue 1900*: 3, 21) (a, left) Anthony J. Cross; (b, right) Zena Corrigan

6.38 (bottom left) Lewis F. Day. 'Tudor' tile, c.1900. Made by Pilkington's Tile & Pottery Co. Shown at the Paris Exposition 1900 and Glasgow Exhibition 1901 as "cloisonné tile in coloured glazes" (*Pilkington Catalogue 1900*: 24, 34, 27; *Pilkington Catalogue 1901*: 36-7) Anthony J.Cross

6.39 (bottom right) Lewis F. Day. Panel of painted tiles. Made by Pilkington's Tile & Pottery Co. Painted in coloured glazes by Lawrence Hall, this pattern was shown at the Paris Exposition 1900 to show "the richness of effect that can be obtained in painted tiles, using modern materials and methods entirely" (*Pilkington Catalogue 1900*: 19, 34) Zena Corrigan

English entries, adding that Pilkington's "have a show of tiles which, if I were not partly responsible for it, I would say was not unworthy of Lancashire".[102] Day's reference to his involvement was very modest, since over half of the seventy-six products exhibited by the firm had been designed by him.

Day's designs shown in Paris reveal his skill in designing for a wide variety of production processes. Several of his designs of flowers and birds were produced as incised tiles. Those patterns were "designed to show the effect that can be obtained by sinking two or three planes to successive depths, so that different thicknesses of coloured glaze really give the pattern".[103] Among the other tile production techniques used for his designs were painting underglaze, printing underglaze, painting in porcelain slip, and embossing.

Day's 'Greek Ivy' design was apparently quite popular for use on the dado portion of a wall and remained in production for a number of years.[104] Printed in two shades of brown, the "skilful adaptation of the Greek ivy-leaf and fret" had been shown at the Building Trades Exhibition in 1897.[105] The same design, this time printed in black under a crimson glaze, was exhibited both in Paris and the following year at the Glasgow International Exhibition.[106] The firm demonstrated how application of various glazes could make tiles look individual. Day appears to have been fond of this design, because he used an illustration of it both in his 1895 article in the *Art Journal* and also in his book *Pattern Design*, in which it was identified as the "brick or masonry pattern".[107]

Another example of Day's use of a foliage motif was the 'Feather Leaf' embossed tile dado.[108] A low-relief design glazed in peacock blue, this pattern for 6-inch square (15.2cm.²) tiles was shown in Paris and a year later in Glasgow.[109] Day was obviously intrigued by the fern motif as a basis of a repeat pattern for the lower part of a wall, because he also used it for a similar Lincrusta Walton dado paper that was produced by Frederick Walton Co. in 1897.[110]

6.40 (above) Lewis F. Day. 'Greek Ivy' printed tiles, c.1895. Shown at the Paris Exhibition 1900, printed underglaze "in black under crimson glaze" (*Pilkington Catalogue 1900*: 27). Made by Pilkington's Tile & Pottery Co. Anthony J. Cross

6.41 (below) Lewis F. Day. 'Brick or masonry pattern' tiles. Made by Pilkington's Tile & Pottery Co. From Day, *Pattern Design* (1903): illus. 90

6.42 (above left) Lewis F. Day. 'Feather Leaf' embossed tile in low relief, c.1895. Shown at the Paris Exposition 1900 "in peacock blue glaze" (*Pilkington Catalogue 1900*: 19, 31). Made by Pilkington's Tile & Pottery Co. From *Art Journal* (1895): 345. Same photo from *Pottery Gazette* 22 (1897)

Angela and Barry Corbett, Pilkington's Lancastrian Pottery Society

6.43 (above right) Lewis F. Day. Majolica opus sectile panel, by 1900. Made by Pilkington's Tile & Pottery Co. From Day, 'Modern Pottery at the Paris Exhibition', *Art Journal Supplement, Paris Exhibition 1900* (1900): 100, No. 8. (Image has been corrected to show unangled panel)

Angela and Barry Corbett, Pilkington's Lancastrian Pottery Society

Exhibitions were a venue in which designers and firms demonstrated their prowess in complex productions, and Day designed two such examples. One dramatic display was a large panel of majolica in opus sectile, a technique in which pieces of relief-moulded tiles with coloured transparent glaze were embedded in resin or mortar.[111] This rhythmic flower and leaf design was illustrated in the *Art Journal*.[112]

A *tour de force* was Day's 'Arab Lattice', two opus sectile panels comprising over 700 separate pieces.[113] Pilkington's *Catalogue* claimed that this ogee-arched and floral design represented "an entirely new departure in English tile work", and not surprisingly, added: "The making, firing, and glazing of so many pieces of intricate shape and of varying size and contour presented difficulties of no ordinary kind".[114] One panel was enriched with the firm's 'Onyx' glazes and the other with 'Sunstone' glazes containing "clouds of golden crystals".[115]

Walter Crane's panel 'The Senses' and tile designs by Voysey, as well as those by in-house artists, were also exhibited. Some of the designs of Crane, Voysey and Day shown in Paris demonstrated the strong linear emphasis, inspiration from organic sources, and undulating lines that had become popular from about the mid-1890s and are suggestive of Art Nouveau. While it would not be an exaggeration to say that Day was disgusted with what he perceived as the lack of restraint in much of the Art Nouveau furniture shown in Paris, he was a master of the flowing yet controlled line and accommodated this to some of the types of designs gaining favour with consumers.

Pilkington's also exhibited Day's encaustic tile pavements, in which patterns in coloured clay were impressed into the body of the tile. This medieval production technique had been revived in the 1830s, and encaustic floor tiles were used throughout the century. Pilkington's manufactured them in highly durable vitreous porcelain and marketed them as a more up-to-date treatment for halls and vestibules "than the stiff Gothic patterns

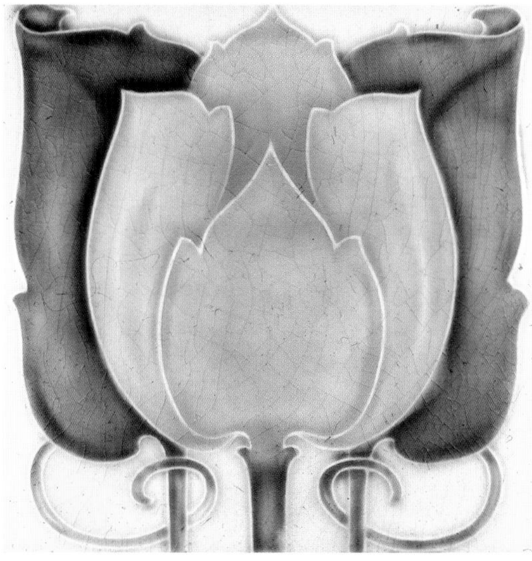

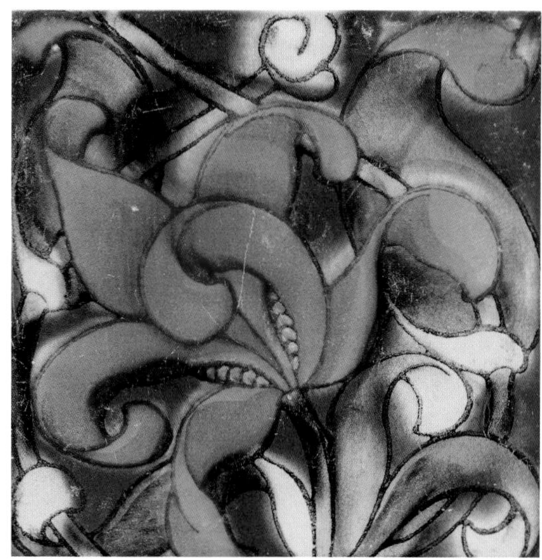

6.44 (above) C.F.A Voysey. Tile, c.1902. Made by Pilkington's Tile and Pottery Co. Hans van Lemmen

6.45 (top right) Lewis F. Day. Tile with lush foliage and flower. Made by Pilkington's Tile & Pottery Co. Pattern shown at Glasgow Exposition 1901 as "painted in rich coloured glazes" by Lawrence Hall (*Pilkington Catalogue 1901*: 28-9) Zena Corrigan

6.46 (right) Lewis F. Day. Tile. Made by Pilkington's Tile & Pottery Co. Pattern shown at Glasgow Exhibition 1901 as "cloisonné tile in coloured glazes" (*Pilkington Catalogue 1901*: 36-7)

Anthony J. Cross

6.47 Pilkington's Tile & Pottery Co. exhibit, Glasgow International Exhibition 1901. Lewis F. Day's 'Anthemion Frieze' tiles surmount the inner portion of the exhibit stand. From Day, 'Decorative and Industrial Art at the Glasgow Exhibition 3', *Art Journal* (1901): 276

Newberry Library, Chicago

6.48 (left) Lewis F. Day. Tile with relief moulded floral design. Made by Pilkington's Tile & Pottery Co. Pattern shown at Glasgow Exhibition 1901 as "cloisonné tile" in coloured glazes (*Pilkington Catalogue 1901*: 36-7) Hans van Lemmen

6.49 a and b (below left and right) Lewis F. Day. 'Heraldic' tiles with lion (left) and griffin (right) motifs. Made by Pilkington's Tile & Pottery Co. Shown at the Wolverhampton Exhibition 1902 (*Pilkington Catalogue 1902*: 18-19) Private collection

which have formed the stock-in-trade of encaustic tile designers".[116] Two examples of these, one of squares with severely conventionalised motifs banded by a plain border, and the other based on roundels of conventionalised leaves with a leafy border, were shown at the Wolverhampton Exhibition in 1902.[117]

It is likely that Day influenced the production of buff faïence lions exhibited by Pilkington's in Paris.[118] Originally designed by sculptor Alfred Stevens for the railings around the British Museum, the lions were reproduced from a mould by Pilkington's and coated in 'Sunstone' glazes. In 1877 Day had purchased a bronze casting of a lion made for the railings from the sale of the contents of Stevens's studio after his death.[119] He greatly admired Stevens and identified him as "the man of the period who came nearest to the great Italians of the Renaissance."[120]

Pilkington's continued to rely heavily on Day's designs for other exhibitions in the early 1900s, and in turn he continued to reiterate the firm's commitment to a marriage of art and industry, praising "the artistic level of design and execution maintained by a firm claiming only to manufacture".[121] Over a third of the wares shown by the firm at the Glasgow International Exhibition in 1901 were Day's designs, many of them having previously been shown in Paris.

The following year the firm exhibited at the Wolverhampton Exhibition. Again, about a third of the tiles shown were designed by Day, and some of them had been shown in the two previous exhibitions.

6.50 (top left) Lewis F. Day. "Embossed tile in coloured glazes", made by Pilkington's Tile & Pottery Co. and shown at the Wolverhampton Exhibition 1902 (*Pilkington Catalogue 1902*: 26-7). Described by Day as "six-inch tile to be fixed brick-wise". From Day, *Pattern Design* (1903): illus. 158

6.51 (left) Lewis F. Day. 'Peony' tile panel, 1902. Shown at the 7th Arts and Crafts Exhibition 1903. From Day, *Nature and Ornament 2: Ornament the Finished Product of Design* (1909): illus. 77

6.52 (above) Lewis F. Day. 'Vine' pattern tiles. Made by Pilkington's Tile & Pottery Co. Shown at the Wolverhampton Exhibition 1902 as "six inch tiles in the Hispano-Mauresque style" (*Pilkington Catalogue 1902*: 12-9). Described by Day as "decorated in coloured glazes separated by a raised outline". From Day, *Ornament and Its Application* (1904): fig. 51

By this time Day had also designed some additional large-scale pieces, including his 'Persian Tree' panel. Featuring a tree with flowers on symmetrically arranged branches, flanked by two flowering plants, the panel was painted by Pilkington artists Miss Tyldesley, Miss Briggs, & T.F. Evans.[122] This was probably also the panel shown at the 1903 Arts and Crafts Exhibition and the 1908 Franco-British Exhibition.[123]

A tile panel designed by Day featuring a wreath of peonies and foliage painted in coloured glazes by T.F. Evans was shown at the 7th Arts and Crafts Exhibition in 1903.

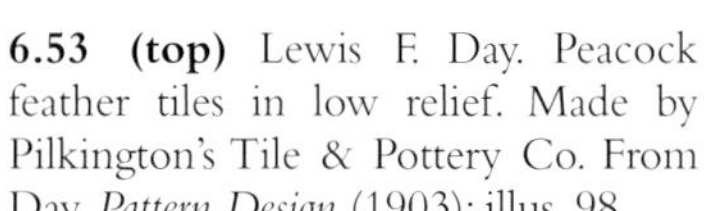

6.53 (top) Lewis F. Day. Peacock feather tiles in low relief. Made by Pilkington's Tile & Pottery Co. From Day, *Pattern Design* (1903): illus. 98

6.54 (bottom left) Mould for peacock feather tile designed by Lewis F. Day. Made by Pilkington's Tile & Pottery Co. Paul Reeves

6.55 (bottom right) Lewis F. Day. Peacock feather tile. Made by Pilkington's Tile & Pottery Co. Paul Reeves

Also exhibited were tiles designed by him and others, painted and modelled by the firm's in-house artists and executed "to meet the conditions of practical manufacture".[124] The *Studio* was enthusiastic, praising Day for the variety, lavish colours and "richly floriated" tiles and panels and adding that the products "afforded an excellent study of what may be done with coloured glazes".[125]

Day rankled some critics at the 1903 Arts and Crafts Exhibition, however, with his relentless push for a better relationship between design and manufacture. In his reports on the Exhibition for the *Art Journal*, Day had highlighted wallpaper manufacturer Jeffrey & Co., textile printers Turnbull & Stockdale, and Pilkington's, describing their exhibits as those in "which the aim has been to work contentedly under conditions imposed by manufacture".[126] He was involved with all three firms, and he had a practice of letting the reader know his connection to firms whose products he reviewed so they could factor that into their appraisal of his remarks. The *Art Workers' Quarterly* challenged his comments: "Surely all repeating patterns should be so designed. Is Mr. Day gently hinting that there are designs in the gallery which look pretty but are quite unpractical?"[127]

Lancastrian Art Pottery

Although tile production remained the firm's main business, in 1904 Pilkington's introduced its Lancastrian Ware, decorative glazed pottery in simple, classical shapes inspired by Greek, Persian, and Chinese pottery.[128] Day influenced the company's choice of shapes for this

The New
English Pottery.
IN A SERIES OF NEW AND
STRIKING GLAZE EFFECTS.

VASES,
TRAYS,
BOWLS,
DISHES, etc.

AN EXHIBITION of Unique Examples of the above will be held in the Graves' Gallery, Pall Mall, W., from June 1 to June 30, 1904.

Pilkington's Tile & Pottery Co.
LTD.
CLIFTON JUNCTION, NEAR MANCHESTER.

6.56 (left) Pilkington's Tile & Pottery Co. 'The New English Pottery'. From *Art Journal* (1904): pl. opp. 160 Newberry Library, Chicago

6.57 (above) Pilkington's Tile & Pottery Co. advertisement announcing the opening of the first exhibition of the firm's new Lancastrian pottery at the Graves Gallery, London, 1904. From *Studio* (1904): back cover

hand-thrown ware, which was exhibited for the first time in June 1904 at the Graves Gallery in London. William and Joseph Burton acknowledged that in this new venture they were "aided by the sympathetic advice and criticism of Mr. Lewis F. Day, the eminent decorative artist" as well as by their own staff.[129]

Day was the only designer so mentioned in the exhibition brochure, and in his 1904 text *Ornament and Its Application*, he illustrated a Persian vase that was a prototype for a series of Pilkington vases.[130] Specific pottery designs by Day have not been identified, however. He also designed the first company mark for Lancastrian Pottery, consisting of the letters 'L' and 'P' and incorporating two bees to represent the Burton brothers.[131] This mark, illustrated in his 1904 article 'The New Lancastrian Pottery' for the *Art Journal*, was transfer-printed onto wares from 1904 to 1905 and impressed from 1905 to 1913.[132]

The Lancastrian ware was enhanced

6.58 (opposite) Lewis F. Day. Lancastrian pottery vase. Made by Pilkington's Tile & Pottery Co.
Pilkington's Lancastrian Pottery Society

6.59 (opposite, inset) Lewis F. Day. Prototype of Lancastrian pottery vase, "modelled to give value to the glaze", based on an example of a glazed earthenware Persian vase in the Victoria and Albert Museum. From Day, *Ornament and Its Application* (1904): fig. 136

6.60 (left) Lewis F. Day. Factory mark for Pilkington's Tile & Pottery Co., used c.1904-1913
Newberry Library, Chicago

with the opalescent, crystalline, textural and transmutation glazes perfected by the firm.[133] Some pieces were decorated by Pilkington's artists with a variety of motifs, including calligraphy, heraldry, animals, birds, mythological characters, and geometric, ship and floral designs popular with British and American firms at this time. Day praised the quality of these glazes and the fact that "no two of their pots come out of the kiln exactly alike. The possessor of a specimen may always flatter himself that it is unique", a quality that was stressed by the firm.[134] Day observed that the effects were "not done in imitation of nature, but in obedience to her laws".[135] The prime achievement of the potters was not that they produced beautiful results by "happy flukes", but rather that they mastered the properties of the materials and the processes of the kiln in such a way as to deliberately produce results that appeared "accidental" and had the "charm of unexpectedness".[136] Day noted that while the effects were spectacular, they did not cross over into extravagance.[137] He placed high value on control and discipline, knowing when one had done enough: "It is curious how little the workman is able to resist the temptation to do all that can be done. He seldom stops to ask if it is worth doing."[138]

Introduced shortly after was Lancastrian Lustre pottery, with an added shimmering effect produced by use of metallic oxides. When the company exhibited at the 8th Arts and Crafts Exhibition in 1906, forty-seven pieces of Lancastrian pottery and thirty-eight items of lustre ware were shown and both types were described in the aggregate as designed by Day, William Burton and John Chambers (Pilkington's chief in-house designer), and thrown and painted by in-house artists. Specific designs by Day for lustre pottery have not been identified. Pilkington's art pottery was sold through prominent outlets including Liberty & Co. and Tiffany & Co.[139] Pilkington's received a Royal Warrant from George V in 1913, and thereafter their wares bore the designation "Royal".[140]

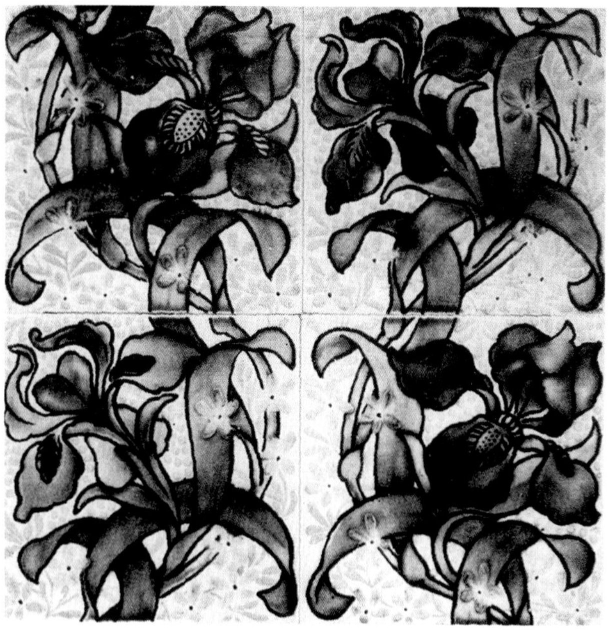

6.61 (above) Lewis F. Day. 'Persian Iris' tiles, by 1902. Painted by W.S. Mycock. Made by Pilkington's Tile & Pottery Co. Shown at the Wolverhampton Exhibition 1902 as "painted in rich coloured glazes" on 6-inch square (15.2cm.²) tiles (*Pilkington Catalogue 1902*: 14-5) and at the Franco-British Exhibition 1908. From Marillier, 'Pilkington's Tiles & Pottery' (1908): 212

Angela and Barry Corbett,
Pilkington's Lancastrian Pottery Society

6.62 (right) Lewis F. Day. 'Persian Tree' tile panel. Painted by Miss Tyldesley, Miss Briggs and T.F. Evans. Made by Pilkington's Tile & Pottery Co. Shown at the Wolverhampton Exhibition 1902 (*Pilkington Catalogue 1902*: 6-7) and the Franco-British Exhibition 1908. From Marillier, 'Pilkington's Tiles & Pottery' (1908): 212.

Angela and Barry Corbett,
Pilkington's Lancastrian Pottery Society

The designer emeritus

Day's relationship with Pilkington's was apparently scaled back around 1905, when Gordon Forsyth became lead artist. Younger designers at the firm were gaining greater recognition, and some of the decrease in the number of designs Day produced for the firm was probably due also to the movement away from pattern in the early 1900s. Glazes and modelling of the surface of tiles – which produced a kind of pattern themselves – replaced some of the earlier fascination with designed pattern.[141] In addition, there are indications that Day suffered some recurrent bouts of illness around this time.[142]

Nevertheless, his designs continued to be featured at exhibitions in the early 1900s. The trade press reported that Pilkington's and Day individually won grand prix awards at the Milan Exhibition in 1906, although specific information is scanty.[143]

At the 1908 Franco-British Exhibition, the firm's predilection for Persian-inspired tiles was seen in its dramatic domed pavilion, which included recessed alcoves decorated with 'Persian Iris' tiles designed by Day and hand painted in richly-coloured glazes by W.S. Mycock.[144] In his report on Pilkington's exhibit for the *Illustrated Review* of the Exhibition, H.C. Marillier commented: "The patterns are English enough in detail, but the colour schemes, of rich cobalt blue, sage green, bright turquoise, and Rhodian red are similar to those employed in the best Oriental work of the fifteenth and sixteenth centuries."[145] The *British Architect* included three illustrations of the Pilkington's exhibit and commented that it exemplified "a well-directed enterprise in the combination of art and science", thus reiterating the firm's mantra.[146]

Day enjoyed a personal friendship with William Burton, with whom he visited on many occasions at The Hollies, Burton's home at Clifton Junction.[147] Both men were of Quaker stock, historians of their craft, lectured extensively, taught, wrote articles and books, and carried on a very active professional life in organisations including the Society of Arts and the Northern Art Workers' Guild. Like Day, Burton was a contributor to the *Manchester Guardian* and served with him on the committee that advised on the rearrangement of the Victoria and Albert Museum in 1908.[148]

The strongest bond of all, however, was the shared vision that they were living in the age of science and that product excellence would come through the fusion of science and art. Day attributed his clear understanding of Pilkington's scientific approach to pottery making to his early first-hand involvement with the firm.[149] He described Burton not only as "an authority on pottery", but as "that *rara avis* among managers of pottery works, a man of science with strong artistic sympathies".[150] Day remarked that the Burtons demonstrated that "science may achieve artistic triumphs" and that this was accomplished by a thorough understanding of the natural properties of their clays and glazes as well as mastery of the processes required to bring about certain effects.[151] He rated the Burtons' commitment to scientific control of production processes more highly than the efforts of those who sought to achieve artistic effects by chance: "Happily they are sensitive to beauty, and they have set themselves to do of deliberate purpose what artists less expert in their trade do sometimes by accident."[152]

On the occasion of the first exhibition of Lancastrian pottery at the Graves Gallery, Day observed: "Art is commonly unscientific in its method, and science is insensible to art."[153] While acknowledging the frequent antagonism between the two fields, Day argued: "It would hardly be overstating the case to say that the artists who have achieved greatness are those who, in addition to the temperament, the imagination, the genius of the artist, have also the science which enables them to make the most of it."[154] He underscored his point by reminding readers that without knowledge of chemistry, potters could not have achieved the innovations and advances in ceramic art that were exhibited at the Paris Exposition of 1900.[155]

Day envisioned the future of the ceramic industry resting not in the hands of the individual studio potter, who could produce a limited number of pieces affordable only to persons of financial means, but rather in the hands of the scientific potter who had a "sense of beauty and some belief in its value – even commercially".[156] The advancement of art in industry was contingent on employing scientific methods of production, and the proper course of action lay "in the direction of art not so intolerant of science as to repudiate system; for it is only systematised art which is available in modern industry; and that, after all, counts for something in the world, despise it as artists may".[157]

CHAPTER SEVEN: CLOCKS AND FURNITURE

"In the department of furniture and decoration, the transitions from style to style, or rather from fashion to fashion, have been more conspicuous than in any other branch of industry." [Lewis F. Day, 1887]

Compared to his designs for wallpaper, tiles and textiles, Lewis F. Day created relatively little furniture. Furthermore, unlike his designs for flat and low-relief pattern, which occupied him throughout his career, furniture designs were only produced from the 1870s to the late 1880s. Nevertheless, furniture represents a significant aspect of Day's career.

Day's clock cases and furnishings exhibited by Howell & James at the international exhibitions in Vienna in 1873 and in Paris in 1878 drew early attention to his work. In a dramatic way, they helped establish his international reputation as a versatile designer. In fact, his clock cases are one of the types of furnishings for which he is still best known. In addition, Day wrote on furniture design throughout his career. In particular, his magazine journalism on furniture shown at exhibitions provides insightful and useful commentary on contemporary styles and preferences in the late 19th and early 20th centuries.

While his involvement with furniture may have taken different forms at various points in his life, he was always intensely interested in it as a major component of the domestic interior. Day studied furniture through the dual lenses of beauty and usefulness, and these two perspectives are consistently reflected in both his designs and his writings.[1] His view paralleled that of William Morris, who said: "Have nothing in your houses which you do not know to be useful or believe to be beautiful." Notions of aesthetics and utility permeated Day's work as a young designer of furniture beginning in the 1870s. They ran as refrains in his writings as he developed into a major journalist and design critic in the 1880s. With an increasingly heavy workload designing and consulting for industry, he did not design much furniture himself after the late 1880s. Nevertheless, his continuing preoccupation with these two requirements of furniture characterise his writings as critic emeritus, as he assessed the state of furniture design and prognosticated its future at the turn of the century.

7.1 Lewis F. Day. Clock case with aluminium dial and ceramic panels representing the months of the year, 1878. Shown at the Paris Exposition Universelle, 1878. Retailed by Howell & James
Michael Whiteway

WELCOMING THE CHALLENGES OF FURNITURE DESIGN

Clock cases

Then in his late twenties, Lewis F. Day energetically threw himself into furniture design in the early 1870s. His earliest pieces were clock cases he designed for Howell & James, the prominent Regent St. retailer of home furnishings. During the 1870s and 1880s, these clocks, along with other types of small furniture with

7.2 Lewis F. Day and Henry Day. Clock case of carved wood, with metal panels of daisies, small painted tiles depicting the phases of the moon and larger ones the seasons. The description refers to the four seasons, but the illustration shows only three. From *Art Journal* (1873): 182, 188 Newberry Library, Chicago

inset plaques in faïence, were among the speciality items marketed by the firm and they became one of Day's specialities, as well.[2]

The clock cases were constructed of oak, walnut, cherry, mahogany or ebonized wood and often featured incised or carved ornament, galleries and stiles with turned terminal knobs. The clock face often incorporated porcelain or metal panels – painted in blue and white – with daisies, leaves, berries, emblems of the seasons, signs of the zodiac, phases of the moon, or figures representing the months of the year.[3] The clock dials were frequently made of brass in the form of a sun or sunflower.

It is not difficult to see why these clocks caught on in the marketplace. They were popular accoutrements to the ebonized Anglo-Japanese furniture then in vogue as well as the current rage for blue and white china. They also allowed consumers to respond to the burgeoning Aesthetic Movement that grew, often imperceptibly, out of the later phase of the Gothic Revival. Sometimes referred to in the art press as 'Early English' or 'Queen Anne' in style, Day observed that by 1878 they had "almost supplanted the old-fashioned ormolu clocks".[4]

An early example of a clock case designed by "Messrs. Henry and Lewis Day" was exhibited at the Vienna International Exhibition in 1873 and illustrated in the *Art Journal* report on the exhibition.[5] Henry Day was probably a relative, but his exact relationship to Lewis and his rôle in this clock's design remain a mystery. Press reports of the clocks shown in subsequent exhibitions refer solely to Lewis Day as the designer. The example exhibited in Vienna featured a dial with a brazen sun in the centre of the clock face and adjacent spandrels with winged symbols of eternity. Four small tiles depicted phases of the moon, and larger tiles the seasons. Narrower metal panels were decorated with daisies and leaves. The stiles, ornamented with simple fluting and carving, culminated in turned knobs. A curved pediment with carved daisy in the centre topped the case.

A more elaborate clock shown at the Paris Exposition Universelle in 1878 featured geometric incised patterning and a dial incorporating a central sunflower.[6] Day worked a number of design elements into the clock case. The clock was surmounted by a roof with fishscale carving, sprockets, and two galleries, one at its base and a smaller one on top. Additional ornamental detail included a pierced skirting and turned stiles terminating in finials.

Day reported on the Paris exhibition as a journalist for the *British Architect*, and about half a dozen of his 'Notes on English Decorative Art in Paris' discussed clocks and furniture shown there. He included illustrations of three of his clocks in his eleventh article.[7] One clock featured painted panels of floral emblems of the four seasons and a sunflower dial encircled with painted fretwork (all in blue and white), simple ribbed stiles and a curved pediment.[8] (See plate 7.3 below and also p.5.) Another included panels of figures, painted in blue and white, representing the twelve months of the year, alternating with panels of stylised leaves. Other design elements included a pediment with carved blazing sun and a "square sunflower dial being engraved on brass".[9] A surviving example includes an aluminium dial, which would have rendered the clock an advanced and expensive piece.

7.3 (above) Lewis F. Day. Clock case with ceramic dial and panels of the four seasons painted in blue and white. From *British Architect* 10 (1878): 127; illus. near 127

7.4 (top right) Lewis F. Day. Clock case. From *Art Journal Illustrated Catalogue of the Paris International Exhibition* 1878 (1878): 106 Newberry Library, Chicago

7.5 (bottom right) Lewis F. Day. Clock case with panels representing the months of the year. From *British Architect* 10 (1878): 127; illus. near 127

7.6 and details (left, above and below) Lewis F. Day. Clock case with aluminium dial and ceramic panels representing the months of the year, 1878. Shown at the Paris Exposition Universelle, 1878. Retailed by Howell & James Michael Whiteway

A third clock, with upper and lower shelves for the display of small ceramic vases, formed part of the firm's exhibit screen, which Day also designed. Day noted that there were a number of other clocks shown by Howell & James, and he referred specifically to one that incorporated the motto "Pleasure and action make time seem short", to another that depicted Shakespeare's seven ages of man, and to one decorated with amorini.[10] Whether they were also designed by him is unclear.

An ebonized clock designed, painted and signed by Day in 1879 features 'The Fowler' on the upper panel and 'The Shepherd' on the lower. The figures were part of a series of panels Day designed on the subject of trades or occupations that also included 'The Woodman', 'The Husbandman', 'The Angler', and 'The Fisherman', among others. The two trade figures on the clock, along with 'The Woodman', were illustrated in the *Architect* in 1877.[11] Apparently Day was fond of these figures, for he also incorporated them into a fireplace design for Maw & Co., and included illustrations of them in some of his books.[12]

7.7 (above) Lewis F. Day. Detail, signature, ebonized clock with figural panels, late 1870s Paul Reeves

7.8 (right) Lewis F. Day. Ebonized clock with figural panels painted by Day, late 1870s. Maker unknown Paul Reeves

7.9 and 7.10 (below left) Lewis F. Day. Cabinet panels with (top) figure of fowler and (bottom) figure of shepherd, c.1877. From Day, *Some Principles of Every-day Art*, 2nd ed. (1894): illus. 14 and 13 respectively

7.11 (above) Lewis F. Day. Ebonized clock with figural panels painted by Day, late 1870s. Upper figure is monogrammed with Day's initials. Maker unknown H. Blairman & Sons Ltd.

7.12 Thomas Harris. Wall clock, c.1878. Retailed by Howell & James. Walnut, with porcelain plaque and enamel dial H. Blairman & Sons Ltd.

The two female figures on either side of the clock also illustrate Day's practice of multiple uses of some of his designs. These figures were originally designed as painted panels for a cabinet.[13] In addition to including them on the clock, Day also used them on two vases that he designed for the Torquay Terra-Cotta Pottery, which were exhibited by Howell & James at the Paris Exposition in 1878.[14] A second clock, very similar to the first, is monogrammed with Day's initials.

The number of clocks that Day designed for Howell & James is unknown. Surviving clock cases are not always marked with the name of the designer, painter, manufacturer or retailer, sometimes making positive identification difficult, if not impossible. Other designers, including architect Thomas Harris, also designed clock cases for Howell & James. In addition, in the 1870s and 1880s a number of firms, including J.W. Benson, Elkington & Co., and Cox & Sons retailed similar clocks, some with cases in wood and others in slate. Further complicating matters is the fact that a manufacturer may have used designs from more than one artist in the production of the case and ceramic panels. It is also clear from surviving examples that the tile panels and the dials as well were sometimes used interchangeably on clock cases.

A good many of these clocks were probably designed for various firms by anonymous artists working with the popular and readily-available motifs of the day, such as sunflowers and daisies, emblems of the seasons, literary references, and proverbs. Illustrations by prominent designers were regularly featured in professional journals and consumer magazines, providing inspiration for the work of others. The close proximity of one retailer to another, as in the case of Howell & James on Regent St. and J.W. Benson at 25 Old Bond St., allowed for quick exposure of one firm's work to the other.

The difficulty in identifying the designer of a clock due to the intermingling of influences and the absence of documentation is exemplified by a clock dating to the late 1870s to early 1880s. This oak clock case features incised stiles terminating in plain knobs, a fretwork apron, and spindled gallery; four square ceramic tiles representing the seasons and four smaller rectangular tiles with a pattern of daisies are painted in blue and white. The clock was retailed by J.W. Benson, and Day is not known to have designed for the firm. Nevertheless, the square tile representing autumn in the upper left corner is almost identical to a tile design by Day that appeared in *British Architect* in 1881. Two other square tiles representing spring and summer are quite similar to ones known to have been designed by Day. The pattern of the slender rectangular panels resembles one of Day's ceiling papers, a diaper of daisies. In addition, Day was fond of using the square spiral form, which is incised on the wood surrounding the dial. In contrast, the plain dial and numerals are very different to those on clocks that have been positively identified as his designs.

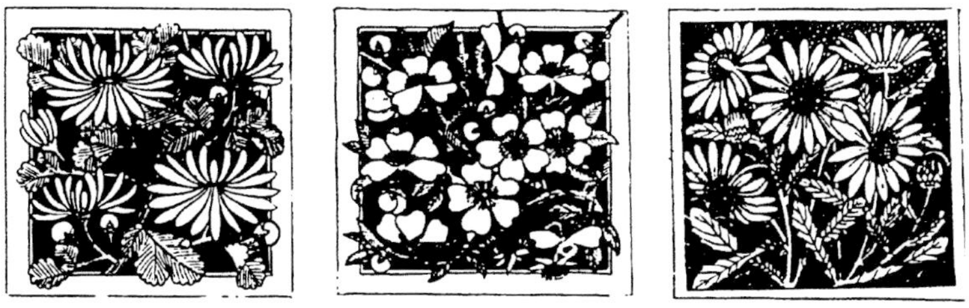

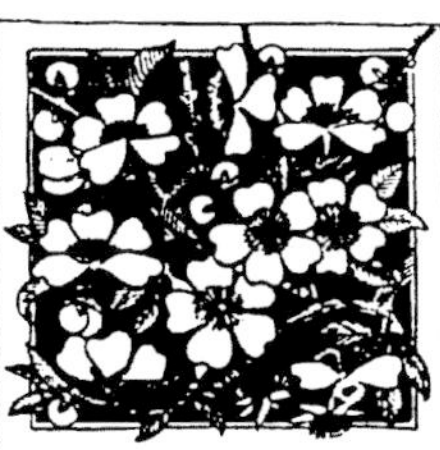

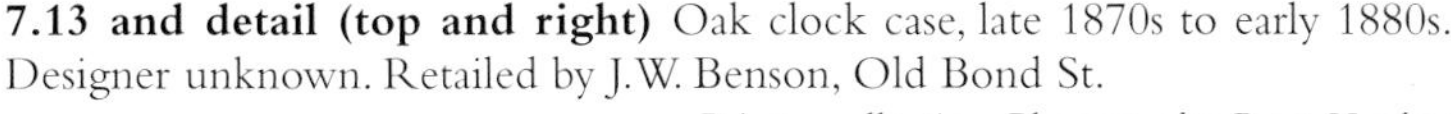

7.13 and detail (top and right) Oak clock case, late 1870s to early 1880s. Designer unknown. Retailed by J.W. Benson, Old Bond St.

Private collection. Photography, Peter Hughes

7.14 a, b and c (above) Lewis F. Day. Tiles, c.1881. From *British Architect* 16 (1881): near 414

Furniture and panels

In the 1870s and 1880s there were a number of prominent architects and designers for whom furniture represented a major area of work. Bruce J. Talbert, Edward W. Godwin and Henry W. Batley were among those who directed a significant amount of their creative effort to designing art furniture. For others, including John Moyr Smith and Lewis F. Day, the amount of furniture designed was much less. Nevertheless, for all these figures, furniture design gave scope to their skills in three-dimensional design, gained them new clients, and provided opportunities for showing their work at international exhibitions.

Day designed furniture for at least three firms. Major difficulties in identifying his furniture are that the pieces are unsigned and there is a lack of documentation regarding the maker of most of the pieces. In addition, aside from reports in the trade and professional press of his

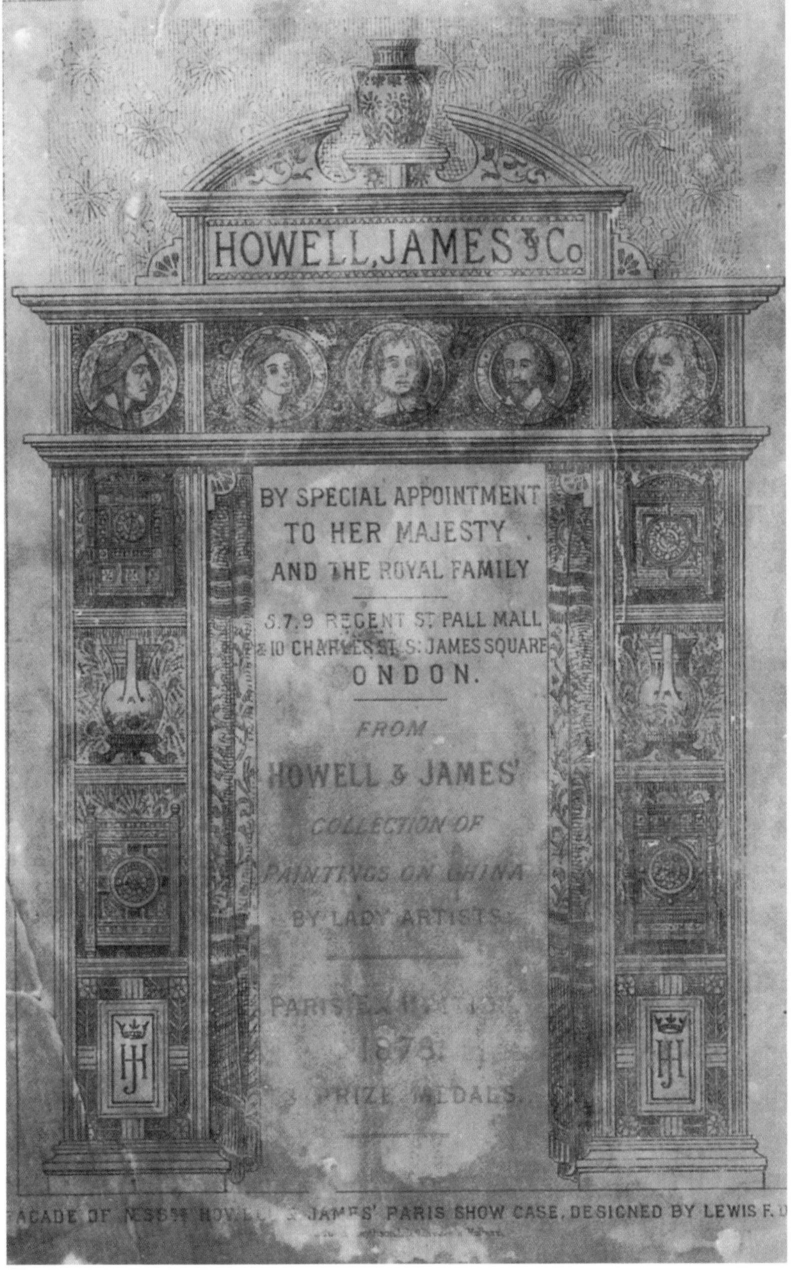

7.15 (opposite) Lewis F. Day. Portion of Howell & James exhibit, Paris Exposition Universelle 1878. From *British Architect* 10 (1878): near 126-7

7.16 (left) Howell & James. Advertisement for façade of the firm's exhibit, designed by Lewis F. Day, Paris Exposition Universelle 1878

The Albert Dawson Collection

furniture shown at major exhibitions, there was little critical commentary on his furniture, since much of it was designed for members of his family.

Most of Day's furniture in this early period was designed around the time of the Paris Exposition Universelle of 1878. Day designed Howell & James's exhibit area for the event, including the cabinets in which pottery was displayed. The store's exhibit area received a great deal of attention in the press, and its connection with Day's name was a huge boost to his growing reputation. The *Art Journal* commented on the occasional furniture offered by Howell & James: "This well-known firm has produced of late some very original small articles of furniture, such as clock cases, china cupboards, and *étagères*, conceived in the spirit of ancient Art of various epochs, into which plaques and medallions in faïence generally enter."[15] It is likely that Day designed some other small pieces of furniture for the store, based on the amount of work he was doing for them at the time and on the fact that he designed furnishings such as cabinets and hanging shelves for his family.

Day also designed furniture for Gregory & Co., Regent St., though he was disappointed with their exhibit in Paris because he felt it could have been arranged more effectively. In his report on the exhibition, he noted: "They exhibit a little fire-screen with fish panels painted in transparent colours on gold, for which I am responsible."[16] The quantity of furniture he designed for Gregory & Co. and the length of his relationship with the firm are unknown. A charming Aesthetic cabinet, designed to hold music or other items, features two painted panels of flowering trees and incorporates tiles monogrammed by Day. Dating to c.1875, it was retailed by Gregory & Co. and several variants exist. Whether the ebonized cabinet itself was designed by Day is unknown, though it should be noted that the flowering trees in the painted panels resemble those in some advertisements he produced for W.B. Simpson around this time, and it is known that Day did design at least one music cabinet for his family.

Day also received a great deal of attention in the press for his collaboration with Henry and John Cooper, Great Pulteney St., on the 'Princess Cabinet': Henry J. Cooper designed the structure of the solid rosewood cabinet and Day the ornamental details. Six panels of the cabinet featured figures from Tennyson's poem 'The Princess' and were painted in oil in tones of red, scarlet, rose, orange, purple and flesh, to harmonise with the warm tone of the rosewood.[17] Day illustrated two of the panels, depicting Princess Ida and Lady Blanche, in his journalistic reports on the exhibition.[18] Decorative details included carved scrollwork of flowers and leaves and repoussé brass mountings on the cabinet doors. Day had realised that the effect of the cabinet would be quite pronounced, so he designed a "refreshing and quiet" setting for it.[19] A rich green velvet was used for the backdrop, chair covers and side curtains, which were enhanced with a border embroidered in coloured silks.[20]

While the *Magazine of Art* criticised the cabinet for having too many illustrative panels "rather hotly painted", the *Art Journal* disagreed, lauding the beauty and refined workmanship of the piece and commending H.&J. Cooper for producing a "harmonious result by the subordination of the painted panels to the general structure".[21] George Augustus Sala, that indefatigable commentator on social and cultural life, included an illustration of H.&J. Cooper's exhibit in *Paris Herself Again* and gave a very detailed and literary description of the six panels. He echoed the *Art Journal's* praise, adding that the painted panels were well-integrated with the overall structure and that the "singularly rich and vivid chromatic result is arrived at without the slightest approach to garishness".[22]

7.17 and detail Cabinet, with tiles monogrammed LFD, c.1875. Retailed by Gregory & Co.
The Albert Dawson Collection

7.18 (right) Lewis F. Day and H.& J. Cooper. 'Princess Cabinet', 1878. From *Art Journal Illustrated Catalogue of the Paris International Exhibition 1878* (1878): 46
Newberry Library, Chicago

7.19 (below) Lewis F. Day. Exhibit area for 'Princess Cabinet', 1878. From George Augustus Sala, *Paris Herself Again* (1879): opp. 320
Trustees of the National Library of Scotland

Decorative panels were popular elements in furniture of the period. The panels could be carved; inlaid with satinwood, boxwood, metals and other materials; or painted with images of historic or literary characters or motifs from nature. These techniques could be used singly or in combination with each other, as is seen in the 'Princess Cabinet'.[23] Day was very interested in the decorative potential of this expensive technique. He cautioned that "if figures are painted on the prominent panels of costly furniture they should be of the very best, and the more these panels are emphasised by elaborate framing, the more imperative it is that they should be worthy of such distinction".[24] Some of Day's earliest designs featured in the trade press were those for painted panels, and they date to the late 1870s. Among these are figural designs of cherubs; well-known characters from Shakespeare, with borders incorporating quotations; and trades or occupations.[25] Whether these designs were all produced for their original purpose as painted panels is unknown, but as has been noted, some were executed for other media.

A pertinent example of Day's use of a design for various media is seen in his 1879 design for the top portion of a cabinet with inlay.[26] It incorporates a frieze of moths and daisies and two large

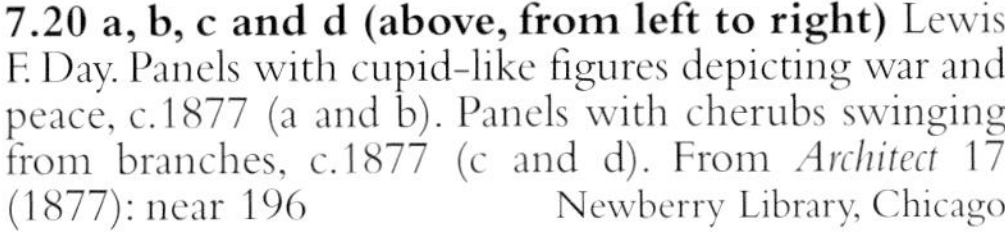

7.20 a, b, c and d (above, from left to right) Lewis F. Day. Panels with cupid-like figures depicting war and peace, c.1877 (a and b). Panels with cherubs swinging from branches, c.1877 (c and d). From *Architect* 17 (1877): near 196 Newberry Library, Chicago

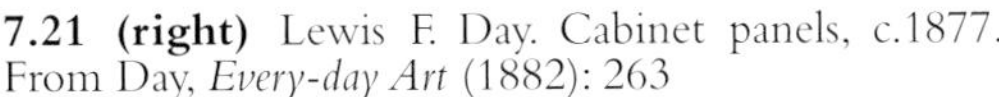

7.21 (right) Lewis F. Day. Cabinet panels, c.1877. From Day, *Every-day Art* (1882): 263

7.22 (bottom right) Lewis F. Day. Panels illustrating "the adaptation of natural forms to ornamental design". From Day, *Instances of Accessory Art* (1880): pl.12 Paul Reeves

7.23 (bottom left) Lewis F. Day. Design for panel, 1892. From Day, *The Planning of Ornament*, 3rd. ed. (1893): pl. 10

panels of flowering plants in urns. Day included an illustration of the left-hand panel, "narcissus compelled into the way of ornament", in his book *Nature in Ornament*.[27] Whether this cabinet was ever produced is unknown. Day later translated the narcissus design into a silk embroidery panel, with no substantial modification.[28]

7.24 (above) Lewis F. Day. Cabinet with panels of flowering plants, 1879. From Day, *Instances of Accessory Art* (1880): pl. 4
Michael Whiteway

7.25 a, b, c and d (below) Lewis F. Day. Painted tiles, 1881. From *British Architect* 16 (1881): 414
Paul Reeves

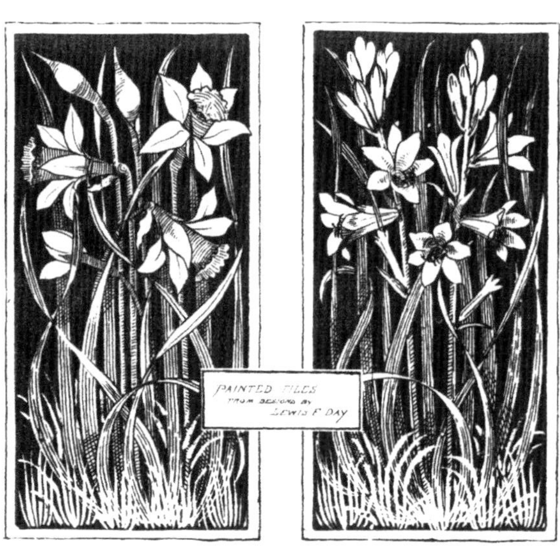

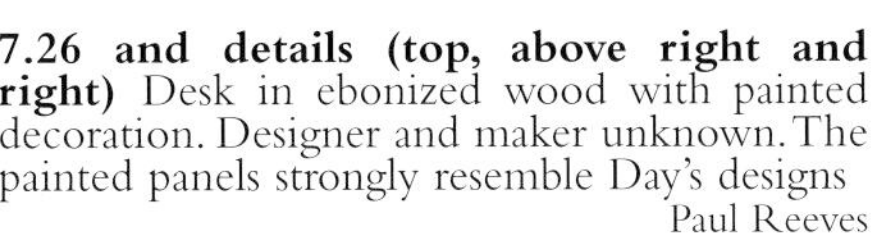
7.26 and details (top, above right and right) Desk in ebonized wood with painted decoration. Designer and maker unknown. The painted panels strongly resemble Day's designs
Paul Reeves

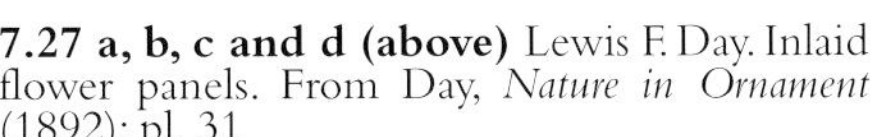
7.27 a, b, c and d (above) Lewis F. Day. Inlaid flower panels. From Day, *Nature in Ornament* (1892): pl. 31

Furniture designed for his family

It is known that Day designed some furniture – including cabinets, hanging shelves, a wall cupboard and sideboards – for members of his family.[29] A mahogany sideboard and two hanging bookshelves were given as a present to his sister-in-law Florence Edith Morrish on the occasion of her marriage to Edmund Strode in October 1880. This cabinet, the lower portion of which is glass-fronted, has six panels with signs of the zodiac painted by George McCullogh and a frieze of daisies and moths, a simplified version of the frieze in his 1879 cabinet design.[30] The bookshelves also incorporate panels with signs of the zodiac. Since the number of zodiac signs in the sideboard and bookshelves totals ten (with Cancer and Sagittarius missing), it is probable that the set originally included one or two other pieces.[31] Day was apparently quite fond of the signs of the zodiac, for he used some of them on tile designs, on an embroidery cabinet in 1888, and in magazine and book illustrations.

Day certainly would have designed some furniture for his own house, and his illustration 'Scheme for Arrangement and Decoration of a Room' probably included some pieces of his own design, in particular the corner cabinet with inset Capricorn panel.[32]

7.28 and detail (above and opposite, top) Lewis F. Day. Sideboard, 1880. Maker unknown. Frieze with inlaid daisies and moths and panels with six signs of the zodiac painted by George McCullogh

Geffrye Museum, London. Photography, John Hammond

7.29 Aesthetic parlour, showing bookshelves designed by Lewis F. Day Geffrye Museum, London

7.30 Lewis F. Day. "Scheme for Arrangement and Decoration of a Room", 1880. From *Magazine of Art* 4 (1881): 185

EMERGING AS A WRITER AND CRITIC

Talking about furniture

For Day, writing about what he did was always as important as the doing of it, and he quickly shared his ideas with the public about the place of furniture in interior schemes. In 1880 and 1881 he penned two series of articles for the *Magazine of Art* that treated various aspects of home furnishing, and the two series were revised and published in 1882 as his second book, *Every-day Art*.[33] This book provides the best single summary of Day's thoughts on furniture at this time, and the basic principles he elucidated remained consistent throughout his career.

As can be seen in his furniture designs of the 1870s and 1880s, Day's own design sources were eclectic, and he was opposed to the imposition of one style as best for home furnishings. Although his vast study of the decorative art of the past had led him to a particular love for the Gothic and Renaissance periods, he was opposed to copying historic forms and insisted that whatever the source of inspiration, the designer should devise his own style.[34] A non-negotiable principle in Day's mind was that whatever the initial inspiration, beauty and usefulness must be combined in furniture design. As was the case with other design critics of the time, including Charles Locke Eastlake, John D. Crace, and Walter Crane, Day spoke of beauty in general terms, citing proportion, scale and propriety of decoration as some of the necessary components.[35]

In agreement with the thinking of A.W.N. Pugin, Day was unambivalent about three characteristics of well-designed furniture: design based on use, sound construction, and freedom from extraneous ornamentation. The overriding principle of design that Day emphasised for all types of applied art was *purpose*: the use to which a piece of furniture would be put dictated its design. His design for a dining room sideboard c.1882 combined the aesthetic components of stylised wood carving and upper and lower figurative panels (the latter featuring his tradesmen figures), with practical features including ample serving, cupboard and drawer space. The piece underscored his contention that a sideboard meant for everyday use should be fit for its purpose and not resemble a "cabinet for 'curios'".[36]

Although no chairs have surfaced that can be positively attributed to Day, he had strong opinions on their design. Since the purpose of a chair was to provide seating, it should not be so lightweight that it was "not to be sat upon by a grown man without danger".[37] Day undoubtedly winced at the thought of lowering his tall frame onto one of the light, spindly occasional chairs that had grown in popularity from the late 1860s. The Sussex range of chairs in ebonized wood with cane seats manufactured by Morris, Marshall, Faulkner & Co. from the 1860s and the Anglo-Japanese side chairs designed by E.W. Godwin c.1875 contrasted with the heavier furniture of the Gothic Revival and spawned imitations by other manufacturers.

Furniture should be soundly constructed, and Day advised that the "expense of good workmanship" would be offset by the savings gained from not buying furnishings one did not really need.[38] Good workmanship cost more but was the best investment – worth far more than "showy manufacture made only to sell".[39] He noted in particular the qualities desired in upholstered furniture: "The chairs and sofa show their framing, and are comfortably padded; they are not overgrown bolsters with iron entrails."[40] He added: "It is a popular superstition to suppose that the most apoplectic-looking chairs are the easiest; but, in truth, it is the form of a chair, and not its padding, that has most to do with its ease."[41] In noting that furniture manufacturers sometimes used padding to hide poor construction, Day likened this to a dressmaker who used the same technique to compensate for lack of a good cut.[42] For the same reason, he was not in favour of wood graining, another deceptive technique that could hide defects in construction.

7.31 Lewis F. Day. Dining room sideboard. From Day, *Every-day Art* (1882): 196

He felt strongly that furniture should also be free of "meretricious" ornament.[43] "As a rule, one may say that the simpler work will be better value than the more elaborate."[44] As was also the case with much of the advice writing by various critics during the period, just what constituted 'meretricious' ornament was never fully defined. For Day it probably meant that all ornamentation should relate to the structure and contribute to a unified, total effect. As an accessory art, decoration fulfilled its purpose when it enhanced or harmonised with the object on which it was used.[45]

Assessing significant developments in furniture design

Day's first foray into exhibition journalism had been his series 'Notes on English Decorative Art in Paris' for the *British Architect* in 1878. Nine years later, the 1887 Royal Jubilee Exhibition in Manchester gave him the chance to pen a sweeping assessment of developments in the decorative arts from the Great Exhibition in 1851 to the fiftieth year of Queen Victoria's reign. In his article 'Victorian Progress in Applied Design' for the *Art Journal*, Day provided a balanced and objective assessment of what had taken place in applied art over the preceding thirty-five years. He noted: "In the department of furniture and decoration, the transitions from style to style, or rather from fashion to fashion, have been more conspicuous than in any other branch of industry."[46] Although his series for the *British Architect* and this article were separated by almost a decade, there was a remarkable consistency in his views about some of the most significant influences on furniture design and manufacture since the Great Exhibition.

A major event was the showing of Sir Rutherford Alcock's collection of Japanese art at the Paris Exposition Universelle of 1867. Day noted the impact of Japanese art: "This fresh Art of Japan was a revelation to all of us", and he added that there were hardly any designers who were not "inoculated more or less with the virus of desire to do likewise".[47] The reaction to things Japanese, "excessive at the time, resulting in a style of Art most un-English", had mellowed by 1887, and the influence of Japan, "now that the fever is past...will affect the design of the near future very favourably; for in workmanlikeness, fitness of treatment, spontaneity, and many other qualities most essential to good ornament, there was everything for us to learn from it".[48] Day's contemporaries also expounded on its influence, among them Christopher Dresser in *Japan: Its Architecture, Art, and Art Manufactures* (1882) and Walter Crane in *Line and Form* (1900).[49]

Day observed that in 1878 in Paris, "nothing was more marked than the influence of Japan upon the exhibits, English and French".[50] Day wrote that next to Thomas Jeckyll, E.W. Godwin was "the most influential convert to Japanese forms" and "an artist of yet higher powers, who accomplished only too little, but who did many things more than well"; he added that Godwin's "Anglo-Japanese furniture, produced by Mr. Watt, set something like a fashion which is not yet extinct".[51] While Day considered the colour scheme of Godwin's exhibit in Paris to be excellent, he had some reservations about the furniture: "If there is a fault to be found with the design of the furniture it is that it is a little too naked in appearance."[52] James McNeill Whistler had assisted Godwin on the decoration of the Butterfly Cabinet, and Day was blunt about what he thought of it. While he thought it cleverly done, it was, "as we might have anticipated, eccentric", and he labelled it "the most frantic specimen of decoration in the furniture of 1878".[53] Other voices in the international chorus of critics criticised the furniture suite as "impractical and flimsy," while yet others praised it for its lightness and elegance.[54]

In his 1887 article Day observed that a real turning point in ideas about furnishing the home was the publication in 1868 of Charles Locke Eastlake's *Hints on Household Taste*: "... one of the few real books on the subject".[55] While Day contended that not all of Eastlake's ideas were original, they were, nevertheless, based on strong convictions and Eastlake did put his own stamp on them.[56] Day attributed Eastlake's greater popularity in America than in Britain to differences in consumer taste: "The fact is the adoption of Mr. Eastlake's principles would consistently involve a recurrence to an altogether simpler and ruder mode of life than finds favour with us."[57] His designs were based on stately and serious examples that when produced looked heavy, and "the mark of the carpenter was too much apparent".[58] Day saw a real incongruity between Eastlake's furniture and current fashions, and since people were not prepared to give up the latter, they gave up the former.[59] Nevertheless, he recognised that Eastlake's teachings would have a long-lasting influence on furniture and particularly credited him with "the suppression of some of the worst and flimsiest forms of upholstery".[60]

Day reserved some of his highest praise for Bruce Talbert, who "for some years made the most decided impression upon the furniture of the period".[61] Not as well-known as others who were less important, Talbert was a "master craftsman" whose *Gothic Forms Applied to Furniture, Metal Work, and Decoration for Domestic Purposes*

(1867) was a valuable resource.[62] While Day thought some of Talbert's work and that of other designers of "quasi Gothic furniture" to be too heavy and characterised by "a too persistent obtrusion of construction", nevertheless he considered "the originality of the design was as marked as its vigour".[63] For Day, the crux of Talbert's excellence as a designer was that he went back to historic examples for inspiration and then adapted them in his own way to produce strong, vigorous work.[64]

7.32 (right) Bruce J. Talbert. Sideboard, 1878. Made by Messrs. Marsh, Jones & Cribb. From *Art Journal* (1887): 185

7.33 (below) Bruce J. Talbert. Sideboard. From *Magazine of Art* 3 (1880): 105

Day was enthusiastic about Talbert's elaborate 'Juno Cabinet', which gained a Grand Prix award for Jackson & Graham at the Paris Exposition in 1878. "There is no elaboration that does not add to the effect – and the result is one of the finest, in my opinion the finest object in cabinet work exhibited at Paris."[65] Despite its massiveness, it "had about it a refinement that reminded one of Greek rather than Gothic Art".[66] Here again Day commented on Talbert's ability to forge from historic inspiration his own style: "The style of the design is what I suppose Mr. Talbert would call 'Old English'. There is much in it that was inspired by Gothic work – something due to Greek influence – and, in the panels at least, something that was learnt from Japan; but it is a complete whole, and although it cannot be catalogued under the head of any historic style it has style – the style of its author."[67] He praised the harmony of the panels with their setting and the "delicacy in the detail that is at times almost Greek", adding that "it does not overstep the limit of consistency".[68]

Day was of the opinion that while Talbert's contribution was significant in wallpaper, textiles and metalwork, his greatest influence was on furniture.[69] He noted Talbert's influence on other designers, including his pupil Henry W. Batley, whose furniture Day seemed to find ingenious, though sometimes rather florid.[70] In observing that Talbert's style was on occasion used and exaggerated by others, Day uttered his famous and tantalising remark: "Talbert was out-Talberted by Mr. Moyr Smith, the most vigourous of his disciples."[71] Regrettably, Day did not say anything further, and the reader was left hanging in suspense as to what he thought of Moyr Smith's work.

Day noted that Talbert also inspired manufacturers, including James Lamb of Manchester. Commending the firm for combining Talbert's influence with their own originality, he added that Lamb "is one of the few provincial cabinet-makers whose name is as well known as that of any of the London firms, and his exhibit at Paris fully sustains his reputation".[72] Day's comments were right on the mark, for the firm had enhanced its reputation in recent decades by securing designs in the 1860s from Charles Bevan for Gothic Revival pieces; for its furniture shown at the international exhibitions in Paris in 1867 and 1878; and for its 'quaint' furniture seen at the Royal Jubilee Exhibition in Manchester in 1887.

While most of the exhibition furniture that Day reviewed was expensive and made for the high end of the market, he did not think that this was the only type worthy of show. Less-expensive furniture served a need, he contested, and there was "no reason why such work should not be represented at an exhibition", provided that the pieces were well-made and useful.[73] Although much exhibition furniture was elaborate, he noted that probably the most desirable furniture for show was something that fell between two extremes: "It is not, on the one hand, ordinary shop work, nor yet is it, on the other, of that extraordinarily elaborate and costly nature that it would be impossible or ruinous to furnish a room up to the same standard."[74]

He highlighted some of Jackson & Graham's work as "simple, sensible and workmanlike, quiet and refined in effect, irreproachable in the matter of taste".[75] Dignified and sober in effect, it was furniture with "which a man of fair means might reasonably furnish his house ... [pieces] you would expect to find in the house of a gentleman, who hated fuss and showiness, but liked to have everything about him thoroughly good".[76] Despite the apparent egalitarianism of this remark, Day was still describing a person who had enough aesthetic education to desire artful furniture and one who, if not rich, at least chose to spend discretionary income on more expensive furniture.

7.34 Lewis F. Day. Embroidery cabinet, c.1888. Oak inlaid with ebony and satinwood and signs of the zodiac painted by George McCullogh. Maker unknown
V&A Images/Victoria and Albert Museum, London, Circ. 349-1955

Remaining involved in furniture design

Designing in the late 1880s

Day had been instrumental in the founding of the Arts and Crafts Exhibition Society, which aimed to improve the state of design and underscore the equal status of the applied arts to architecture and the fine arts. The Society was also founded to provide a means for designers, craftspersons and manufacturers to publicly exhibit their work.[77] At the Society's first exhibition in 1888 at the New Gallery, Day exhibited an

embroidery cabinet, probably designed for his wife and daughter in about 1888. Constructed in oak with inlaid ebony and satinwood, the cabinet featured panels with the twelve signs of the zodiac painted by George McCullogh, who had painted the zodiac panels on the sideboard Day had designed in 1882. The usefulness of the cabinet is seen in the array of small cubicles inside for storing threads and yarns. It may also have had a glazed cupboard or display case that sat on top.[78] Dating to about the same time is a mahogany sideboard featuring a convex mirror and painted panels of fruit and foliage.[79] It is not known where these pieces were made, nor by whom.

From the early 1890s, Day had a very heavy workload as a designer and consultant to industry. His business relationships – particularly those with textile printers Turnbull & Stockdale, wallpaper manufacturer Jeffrey & Co., and Pilkington's Tile & Pottery Co. – left him little time to design furniture himself. His interest was undiminished, however, and he directed his energies to mentoring students and continuing to critique furniture design and manufacture.

7.35 (above) Lewis F. Day. Sideboard, c.1888. Maker unknown. Mahogany, with painted panels of flowers and fruit

V&A Images/Victoria and Albert Museum, London, Circ. 350-1955

7.36 (above right) Lewis F. Day. Panel with dandelion, 1890. From Day, *Nature in Ornament* (1892): pl. 90

Focusing on students

Day produced a number of designs for small accessories such as bellows, frames, and panels for furniture and doors that were executed by students at the School of Art Woodcarving in South Kensington. A number of these pieces, many carved in oak and walnut by Maria E. Reeks, were exhibited at five of the Arts and Crafts Exhibitions in London between 1888-1903 and at the Manchester Arts and Crafts Exhibition in 1895.

Reeks, who was tutored by Day, was first a student-teacher, then, as of 1901, was manager of the School; she became a close friend of the Day family.[80] Two designs dating to 1890, one of oak leaves and acorns and the other of a dandelion, were

illustrated in *Nature in Ornament*, and both were carved into oak panels by Reeks c.1905.[81] The dandelion design could be rendered effectively through carving and provided for the contrasting of plain and carved surfaces "to make the most of the surface of the wood".[82]

Day's rhythmic designs for Comeragh Court – one of panelling for a chimney-piece and the other for a pierced panel in a niche in the overmantel – were executed by student Ellen Dakin and exhibited in 1908 at the Ideal Home Exhibition at Olympia, and photographs of these appeared in the *Builder* in 1909.[83]

Day's relationship with the School of Art Woodcarving extended far beyond providing designs for students. Along with Walter Crane and Sir Edward J. Poynter, who became President of the Royal Academy in 1896, Day served on the Committee of Management.[84]

In response to the School's request to the Society of Arts, in mid-1890 Day gave a series of three evening lectures entitled 'Design Applied to Wood-Carving' to instruct students in design principles as they applied to this medium.[85]

The lectures focused on the importance of system and planning; the arrangement of line and mass, a major requirement for carvers; and reticence and simplicity as antidotes to over-elaboration in design. Day detailed practical issues related to designing in high and low relief for specific applications, including panels, pilasters, columns, friezes, and mouldings. He also advised on the use of devices such as arabesques and grotesques, cartouches, strapwork, and wreaths. He traced the treatment of woodcarving, carpentry and joinery in specific historical periods and showed examples in Gothic, transitional, Renaissance and French styles. While encouraging the study of historic forms, he urged students to adapt them and develop their own style, a quality that he felt was lacking in much of the School's work.[86] Day was not unique in his view that students needed more training in designing for high and low relief. Crane devoted considerable discussion to this subject in *Line and Form*.[87]

Critiquing furniture design in the 1890s

Day continued his magazine journalism well into the 20th century, and some of his most thought-provoking writing on furniture was contained in his reports on the Arts and Crafts Exhibitions of 1893 and 1896. Day was on the Selection Committee for the 1893 Exhibition, and he commented that much of the furniture sent in for exhibit could not be accepted, because it either demonstrated good workmanship but banal design or good design but amateurish workmanship.[88]

7.37 Lewis F. Day. Detail of chimneypiece and niche panelling designed for Comeragh Court, c.1908. Carved by Ellen Dakin. From Day, *Nature and Ornament* 2 (1909): illus. 7

Day contended that furniture design at this point was at a "standstill", "left to languish" between two opposing trends: tradition and novelty. The former was exemplified by "those who have lapsed into dull contentment with time-honoured shapes, no matter what, so they be traditional".[89] Using the excellent photogravures of historic furniture that were readily available, the majority of rival manufacturers followed a safe and economical plan of simply reproducing them, sometimes even advertising the reproductions as "absolute copies of genuine examples" of a particular period.[90] Manufacturers would "resuscitate old forms" based on what was currently in fashion, rather than on the intrinsic merits of the design.[91] Day protested that some old work was not beautiful, and much of that which was "will pass no longer for comfortable or convenient".[92] He noted that reproducing a Chippendale settee with "three chairs 'all in a row,'" was to ignore recent developments "in the direction of ease and material comfort".[93] He opposed mindless copying, and urged that rather than working in imitation of a past period, designers should work in its manner or spirit.

7.38 Catharine Weed Barnes Ward. 'Modern London – The Thames Embankment'. From *Art Journal* (1898): 284

Day observed that even Gillow & Co., who he praised for the "simple and delicate design" of their furniture in the style of François Premier – the period when French design was "at its best" – were also making furniture in the "pretentious" and "frivolous" styles of Louis XIV to Louis XVI.[94] He contended that, while collectors of antique furniture might want some reproductions to fill in gaps in their collections, those persons were few in number and did not justify the production of large quantities of this furniture.[95] Such pieces were "an extravagance in the way of workmanship and finish which, whilst it may suit to perfection the taste of the millionaire, and especially of those who would be taken for millionaires, makes it absolutely impossible to popularise it, for it depends for its charm entirely upon that exquisite execution which must in the nature of things be exceptional".[96] While reviving French styles might be a "commercial expedient" for British firms, it was also a risky business strategy, for if their British customers came to prefer French styles, they might well conclude that they should "go straight to France" for them.[97]

The second trend Day noted in 1893 was the chasing of novelty for its own sake, seen in the work of those "who strain perpetually after some new thing – any new thing".[98] Three years later he complained about the same thing in his two-part coverage of the 1896 Arts and Crafts Exhibition for the *Magazine of Art*. In striving to "leave the rut of convention", one could take a "passion for originality-at-any-price" and "sacrifice all claim to beauty and revel in absolute ugliness"; but for objects to satisfy over the long term, the "the newly-won individuality" must be combined with "a return to the acknowledged canons of beauty".[99] While

Day agreed that simplicity was an antidote to "unconscious and thoughtless" use of ornament, even that had to be done in moderation to produce a pleasing product: "Doubtless, the newly-born passion for simplicity and purity of design has led many members of the society into a self-conscious baldness that has resulted in what is dubbed the 'rabbit-hutch school'."[100]

Overall, Day was a bit more cheerful by 1896, observing that the efforts of the Arts and Crafts movement to foster good design were bearing some fruit: "The exhibition is not only better artistically, it is saner aesthetically than any that have gone before", and this was seen "in a greater reticence than was formerly the case, greater manual skill, more highly-developed fancy and imagination, and a more defined unity of idea and intention".[101] He found a great many examples of stellar work, and among the furniture he singled out as particularly noteworthy were Edgar Wood's simple bedstead; C.F.A Voysey's mantel, fireplace and "quaint and characteristic designs for clock- and barometer-cases"; Mackay Hugh Baillie-Scott's novel Broadwood pianoforte; and W.A.S. Benson's metalware and electric hanging lamp.[102]

Day remained somewhat sceptical, however, about the extent to which furniture, wallpaper, pottery and other objects shown at these exhibitions would influence general manufacture. Although exhibitors including Jeffrey & Co., Turnbull & Stockdale and Liberty & Co. found a significant market for their artful goods, Day questioned whether there would be a trickling down effect to other manufacturers. While such furnishings could be appreciated by persons of taste and judgment, they might have "little effect on the ordinary trades whose hide-bound Unions" pushed standardisation of products "for the equalisation of wages".[103] To compound matters further, both designers and craftsmen were "wholly out of touch" with purchasers, who often did not pay enough attention to the furniture in their homes.[104]

Reflecting on the future of furniture design

Incensed by Art Nouveau

By the turn of the century, Day had not been designing furniture himself for over a decade, though he was unrelenting in his commentary on the state of furniture design and manufacture. By the time of the Paris Exposition Universelle in 1900, Day felt that "of sane and serious recognition of the new century there is very little".[105] He continued to lament the same two trends he had identified in the early 1890s that were retarding the development of good furniture design. "Indeed modern effort takes one of two opposite directions – either it falls back into cowardly exercises in some traditional manner or it runs to rather daring innovations."[106]

Day thought that Art Nouveau exemplified the seeking of novelty for its own sake, and he scathingly attacked the lack of restraint of the French furniture exhibited at the Paris Exposition.[107] He argued that Art Nouveau's revolt against tradition "distinctly recalls the old period of French license", and the exaggerated forms, asymmetry, and lines "without aim or order" resulted in "forms attractive only in the sense that you can't help seeing them, and resenting their self-assertion".[108] He ranted about the disregard for the two qualities he most valued in furniture design: "It is the delirious art of men raving to do something new, oblivious in their rage alike of use and beauty."[109] His disgust was palpable: "And so we have furniture not built on any theory of refined proportion or of constructive fitness, of usefulness or comfort, but deliberately fantastic."[110] He wondered how anyone could want to sleep in beds or sit on chairs with such exaggerated shapes.[111]

It is not surprising, then, that Day strongly opposed acceptance by the Victoria and Albert Museum of the bequest of Art Nouveau furniture by dealer and collector George Donaldson. The bequest was of furniture from France, Germany and other countries that had been exhibited in 1900 at the Paris Exposition. Although he credited Donaldson with "the most generous intentions", Day maintained that the acceptance of the bequest was not in keeping with the mission of "our great storehouse of practical and industrial art".[112] Day roundly criticised the Board of Education – the museum's administrative agency – for deviating from its educational mission of preserving "for our instruction and enlightenment the best that has been done", and for putting this furniture in a prominent place, where impressionable design students could see and imitate it.[113]

This was a particularly sore point for him. In the 1890s and early 1900s Day was very busy teaching and examining student work, and the design principles he emphasised were being contradicted by the very museum to which he took his students to study. He was incensed that Renaissance cabinetwork had been displaced to make room for these "ill-mannered specimens of upstart art" and by the plan of the Circulation Department to send them for exhibit to manufacturing cities around the country.[114] He was not the only critic exorcised over this matter, for discussion raged in the pages of consumer and professional publications including *The Times*, *Manchester Guardian*, *Morning Leader*, *Builder*, *Journal of Decorative Art*, and *Magazine of Art*. Response to the acquisition was overwhelmingly negative, and the furniture was soon exiled to the branch museum at Bethnal Green, where it was exhibited with a warning to students not to copy it.[115]

Reviewing later Arts and Crafts furniture design

Day was relieved that the British work exhibited at Paris was "not so wild, nor yet so willful" as that of the French.[116] In his report on the 1903 Arts and Crafts Exhibition for the *Art Journal* he commented that it was "satisfactory in the interests of sane design that the Society should so plainly have pronounced against the swishing line and other features of the new rococo".[117] However, he was less satisfied with a declining respect for tradition: "The *personal* note is too much insisted upon – as if the temperament of the artist were the one thing caring for, and technique were not of much account."[118] He disagreed with this trend: "It is an axiom in art that the artist should keep himself in the background; and in the Arts and Crafts, which are in their very essence subsidiary, the obtrusion of the artist's personality may very easily become exasperating."[119]

While he fully supported a simplicity that resulted "from the rejection of whatever is redundant or excessive in design", some simple designs lacked "the sense alike of proportion, of scale, and of propriety of decoration".[120] Simplicity of form should be accompanied by beauty and appropriateness for use.[121] Day judged that too much of the furniture was "simple joinery" which, while well-crafted, was "too deliberately archaic".[122] As an example, he mentioned that Voysey's furniture shown at the exhibition looked like it belonged "less to the house than to the outbuildings", and while a designer had

7.39 W.A.S. Benson. Interior of exhibit, Glasgow International Exhibition, 1901. From *Art Journal* (1901): 241 Newberry Library, Chicago

the right to create the kind of furniture he wanted for his own house, Day felt it could well be too extreme for popular taste.[123]

He was not totally discontent with the current state of affairs in 1903, however. While he noted that with the coming of the new century, the work of some established designers was not represented, their place was being taken by lesser known members of the younger generation, some of whom were producing "good designs and excellent workmanship" and were designing for prominent manufacturers.[124] Among the exhibits he praised in his report on the Arts and Crafts Exhibition were E.W. Gimson's "beautifully finished letter cabinet"; C.R. Ashbee's design for a Broadwood piano case, "certainly a more manageable piece of furniture than the awkward harp shape" of the grand piano; and the work of some prominent manufacturers and retailers including Heal & Son and Liberty & Co.[125]

Some of his greatest praise, however, was reserved for W.A.S. Benson, whose work Day regarded highly. He commended Benson's

7.40 George Walton. Interior of exhibit, Glasgow International Exhibition, 1901. From *Art Journal* (1901): 273 Newberry Library, Chicago

display at the 1903 exhibition, saying that his firm "decorated up to their furniture".[126] While he felt Benson's furniture was not quite as comfortable as might be desired, it was "refined and quaint", with "artistic use of metal framing in the glass doors of cabinets and bookcases"; his electric light fittings, more advanced than those of others, "shall strike one as at last obviously the right thing".[127] Noting as well the great vitality of Benson's electric light fittings, Day praised him for work that "hits the mean between art and manufacture".[128]

Looking to Glasgow

Day's five-part series 'Decorative and Industrial Art at the Glasgow Exhibition' of 1901 for the *Art Journal* revealed his belief that some of the most significant work in furniture design was coming from Glasgow. He made passing references to Charles Rennie Mackintosh's individualistic design for the Glasgow School of Art and the work of decorative artists that was "seen to better advantage in the decoration of Miss Cranston's tea rooms in the city than at Kelvin Park".[129] Day looked to other sources, however, for real advancement in furniture design.

He singled out the firm of Wylie & Lochhead, who furnished a series of rooms that showed "the effort that is being made, and made especially in Glasgow, to break new ground in design".[130] In striving for simplicity, they produced furniture "which while the lines are mostly straight up, are distinctly graceful".[131] Day was similarly impressed with the work of architect and furniture designer George Walton. Day included a number of photographs and considerable discussion to Walton's exhibits, and praised him for his simplicity, absence of pretence and his effort to do something new in design.[132] Two years later Day said much the same thing, noting that at the 1903 Arts and Crafts Exhibition, Walton's exhibit had "distinction", demonstrating "elegance in his slender-legged furniture, for the thoroughly good workmanship of which Messrs. Henry and Co. deserve credit".[133] In Day's judgment, these were apt examples of achieving something new while not abandoning tradition, of producing furniture that was useful and beautiful.

Despite examples like these that demonstrated new approaches in blending usefulness and beauty, Day contended that much furniture design still did not achieve a "happy mean" between mindless repetition of historic designs on the one hand and novelty at any price on the other.[134] This happy mean was, in his opinion, what was most desired by the public.[135] While in their boredom with tired examples from the past the public might "welcome some wild freak of decoration", they would soon find it difficult to live with and abandon it, returning "in a more resigned mood to the tame copy of no matter what historic style ... [for] it is possible to live with it".[136]

He contended that a happy compromise could be achieved if both designers and manufacturers used the Arts and Crafts Exhibitions as "an opportunity of trying upon a more advanced public ventures in design for which their customers, perhaps (and certainly their salesmen), are not ready, and the manufacturers themselves do not understand".[137] He added that "one cannot but regret that the efforts of furniture reformers are not more in the direction of supplying the wants of persons not very extreme in their tastes – so that they might have some effect upon production generally".[138]

CHAPTER EIGHT: TEXTILES

"The texture of a material makes all the difference in the kind of pattern appropriate to it."
[Lewis F. Day, 1904]

8.1 Lewis F. Day. 'Daffodils' printed velveteen, c.1888. Made by Turnbull & Stockdale. Block printed V&A Images/Victoria and Albert Museum, London, T.75-1967

Textile design was a major activity for Lewis Foreman Day from the mid-1870s to 1910, and during that thirty-five-year period he produced an astounding number of patterns for silk, wool, cotton, and linen fabrics. They found their way into thousands of homes in England and abroad as curtains, furniture coverings, table linens, carpets and other soft furnishings. Day had business connections with some of the most prominent and innovative textile manufacturers and retailers of the period, and he was friends with many leading contemporary textile designers. As a writer of design textbooks and a journalist, he had a great deal to say about textile design and manufacture. His activities were situated in the changing face of Britain's textile industry.

Textile production, long premier in the British economy, underwent a major transformation in the last quarter of the 19th century. Much of Britain's production of printed and woven textiles – including high-quality worsted, damasks, and silk fabrics – was exported. While in the late 1860s textiles represented 72% of Britain's manufactured exports, that figure had slowly declined to 51% by the eve of World War I, as Britain faced stiffening competition from France, Germany, and the United States.[1]

These competitive pressures, felt from the 1830s, spurred technological developments designed to reduce the time and cost of producing goods. Looms powered by steam were increasingly used to boost output of various types of woven fabrics, particularly for large production runs and contract weaving. Mechanised roller printing made long, high-speed production runs possible and gradually replaced the older method of printing by hand using carved wooden blocks. Chemical dyes, the first of which, a purple, was discovered in 1856 by the Englishman William Henry Perkin from coal-tar, were initially harsh colours that worked well only on silk or wool; further refinements led to better colours and increased dyeing capability for cotton.[2] By the end of the 1880s, only some of the most expensive fabrics continued to be hand printed and vegetable dyed. Many manufacturers who continued to produce hand-woven or hand-printed textiles also produced less expensive machine-made versions to appeal to a larger segment of the market. After 1860, textile manufacturers produced less on speculation and more on commissions from wholesalers and retailers.[3] Through their direct contact with customers, retailers were in a good position to gauge current demand, identify emerging buying trends, and influence future demand.

8.2 (top) William Morris's Merton Abbey Works, Surrey. From Day, 'William Morris and His Art', Easter Art Annual, *Art Journal* (1899): 2

8.3 (bottom) Block printing by hand at William Morris's Merton Abbey Works, Surrey. From Day, 'William Morris and His Art', Easter Art Annual, *Art Journal* (1899): 6

To position himself in this challenging environment, Day used the same strategy as he did for designing wallpaper and tiles. He established himself with firms that produced expensive, hand-made goods; capitalised on the cachet of these commissions to secure additional clients; and then exploited the potential of machine production to produce well-designed furnishings affordable to those of more moderate means. He thus embodied in a microcosm the practice of high-end firms that produced both hand-manufactured and machine-made products to meet various price levels in the market. Day's fascination with textiles permeated his work from the early days in tapestry design through his years as a virtuoso designer of a wide variety of printed and woven textiles, carpets, embroidery and lace. It flowed through his commentary as a journalist and industry critic who identified problems and articulated future directions for the textile industry. Most significantly, as designer, art director and board member with the major textile printing firm Turnbull & Stockdale, Day came closest to the realisation of his dream of a marriage of art and industry.

Day's entrée to textile design

Tapestry

Day began designing textiles in the mid to late 1870s, when firms were gearing up for the Paris Exposition Universelle of 1878. One of the first firms for which he designed – the Royal Windsor Tapestry Manufactory – was a new enterprise trying to make its mark in the revival of hand-woven tapestry manufacture. The firm had been founded in 1876 by H.C.J. Henry, a Frenchman and art advisor to Gillow & Co., who employed some workers from the French Aubusson factory and began producing heavy hand-woven fabrics with rich and complex pictorial designs.[4] The Royal Windsor Tapestry Manufactory and William Morris's works at Merton Abbey on the River Wandle near Wimbledon became major centres that exemplified the revival of interest in tapestry manufacture during this period.[5]

Shortly after the firm's founding, Day supplied a few cartoons, or large-scale drawings, for tapestries. The second recorded tapestry produced by the firm, dated April 1877, bore the arms of Prince Leopold, the first Duke of Albany, youngest son of Queen Victoria and patron of the manufactory.[6] The tapestry – 1ft. 8in. square

(50.8cm.[2]) and woven from Day's design – was presented to Prince Leopold on his 25th birthday, 7 April 1877; it was exhibited at Windsor Town Hall in December 1878, but does not appear to have survived.[7] Day provided at least two other designs, one that commemorated the first exhibition of the company's work held in Windsor Town Hall in December 1878, and the second a heraldic panel, but whether these designs were ever produced is unknown.[8]

There is no evidence that Day designed any of the firm's tapestries exhibited at the Paris Exposition in 1878, though it is clear from his journalistic reports on the exhibition for the *British Architect*, which launched his career as a design critic, that he had quite a bit to say about the firm and the revival of hand-woven tapestry manufacture. The Royal Windsor Tapestry Manufactory won a gold medal at the exhibition for its 'Merry Wives of Windsor' tapestry, and Day praised the "decorative restraint" and "sense of fitness" of the firm's work.[9] He was sceptical, however, about the viability of reviving "such an elaborate and costly style" of furnishing.[10] A surviving catalogue from the Windsor firm lists sofa coverings at £80 and tapestry screens ranging from £115 to £150, unaffordable for an average middle-class family with a yearly income of between £300 and £800.[11]

Day pointed out that, from an aesthetic perspective, the chief merit of old tapestries was the high quality of the drawings produced by talented artists, and present-day painters were unlikely to be attracted to tapestry design when picture painting was much more remunerative.[12] On a practical level, the medieval necessity for tapestries was no longer a factor in contemporary life: "If we want warmth and comfort, some less costly stuff would answer every purpose, and if we want allegory, history, or portraiture, it would be in every way simpler and better to paint upon the wall, on canvas, or on panel."[13]

Day's assessment of the lack of viability of reviving manufacture of hand-woven tapestries was partially confirmed. Although

8.4 Lewis F. Day. Cartoon for tapestry incorporating the Arms of the First Duke of Albany, 1877. Made at the Royal Windsor Tapestry Manufactory, for presentation to the First Duke of Albany
V&A Images/Victoria and Albert Museum, London, E.1034-1925

Morris's Merton Abbey works lasted with limited production until 1940, the Royal Windsor Tapestry Manufactory was beset with financial problems; it ceased production in 1895 and was liquidated in 1904.[14] Day's assessment was also reflected in the direction of his own work. Although he reportedly produced some tapestry designs for the upscale department store Howell & James, specific tapestry designs have not been traced, and Day did not pursue pictorial tapestry design after c.1880.[15]

Early woven textiles

While his work in tapestry design was short-lived, other types of woven textile design occupied him throughout his career. By the time of the 1878 Paris Exposition, Day had designed woven fabrics for William Fry & Co. of Dublin, a manufacturer of woven silk and wool fabrics for curtains and upholstery. Exact details of Day's relationship with the firm are unknown, but in his journalistic reports on the exhibition, Day recounted that he came across the exhibit of one of Fry's

competitors "who have impressed their existence upon me by exhibiting an impudent reproduction of a peacock design of my own, which was made for silk and produced by Wm. Fry & Co., of Dublin".[16] He was highly indignant: "If there had only been a grand gold medal for cool appropriation of other people's designs, what keen competition there would have been among our manufacturers for the honour!"[17]

William Fry & Co. advertised their plain and figured wares as "Art Wares" in keeping with Aesthetic Movement notions that useful household items could also be artistic.[18] The firm's silk damasks, as well as their less expensive silk and wool fabrics (terries) and silk and linens (poplins), were touted in the contemporary press for the quality of the fabric and for the excellence of designs that the firm offered in a variety of natural and conventionalised styles.[19] The firm regularly exhibited at trade and industrial exhibitions and by the early 1870s had won sixteen prize medals, including a first-class medal at the Paris Exposition Universelle in 1867.[20]

As was common practice with many firms of the period, William Fry & Co. was reluctant to disclose the names of its designers.[21] However, in 1880 one of Day's designs received particular attention in the *Architect*, a publication to which he was already well-known. In the interests of reviving the poplin trade in Dublin, the Duchess of Marlborough encouraged firms to submit for her consideration designs for curtains for Dublin Castle.[22] William Fry & Co. submitted the winning design: a heraldic design by Day. The firm also produced it as a silk damask for curtains and coverings at Windsor Castle

8.5 (top left) Lewis F. Day. Heraldic design for curtain, 1880. Made by William Fry & Co. for Windsor Castle. From Day, *Every-day Art* (1882): 141

8.6 (bottom left) Lewis F. Day. Curtain fabric with heraldic design (fragment), 1880. Made by William Fry & Co. for Windsor Castle. Silk damask
National Archives, United Kingdom, BT 44/30 No. 344971

and Osborne House.[23] Patronage from royalty and the aristocracy certainly enhanced a firm's reputation in the industry and also helped a designer to secure additional commissions.

Day used his winning heraldic design in his second book, *Every-day Art*, to emphasise that a designer must constantly bear in mind the relationship of form and colour. "The texture of a material makes all the difference in the kind of pattern appropriate to it," he explained, and noted that "the pronounced pattern of the curtains illustrated, is calculated not to be altogether lost" even in the one-coloured fabric in which it was produced but would "just break the monotony of a flat surface without itself being obvious".[24] Apparently, Day was also engaged by the firm to prepare a special heraldic design for H.R.H. the Prince of Wales, though this design has not been traced.[25]

8.7 Lewis F. Day. 'Old Leno Weave – Corn & Butterflies'. Made by Alexander Morton & Co. Hand-woven Madras muslin. From *Art Journal* (1900): 9
Newberry Library, Chicago

THE VIRTUOSO DESIGNER: WOVEN AND PRINT TEXTILES, CARPETS, EMBROIDERY AND LACE

Woven textiles

Day used these early experiences in textile design and his growing reputation in journalism as a springboard to broaden his client base and to increase his repertoire in designing many types of textiles. In the late 1870s and early 1880s Day extended his client list to include prominent firms located in the north of England and Scotland, major centres of wool production. In 1886 the *Journal of Decorative Art* reported that he designed curtains for several companies that manufactured worsteds, woollens and silks: McCrea of Halifax; Barbour, Miller & Anderson of Glasgow; and Cowlishaw, Nichol & Co. of Manchester, a major contract weaver.[26] However, these designs have not been traced.

During the 1880s and 1890s Day continued to position himself with high-end firms that were responding to consumer demand for diverse styles and innovative fabrics. One of these, Alexander Morton & Co. of Darvel, Scotland, manufactured Madras muslins, chenille curtains, woollen fabrics, double-cloth (two cloths woven as one), and carpets that were retailed by Liberty & Co., Maple & Co., Morris & Co., and Wylie & Lochhead in Glasgow.[27] Founded in the late 1860s, the Morton firm employed their own designers, but also purchased designs from leading figures including Bruce Talbert, Arthur Silver, Harrison Townsend, Heywood Sumner, Lindsay Butterfield, C.F.A. Voysey and Day, whose designs appeared from the 1880s.[28] Many of the firm's samples of these designers' work were destroyed in a fire in 1914, so evidence must be pieced together from surviving examples, references in the contemporary press, and information supplied by descendants of the Morton family.[29]

In commending the firm for the stylistic diversity of its product line, critic James Caw observed that in contrast to Talbert's "Tudor or Early English" designs for the firm, Day's designs of flower and fruit motifs were "managed with a certain freedom and grace, now and then suggestive of Japanese influence".[30] Day's curtain design "Old Leno Weave – 'Corn and Butterflies'" (date unknown) exemplifies the traditional hand-woven Madras muslin that was one of the firm's specialities.[31] Transparent Madras muslins (also referred to as lenos) were soft cotton fabrics, hand-woven on Jacquard looms in natural colours with the opaque pattern woven in colour.[32] Jacquard looms employed a mechanism that used sets of perforated cards to regulate the raising and lowering of warp threads to form patterns, which could be complex and incorporate several colours. Day's design, comprised of a border of cornflowers enclosing a filling with an overall pattern of butterflies flitting among leaves, is well-suited to the light and delicate fabric.

This pattern illustrates Day's expertise in the adaptation of nature to purpose and to designing within the demands and limitations of particular materials. These qualities were recognised by the Mortons, who included two of his books, *Nature in Ornament* and *The Application of Ornament*, in their reference library.[33]

From the 1890s on, Day also produced designs for Arthur H. Lee & Sons (also known as A.H. Lee & Sons). Established c.1888 by Arthur H. Lee, a member of a prominent textile family, the firm was located at Warrington, Lancashire, and from 1904 at Birkenhead, then in Cheshire. The firm manufactured Jacquard-woven wool, silk and cotton fabrics that were used for curtaining, wall hangings, portières, and upholstery. Some of the firm's heavyweight fabrics were further enhanced by colours block-printed by hand. 'Tapestry fabrics' were a speciality of the firm and reflect the extension of the term 'tapestry' during this period beyond its original meaning of hand-woven pictorial fabrics to include "heavy, mainly woollen cloth (machine-made in Britain from the late 1850s) with a warp-faced pattern and also to machine-made pictorial hangings".[34]

The firm secured designs from freelancers including Lee's brother-in-law, the influential architect and designer G. Faulkner Armitage, Walter Crane, A.H. Mackmurdo, George Haité, C.F.A. Voysey and Day.[35] Three woven hangings designed by Day were shown by the firm at the 4th Arts and Crafts Exhibition in 1893 and were singled out in the press as "handsome fabrics".[36] The firm exhibited two of his tapestry fabrics – one in cotton and the other in wool – at the Manchester Arts and Crafts Exhibition in 1895, and a wool tapestry hanging at the 5th Arts and Crafts Exhibition in London in 1896. A surviving tapestry fabric designed in 1904, featuring a Renaissance-inspired ogival structure with interlacing flowers and foliage, is characteristic of the historical reproduction designs that the firm produced around that time.[37] Day frequently sought inspiration from Renaissance textiles for his own designs for woven fabrics, and he included illustrations of some of them in his books.

8.8 Lewis F. Day. Design for woven textile, 1893. From Day, *The Anatomy of Pattern*, 4th ed. (1896): pl. 21

Printed textiles

It is likely that Day designed some printed textiles during the 1870s, but no examples are known to have survived. In the 1880s, however, he designed some patterns for Thomas Wardle & Co., of Leek, Staffordshire, a printer of silk, cotton, wool and velveteen fabrics. The commercial side of Wardle's business was based on modern scientific methods and technology (including synthetic dyes), and its success helped subsidise an experimental workshop, in which vegetable dyes and block-printing were used.[38] Wardle, who printed some of Morris's designs, also purchased designs from Walter Crane, W.R. Lethaby, John D. Sedding, and Day.[39] Wardle marketed his high-quality fabrics through shops including Heal & Son, Howard & Sons, Liberty & Co. and Story's as well as his own shop Wardle & Co. in New Bond Street.[40]

Fascinated by the textiles of the East, Wardle sought ancient and modern Persian and Indian designs and fabrics during his travels. In these and old Italian and Sicilian textiles he found inspiration for his own silks, cretonnes and velveteens.[41] Wardle's printed velveteens became a house speciality, and Day's design for a printed velveteen inspired by "old Persian tiles" reflects the interest in Eastern influences that the two men shared.[42] In this design, floral bands form ogival compartments with central medallions and trailing flowers.

Wardle & Co. exhibited two printed cotton velvets designed by Day at the 1890 Arts and Crafts Exhibition in London. At the Manchester Arts and Crafts Exhibition in 1895, Day's hand-printed velveteens and cretonnes were shown, along with those designed by Crane, Lethaby and others.[43] However, Day's work in printed textiles was dominated by his relationship with Turnbull & Stockdale.

8.9 (top right) Lewis F. Day. Printed velveteen, 1888. Made by Thomas Wardle & Co.
Whitworth Art Gallery, University of Manchester, T.10165

8.10 (bottom right) Lewis F. Day. Printed velveteen, c.1888. Probably made by Thomas Wardle & Co.
V&A Images/Victoria and Albert Museum, London, T.78-1953

8.11 (top left) Lewis F. Day. Design of asters and foliage, 1891. Possibly made as a carpet by Brinton's © Brintons Ltd. With permission

8.12 (top right) Lewis F. Day. Design for 'Bunches' pattern. An accompanying tag, which appears to be in Day's hand, says "two colour reversible 'Bunches'", indicating it may have been intended for a reversible furnishing fabric. Possibly made as a carpet by Brinton's. At the Manchester Arts and Crafts Exhibition in 1895 Jeffrey & Co. exhibited a wallpaper named 'Bunch,' and the catalogue for the exhibition noted that a matching cretonne was available. This may be the same pattern as 'Bunches' © Brintons Ltd. With permission.

8.13 (bottom left) Lewis F. Day. Design of waving stems bearing five-petalled flowers, c.1903. Marked in Day's hand, "Work from other drawings". Possibly made as a carpet by Brinton's © Brintons Ltd. With permission

8.14 (bottom right) Lewis F. Day. Design for pattern "in which the wave-lines divert the eye from the vertical". From Day, *Pattern Design* (1903): illus. 131

Carpets

With surface decoration the major focus of Day's design work, it is likely that he also produced carpet designs. A firm for which he may have designed is John Brinton & Co. of Kidderminster. Founded in 1783, the firm manufactured Brussels, Axminster and Wilton carpets. Brinton's catered to the upper-middle and upper end of the market; its goods were retailed by Maple & Co., Liberty & Co., and probably Heal's, as well as being marketed abroad.[44]

While it was not customary practice for the firm to use outside designers, Christopher Dresser is known to have designed for Brinton's and it is plausible that Day may have, as well.[45] Although the firm's production records, order books and correspondence from this period no longer exist, about a half-dozen designs by Day dating from c.1890-1909 have survived. How these designs were acquired by Brinton's and whether they were produced as carpets are unknown. Some of Day's designs were produced as both textiles and wallpaper, and it is conceivable that the designs in Brinton's possession, which include a couple of patterns that were produced as cretonnes, were also manufactured as carpets. They may have been intended for Wilton carpets, which had a cut pile and a soft, velvety appearance.[46] Due to the large quantity of yarn used in their manufacture on a power loom, Wilton carpets were more expensive than Kidderminster flat-woven carpeting.[47]

In line with a number of contemporaries, Day contended that carpets should not have a directional design that would cause design elements to appear "upside down" from particular vantage points in a room.[48] He also stressed that large surfaces in a room should form a relaxing backdrop for the eye. Day's overall pattern of asters and gently swaying leaves with serrated edges would have met these criteria.

A second design, dating from c.1903 and characterised by free-flowing and sinuous lines suggestive of Art Nouveau, was described by Day as a "pattern in which wave lines divert the eye from vertical", by the device of "carrying the eye alternately from left to right and right to left".[49] An illustration of this was included in *Pattern Design*, where it was identified as a design for printed cotton.[50]

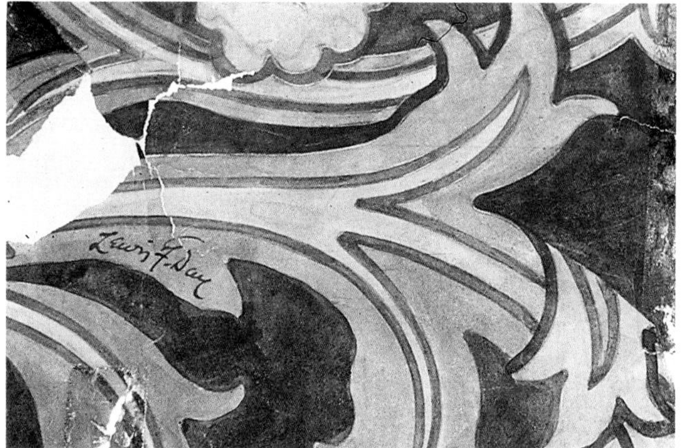

8.15 (top) Lewis F. Day. Detail of design of scrolling leaves and carnation-like flowers, showing signature. Possibly made as a carpet by Brinton's

© Brintons Ltd. With permission

8.16 (bottom) Lewis F. Day. Design of scrolling leaves and carnation-like flowers. Possibly made as a carpet by Brinton's © Brintons Ltd. With permission

8.17 (top) Lewis F. Day. Cabinet panel, "Narcissus compelled into the way of ornament", 1879. From Day, *Nature in Ornament* (1892): illus. 70

8.18 (bottom) Lewis F. Day. 'Narcissi' panel, designed 1879. Cotton sateen embroidered in coloured silks, c.1880 Whitworth Art Gallery, University of Manchester, T.1985.112

Embroidery and lace

Although Day's principal contribution to textile design rests in his patterns for woven and print fabrics that were serially or mass-produced, he also created numerous embroidery designs. He began collecting samples of embroidery from around the world before his marriage in 1873 and continued this practice with his wife, Temma.[51] Day used embroideries as sources of inspiration for his textile and wallpaper designs and also regarded them as worthy examples of applied art in their own right.

Needlework was a popular and creative outlet for women in an era in which they were quite circumscribed professionally and socially. In discussing the capacities of embroidery as applied art, the *Art Workers' Quarterly* observed that "decorative embroidery contains all the necessary elements of Art: it may exercise the imagination and the fancy; it requires education in form, colour, and composition, as well as the craft of the practised hand, to express its language and perfect its beauty".[52] Day was of the same opinion, and his primary interest was on the *design*, which should provide an appropriate structure for high-quality needlework. He stressed that there had to be sufficient quality in the design of the embroidery to justify the hours of labour and the expense of the materials.[53] He included a graceful design for an embroidered panel showing "narcissus compelled into the way of ornament" in *Nature in Ornament*.[54] The original design dates to 1879 and was initially intended for a cabinet panel.[55]

To provide a reference book in which design principles were fused with technical instruction, in 1900 Day co-authored *Art in Needlework* with Mary Buckle, a highly skilled embroideress, as technical advisor.[56] Photographs of items in the Days' collection were included in the book, and some of the stitch illustrations had been exhibited at the 1899 Arts and Crafts Exhibition. Described by the art press as "one of the most practical and most entertaining books on art needlework that have ever been brought before us", the text was praised for its usefulness, technical accuracy, and extensive examples; the book went through three editions by 1907.[57]

Many of Day's embroidery designs were executed by wife Temma, daughter Ruth, and Mary Buckle, as well as friends and relatives; twenty-four of the resulting pieces were exhibited at the Arts and Crafts Exhibitions in London from 1890 to 1906. These screen panels, cushions, fans, doilies, cabinet curtains, chair backs and bed coverings were mostly worked in silk embroidery. An elegant blue and white cushion cover, designed by Day and meticulously hand-embroidered in silks by Temma Day, was exhibited at the 1906 exhibition and featured in the *Art Journal*.[58] In *Nature and Ornament* Day used this as an example of an abstract design in which recognisable characteristics of nature have been removed, but which, nonetheless, "contains suggestions of foliation".[59] This design reflects Day's belief that "excepting in purely geometric pattern, something in the nature of growth is to be desired in ornament, even the most abstract".[60]

Some of Day's embroideries were also shown at the 1904 Louisiana Purchase Exposition in St. Louis in the Lace and Embroidery Court, a collective exhibit of examples from Great Britain and Ireland.[61] Day also produced several designs for lace cuffs and collars. One of these is possibly the collar in Devonshire lace that was executed by the Devon Cottage Lace Industry and exhibited at the 1910 Arts and Crafts Exhibition.[62]

8.19 (top right) Lewis F. Day. Cover, *Art in Needlework* (1900)

8.20 (above, left) Lewis F. Day. Crewelwork in pattern of scrolling foliage, flowers and butterflies. Embroidered by Temma Day in crewel stitch in twisted silk, 1890s. From Day and Buckle, *Art in Needlework* (1900): illus. 15

8.21 (above, centre) Lewis F. Day. Conventional ornament in embroidery. Probably embroidered by a relative or friend. From Day, *Nature and Ornament 2: Ornament the Finished Product of Design* (1909): 6

8.22 (above, right) Lewis F. Day. Needlework with heart shapes and flowers. Embroidered by Mary Buckle in satin stitch and fine cording, 1890s. From Day and Buckle, *Art in Needlework* (1900): illus. 93

8.23 (right) Lewis F. Day. Cushion cover. Embroidered by Temma Day, c.1906. From Day, *Nature and Ornament 2: Ornament the Finished Product of Design* (1909): 10

8.24 (below) Lewis F. Day. Honiton lace collar, c.1900. Possibly the example worked by the East Devon Cottage Lace Industry and shown at the 9th Arts and Crafts Exhibition in 1910

V&A Images/Victoria and Albert Museum, London, T.82-1946

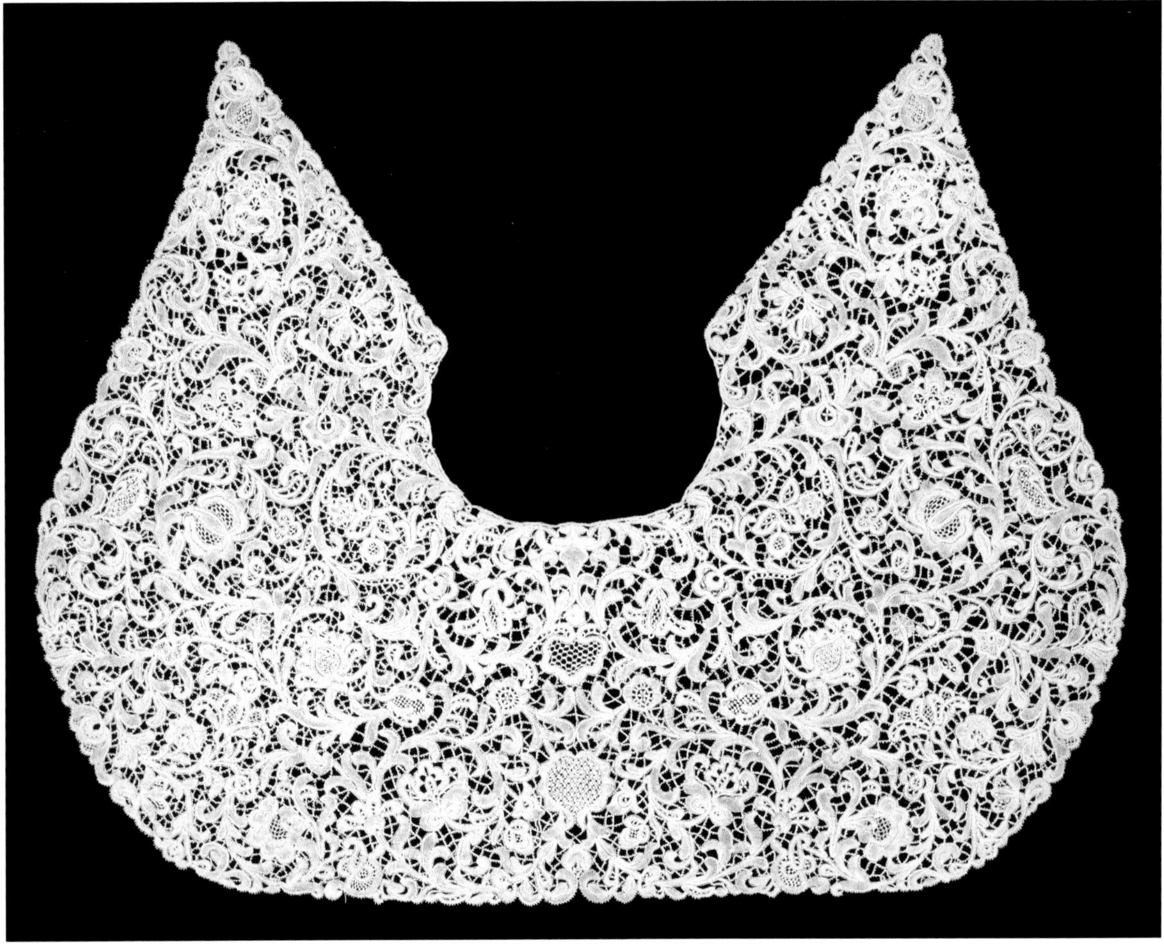

The journalist & critic: Day's assessment of the linen damask industry

Lamenting the look of linens

As a prolific journalist and author of textbooks, Day commented on many aspects of textile design and production. An issue that particularly vexed him was the state of the linen damask weaving industry, and he devoted considerable efforts as a critic, designer and consultant to addressing industry problems. In his 1887 article 'Victorian Progress in Applied Design', which coincided with the Royal Jubilee Exhibition, he referred to linen damask weaving as one of the "most conservative of industries".[63] His opinion had not changed eight years later, when he described it as one of those industries "which seem to be persistently conservative, to lag behind in the race for artistic development, and to be content always with models which might have done duty for design a generation or two ago".[64] Other critics agreed with Day: design educator George Trobridge commented in the *Magazine of Art* that "damask weaving has perhaps been less influenced by the recent renaissance of decorative art than almost any other branch of manufacture".[65]

Male and female critics alike blamed the lack of progress in the industry on two parties: women and manufacturers. While architects and decorative artists influenced taste in interior decoration and furniture, the arbiter of taste in household linen was the housewife, who was content with familiar old patterns.[66] Many of these patterns were fussy designs, with consumers favouring roses, ivy, ferns and scenic designs with shading, relief and perspective that made them look "realistic".[67] Such designs disregarded "the obvious propriety of flat design for tablecloths and the beauty resulting from well-balanced distributions of warp and weft".[68] Critic Rosa Crandon Gill echoed these remarks, advising that "the cloth's pattern ought not to represent depth beyond depth, or lifelike things in the round" and that flowers and animals "should be wholly or semi-conventionalised".[69] Manufacturers were faulted as well, for they catered to consumer preferences for fussy patterns rather than trying to shape public taste by offering linens with appropriate designs.[70]

One firm that Day publicly exempted from these criticisms was John Wilson & Sons, and Day's design work for the firm – along with his writings and consulting work – reveal his determination to help improve matters.[71] John Wilson & Sons of Bond St. (and later Regent St.) was a retailer of a wide variety of household linens, including damask tablecloths and napkins, lace window hangings, Madras muslins and stencilled cloths. John Wilson was a highly respected designer, and he and his firm were frequently singled out in the art press for their commitment to product excellence.[72] Day viewed John Wilson & Sons as an industry leader that would help lift linen manufacture "out of the slough of commonplace".[73]

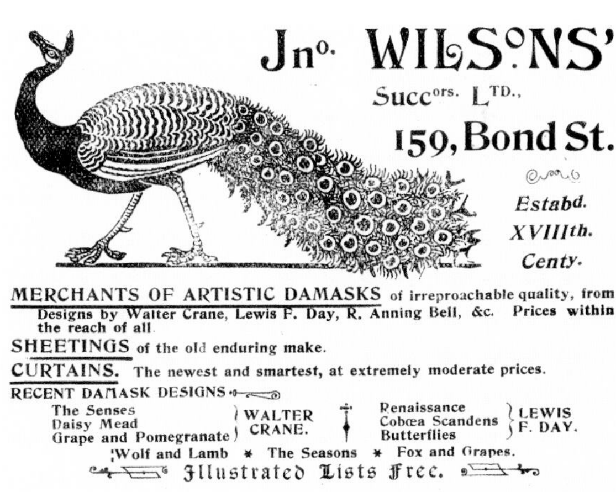

8.25 John Wilsons' Successors Ltd. Advertisement. From Day, 'William Morris and His Art', Easter Art Annual, *Art Journal* (1899): inside front cover. In 1899 the firm changed its name from John Wilson & Sons to John Wilsons' Successors Ltd.

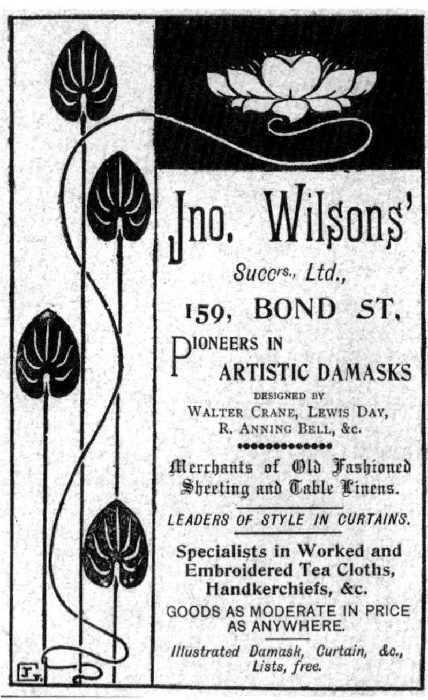

8.26 (top) John Wilsons' Successors Ltd. Advertisement. From *Royal Academy Pictures* (1899): inside front cover

8.27 (bottom) Walter Crane. 'The Senses' tablecloth, c.1891. Made by John Wilson & Sons. Linen damask. From Walter Crane, 'The Work of Walter Crane'. Easter Art Annual, *Art Journal* (1898): 25

Most of the firm's damasks were woven in Belfast on Jacquard looms, which employed a mechanism using sets of perforated cards to regulate the raising and lowering of warp threads to form patterns. Complex patterns and intricate designs required the cutting of many hundreds of cards, thereby making such designs expensive.[74] Less expensive goods could be produced by making one group of cards control several sets of threads to repeat a portion of the design or by using existing sets of cards in different combinations.[75] The firm's more expensive fabrics were produced on hand-looms, while others were machine-made.[76] By offering various price levels of goods, retailers could appeal to a larger market. Enticed into shops by the promise of less expensive goods, some customers could be converted to the more expensive lines.[77]

Day's designs for John Wilson & Sons

While John Wilson & Sons claimed roots in the 18th century and revered tradition, it commissioned designs from prominent figures of the day, including Christopher Dresser, Walter Crane, R. Anning Bell and Day, whose work for the firm spans the 1890s to the early 1900s. In contrast to firms who wished to keep their designers' names a secret, Wilson's capitalised on the cachet of these connections and used their names in advertisements.[78] The firm astutely marketed their goods by appealing simultaneously to the consumers' respect for tradition and their desire for the latest patterns from leading designers.

Reports on John Wilson & Sons's products in the *Art Journal* in the 1890s and 1900s captured the stylistic diversity in table linens that helped the firm satisfy consumers' varying tastes. One design, by Dresser, incorporated owls and storks.[79] Bell's 'A Midsummer Night's Dream' featured human figures and fairies in a tribute to Shakespeare. Crane's 'The Five Senses', regarded by Day as "a *tour-de-force* in damask", included human figures, animals and birds.[80]

Day's designs were usually inspired by nature, as exemplified in his 'Thistle Centre', which incorporated a border and centre of intricate scrolling leaves and thistles. This pattern was also available with a secondary border of strawberries and leaves.[81] Day included an illustration of a very similar strawberry border in *Nature in Ornament* and described it as one in which the characteristics of the plant had been retained while conventionalising it to suit the purpose of ornament.[82] The designs of Day, Crane and Bell were woven on handlooms.[83]

A lustrous, high-end fabric, linen damask carried connotations of gentility and refinement. The flax fibre from which it was woven was also strong and could withstand vigorous use and many washings, an indispensable requirement for table linens. Day strongly recommended a flat, simple, bold pattern that displayed the fine textural quality of the fabric, the feature that the connoisseur of table linen most appreciated.[84] Bold patterns with broad surfaces would provide contrast to large areas of plain ground.[85] Since the gloss of the flax fibre reflected light in different ways, depending on the direction in which the rays fell, several contrasting shades would result, thus making the most of the rich body of the linen.[86]

Day's table-cloths and napkins possessed "every feature that a cloth in general use should have, as there is none of that fussiness which decorators know as a 'busy' pattern", Rosa Crandon Gill observed.[87] In the 1890s, table linen patterns in Renaissance styles were popular, and Day drew on that period for inspiration for his 'Renaissance Wreath' tablecloth and serviette, which featured scrolling foliage and leaves with turn-over treatment.[88] Serviettes, which measured 21in. by 31in. (53.3cm. x 78.7cm.), had the same pattern as the tablecloth, though with only one border, the middle often being a combination of the cloth's filling and other border.[89] In this pattern, the centre of the serviette is a combination of the scrolls and leaves of the border, with little festoons repeated from the cloth's filling. This may have been the design exhibited by the firm (by then renamed John Wilson's Successors Ltd) in 1899 at the 6th Arts and Crafts Exhibition.

8.28 (top) Lewis F. Day. 'Thistle Centre' tablecloth. Made by John Wilsons' Successors Ltd. Linen damask. From *Art Journal* (1905): 189 Newberry Library, Chicago

8.29 (bottom) Lewis F. Day. Design for tablecloth. Made by John Wilson & Sons. Linen damask. From *Magazine of Art* 24 (1900): 10

8.30 (top left) Lewis F. Day. 'Renaissance Wreath' Serviette, c.1891. Made by John Wilson & Sons. *Art Journal* (1891): 179 Newberry Library, Chicago

8.31 (bottom left) Lewis F. Day. 'Ornamental Lily' doilies, 1890s. Made by John Wilson & Sons. Silk and linen damask
Geffrye Museum, London, 0441-6, Box 38

8.32 (below) Lewis F. Day. Design for 'Coboea Scandens', c.1891. Made by John Wilson & Sons. Linen damask. From Day, *Nature in Ornament* (1892): pl. 89

Day included an illustration of another pattern, 'Coboea Scandens', a loose arrangement of the cup-and-saucer vine, in *Nature and Ornament*. He pointed out that while the plant would grow that way, he made it conform to the requirements of the Jacquard loom and chose details that would be produced in two textures upon the ground, adding that "the form goes about as far in the direction of nature as I am personally inclined to go".[90]

While Wilson's contention that their goods were "within the reach of all" is a classic example of advertising hyperbole, some of Day's designs were cited in the art press as affordable to a broader consumer base. For example, nearly all his designs for tablecloths could accommodate insertion of a monogram or coat-of-arms.[91] This eliminated the expense of having an entire cloth designed new, which could cost upwards of £80 due to the large number of cards that would need to be cut for its weaving on the Jacquard loom.[92] Three of his all-over fruit patterns, which featured pomegranates, filberts, and olive branches, were described as moderately priced, though no prices were quoted.[93] An undated marketing brochure from Wilson's

8.33 John Wilson & Sons. Advertisement. From Easter Art Annual, *Art Journal* (1897): inside front cover

containing an article written by Day on Crane's 'The Five Senses' tablecloth, also advertised Crane's 'Flora's Retinue' doilies and Day's 'Ornamental Lily' doilies at 18s. 6d. a dozen in white or coloured silk and linen damask.[94]

Day was recognised as a designer who had a thorough knowledge of the requirements of the material, methods of production, and the product's use.[95] From his early days as a designer, he was fascinated by the intricacies of damask design and stimulated by its production challenges. He always insisted that, no matter what the task, the designer should accept the conditions of a situation, figure out what needed to be done, and make the challenges work in one's favour.[96] "The reversing or folding over of the pattern (necessitated, if not by the Jacquard loom, by its economic use) places, of course, some restriction upon the designer; but it is the business of the designer to adapt himself to conditions."[97]

The designer was required to produce a precise drawing of the pattern, because the design would be transferred to squares on point paper and then programmed into the loom. Although the design might appear harsh on paper, when it was produced, the sheen of linen damask would soften the forms.[98] Bearing in mind that the fabric would be produced to fit tables of various sizes, the designer had to use ingenuity in providing supplementary sections that co-ordinated with the original panel.[99] While some might balk at these demands, Day brooked no complaints: "A designer, whatever his natural gift, is of no practical use until he is at home with the conditions of manufacture."[100]

Neither Day nor his fellow-critics believed that the old patterns would disappear quickly from manufacturers' pattern books.[101] While he admitted that some people might think "it is a waste of energy" to spend so much effort on designing "a mere dinner cloth", Day insisted that frequently used household articles should be worth looking at, a view shared by other Arts and Crafts designers.[102] "It is only from such efforts as this that we can look for any impetus in the direction of improved design in damask."[103]

Day and other industry critics recognised that unless new designs were also commercially successful, manufacturers would keep relying on old ones, to the detriment of Britain's domestic and export trade.[104] His expertise was well-recognised in the weaving centre of Belfast. Prompted by the need for high-quality damask designs that were also commercially successful, in 1899 the Belfast Government School of Art conducted student competitions, with substantial prizes funded by local firms. Day served as judge for some of these and gave two public lectures on design, "which aroused a considerable amount of interest".[105]

REALISING THE DREAM: DESIGNER, ART DIRECTOR AND BOARD MEMBER WITH THE TEXTILE PRINTING FIRM TURNBULL & STOCKDALE

Lewis F. Day's long association with the textile printing firm Turnbull & Stockdale was one of the most important business relationships of his career. His prolific design work for the firm represents the bulk of his *oeuvre* in printed textiles. In his multiple rôles, he helped the firm – a late-comer to the Lancashire cotton trade – become a leading manufacturer of printed textiles. While Day accrued financial benefits from the relationship for twenty-five years and secured a wide distribution of his own work in Britain and abroad, he also developed a valued friendship with William Turnbull and learned much from him.[106] Most importantly, Day's relationship with Turnbull & Stockdale embodied his major professional preoccupation: the marriage of design and industry. As he put it: "The best work of all can not be arrived at until the artist and manufacturer are convinced that their interest is one."[107]

The early days

The last quarter of the 19th century and the early years of the 20th century saw increased popularity and demand for household furnishings made from cretonnes (a term applied in this period to all types of printed cottons), velveteens, and new reversible fabrics. Seizing this opportunity, in September 1881 William Turnbull founded W. Turnbull and Company in Bury, Lancashire, to produce machine-printed textiles. Turnbull's family had been calico printers for generations, and by the age of thirty he already had a great deal of practical experience in cotton printing. Turnbull read the writings of John Ruskin and Thomas Carlyle and greatly admired William Morris and other figures of the Arts and Crafts movement.[108] Recognising that a thorough knowledge of chemistry was absolutely essential to "do for machine printing what William Morris had already begun to do for hand work", he pursued studies in chemistry while continuing to work.[109]

In September 1882, Turnbull entered into a partnership with William Stockdale, a close friend and fellow student who was a strong mathematician and an astute businessman.[110] The commission side of the business, through which the firm bleached, dyed and printed the dress and shirt fabrics of other firms, helped finance the merchant side, the firm's own "distinctive artistic and decorative fabric line".[111] The fledgling company, now renamed Turnbull & Stockdale, adopted the corporate philosophy of producing "something better" than products currently on the market.[112] This strong commitment to both technical excellence and high-quality design became a hallmark of the firm.

8.34 Photo of Turnbull & Stockdale Mill, Doctor's Lane, Bury, 1881-85. From Turnbull & Stockdale, *Jubilee* (1931): 12

The decision to secure Day's services soon after the firm's founding was one that critically affected its future growth. Players in a highly competitive market, Turnbull & Stockdale sought to establish its corporate identity and protect its product line by registering a number of its designs, beginning in early 1884. Day's 'Victorian Renaissance' design, an elaborate combination of vase, candelabrum and grotesque motifs, was the first registered.[113] His professional connections undoubtedly helped the firm make a high-profile entrance into the marketplace: the fabric was retailed by the prestigious department store Howell & James of Regent St., for whom he had designed since the early 1870s, and was featured in the *Furniture Gazette*, which regularly covered his work.

The key to the firm's expansion was innovation in the development of new forms of printed textiles, including reversibles, indigo discharge, rainbow and fadeless fabrics. By 1885 the firm had outgrown the original plant in Bury and moved to nearby Stacksteads, where a dyeing plant was added and manufacturing capabilities were increased.[114] The firm installed a duplex machine for printing reversible fabrics and in 1885 registered its first reversibles, including a design by Day.

A member of the team

An important milestone occurred c.1888-1889 when Day became the firm's art director, a rôle that both he and the firm publicised.[115] He was, undoubtedly, thrilled by this appointment, for while in his 1887 article 'Victorian Progress in Applied Design' he credited the firm for the excellence of their reversible fabrics, he added that many of them were "too directly inspired by Japan".[116] From this point on, Day supervised the creative output and helped ensure a unified and distinctive product line.[117] Around the same time, a department for hand block printing was opened and the firm's product line expanded.

Turnbull & Stockdale exhibited at the first Arts and Crafts Exhibition in 1888, clearly reinforcing their position as a textile manufacturer of artistic goods alongside Morris & Co., Thomas Wardle, and Templeton & Co. of Glasgow. Since Day had been intensely involved in the formation of the Arts and Crafts Exhibition Society and on the Selection Committee for the 1888 Exhibition, he would have been highly influential in the firm's presence there.

In addition to positioning itself at high-profile events such as this, the firm helped offset the disadvantage of being a late-comer to the textile printing industry by

8.35 Lewis F. Day. 'Victorian Renaissance' furnishing fabric, 1884. Made by Turnbull & Stockdale and retailed by Howell & James. From *Furniture Gazette* 22 (1884): ff. 356

offering consumers a wide selection of machine-printed and hand block-printed fabrics. Product diversity was achieved by capitalising on Day's own enormous versatility, along with using freelance designers with very different styles. The firm bought designs from a number of prominent designers including C.F.A. Voysey, Lindsay Butterfield, Harry Napper, Sidney Mawson, Alfred Carpenter, and possibly Christopher Dresser.[118]

When the firm became a limited company in 1892, Day was given a seat on the Board of Directors, a highly unusual and very formal recognition of the importance of creative direction to corporate success.[119] This appointment also enabled him to increasingly influence

8.36 a and b C.F.A. Voysey. Textiles. From 'Cretonnes, Printed Velvets and Linings', Turnbull & Stockdale sample book, c.1892-5

Nordiska Museet, Stockholm
Erik Folcker Collection, 313.052

production techniques and marketing, as well as to direct product design. Day firmly believed that the designer should not view himself as autonomous, but should work with others as a member of the manufacturing team, and this appointment was the ultimate realisation for him of that belief.[120]

The combined talents of Turnbull, Stockdale and Day became a potent mix for the further development of the technical, business, and creative aspects of the firm. Having outgrown the Stacksteads premises, in 1896 the firm purchased Rosebank Printworks at Ramsbottom, operating the two sites concurrently until 1906, when all the operations were consolidated at the expanded Rosebank facility.[121] A dye-works was added in 1900, a weaving shed in 1908, and in 1910 the firm produced its first 'fadeless' dyed fabrics.[122]

The firm's technical and creative advances were accompanied by expansion of distribution, marketing, and promotion. In 1892 Turnbull & Stockdale contracted with William T. Bennett to be its London agent and help expand distribution options.[123] The firm also secured marketing representatives in other British cities, including Manchester, Birmingham and Glasgow, as well as in major cities in Europe and around the world. A number of high-quality shops and department stores carried the firm's textiles, and Turnbull & Stockdale became contract printers to Heal's, Maple's, Goodyer's and Liberty & Co.[124] The variety and high quality of their fabrics frequently garnered favourable press coverage for the firm.[125]

As art director, Day supervised Turnbull & Stockdale's exhibits at major trade and industrial exhibitions at home and abroad. The firm also energetically promoted its fabrics at the Arts and Crafts Exhibitions held in London and the Manchester Arts and Crafts Exhibitions in 1891 and 1895. Of particular importance was the Paris Exposition Universelle in 1900, where the firm won gold and silver medals for its block-printed and machine-printed furnishing fabrics including cretonnes, printed

8.37 Irwell Bank Print Works, Stacksteads, in operation from 1886-1906. From Turnbull & Stockdale, *Jubilee* (1931): 12

8.38 (above) Photo of Lewis F. Day, early 1900s. From Turnbull & Stockdale, *Jubilee* (1931): 26

8.39 (top right) Photo of Rosebank Print Works, in operation from 1896. From Turnbull & Stockdale, *Jubilee* (1931): 16

8.40 (centre right) Chatterton weaving shed, in operation from 1908. From Turnbull & Stockdale, *Jubilee* (1931): 34

8.41 (bottom right) Turnbull & Stockdale's sales room at Roxburghe House, Regent St., London. From Turnbull & Stockdale, *Jubilee* (1931): 48

velveteens, and sateens.[126] At the St. Louis Exposition in 1904, the firm's printed hangings graced the entrances to the Royal Commission exhibit.[127] Day directed the creative side of the business until sometime in the early 1900s. By 1914 (four years after Day's death) William Turnbull's second son, also named William, had assumed the artistic directorship.[128]

Day's designs for Turnbull & Stockdale

Day produced scores of designs for the high-quality cretonnes, reversible fabrics and printed velveteens for which Turnbull & Stockdale became known. He drew inspiration from nature, historic ornament and the cultures of the East, and he was unapologetically eclectic. His excellent draughtsmanship, facility in using different methods for organising a pattern, and his thorough knowledge of production techniques reveal his skills as a designer and illustrate his value to Turnbull & Stockdale.[129] While remaining within the mainstream of textile design of the period, Day created designs that satisfied diverse tastes in the marketplace.

8.42 **(top left)** Lewis F. Day. Cover, 'Cretonnes, Printed Velvets and Linings', Turnbull & Stockdale sample book, c.1892-5

Nordiska Museet, Stockholm, Erik Folcker Collection, 313.052

8.43 **(bottom left)** Lewis F. Day. Renaissance-inspired design printed on cotton repp, 1898. Made by Turnbull & Stockdale. Machine-printed. From *Art Journal Supplement*, Paris Exhibition 1900 (1900): 346

Angela and Barry Corbett

Day particularly drew inspiration from the Gothic and Renaissance periods for examples of how natural forms were adapted to purpose while retaining the life in them.[130] Day's first registered design was inspired by the Renaissance, and he designed a number of patterns with formal repeats that drew their inspiration from 15th- and 16th-century textiles. In the example above, stylised plants are arranged in a formal turn-over that repeats twice in the width. It was produced as a two-colour machine-printed cotton and was exhibited at the Paris Exposition of 1900.[131]

Like William Morris, whom he greatly admired, Day's textile designs in the 1880s and 1890s often incorporated scrolling foliage.[132] His ability to disguise repeats – which he admitted was a very difficult thing to do – is illustrated by one of his best-known roller-printed cottons of the period, 'The Grotesque', which features a mythical creature metamorphosing into swirling foliage.[133] Day, who did not favour the use of animals in repeat pattern because they were difficult to conventionalise without losing their character, was fond of grotesques because they allowed him to blend fanciful creatures with foliage to suit the purposes of his design.[134] Designed in 1886, the fabric was probably shown at the first Arts and Crafts Exhibition in 1888 and was also produced as a reversible fabric. Several of Day's designs, including the 'Grotesque', were illustrated in the *Art Journal* in 1891, which commented: "Mr. Lewis Day does not rush to meet every new fashion, but tries to produce designs of intrinsic merit."[135]

Turnbull & Stockdale became well-known for pioneering duplex fabrics, which featured the pattern printed on both the face and back of the cloth, making it reversible. In one design (plate 8.48), the reversibility of the fabric is echoed by the leaves in the pattern, which are patterned on both sides. Inspired by 15th- and 16th-century Gothic work

8.44 (opposite, top right) Lewis F. Day. Printed cotton, 1888. Made by Turnbull & Stockdale. Roller printed

V&A Images/Victoria and Albert Museum, London, T.16-1954

8.45 (opposite, bottom right) Lewis F. Day. Printed cretonne, 1907. Made by Turnbull & Stockdale. Machine printed

Whitworth Art Gallery, University of Manchester

8.46 (top right) Lewis F. Day. Pattern of small snails and vine leaves diapered "with arabesque in the place of veining". Made by Turnbull & Stockdale. From Day, *Nature in Ornament* (1892): pl. 61; 125

8.47 (bottom right) Lewis F. Day. 'Grotesque' printed cotton, 1886. Made by Turnbull & Stockdale. The firm registered this 28 Dec. 1889 as a duplex reversible fabric (BT50/112 #117343). Reproduction, renamed 'Wyvern', by Watts of Westminster

Paulo R. DeAndrea, PRD Photography

8.48 (top) Lewis F. Day. Reversible cretonne. Pattern 903-09 in 'Cretonnes, Printed Velvets and Linings', Turnbull & Stockdale sample book, c.1892-5
Nordiska Museet, Stockholm, Erik Folcker Collection, 313.052

8.49 (above) Lewis F. Day. 'Daffodils' cretonne. Made by Turnbull & Stockdale, c.1892-5
Nordiska Museet, Stockholm, Erik Folcker Collection, 317.518+ and 312.595

8.50 (left centre) Lewis F. Day. Design for printed velvet. From Day, *Pattern Design* (1903): illus. 125

8.51 (left) Lewis F. Day. Design for printed velvet "with colour in broad masses". From Day, *Ornament and Its Application* (1904): illus. 36

8.52 (opposite, top) Lewis F. Day. 'New Dot' printed cotton, c.1898. Made by Turnbull & Stockdale. Indigo discharge and roller printed
V&A Images/Victoria and Albert Museum, London, T.17-1954

8.53 a and b (opposite, bottom) Lewis F. Day. Cretonne, c.1890. Pattern 964-70 in 'Cretonnes, Printed Velvets and Linings', Turnbull & Stockdale sample book, c.1892-5
Nordiska Museet, Stockholm, Erik Folcker Collection, 313.052

that featured the turning over and curling of the edges of foliage, Day elaborated on nature, incorporating leaves "enriched with patterns which take the place of natural veining".[136] This pattern was available in seven colourways.

Printed velveteens were popular during the 1880s and early 1890s, and as critic Aymer Vallance commented about English fabrics, "in respect of decorative composition we have no need to fear being out-done".[137] Day designed a number of printed velveteens with conventionalised floral patterns. 'Daffodils', dating from c.1888, featured clusters of blooms arranged in a drop repeat; it was exhibited at the Paris Exposition of 1900 and was also available as a cretonne.[138]

One of the firm's specialities was indigo discharge printing, by which indigo-dyed fabric was either block printed or roller printed with a bleaching paste that removed the dye from the ground to form a pattern. Subsequently, additional colours could be printed on the fabric. Day felt that discharge printing posed some specific challenges to the designer. While the process could produce deep rich colours, it could also result in some impurities that would show on broad surfaces: "Hence the narrow lines and dots so familiar in discharged prints."[139] Day warned designers to be aware of conditions and problems like this that could arise during the production process and affect the original plan.[140] He often made notes on his designs, giving specific directions for their manufacture. Day's 'The New Dot', with its delicate filigree of leaves and tiny blossoms superimposed over a background of tiny dots, was well-suited to the indigo discharge method of printing and was shown at the 1900 Paris Exposition.[141]

Some of Day's textile designs from the 1890s on show an increased emphasis on flowing lines and sinuous stems, stylistic characteristics usually associated with Art Nouveau, a movement that Crane

referred to as "that strange decorative disease" and Day called the "new artistic revolt against order".[142] Day used undulating lines of natural forms in his pattern for a printed velveteen featuring a swirling trumpet-like flower, a form that evidently interested him because he also used it as a key element in a tile panel produced by Maw & Co., c.1887.[143] The design was also produced as a cretonne, available in seven colourways. It was illustrated in the *Art Journal* and in Julius Hoffmann, Jr.'s *Für das Kuntsgewerbe* [*For the Arts and Crafts*], "one of the first German publications dealing with what were then called the modern naturalistic styles".[144]

8.54 (above) Lewis F. Day. 'Tulip Tree' cotton, 1903. Made by Turnbull & Stockdale. Roller printed
V&A Images/Victoria and Albert Museum, London, T.23-1954

8.55 (left) Lewis F. Day. Tulip frieze. From Day, *Nature in Ornament* (1892): pl. 85

Photographs and illustrations in the late 1890s and early 1900s reveal a revival of interest in patterns inspired by 16th- and 17th-century crewelwork embroideries, following the general trends of the period. Designing this type of pattern was second nature to Day, with his thorough knowledge of historic embroideries. His English crewelwork patterns manufactured in printed linen were exhibited by the firm at the St. Louis Exposition in 1904 and the 8th Arts and Crafts Exhibition in 1906.[145]

In response to changes in consumer taste around the turn of the century, some of the firm's fabrics illustrate the move to simplification in design that characterised interior schemes at that time. Day's 'Tulip Tree' design was in keeping with this trend. The loose, meandering arrangement of stylised stems, leaves and flowers was given added interest by its rendition in shaded tones of gold, red, blue and green.

Turnbull & Stockdale was a contract printer to Liberty & Co., and in the early 1900s Day designed some patterns that were retailed exclusively by the store under its own name. Two of these patterns drew their inspiration from Eastern textiles: 'Agra', an airy design in delicate hues, and 'Indian', an exuberant pattern based on 18th-century Indian chintz. His floral design of the same period reflects the enduring popularity of patterns inspired by English gardens.

8.56 (top left) Lewis F. Day. 'Old English' printed linen. Made by Turnbull & Stockdale. From *Studio Yearbook* (1907): 158 Newberry Library, Chicago

8.57 (bottom left) Lewis F. Day. Floral design, 1908 © Liberty PLC. With permission

8.58 (top right) Lewis F. Day. 'Agra' printed cotton, c.1905-6. Made by Turnbull & Stockdale for Liberty & Co.
Whitworth Art Gallery, University of Manchester, T.1986.23

8.59 (centre right) Lewis F. Day. 'Blue Bramble' printed cotton, 1901. Made by Turnbull & Stockdale
Arthur Sanderson Ltd., T84

8.60 (bottom right) Lewis F. Day. 'Indian', 1909. Made by Turnbull & Stockdale for Liberty & Co. Contemporary reproduction, renamed 'Dante', made by Liberty & Co. © Liberty PLC. With permission

Fabrics featuring stencil-like designs of flowers and leaves reduced to basic shapes by flattening or squaring their edges became quite popular from c.1899 to 1910. Surviving records of Heal's, for which Turnbull & Stockdale was a contract printer, indicate that sales of these patterns were quite healthy. In the late 1890s, Heal's offered these cretonnes priced from 8½d. to 4s. per yard; Turnbull & Stockdale's fabrics, which included Day's designs, seem to have been priced near the middle of that range.[146]

Day's views on the future of cotton printing

Changes in the scale and methods of textile printing from the mid-19th century on provoked vigorous debate in the press about a perceived drop in manufacturing standards and product quality. Day's analysis of the state of the cotton printing industry and its future direction were most fully expressed in two articles he wrote in the 1890s: 'Progress in Cotton Printing' for the *Art Journal* and 'Cotton Printing', which appeared in the catalogue of the Northern Art Workers' Guild Exhibition in 1898.[147] The latter was also reprinted a year later in the American publication *House Beautiful*, thereby disseminating his ideas more widely to the interested public as well as industry professionals.[148] These articles reveal both Day's acceptance of the realities of textile manufacture in the late 19th and early 20th centuries, and his balanced views about the strengths and weakness of old and new methods of dyeing and printing.

The older process of producing vegetable-dyed fabrics, viewed by some of Day's contemporaries as more artistic due to their soft colours that faded "in artistic proportions", cost twice as much as artificial dyeing.[149] Day felt that vegetable dyes were well-understood and there was "nothing more to learn" from them.[150] He dismissed the notion that everything printed by vegetable dye was inherently superior to those printed by synthetic dyes. The bad reputation of chemical dyes was not attributable to the dyes themselves, he argued, but rather to

8.61 Lewis F. Day. Printed cotton, 1901. Made by Turnbull & Stockdale. Indigo-discharge and block printed
Arthur Sanderson Ltd., T81

constant changes in fashion that sometimes led to a vogue for hideous colours.[151] The future lay not in damning Perkin for his coal-tar investigations, but in continued trial-and-error experiments with chemical dyes, which offered a much greater variety of colours.[152] Chemical dyestuffs also dried quickly and allowed for subsequent printing of colours by block and roller to happen almost immediately, thus saving manufacturers time and money.[153] Day was probably indirectly, and negatively, comparing Britain with Germany, which by the end of the 19th century led the world in the development of dyestuffs.

Day also observed that textile firms were missing a business opportunity by failing to exploit the potential of resist and discharge printing. In the former, cloth was printed with a substance that resists colour when the cloth is dyed; in the latter, an acid was printed onto dyed cloth that "eats out" the colour and "exposes the natural white of the fabric".[154] Resist and discharge printing produced a deep and rich ground-colour that was fuller because it was dyed rather than printed.[155] In addition, these processes were very versatile because they could be used with vegetable or synthetic dyes and with hand block or roller printing.

Lewis Day contended that mechanised printing by engraved copper roller offered the potential for benefit as well as misuse.[156] It was misguided to dismiss roller printing by machine as inferior because it did not produce the same effects as block printing by hand, he counselled. The challenge to both designer and manufacturer was that the two methods required different kinds of designs and colour schemes to capitalise on their strengths. Wood-block printing by hand produced a softer line "and freshness and brightness of tint".[157] Printing by engraved copper roller had the capacity to render greater accuracy in the fitting of the joints and ensure continuity of line through long production runs.[158]

Although the initial expense of engraving a copper roller was quite high, costs were more than recouped because roller printing made high-speed, long production runs possible. Consequently, economics rendered hand block printing an ideal incapable of realisation in modern manufacture, as evidenced by its sharp decline by the 1890s.[159] Day's ultimate verdict on the current state of the printed textile industry and its future direction would have struck some of his contemporaries as very harsh: "The men, therefore, who are doing most for the future of this textile industry are those who are persistently trying to get all that is possible out of roller printing, and not the little band of retrograde craftsmen whose ideal is that of other times and other possibilities."[160]

8.62 (top) Hand block printing, Turnbull & Stockdale. From Turnbull & Stockdale, *Jubilee* (1931): 22

8.63 (bottom) Cretonne-printing machine. From Turnbull & Stockdale, *Jubilee* (1931): 18

SCHEME FOR ARRANGEMENT AND DECORATION OF A ROOM

CHAPTER NINE: THE DOMESTIC INTERIOR

"We are too much accustomed, in these days of locomotion, to look upon our dwellings as mere halting-places between the stages of the journey through life, and to treat them with as little respect as if they were inns or railway stations." [Lewis F. Day, 1882]

9.1 Lewis F. Day. 'Scheme for Arrangement and Decoration of a Room', 1880. From *Magazine of Art* 4 (1881): 185; also in Day, *Every-day Art* (1882) 216

The domestic interior was the stage on which Lewis Foreman Day lived out his personal and professional life. His home and studio at 13 Mecklenburgh Square, his residence for over thirty years, was a gathering place for friends and colleagues and an anchor for him during a lifetime of heavy travel.[1] In addition to citing his profession as a decorative artist and designer, he sometimes referred to himself as a decorator, and most of his designs were for components of home furnishing: textiles, wallpaper, ceramics, furniture.[2]

Walter Crane underscored the importance of his friend and colleague's work as an interior decorator: "A good deal of his best effort went to the designing of decorative schemes for rooms and houses."[3] The trade and professional press referred to his schemes for public interiors and model rooms erected for exhibitions.[4] In 1886 the *Journal of Decorative Art* highlighted some of the many firms for which Day designed home furnishings and remarked: "Formidable as this list appears it does not by any means exhaust Mr. Day's energies, as a considerable part of his time has been occupied in actual decoration. Much of this is of a domestic character, undertaken direct by Mr. Day, but no inconsiderable amount has been done for various decorating firms, which it would be a breach of confidence to further refer to."[5]

While disappointing, it is not surprising that no documented connections to specific domestic interiors have been traced. Commissions from decorating firms would have been executed under the company's name – not Day's – and commissions from private individuals are not likely to have been recorded by them. Day's log books and correspondence have not survived, and while in his articles and books he named some of the manufacturers for whom he designed various types of furnishings, he did not mention specific commissions for domestic interiors.

Despite all this, Day's ideas about interior decoration are amply revealed in his advice to consumers and professionals in his lectures, magazine articles, and books and the accompanying illustrations.[6] It is evident from his writings that he was engaged in domestic interior decoration by at least the late 1870s. He was constitutionally incapable of not talking about his design work. Putting his thoughts on paper not only allowed him to work out his ideas about interior decoration, it helped establish his reputation as a decorator with the public. As he once remarked, people might not know the name of the person who designed their wallpaper or carpet, but they would recognise the name of an author.[7] Day's approach to interior decoration was revealed in his analysis of his audience and the problems they faced in furnishing their homes; his general guidelines for decorating various rooms; and his advice on the relationship between the client and interior decorator.

INTERIOR DECORATION AND THE MIDDLE-CLASS CONSUMER

The milieu of advice writing

The period from 1870 to 1915 witnessed enormous demographic, economic, technological and social changes, many of which affected home furnishing by a burgeoning middle class. Middle- and upper-class families could choose from many types of accommodation, and with some financial means to decorate their homes, had their appetite for furnishings whetted by the stimulants of availability and advertising.[8] Arts professionals and opinion leaders, alarmed about a perceived decline in public taste, seized the mantle of educator. What had been a trickle of writing on taste and home furnishing earlier in the century escalated to a veritable flood by the 1880s. This unprecedented interest of professionals and the public in interior decoration resulted in a specialised genre of domestic advice writing.

An amazing array of writers took pen to hand, advising consumers on how to create the ideal home. They ranged from architects Charles Locke Eastlake and Robert W. Edis, to art critic Clarence Cook, to editor William Loftie, to aesthetically aware lay persons like Eliza Haweis, Jane Frith Panton and Dorothy Constance Peel.[9]

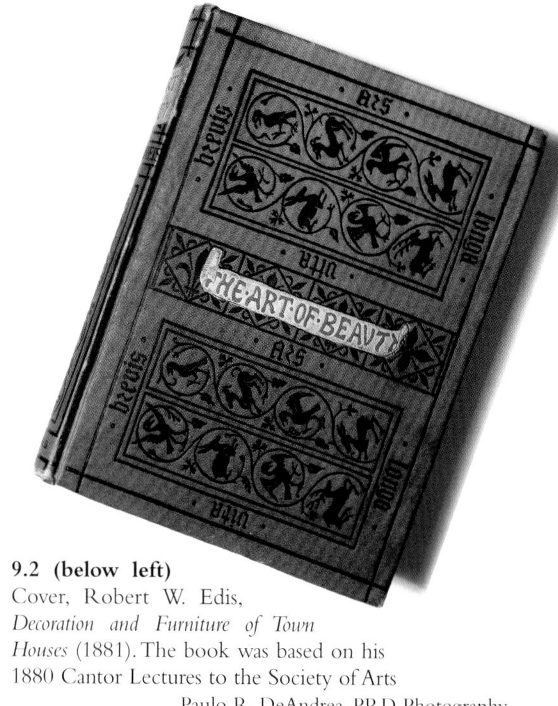

9.2 (below left) Cover, Robert W. Edis, *Decoration and Furniture of Town Houses* (1881). The book was based on his 1880 Cantor Lectures to the Society of Arts
Paulo R. DeAndrea, PRD Photography

9.3 (above) Cover, Mrs. H.R. (Mary Eliza) Haweis, *The Art of Beauty*, 1878. The book was based on her previous articles for *St. Paul's Magazine*
Paulo R. DeAndrea, PRD Photography

While they directed their remarks primarily to the middle class, that group was certainly not homogeneous. Factors considered in defining this group – income, occupation, education, and manner of living, including the keeping of servants – differed greatly among members described as "middle". At the low end of the scale, an annual income of £160 was the threshold to pay income tax, and an annual income of at least £200 was required to set up housekeeping and employ one servant.[10] With an income of around £500, one could rent a house in the country and employ three servants, while more highly-paid professionals earning £900 or more could afford a larger London house and keep four servants.[11] Most of these writers seem to have been directing their advice to readers with an annual income of about £300–£800, which would have allowed for some discretionary income for home furnishing. The cost of furnishing a house varied greatly, depending on its size and the

number and quality of furnishings chosen, but as house furnisher A.R. Dean pointed out, the cost of furnishing an eight-room house could be well over £100.[12]

Day joined the dialogue in the same way Eastlake and Cook initially did, by writing a series of magazine articles on home furnishing that were subsequently published as a book. He penned two series of articles that ran in the *Magazine of Art* from 1880 to 1881, and these were revised and published in 1882 as his second book, *Every-day Art*.[13] Like the other writers mentioned, he seems to have directed his comments to those making at least £300 to £350 per annum. This was also the audience to whom his heavily illustrated book would have appealed at its selling price of 7s. 6d., which was in the middle price range for books of this type. Day's approach to interior decoration, the problems he identified, and the remedies he offered all suggest that he was quite in the mainstream of advice writing of the 1870s to 1880s; he was, however, notable for his thorough understanding of his audience and his practical suggestions for achieving fitness for daily living.

Analysing his audience

Day identified several problems his readers faced in decorating their homes, the first of which was frequent moves from one residence to another. While he had a generally positive attitude toward the age in which he lived, he admitted that one of its negative characteristics was "restless ambition" brought on by so much rapid change.[14] "We seem to be... becoming more and more nomadic in our mode of life," he complained.[15] Homes were regarded as temporary resting places, as inns or railway stations in the journey of life, he observed, and were not revered as the site of many of life's major events: beginning married life, birth, and death.[16] Houses were often rented for short periods of seven years or so, and residents held back from making improvements to comfort and appearance, seeing no benefits in bettering property for later tenants.[17] Day advised that rather than taking a house they would soon outgrow, newly-married couples of moderate means should take a house somewhat larger than they immediately needed, but should not fill it with superfluous furniture they could ill afford.[18]

Day was aware that his readers often inherited decorating problems not of their own making. Many people lived in houses constructed by speculative builders, and some of the structural qualities of the houses, room arrangements and existing decorations could be less than ideal. The builder may have selected wallpapers on the basis of cheapness, novelty of design or a sizeable trade discount rather than on the merits of the pattern.[19] Wallpaper and carpet patterns that the builder had selected from a small swatch on a roll could look discordant with each other and with the occupants' own furnishings when installed.[20] In addition, householders might already be encumbered with ill-assorted furnishings that they had inherited or received as gifts, and it could take years to weed out unsuitable pieces.[21]

The biggest obstacle in home furnishing, however, was letting oneself be seduced by the latest fashions or the opinions of others.[22] Advice writers sometimes addressed their readers in a rather didactic tone with veiled references to the connection of home furnishing and one's character, and Day was no exception. Some of his remarks reflected the Quaker admonitions against vanity, frivolity, catering to the opinions of others, and spending money unwisely that had been instilled in him in his youth. Pointing out that the concern of art was beauty, not fashion, he cautioned his readers against spending limited financial resources on furnishings that could seem very old-fashioned in a year or two and of which they may soon tire.[23]

He urged his readers "to turn a deaf ear to the puffery of the latest novelty, and permit themselves to like or dislike without reference to what Mrs. Somebody may think".[24] Stressing that interior decoration

A PLEA FOR

ART IN THE HOUSE,

WITH SPECIAL REFERENCE TO THE ECONOMY OF COLLECTING WORKS OF ART, AND THE IMPORTANCE OF TASTE IN EDUCATION AND MORALS.

BY

W. J. LOFTIE,

B.A., F.S.A., AUTHOR OF "IN AND OUT OF LONDON."

London:

MACMILLAN AND CO.

1876.

should be determined by their way of life, he encouraged them to surround themselves with the things they cared about and enjoyed.[25] An astute manager of money himself, Day recognised that people may spend portions of their income differently. "No man is justified in his own eyes in giving more for a thing than it is worth to him", and while liking a thing did not make it beautiful, it did, he contended, make it worth having, and people ought to follow their own sense in this.[26]

Day suggested that before beginning to decorate, people should try to educate themselves about decoration and style. Reading a brief introduction to historic styles, such as Ralph N. Wornum's *Analysis of Ornament*, could help ensure consistency and save time for those not using a decorator's services.[27]

Day believed that historic styles should be adapted to present-day homes, and if the householder opted not to use them, it should be by informed choice rather than through ignorance.[28] Day's views on home furnishing revealed his innate eclecticism, founded on the right of each individual to personal choice. They also reflected his belief that his readers could cultivate a sense of taste, a point of agreement with decorator John D. Crace.[29] However, like many other critics of the period, Day and Crace referred to "taste" and "beauty" very generally in terms of fitness, proportion, and moderation rather than providing a specific definition.[30]

The desired result of decoration: fitness for daily living

One underlying theme prevails in Day's advice: interior decoration based on fitness for daily living. Three indispensable qualities in a well-furnished home were fitness for purpose, restfulness and comfort.[31] "The consideration of use, wherever it occurs in decoration, over-rules all others," he observed, and the purpose of the room was most important, not its name.[32] Day was in the mainstream of advice writers who advocated using rooms for multiple purposes, rather than setting them aside for one specific use, as had been common earlier in the century. One's daily habits and schedule were important factors to consider. A person might not "see any particular advantage in consuming his breakfast in one room and his dinner in another", and a family's needs might be better served by combining a dining room and sitting room.[33] If a room was used mostly in the evening, it should not be "so light as to appear cold or naked" nor so dark as to require gas lighting, "which means heat, foul air, heaviness, and general discomfort".[34]

9.4 (top) Cover, William J. Loftie, *A Plea for Art in the House* (1876). This was the first of the 'Art at Home' series of home-decorating manuals published by Macmillan & Co., 1876-8

9.5 (centre) Title page, William J. Loftie, *A Plea for Art in the House* (1876)

9.6 (bottom) Cover, Ralph N. Warnum, *Analysis of Ornament*, 7th edition (1882). First published in 1855 Paulo R. DeAndrea, PRD Photography

Rooms should convey a sense of restfulness, explained Day: "In a home one wants, before all things, repose. Rest for the eye, as well as for the limbs, is implied in the ideal of home comfort."[35] Qualities that contributed to restfulness were mellow tones, restraint in decoration and incorporation of plain surfaces, for much of decoration served as a background to other furnishings.[36] Startling designs and strong colours used in public lobbies or restaurants would be difficult to live with at home, and rather than stunning the viewer by its originality, the ideal domestic interior should express a satisfying unity of effect.[37]

Day also valued comfort highly. A comfortable home would seem to have grown around its residents naturally and beautifully, like a shell, he suggested.[38] Interior decoration should facilitate, not hinder the daily life and habits of those who lived there: "There is no excuse for the house that is picturesque but inconvenient, or the room that is made beautiful at the cost of homeliness."[39] Furnishings should be lived with and enjoyed even if that resulted in occasional loss, for "a thing of beauty is not a joy if you are for ever afraid that harm shall happen to it".[40]

Day wholeheartedly agreed with William Morris's "golden rule": "Have nothing in your houses which you do not know to be useful or believe to be beautiful." In his review for the *Art Journal* of Morris & Co.'s redecoration of the Kensington home of wealthy businessman and noted patron of the arts A.A. (Aleco) Ionides, Day remarked: "It is one great charm of the whole house that it strikes one unmistakably as a place to live in. It is stored full of beautiful things; but they take their place, and are not, as it were, on exhibition; it has none of the air of a museum."[41] Fitness for purpose and beauty, which included "grace of form and harmony of colour", said Day, were completely compatible, and interior decoration was "or should be, art controlled by common sense".[42]

General guidelines for interior decoration

Walls, ceilings and woodwork

Day framed his advice on room decoration in the form of general principles that could be applied widely across rooms having different characteristics and dimensions. While rooms should be decorated for their purpose, all rooms used for a similar purpose did not have to be decorated alike.[43] Entrance halls, for example, should appear welcoming and friendly and provide a clue as to what might be expected in the tone of other rooms of the house.[44] Halls could range in size from a narrow passageway to a full waiting room and often presented particular challenges related to their size, proportions and the presence of a staircase.[45] Larger ones could be decorated with more dramatic colours or patterns that would be hard to live with in main rooms of the house.[46]

Small or poorly proportioned halls should be treated more simply to avoid emphasising their poor qualities. Day showed how this could be done in *Every-day Art*. Lamenting the depressing "dreary breadth of ill-considered wall and ceiling space, the well scooped out of the stairs, the abrupt conclusion of the cornice", he suggested several practical remedies: dividing the wall horizontally to relieve monotony and steady the eye, and adding decorative bands to break the ceiling and soffits of stairs into panels.[47] Inoffensive woodwork painted in a more prominent colour and panes of glass added in the door would help distract attention from "the graceless curve of the ceiling above and its awkward junction with the side wall," he added.[48]

For a hall and staircase in a moderately-sized house, Day suggested a "slightly severe" wallpaper pattern such as his symmetrical arrangement of daisies, stylised brushwork leaves, and rope-like twists within a rectangular framework.[49]

9.7 (top) Lewis F. Day. Poorly proportioned hall before decoration. From Day, *Every-day Art* (1882): 194

9.8 (bottom) Lewis F. Day. Hallway decorated to offset poor proportions. From Day, *Every-day Art* (1882): 195

The decoration of the main rooms of the house could be suggested by important pieces of furniture or distinctive features of the interior architecture such as arches, a moulded ceiling, or dramatic chimney-piece.[50] Day contended that wallpaper was the simplest, most effective and most economical method of covering a wall and, like many of his contemporaries in the 1870s and 1880s, he favoured the tripartite arrangement of dado, filling and frieze for rooms that had heavy use.[51] Since the lower part of the wall was subject to the most wear and tear, the dado should be in a dark colour that would also help unify the pieces of furniture and create a snug feeling.[52] A freer and more flowing design was suitable for the wall above, but he cautioned that the various patterns used in a room must harmonise with each other, lest one pattern dominate the entire scheme.[53] Day later modified his view and conceded that the two-part wall treatment of frieze and filling, which had increased in popularity in the 1890s, could be a suitable option.

The depth of the frieze, stated Day, should be based on the height of the room and be compatible in tone and pattern to the wallpaper. A well-chosen frieze would keep lines of the wallpaper from seeming to disappear behind the cornice, and by pulling the eye upward toward the ceiling, could create the impression of greater height.[54] Painting the cornice in shades of an intermediate colour would connect the wall and ceiling, and mouldings that were very nondescript could be stencilled to offset their deficiencies.[55] The ceiling was most suitably treated by distemper or papering with a simple diaper or non-directional pattern.[56]

On the decoration of woodwork, Day dismissed as a sham the common practice of wood graining. While he noted that the practice of painting an inferior wood to imitate the grain of a more expensive wood had been condemned on moral grounds as deceptive, the technique was also paltry and showed a lack of inventiveness.[57] Wood graining could hide structural defects like "yawning gaps in the joinery", and even if graining was done competently, it was not an economical choice, because the cost of good graining could approach that of the wood itself.[58]

He suggested severable more suitable options. A flat paint treatment on woodwork produced a soft tone, while a varnished one afforded durability, which could be further enhanced by painting woodwork in two or three shades of colour in keeping with the tone of the dado.[59] A transparent coating would allow the colours to run into each other, providing variation of tint that would render nicks and marks less visible, and mottling woodwork would allow for easy touch-ups.[60] Decoration of mouldings and panels should harmonise with the wallpaper, with hand-painting reserved for door panels and window-shutters that were seen at closer view.[61]

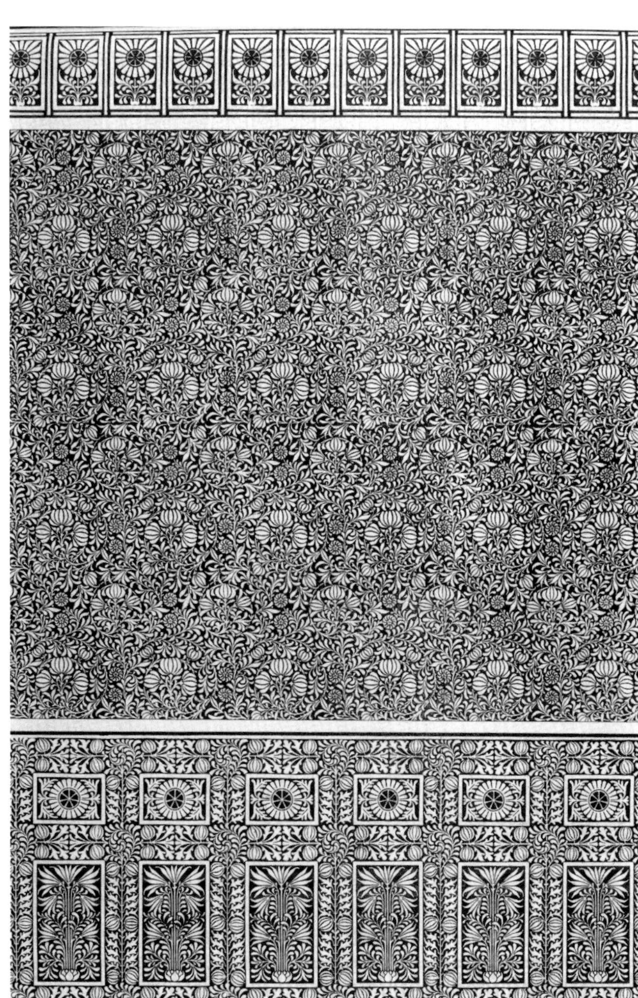

9.9 (above) Lewis F. Day. Hall and staircase paper, 1877. From Day, *Every-day Art* (1882): 192. The paper was block-printed by Jeffrey & Co. for W.B. Simpson & Sons. PRO, BT43/102:#316483, reg. 19 November 1877

9.10 (right) Lewis F. Day. Tripartite wall decoration featuring 'Indian' filling paper with accompanying dado and frieze. From *Architect* 26 (1881): pl. opp. 278

Trustees of the National Library of Scotland

9.11 Lewis F. Day. Detail, 'Indian' wallpaper, an all-over pattern "showing the cross-lines upon which it is planned". From Day, *The Anatomy of Pattern*, 4th ed. (1896): pl. 5; ix

9.12 Lewis F. Day. Detail, 'Indian' wallpaper. From Jeffrey & Co., *Selected Hand-Printed Wall Papers* (1894-5)

Nordiska Museet, Stockholm, Erik Folcker Collection, 310.405

9.13 (top left) Lewis F. Day. Tripartite wall decoration in hall. From Day, *Every-day Art* (1882): 238

9.14 (bottom left) Lewis F. Day. Dado paper for a hall. From Day, *Every-day Art* (1882): 193

9.15 (top right) Lewis F. Day. Ceiling paper featuring diaper of daisies. From Day, *Every-day Art* (1882): 62

9.16 (bottom right) Lewis F. Day. Ceiling paper. From Jeffrey & Co., *Selected Hand-Printed Wall Papers* (1894-5)

Nordiska Museet, Stockholm,
Erik Folcker Collection, 310.405

9.17 Lewis F. Day. Ceiling treatment showing decoration of frieze and cornice. From Day, *Every-day Art* (1882): 173

9.18 (above left) Lewis F. Day. Painted door panels, "showing the influence of the proportions of the panels upon the design of the decoration". From Day, *The Planning of Ornament*, 3rd ed. (1893): pl. 6; ix

9.19 (above right) Lewis F. Day. Painted door panels. From Day, *Instances of Accessory Art* (1880): pl.28 Paul Reeves

Window and floor coverings

Day advocated simple window treatments such as a stout brass pole or a simple cornice from which curtains hung in straight folds almost to floor.[62] Simple drapery and rich fabrics had "grace and dignity", he said, unlike drapery that was looped up, or embellished with "superfluous cords, tassels, or fringes", a practice frequently criticised in the contemporary press.[63] Other fabrics used in the room should also be arranged simply, for "the toilet-tablet 'got up' in muslin and pink satin as if it were going to a ball, is not a triumph of art", he caustically remarked.[64] His recommendations were also based on the rising concerns in the 1880s about the deleterious effects of accumulated dust and dirt on health: "In manufacturing and other large towns, cleanliness and health alike recommend that as little stuff as possible be introduced into a room."[65]

This applied to floor coverings, as well. Carpets nailed down over the entire floor held the dust, whereas rugs could be picked up and shaken daily, saving the wear that comes from frequent brushing.[66] Persian rugs were an ideal floor covering for floors that were polished, stained, varnished or painted.[67] Floor coverings should be arranged for comfort and warmth, and an unobtrusive pattern with "blurred and broken colour" was more serviceable than a plain ground, which would reveal stains and wear.[68]

Furniture

Day's advice on furniture was eminently practical. First, consumers should buy only what was really needed for their way of life, not "things for which they have no use and no excuse but custom".[69] Second, while individual pieces should be compatible, shoppers should avoid buying a suite of furniture from one store, particularly for a dining room that would also be used as a sitting-room where the family would spend considerable time.[70] Running counter to advice in store catalogues that promoted purchase of entire rooms – even entire houses – of furniture, Day cautioned against rashly ordering furniture on the basis of how attractive it looked in the showroom.[71] Furniture should be soundly constructed, for the expense of well-crafted items would be offset by the savings gained from not buying unnecessary ones.[72] Architect Robert Edis shared this opinion, observing that "furniture of thoroughly good art design, comfortable in shape, and good in workmanship, may be made without any extravagant outlay".[73] Edis, Loftie, Day and other writers on home furnishing frequently reminded their readers that furniture should also be free of excessive decoration, and in general simpler pieces would be a better value than more elaborate ones.[74]

9.20 (above) Oetzmann & Co. Advertisement. From Christmas Number, *Art Journal* (1897)

9.21 (opposite, top) Maurice B. Adams. Dining room sideboard. Made by Jackson & Graham. From Edis, *Decoration and Furniture of Town Houses* (1881): pl. 8

9.22 (opposite, bottom) Lewis F. Day. Straight-lined fireplace design, 1878. From Day, *Every-day Art* (1882): 255

Straight-lined fireplace design.

MAPLE & CO
Designers and Manufacturers of
FIRST-CLASS FURNITURE
AND
INTERIOR DECORATIONS
THE LARGEST AND MOST CONVENIENT FURNISHING ESTABLISHMENT IN THE WORLD.
❋ BEDROOM SUITES IN SOLID OAK. ❋
Example of a "TUSMORE" BEDROOM SUITE in Solid Oak.
The Largest Selection of BEDSTEADS and BEDDING in the World.
A Special Design Book of "QUAINT ART BEDSTEADS" sent post free.
MAPLE & CO Tottenham Court Road London
Rue Boudreau Paris MAPLE & CO
AD. XIII

9.23 (top) Oetzmann & Co. Advertisement. From *Royal Academy Pictures* (1901)

9.24 (bottom) Maple & Co. Advertisement. From *Studio* 19 (1900)

Particular decorating challenges

Day remarked that the biggest sacrifices in both space and expense were made in the drawing room because persons who did not do much formal entertaining often felt compelled to have "a room of state, which is only a costly encumbrance".[75] He noted that the "chilling conventionality" of the room was seen "in the pinafores in which the furniture is carefully covered up"; decorator John Crace also criticised the sterile and lifeless quality often found there.[76] For those who wanted a drawing room, Day recommended that it be "light, easily illuminated, delicate and not too serious in its general tone", since it was used for more superficial rather than intimate social interactions.[77]

While a library was a luxury for many families, it could serve as an indispensable office for persons with literary or business interests.[78] One of the most important requirements of a library was convenience. Day found it ironic that many home libraries were "dingy and comfortless" rooms that actually hindered reading and were rarely used, while the breakfast or dining room where the family spent their time was not seen as a place for books.[79]

Since bedrooms were in the private part of the house and were infrequently visited by outsiders, they often received short shrift in the decorating process. Self-respect dictated that they receive more attention, insisted Day: "A fine house with mean bedrooms is no better than a smart dress and shabby underclothes."[80] Along with other advice writers, he noted that the use of the bedroom during periods of illness and convalescence prohibited oppressive or agitating wallpapers, and "harmlessness" in a pattern was "a positive merit".[81] "Who has not at some time in his life been confined to a room in which the wallpaper oppressed him like a nightmare? The rosebuds *would* resolve themselves into grotesque faces, peeping out at him from wherever he turned his eyes. Or the pattern became an arithmetical puzzle, never to be solved: when darkness came it brought no relief, and he found himself lying awake half through the night, mechanically counting phantom figures."[82]

9.25 (left) Maurice B. Adams. Bedroom furniture. Made by Holland & Sons. From Edis, *Decoration and Furniture of Town Houses* (1881): pl. 19

9.26 (below) Lewis F. Day. Design for panels of piano front. From Day, *Every-day Art* (1882): 258

Sitting and living rooms were often the most frequently used rooms in the house, so, reasoned Day, they should be furnished to meet the practical needs of the household.[83] Variety in seating allowed for changes in position and relaxation, and while the fabrics covering chairs did not have to be the same, they should harmonise and not be so expensive that covers were needed.[84] Day noted that although velvet hung and wore well, it was not a good choice for chair seats because it clung too much to be comfortable.[85] Since this room was meant to be homely, special interests of the household could be reflected in items such as a piano, pictures, photographs or collections, which should be chosen for their quality, "proportion, scale, and general effect".[86]

Day saw limitless options for devising a comfortable scheme of decoration based on one's needs and preferences.[87] If the householder was a book-lover, for example, some low bookshelves on either side of the fireplace would provide storage space and be in easy reach.[88] Adding to one's comfort would be a fender high enough to warm the feet, a light behind the reader's back for reading, and a moveable desk beside an easy-chair for taking notes.[89] Day considered that a work of art over the mantel was preferable to a mirror.[90] Influenced no doubt in his upbringing by Quaker admonitions against vanity, Day heartily disliked mirrors: "The perpetual nuisance of seeing oneself reflected at every turn in a mirror more than outweighs any convenience there

might be in it"; if a mirror were absolutely necessary, then it should be hung out of the way "so that one could not see oneself in it without deliberate intention".[91] Other small decorative items – a clock, andirons, candlesticks and so forth – could add interesting detail, but should look like they belonged together rather than having "met by accident".[92]

A room needed to be lived in for a while, cautioned Day, because despite all this careful planning, a few conveniences would likely be overlooked.[93] Also, explained Day, when the novelty of a newly decorated room wears off, people begin to incorporate "those familiar and necessary comforts that make home homely", and "habit and convenience effect, perhaps, at last what it should have been the first object of art to produce – oneness and repose".[94] If the occupants were satisfied with the end-results of their decoration, the room would continue to grow on them and they would be reluctant to make big changes over the years.[95]

9.27 (above) Maurice B. Adams. Dining room furniture and decoration. Designed by Robert W. Edis, architect. From Edis, *Decoration and Furniture of Town Houses* (1881): pl. 16

THE RELATIONSHIP BETWEEN THE CLIENT AND DECORATOR

By 1890 *Every-day Art* was out of print, and Day considered whether to have it reprinted. The book had taken its place in the dialogue on home furnishing and established him as an authority on interior decoration. Undoubtedly, it had garnered him decorating commissions, as well. He realised, however, that over the eight years since it had been published, tastes in furnishing had changed and he had changed, too. Having secured an international reputation as a major designer, by the late 1880s he was turning out a large volume of work for eminent firms. He had also moved into a period of great intellectual development and had written the first three of his *Textbooks of Ornamental Design*. The second part of *Every-day Art* contained specific recommendations on decorating, and believing that it was outdated and of little interest, Day dropped it and revised the first section alone. The revised text, published as *Some Principles of Every-day Art* by B.T. Batsford in 1890, was intended as the introductory book to his series of *Textbooks*.

Day's professional audience

Although he certainly had discussed the rôle of the decorator in his earlier writings, from the 1890s on, most of Day's advice was directed to professionals rather than the general reader. He was unusual among his peers for the attention he devoted to the professional development of interior decorators. Through his sought-after lectures to groups such as the Master House Painters and Decorators Association and the Institute of British Decorators, Day – a lifelong learner himself – encouraged his audience to continue to develop their technical and managerial skills. He spoke as a member of the profession he was addressing, and these lectures were reported on in both the professional and the general press. His lecture, 'The Art and Trade of House Decoration' to the Master House Painters and Decorators Association, was published in the *Journal of Decorative Art* and was also paraphrased in general interest publications including *Scientific American & Building Monthly* and *House Beautiful*.[96]

Consumers needing decorating assistance had a number of options from which to choose. These ranged from getting advice on the selection of one particular type of furnishing to complete management of the entire decorating process. Some manufacturers, such as wallpaper manufacturer Jeffrey & Co., advertised that the public could visit their showrooms to see a variety of papers and get advice. A number of stores, including Liberty & Co., Oetzmann & Co., and Maple & Co., offered decorating services. Many people in the middle and upper income brackets sought assistance from decorating firms, which ranged from large firms catering to an affluent clientele, to smaller companies serving customers of more modest means. Day's advice to decorators centred on effective management of the decorator-client relationship. He continually emphasised that the success of the interior decorating project depended in large measure on the parties collaborating effectively during critical aspects of the process. These included determining the scope of the project; having mutual understanding of its financial implications; and negotiating practical issues.

9.28 Lewis F. Day. Cover, *Some Principles of Every-day Art* (1890)

Collaboration between decorator and client

Day always came back to the point that the purpose and parameters of the decorating project should be based on the needs and preferences of the householder and family.[97] To ensure that the parties adhered to this purpose and to provide unity and consistency in decoration, someone must take charge of the task, which taxes "time, temper, and taste".[98] If this seemed too daunting to do personally, the householder should locate a trustworthy decorator and "instruct him fully, tell him your pet ideas, as you would confide your symptoms to a physician", a rather humorous analogy.[99] Even when using an interior decorator, it still remained the responsibility of the client to determine what he or she wants.

Oftentimes a client relied too heavily on the decorator to make decisions, and the completed room would reflect the taste of the decorator rather than the client.[100] Even clients who claimed to have little interest in decorating and left decisions to the decorator could soon realise discomfort from a room that is "too sombre or too spick-and-span" for their taste.[101] In his review of the redecoration of the Ionides's home at 1 Holland Park Road by Morris & Co., Day commented: "We have here a really beautiful house, full of beautiful things, an ideal interior in its way; but it is the idea of its owner, not the idea of the artists he has called to his help, that it realises."[102]

The decorator's rôle was to translate the wants and preferences of the client into decorative shape.[103] Day observed that while the primary business of the decorator was to serve the client, not create a *tour de force* in art, that did not mean that the decorator was simply an executor of the client's directions.[104] The decorator who kept in mind the client's preferences and not just his own predilections, should at the same time be able to demonstrate his decorating talents.[105] The decorator, after all, was likely to know more than the client whether the idea would work out satisfactorily and how the client's initial idea might be improved.[106] Since some of the client's ideas would prove impractical or be too expensive, it would ultimately be a question of the relative importance of the idea in the client's mind and how far the latter was willing to go in pursuing it.[107] Give and take between client and decorator was inevitable, and weighing personal choice against the decorator's objections, the client should either give up the idea, override the objection, or seek another way to accomplish it.[108]

While Day believed that one of the most common reasons a decorative scheme did not work out well was that the parties had not remained focused on the family's needs, he observed that "practically two-thirds at least of the decorator's work is to make the best of the bad bargain which has been made for him by the manufacturer, builder or architect".[109] The ultimate professional challenge for decorators was to adapt themselves to the conditions and parameters of their work. Since interior decoration was not an independent art, it consisted "in doing the definite thing to be done, often in making the best of what promises to be a bad job".[110] With his characteristically positive attitude toward surmounting obstacles, Day concluded that difficult jobs offered the chance to stretch one's talent and skills in a way that would not have occurred but for the problem.[111]

The decorator was also required to assist the client in having a clear understanding of the financial implications of a project. Often clients would not know the relative cost of things.[112] A job estimate would invariably be higher than was originally anticipated by the client, leaving the decorator with the question of how to reduce this "to reasonable proportions".[113] While the usual answer was to eliminate craftsmanship and go with straight contract work, Day counselled that thoroughly good workmanship was always the best choice, and project costs could be controlled by eliminating "excess, elaboration, lavishness", things not necessary to the decorative scheme.[114]

The decorator and client also had to navigate the shoals of specific practical issues. The consumer could be confused by the terminology and jargon used in the process of decorating, as well as by the vast array of options available.[115] In awe of professional expertise, a client might be reluctant to disagree with the decorator's opinions.[116] Day sympathetically remarked: "Often customers are wearied and fatigued by being shown an endless succession of things until their brains are in a perfect maze of bewilderment, and they settle on something out of sheer exhaustion."[117] The choice of textiles and wallpaper could be especially confusing because patterns selected from showroom samples did not give the buyer a real idea of how they would look on an entire floor or wall.[118] Nor did the effect of a pattern the client may have seen in a small room necessarily translate well into a larger one. Decorator John Crace complained: "There are people who, having visited some pretty country vicarage, and been charmed with the paper that adorned walls of some cosy room 9ft. or 10ft. [2.7m. - 3m.] high, insist on applying the same paper to their own town drawing room, 13ft. high [3.9m.] or more; or who can't endure life without a dado, regardless of the proportions of their own room."[119]

Day pointed out that the decorator would know that some papers with meticulous detail that looked good in the sample book would not look pleasing on the wall, while designs that appeared plain or uninteresting could produce a broad and dignified effect when installed.[120] Although consumers might not accept the decorator's preference to their own, they would generally listen to reason if the decorator explained why one pattern would not hang well and why the other one would.[121] Likewise, if a client had already decided on a certain colour in a room, the decorator could provide guidance on the precise shade.[122] While customers wanted to choose, they also ultimately wanted to save themselves time and aggravation. Day suggested that decorators put together their own sample book of designs they knew worked well, and revise it yearly.[123]

Day's challenge to decorators

As a decorator himself, Day was well-versed in handling clients' demands, and the tone of his lectures and writings is one of encouragement. Nevertheless, he did not mince his words when berating practices that he deemed unworthy of a conscientious professional. A decorator could benefit himself financially at the consumer's expense, and Day identified two common ways decorators did disservice to a client. First, touting 'art' could become a means to an end: "He provides novelty under the guise of art since novelty is what sells and sells more readily."[124] Conversely, the decorator could espouse risk aversion; wanting to secure a solid percentage of profit and, knowing that the client has a budget or top limit in mind, the decorator could recommend things "only as are safe and bear a distinct and assured profit".[125] Foregoing the option of a special treatment that might enhance a particular feature of a room, the decorator offered wallpapers that were very safe and simple and used only ordinary workmen who gave neither trouble nor anxiety.[126] Day encouraged decorators to widen their experience and try new materials, techniques, and ways of executing things, provided that the client was willing.[127]

Day did, however, respect the fact that decorators were people of business, who needed to turn a profit: "The mere fact of a man's going into business implies that he expects to make a living out of it. But the hope of art in it depends upon his caring for this particular trade, preferring it to any other."[128] He pointed out that art was inherent in the decorator's profession, for "the moment the consideration of beauty (apart from utility) enters into the calculations of the workman, he touches on the domain of art".[129] Many decorating firms were not large enterprises, and Day felt that the marriage of art and commerce was more readily achieved in smaller businesses: "Art has flourished best in trades of no great magnitude – trades small enough to be conducted by, if not an artist, a man not so engrossed in business operations as to have no time or temper to go into questions of art."[130] He concluded: "The possibilities of art are greater, I think, in the case of small masters than of big employers, working for the million."[131]

CHAPTER TEN: COLLEAGUES AND STUDENTS

"We pride ourselves upon our individuality, but absolutely independent we are not...Polite society makes the artist something of a man of fashion, just as the companionship of fellow artists kindles and strengthens in him the spirit which produces." [Lewis F. Day, 1901]

10.1 Lewis F. Day. From *Year's Art* (1900)

Lewis Foreman Day's fierce independence was balanced by a strong sense of belonging to a wide community of professionals working in the applied arts. His associative behaviour was the antithesis of that of a loner. Throughout his life he was able to work collaboratively with others toward common goals, while simultaneously maintaining his own ideological independence. This combination of energetic involvement with others and intense individualism was cited by his contemporaries as among his most distinguishing characteristics.[1]

Day demonstrated his sense of affiliation with others through two main venues – professional organisations and the design education system, which were inextricably linked. By actively participating in professional organisations, Day found camaraderie; forged alliances with other key figures in design and industry; tested his ideas about design and the rôle of the designer; and marketed himself to prospective clients. Through teaching and lecturing, judging student work, mentoring students – who would became well-known designers in their own right – and evaluating schools of design, he helped prepare the next generation of designers to work in industry. Day clearly received a great deal of professional growth, satisfaction, reputation, and income from the design profession, but he also gave a lot back, both to his peers and students.

Professional activities: balancing independence with collaboration

A collaborator from the beginning

Associationism – the joining of professional, religious, philanthropic or other types of organisations – was a defining form of social behaviour in the 19th century. It has been estimated that during the later Victorian period, it was common for people to belong to several organisations.[2] Day was a good example of this, and one can only marvel at both the sheer number of professional organisations to which he belonged – some of them for long periods of time – and the level of activity he sustained despite a busy career as a designer and writer.

From his early days as an employee of stained glass firms, Day sought out other professionals. Beginning in the 1860s, he attended meetings of the Architectural Association, whose members met fortnightly for fellowship and mutual study of the practical aspects of their work.[3] Young members benefited from the experience of prominent architects and decorative artists and from the opportunities such contacts brought to get work. Day expressed his independent thinking in discussions, but was also energised by interacting with others, as he commented years later: "We pride ourselves upon our individuality, but absolutely independent we are not...Polite society makes the artist something of a man of fashion, just as the companionship of fellow artists kindles and strengthens in him the spirit which produces."[4]

In 1868, when employed by the stained glass firm Clayton & Bell, Day won a prize for his essay 'The History and Application of Stained Glass'.[5] This was the earliest reference to Day in contemporary periodicals and harbingered his dual career as designer and writer. He later presented two other papers on stained glass to the Architectural Association: 'Stained Glass: Its Application to Domestic Architecture' (1872) and 'Some Lessons from Old Glass' (1886).[6]

In the 1860s, Day also belonged to the Quibblers – a society of young art and design students – which numbered among its members the illustrator and designer Walter Crane, and the architect R. Phené Spiers, who would remain lifelong associates and friends.[7] By 1869 they had refashioned themselves as the Associated Arts Institute, which met for discussion, presentation of papers, and exhibitions of drawings.[8] The group broadened its scope to include both amateurs and professionals. Its philosophy was that amateurs could learn from the practical experience of professionals, and the latter, in turn, could benefit from "learning the opinions of intelligent lovers of art" who may be free of "professional prejudices" that had been "acquired in special schools".[9] Day might well have influenced this inclusive approach, because throughout his life he encouraged learning by anyone who wanted to know more about a subject and he directed much of his writing to general interest readers as well as professionals. Despite its lofty aim, the group appears to have dissolved in the early 1870s, though its members became active in other organisations.

10.2 G.F. Watts, R.A. Portrait of Walter Crane. From Easter Art Annual, *Art Journal* (1898): 32

The Society of Arts

One of Day's most important and enduring memberships was with the Society of Arts, which he joined in January 1879. The mission of the Society – "The Encouragement of the Arts, Manufactures, and Commerce of the Country" – drove it to foster the practical applications of art and science to industry. It also granted awards for inventions and industrial improvements that promoted employment and increased British trade and commerce.[10] When in 1886 the Applied Arts Section of the Society was formed to focus more intensively on industrial applications of the arts, Day became one of the original members of its Committee.[11] This was a natural fit with Day's preoccupation with the marriage of design and industry and his belief that the rôle of the designer was situated at the nexus of art and

10.3 (left) Society of Arts, Adelphi, London, 1990s

10.4 (above) Plaque near entrance to Society of Arts, stating the Society's mission, 1990s

commerce.[12] He became lifelong friends with kindred spirits Sir George Birdwood, Section chair, and Henry Trueman Wood, Secretary of the Society. In 1897 Day was elected a member of the Council, and from that year until his death he served continuously in either that capacity or as Vice President, except for those intervals required by the Society's rules.[13]

Day's high level of participation was also reflected in the significant number of lectures he gave to the Society of Arts from the early 1880s through to 1908, beginning in February 1882 with 'Stained Glass Windows: As They Were, Are, and Should Be'.[14] In late 1886, Day delivered his first series of the high-profile Cantor Lectures, centred on 'The Principles and Practice of Ornamental Design'.[15] These four, hour-long lectures were an important milestone for him, because they gave him the opportunity to formulate many of his fundamental ideas about design and ornament in front of an audience and benefit from their questions and comments. Day's textbooks *The Anatomy of Pattern* and *The Planning of Ornament*, published by B.T. Batsford in 1887, and *The Application of Ornament*, published the following year, were largely based on these lectures.

Day chose diverse topics and was an energetic lecturer, posting diagrams and designs on the walls to underscore his main points. In April 1888 he lectured on 'Craftsman and Manufacturer', enumerating current problems in industry and emphasising that in order to produce the best products, designer and manufacturer must work as one.[16] In May 1890 he gave a three-part series of lectures on 'Design Applied to Wood-Carving', given at the request of the School of Art Woodcarving at South Kensington, which had asked the Society to supply instruction to their students.[17] In the 1890s he also presented two additional courses of Cantor Lectures: 'Some Masters of Ornament', a four-part series in April and May 1893; and 'Design in Lettering', four lectures given in May, 1897.[18] Parts of the latter lectures were incorporated into his books *Alphabets Old and New* (1898) and *Lettering in Ornament* (1902). Day was awarded two silver medals for his lectures to the Society: one in 1898 for 'The Making of a Stained Glass Window', and a second about a decade later for 'How to Make the Most of a Museum'.[19]

Day also applied his graphic skills to benefit the Society. He designed the July 1893 Address to H.R.H. the Prince of Wales, President of the Society of Arts, on the marriage of their Royal Highnesses the Duke and Duchess of York, Prince George and Princess May.[20] In 1904 he designed a new cover for the Society's *Journal* which was used until 1911.[21] In March 1910, Day chaired a meeting at which Noel Heaton lectured on 'The Foundations of Stained Glass Work'; since Day's first lecture to the Society in 1882 had been on the subject of stained glass, it seems appropriate that it was also the subject of the last meeting that he chaired, just a month before his death.[22]

FOUNDING NEW ORGANISATIONS

The Fifteen

In the 1880s Day not only belonged to, but helped found several organisations. In January 1881 he instigated the establishment of 'The Fifteen', a group of architects, artists and designers (some of whom had belonged to the Quibblers) who met to discuss the relationship of art and design to everyday life.[23] Member Walter Crane recounted that Day hosted the first meeting at his house on "Hurricane Tuesday", during which the winter blizzards and drifting snow were so severe that Crane himself was unable to attend. Held monthly from October to May at members' homes or studios, the meetings were convivial affairs, with the host of the evening providing refreshments and leading a discussion on some aspect of decorative art.[24] In addition to Day and Crane, among the Fifteen were Henry Holiday, Hugh Stannus, John D. Sedding, and Hugh Arthur Kennedy, with William Morris designated an honorary member.[25] Crane noted that membership fluctuated and apparently never actually numbered fifteen; rather, the group had taken its name from "a popular puzzle with which people were wont to exasperate their spare moments about this time – some trick with fifteen numbers and one blank in a square box".[26]

The Art Workers' Guild

In 1884, most of the members of the Fifteen were absorbed into a group with much broader objectives and a larger constituency.[27] They joined with architects from the St. George's Art Society, many of whom were pupils of Richard Norman Shaw, to form the Art Workers' Guild to promote unity of the arts and fellowship.[28] Though not one of the five founder members, Day was among those first invited to attend early meetings in January and March 1884, at which the mission of the new Guild and qualifications for membership were defined; along with W.R. Lethaby and W.A.S. Benson, he was elected to the Provisional Committee, which organised the new society from 1884 to 1887.[29]

The early members sought to combat the negative effects of industrialisation. Chief among their concerns were the increasing separation of art, architecture, design, and craft, and the foisting of poorly designed and manufactured objects onto

10.5 Art Workers' Guild, Queen Square, London, 1990s

the public in the interest of profit. The Guild's belief that existing organisations such as the Royal Academy and the Institute of British Architects had neglected to address the increasing separation of art and architecture prompted them to raise the banner of unity among the arts.[30] Never one to be content with simply complaining about things, Day was of like mind with other colleagues that if an existing organisation did not meet present needs, the best course of action was to move forward and found a new one. While the Guild took an avowed position against the seeking of publicity, a number of its members – among them Crane, Lethaby and Day – had very public rôles in the arts.[31] Designer Heywood Sumner, one of the earliest members and Master in 1894, commented that those looking for a capable person to serve in a public position related to the arts would find that person at the Art Workers' Guild.[32]

Day was Treasurer from 1884 to 1887, which certainly was an apt use of his mathematical skills. He was elected Master of the Guild in 1897. On concluding his term of office he promoted the idea of an Art Workers' Guild 'club' to foster greater socialisation and discussion of current publications, but it did not materialise due to insufficient support, lack of space and cost.[33]

It is not surprising that he was also an honorary member and officer of the Northern Art Workers' Guild, which Walter Crane had inaugurated in Manchester in July 1896, modelled on its London predecessor.[34] Day had extensive business relationships with Maw & Co., Turnbull & Stockdale, and Pilkington's Tile & Pottery Co. – all manufacturing firms located in the North. Although designated as an honorary member, Day was active in the Guild. Some of his furnishings were shown at the 1898 exhibition, and his perceptive article 'Cotton Printing' was included in the exhibition catalogue.[35] He contributed an essay, 'Design and Handicraft', to the catalogue of the 1903 exhibition and remained on the officers' list until at least 1904.[36]

10.6 Edward R. Hughes. Portrait of Lewis F. Day, 1900. Day was Master of the Art Workers' Guild in 1897, and the portrait hangs above the fireplace at Art Workers' Guild. 1990s

By kind permission of the Art Workers' Guild, London

Arts and Crafts Exhibition Society

Some members of the Art Workers' Guild believed that an important means of strongly demonstrating the equal status of the applied arts to architecture and the fine arts was through exhibitions. They envisioned a way in which professionals and amateurs could exhibit their work in a suitable venue, with recognition to designer, manufacturer and executant. The Guild was not an option due to its aversion to publicity, and they had given up on the Royal Academy because selection of objects for exhibition was determined by a jury of academicians who were biased in favour of painting and the fine arts.[37] So it was that a group, comprised mostly of members of the Art Workers' Guild, began planning an exhibition society in early 1886, holding the first meeting in a little room at the Charing Cross Hotel.[38]

Walter Crane later commented that Day was among the most energetic workers of

10.7 (above left) New Gallery, Regent St., London. Entrance to the Competition Room. From *Art Journal* (1898): 29

10.8 (above right) Arts and Crafts Exhibition Society. *Catalogue* cover, Fifth Exhibition, 1896

the new group, intensely involved in both organising the society and implementing the exhibitions.[39] He was a member of a Provisional Committee for this "Combined Arts Society", later renamed the "Arts and Crafts Exhibition Society"; Day seconded the proposal to change the society's name.[40] To be eligible for membership, persons had to be actually engaged in the arts as designers or workers.[41] The early members determined several distinguishing parameters: the exhibitions would illustrate application of the arts in a variety of materials and uses; designers and craftsmen would show under their own names; and although objects would not be sold at the exhibitions, prospective purchasers would be directed to the exhibitors.[42]

Walter Crane was elected President and W.A.S. Benson Honorary Treasurer. The important Selection Committee, which included Day, William Morris, Philip Webb, Heywood Sumner and Mervyn McCartney, judged the quality of work submitted and the space available for exhibiting.[43] "After prolonged incubation", as Walter Crane put it, the society held its first exhibition in 1888 at the New Gallery.[44] Day and Emery Walker also helped expedite the printing of the 1888 exhibition catalogue, which had been beset by logistical problems from the start.[45]

While initially the exhibitions were held annually, from 1890 they were scheduled every three years until the early 20th century, when they were held periodically. Lectures were offered in tandem with the exhibitions to publicise the aims of the Society and promote public appreciation for applied art. Exhibition catalogues were an educational tool as well, for they also contained essays. Day lectured on 'Ornament' at the 1889 exhibition and contributed an essay 'Of Designs and Working Drawings' to the exhibition catalogue.[46] The 1893 exhibition featured lectures by William Morris, Selwyn Image, Walter Crane, W.B. Richmond and Day, who spoke 'On Some Ornamental Offshoots of the Italian Renaissance'.[47] As a well-known journalist and design critic, Day also reported on some of the Arts and

Crafts Exhibitions for the *Art Journal* and *Magazine of Art*.

Day was a member of the Selection Committee for the first six exhibitions, but in 1896, he resigned. Although the specific incident that triggered his resignation is unclear, he was obviously very upset. He stated in his resignation letter that the Committee was not seriously judging ornament and pattern, that manufacturers were not being encouraged, and that the Committee was more concerned with how the galleries looked than the opinions of exhibitors.[48] Despite the Committee's appeal to him to reconsider, Day did not budge from his decision. He did, however, continue to exhibit at each of the shows until 1910, the year he died. In his preface to the 1912 Arts and Crafts Exhibition Society catalogue, Walter Crane paid tribute to Day, describing him as "a learned writer and lecturer ... a lucid and able teacher ... an accomplished and facile designer and decorator," and, he added: "I have lost an old and valued friend".[49]

Although those who espoused Arts and Crafts ideals shared concerns about the effects of industrialisation on design and society, they held a range of opinions on suitable remedies. Ultimately, each person arrived at an individual response or accommodation.[50] While Day had joined with his Arts and Crafts colleagues to improve design and manufacture, he was firmly grounded in the present and had no desire to turn back the tide of industrial progress. Rather, through the Exhibition Society and other vehicles, he sought to promote a better relationship between designers and manufacturers. He agreed with Morris, Crane and others on the need to improve society, but did not accept their proposed remedy: "Many of us recognise, of course, the intimate relationship of art to life, without arguing from that the necessity of socialism," adding that they, while generally accepting Morris's "diagnosis of the social anemia of the century-end, have no very great faith in his remedy".[51]

10.9 William Morris. From *Magazine of Art* 19 (1896): 56

Pursuing other professional interests

While his main energies were channelled through the Society of Arts, the Art Workers' Guild, and the Arts and Crafts Exhibition Society, the indefatiguable Day also found time to pursue other special interests. From its founding in 1894 to c.1900, he served on the committee of the Society of Illustrators.[52] His strong interest in illustration is amply evidenced through the advertisements he designed for clients; his magazine, catalogue and book covers; the illustrations, which were such a prominent feature in his books; and his texts on lettering. He also frequently lectured to various professional and trade organisations around the country, among them the National Association of Master House Painters and Decorators of England and Wales (1902) and the Institute of British Decorators (1902 and 1904). In 1904, Day was elected a Fellow of the Society of Antiquaries, resigning shortly before his death.[53]

Design education: preparing the next generation of designers

Although Day occasionally lectured to students in various venues throughout Britain from early in his career, it was in the early 1890s that he became more regularly involved with the educational establishment. From that time on, he energetically applied his knowledge and vast practical experience to helping prepare the next generation of designers and effect positive change in the British design education system.

Design education in Britain

From the 1830s on, the Government – seeking to advance British competitiveness – established schools of design to train students to work in industry, thereby raising the overall standards of design and manufacture. The design education system that evolved can be likened to a wheel, with the School of Design in South Kensington, London as the hub, and as the spokes the National Course curriculum required of all students, including those in schools of art throughout the country.[54] The School of Design – operating from 1864 as the National Art Training School and from 1896 as the Royal College of Art – educated art-teacher trainees and those preparing for careers in industry. Students throughout the country took classes at variety of venues, including elementary day schools, evening continuation schools, teacher training colleges, schools of art, the National Scholars programme, and summer courses at the National Art Training School. Tuition costs were defrayed by student fees, grants, scholarships and awards based on performance at standardised examinations and competitions. The National Course required that all students in the system progress through a highly-structured curriculum of drawing from two- and three-dimensional forms, to modelling, design, and technical classes in applied arts areas, such as textiles, metalwork, and porcelain.

The growth and eventual scope of national art and design education in Britain is attested to by the increase in the number of art schools from fewer than 20 in 1852 to 284 by 1897.[55] The number of students receiving art instruction through the government's Department of Science and Art escalated from 55,000 in 1857 to 2.6 million by 1897.[56] However, the wheel did not always roll smoothly toward improved manufacture; throughout the years the South Kensington system was criticised on a number of fronts, including the rigid nature of the National Course curriculum, the ineffectiveness of both the administration and teachers, and the increasing emphasis on the fine arts.[57] Walter Crane, Director of Design at the Manchester School of Art from 1893 to 1896 and Principal of the Royal College of Art from 1898 to March 1899, criticised the "rather cut and dried and wooden courses prescribed by the Department".[58]

The grants in aid of art instruction made to schools by the Department were based on payment by results: student performance in examinations that were part of the National Course curriculum. Day scathingly referred to this system as "a standing temptation to masters to cram their pupils instead of teaching them".[59] Critics contended that the National Art Training School had veered away from its original mission of training designers for industry and focused instead on the fine arts, which was supported by the fact that by 1888 more than 75 percent of the students were in fine art.[60]

Day the educator: teaching, lecturing and curriculum development

Despite his very heavy work schedule in the 1890s, Day immersed himself in an array of educational activities: he examined student work in painting and ornament; he lectured on practical design and ornament to the National Scholars at South Kensington, at the National Art Training School in 1895, and from 1896 to 1899 at the Royal College of Art; and taught two

courses at the Royal Institution.[61] He was a lively lecturer, speaking with force and conviction and enlivening his presentations with many lantern slides.[62]

Day had not attended design school, but had educated himself through study and workshop experience. He was deeply interested in developing a less rigid and more effective curriculum, and in 1893 he introduced his syllabus for students studying for the examinations in design.[63] Nevertheless, it was his textbooks on design, the first of which was published in 1887, that made his knowledge and practical advice available to a wider student audience. Day's very useful and practical textbooks, which were officially approved by the Board of Education, went through many editions and were used in design schools for decades.

Examining and judging student work

From 1890 until at least 1908, Day was an examiner for the National Art Competition, held annually by the Department of Science and Art and from April 1900, by its successor, the Board of Education.[64] Day, William Morris, Walter Crane and William De Morgan were among those who periodically served as examiners for students' work submitted for the competition. Day's expertise in design and his knowledge of the practical realities of manufacture are evident in the number of areas in which he judged students' work over two decades: interiors; book covers and illustration; textiles (printed and woven textiles, damasks, laces, embroidery); carpets and linoleum; metal and ironwork; stained glass; wallpapers; ceramics (tiles, pottery); mosaics; jewellery; stencils; and painted hangings. Gold, silver and bronze medals were given to the winners, and books – including those written by Day – were also awarded as prizes.

The National Art Competition drew substantial coverage in the art press, and Day wrote a number of articles on these events for the *Art Journal*, *Magazine of Art*, and *Manchester Guardian*. His journalism revealed his views on administrator and teacher performance and the fine arts emphasis that had drawn considerable criticism. Day noted that while the performance of students in the National Competition reflected to some extent the quality of teaching in the schools, it depended more on the degree of talent of individual students.[65] Exceptionally gifted students would be likely to do well without a great deal of teaching – as "genius somehow finds out its way".[66]

Day argued that, since "the very highest awards mark rather the fluctuations in the crop of individual talent than the current state of teaching", the quality of teaching was more clearly reflected in the work of the majority of students who garnered the smaller prizes.[67] "A gold medallist is a sort of *rara avis*," he commented, "hatched perhaps in the scholastic nest, but hardly belonging to it", and more credit may be given to the school that it really deserves.[68] He also felt that performance by students of more moderate ability was more significant for the eventual improvement of manufacture than "the superlative merit of Gold Medallists, who will in all probability drift eventually into painting, sculpture, or some other form of art remote from manufacture".[69]

Day's attention remained firmly fixed on the mission of the system to train young people to design for industry. He observed that while there was not a great deal of originality demonstrated in the competitions, "originality is a very rare thing; and, after all, it is not the business of the Department to produce it. All that the schools can do is to turn out good workmen, and give invention a chance of expressing itself with full effect".[70] Although acknowledging the necessity of student examinations, Day judged them to be "at best a very fallacious test of capacity".[71] The real test of competence was for students to demonstrate proficiency in all the steps from the initial design through to its production. He was pleased to observe that by 1899 a major improvement had taken place, largely due

10.10 Beatrice Waldram. From *Arts and Crafts* 4 (1905-6): 75
Trustees of the National Library of Scotland, Edinburgh

to examiners' demands: more practical work was submitted, often accompanied by "executed work for comparison with the design, so as to show how it works out, which of course is the best possible test of its fitness for supposed purpose".[72]

Day was in high demand as an evaluator of design education programmes. He evaluated provincial schools of art and did a tour of inspection of schools in 1898.[73] Other educational and professional groups, including the School of Art Woodcarving, the English Silk Weaving Company and Spitalfields Silk Association, frequently requested his help in judging student and exhibition work.[74]

Mentoring young designers

Although Day's primary influence on design education was through his textbooks on design, he had a personal impact, as well. Newspaper accounts of his death frequently referred to his generous gift of time and attention to others and his personal qualities as a teacher, describing him as "unwearied in giving private help and counsel to young artists who came to him".[75] His lectures and advice "were keenly appreciated by his students, many of whom came to know him as the kindest of friends as well as an inspiring teacher".[76] His advice was seen as helpful, practical and objective, and other well-known designers were proud to be able to say they had been taught by him.[77]

A number of British and American students tutored by Day became well-known designers, including designer and metal craftsman Omar Ramsden.[78] Beatrice Waldram, employed as Day's assistant from c.1898 to 1904, refined her techniques under his guidance and later went into business for herself.[79] Louisa Pesel, a designer and embroideress, who later became well-known in professional and educational circles in both England and Greece, trained under Day.[80] The prominent Chicago interior decorator of the late 1890s, Alice E. Neale – "the pioneer in the profession in the west" – studied design in London under both Day and Walter Crane.[81] Another American, Dorothea Warren O'Hara, was a successful china painter, writer and teacher who studied under Day prior to establishing herself in New York around the turn of the century.[82]

Day also tutored graduate students from the Philadelphia School of Design who had been awarded P.A.B. Widener European Fellowships for Practical Design. The Widener students received a year's study abroad that included tutoring from a professional designer, studio experience, and study in applied arts at the Victoria and Albert Museum.[83] Day was the first tutor for the programme, directing the studies of five fellowship recipients from 1900 to 1904; included in this group was Mary S. Braid (Hartman), who went on to become a textile designer and an instructor at the Philadelphia School of Design.[84] Illness forced Day to relinquish this responsibility to Lindsay Butterfield in 1905.[85]

Retaining his sense of community in later years

Rearrangement of the Victoria and Albert Museum

Propelled by his agenda of promoting the marriage of design and industry, Day continued to contribute to the design community even in his last years. In 1908 the Victoria and Albert Museum decided to reevaluate the arrangement of its collections, in preparation for the opening of its new building designed by Aston Webb to the east of Exhibition Road.[86] While the Museum had been founded to encourage manufacture and decorative design, the collections had widened, the parameters had become less defined, and its function obscured.[87]

A Committee of Rearrangement was appointed in February 1908 and included Day, W.A.S. Benson, Harry Powell of the glassmaking firm James Powell & Sons, J.C. Wedgwood, and museum administrator Cecil H. Smith. William Burton, managing director of Pilkington's Tile & Pottery Co., architect Reginald Blomfield, and Sir Charles Dilke were also involved in the project.[88] The committee was charged with preparing a plan that would facilitate study of the collection by designers, craftspeople, manufacturers and students involved in commercial manufacture, and to advise on the future development of the Museum.[89]

The Museum's exhibits had been arranged by material and technique.[90] Around the turn of the century, some museums were acquiring period rooms, rethinking their methods of arrangement of artefacts, and considering arrangement by period and style, to provide interest and appeal to a wider audience.[91] The Committee had only five months to evaluate this issue and make its recommendations so that structural issues relating to the nearly completed new building could be accommodated.[92]

After their brief study, the Committee concluded that the Museum should be arranged primarily for those who used it as a museum of industrial art, as a learning resource for designers and manufacturers, rather than as a vehicle for educating the public about the history of objects.[93] The aim, they decided, was not to turn the institution into a "Museum of Commercial Products", but rather to improve the quality of design for manufacture; therefore the Committee recommended continuing the system of classification by materials, incorporating the development of design and methods of workmanship.[94] The Committee's recommendations provoked some negative reactions in the trade and popular press.[95]

10.11 Aston Webb. From *Magazine of Art* 22 (1899): 332

It is not surprising that Day "greatly influenced the scheme which was eventually adopted".[96] He had invested heavily, both emotionally and intellectually, in this issue. The study of museum collections had been such an important part of his own self-education and was the focus of much of his leisure time, as well as being one of his teaching methods. Several months before the Committee's report was issued, Day gave his lecture 'How to Make the Most of a Museum' to the Society of Arts; intriguingly, the meeting was chaired by

10.12 The Ceramic Gallery, Victoria and Albert Museum, London. From *Art Journal* (1887): 223

Aston Webb.[97] Day's wealth of knowledge was evident in both his detailed analysis of the practices of Continental museums and the relationship of physical aspects, such as size of display cases, colours used in the galleries, labels, and lighting on the display of objects. The core of his lecture, however, was the idea that the "order of arrangement should be that rather of artistic and technical development than of historic periods".[98] While he realised that it was not possible to satisfy everyone, he felt it important that a museum of applied arts should be arranged for those who want to study the development of particular arts, and "the purpose of those who want to learn is only half served by the too popular show place".[99] While admitting that his view was "prosaic", he contended that "a museum is not a story book but a work of reference", and one should "acknowledge its strictly utilitarian purpose".[100] The Society of Arts awarded him a silver medal (his second from the Society) for this lecture.[101]

The gist of many of these points was also incorporated in an article Day penned for the *Manchester Guardian*.[102] He reiterated these ideas at the Third International Art Congress in 1908. In a discussion on 'Museum Co-Operation in Art-Teaching', he expressed his strong view that museums were places to teach and should be arranged to accomplish the education and training of students, rather than being organised to draw in public crowds.[103] If, as some teachers said, students were bewildered by a museum, it was because they came unprepared, and it was the duty of teachers to prepare them.[104]

The Design Club

In 1909 Day was instrumental in the founding of the Design Club to bring together designers for industry with manufacturers and retailers, who were lay members. Obviously this activity played right to the heart of Day's beliefs that design occurred where art and commerce met, that design was not an autonomous activity, and that availability of high-quality products depended on designers, manufacturers and retailers working together. The opening of the Club's premises at 22 Newman St. in February 1909 was advertised in the professional press with an invitation designed by C.F.A. Voysey – featuring head, heart and hand – and the announcement that Day and Arthur Lasenby Liberty would deliver the keynote addresses.[105]

Lindsay P. Butterfield was Secretary of the group, and among the designers, manufacturers and retail firms who bolstered membership to over 100, were Walter Crane, Ambrose Heal, Jr., William Burton of Pilkington Tiles, Metford Warner of Jeffrey & Co., and principals from Alexander Morton & Co., Alexander Rottman, Josiah Wedgwood, A. Sanderson & Sons, F. &. C. Osler, and Heal & Sons, Ltd.[106] Day was chairman of the Committee until just before his death.[107] The Club closed shortly before World War I.[108]

Day and design education at the turn of the century

In the last two years of his life, Day took advantage of three special opportunities to advance his ideas about preparing designers for industry. The first of these was the presentation of his paper 'Design' at the London County Council Conference on the Teaching of Drawing in Elementary and Secondary Schools, held in 1908 to assess theory, practice, and methods.[109] That same year Day lectured on 'Art Teaching in Relation to Industrial Design' at the Third International Art Congress for the Development of Drawing and Art Teaching and Their Applications to Industry, a huge event that garnered attendance of over 1,800 attendees representing 38 countries.[110] The third opportunity came in the autumn of 1909, when

THE·COMMITTEE·OF
THE·DESIGN·CLUB
REQUEST·THE·PLEASURE
OF·YOUR·COMPANY·ON
THE·OCCASION·OF·THE
OPENING·OF·THEIR
PREMISES·AT·22·NEW-
MAN·STREET·W·ON
TUESDAY·THE·16TH·OF·FE
BRUARY·1909·AT·8·PM
BY·LEWIS·F·DAY·AND
A·LASENBY·LIBERTY.
SMOKING·CONCERT.

THE·DESIGN·CLUB
22·NEWMAN·STREET
NAME
INTRODUCED·BY
FEBRUARY·16·1909

The mystical symbol at the top is intended to express the essentials of design—Head, Heart, and Hand, "the head crowned with the band of restraint." The meaning of the symbol is better than its decorative effect, which is not very attractive; but the writing (which includes nearly all the letters of the alphabet) is a fine example of script.

10.13 C.F.A. Voysey. Invitation to the opening of Design Club in 1909. From *Builder* 96 (1909): 236
Newberry Library, Chicago

10.14 Board of Education. Heading from notice to students of the Royal College of Art (1904)

Board of Education, South Kensington.

ROYAL COLLEGE OF ART.

COUNCIL OF ADVICE.
Sir W. RICHMOND, K.C.B., R.A. T. G. JACKSON, R.A. T. BROCK, R.A. WALTER CRANE, R.W.S.
PRINCIPAL AND HEAD MASTER.
A. SPENCER, A.R.C.A. (London).

Professor of Modelling.
E. LANTERI.

Professor of Architecture.
A. BERESFORD-PITE, F.R.I.B.A.

Professor of Design.
W. R. LETHABY.

Professor of Painting.
G. MOIRA.

Day was appointed by the Board of Education as Visitor to the Royal College of Art. He was charged with the task of evaluating the structure and effectiveness of the School of Design, directed at the time by W.R. Lethaby, which in 1901 had been reorganised into four schools: Architecture, Painting, Sculpture and Design.[111] On the face of it, these three occasions appear quite disparate; however, running through them all were several major themes of central importance in Day's thinking.

As ten years had passed since his last inspection of schools for the Board of Education, in preparation for his lecture for the Third International Art Congress, Day contacted art educators and manufacturers, particularly those in industrial districts, to bring himself up-to-date on recent developments in design education. While concluding that the skills of young people looking for employment had vastly improved, Day thought some schools continued to follow directions that deviated from their mission of preparing designers for industry.

The first of these was an over-emphasis on fine arts training for which the system had been criticised for years, and which Day contended bred reluctance in students to look for employment in industry. The second – a handicrafts orientation – had led "further to divert the energies of teaching away from industry", for while Day agreed that this approach fostered skill and craftsmanship in individuals, he contended that it ignored the realities of designing for manufacture.[112] "It has become the fashion to exalt handicraft at the expense of design," he observed.[113] These were among the very criticisms he levelled at the Royal College of Art: the pictorial emphasis of many of the required exercises; the neglect of practical application of the work to industry; and an over-emphasis on handicrafts.[114] His critical comments somewhat tempered by advice from the Board that the report might be made public, Day nevertheless gave a frank assessment of the College's programmes.[115] At the heart of Day's concerns was the disservice to students that resulted from current practice in design education. Training skewed either to the fine arts or crafts unrelated to the demands of manufacture produced the same net result: scores of young people unable to earn a living in either the fine arts or in narrow areas of craft specialisation for which there were few to no opportunities for employment.[116]

A closer working relationship with industry would help design schools stay true to their mission, Day advised. While schools did not have to teach all particulars of a trade, ideally they would have some connections with firms that could help acquaint students with work in various industries.[117] "Manufacturers are apt to take too narrow a view of artistic education, schools too impractical a view," Day commented; and while he did not believe commercial influence should predominate, he did feel that industry "should be fairly represented" in schools, including on the governing boards.[118] The benefits of such cooperation between art schools and industry were seen in factories such as Delft in Holland, Rörstrand in Sweden, and the Royal Porcelain Works at Copenhagen where "painters and modellers are drawn from the state schools".[119]

Day was convinced that a combination of design education instruction in school

and practical training in a workshop was the most effective option for training designers.[120] Effective design education was not so much *technical* education as *practical* education that taught students how to design under conditions that would affect how and whether designs worked out well when produced. Although originality and invention could not be taught, planning a design and how it could be executed under practical conditions could and ought to be taught.[121]

Day viewed design as both art and problem-solving and observed that even elementary school children could enjoy being introduced to this concept. Children took naturally to geometric forms and could develop patterns by experimenting with them, rather than beginning with a difficult task like designing ornament from plant growth.[122] Experimenting with forms would also help them plan out a design, a skill of paramount importance in Day's mind. "Every design is the building up of a scheme, every practical design is the solution of a problem," he said, explaining that children would attack a problem eagerly if a teacher interested them in "playing the game".[123] If the design or a portion of it could be produced in needlework, cut stencils, and so forth, so much the better, for the student could then see how the design worked out.[124]

While older design students might not know exactly what they would be designing when employed, Day felt that the specific application was secondary to learning how to design "under strictly practical conditions", which would make them adaptable in working in industry.[125] This underscored Day's cardinal belief that one could be true to one's art and be commercially competent, as well. Instead of starting with craftsmanship in wood-work, metalwork, or other materials, students should be taught to design. Day's recommendation was to "*teach a craft incidentally to design*, that is to say, with the purpose of enforcing the dependence of design upon conditions of production, and of accustoming the student to work under such conditions".[126] Ideally, teachers would have had practical experience in designing for industry themselves, although he admitted that was not usually the case: "It is only by exception that one finds a man at once practical workman, educated artist, and efficient teacher."[127] In lieu of that, instruction might need to be provided by two persons – a designer and a workman.

Day believed that schools had a responsibility to prepare students for life as adults. That included providing skills training in types of work for which students could realistically hope to earn a living, not in areas demanding such exceptional skills or in narrow specialised areas with few opportunities for employment.[128] In Day's mind this was not just an issue of professional training, but was one of character development as well, for industry "does not want craftsmen too proud of their invention to carry out any design but their own, or to adapt themselves to the necessities of industrial production".[129]

By the early 1900s, educational theorists ran the gamut from proponents of free expression by the student, unhampered by required exercises and teacher criticism, to advocates of more guided instruction from the teacher. Day took his position with the latter group. His no-nonsense approach to education undoubtedly stemmed from his own strict upbringing, and he apparently saw no need to alter this view in adulthood. If the teacher was not going to give students some direction, what was the point of teaching?[130] Simply letting young people follow their own preferences did them a disservice, because one did not get to do whatever one liked in the real world: "The purpose of education is to fit young people for life – and for the life there is a reasonable chance and likelihood of their living – not for the ideal life beyond the reach of all but the very few."[131] Day's ideas about education and the development of the whole person continue to resonate today.

ENDNOTES

Chapter 1: The Life of Lewis Foreman Day (1845-1910)

1. 'Lewis Foreman Day', *Journal of Decorative Art* 6 (1886): 891. This article was based on an interview with Day and, although unsigned, may have been written by W. Sutherland, publisher of the *Journal of Decorative Art.*

2. Lewis F. Day, 'Victorian Progress in Applied Design', *Art Journal* (1887): 185; Lewis F. Day, 'Decorative Art at the Paris Exhibition 3', *Manchester Guardian* (26 June, 1900): 12; Walter Crane and Lewis F. Day, *Moot Points: Friendly Disputes on Art & Industry* (London: B.T. Batsford, 1903), 11; Lewis F. Day, 'Decorative Art 12', *British Architect* 10 (1878): 253.

3. The biographical facts of Day's life have been gleaned from standard reference sources, including: census data; birth, marriage and death records in the Family Records Centre; parish registers; probate records; poor rate books; and Post Office directories, and will not be individually cited.

4. The name Rye Terrace was abolished in 1880 and the entire street was renamed Peckham Rye and renumbered. No.12 Rye Terrace is now known as 149 Peckham Rye. I am grateful to local historian Ron Woollacott for this information and much of the background on the area.

5. Ron Woollacott, A *Historical Tour of Nunhead and Peckham Rye.* (Nunhead: Ron Woollacott, 1995), 30.

6. In 1880 Beaufort House was renamed 125 Peckham Rye. It was demolished in the 1930s and replaced by an apartment block called Brookstone Court.

7. Samuel Smiles, *Self-Help: With Illustrations of Character and Conduct* (London: John Murray, 1859). The book went through numerous editions thereafter.

8. Obituary, 'Lewis F. Day', *Manchester Guardian* (19 April, 1910): 8; Joseph J. Green, 'The Late Lewis Forman [*sic*] Day', *The Friend* 50 (20 May, 1910): 329. Joseph Green was a member of the Society of Friends and was related to the Day family.

9. Elizabeth Isichei, *Victorian Quakers* (London: Oxford University Press, 1970), 170-1.

10. Green, 'Late Lewis Day', 329.

11. Green, 'Late Lewis Day', 329.

12. *Extracts from the Minutes and Epistles of the Yearly Meeting of the Religious Society of Friends, Held in London from Its Institution to the Present Time. Relating to Christian Doctrine, Practice and Discipline.* 5th ed., 1871, with Supplements. (London: Friends' Book Depository, 1871), Printed Epistle (1860), 121; Printed Epistle (1853), 120.

13. *Extracts*, Printed Epistle (1819), 109; Printed Epistle (1692), 105; *Rules of Discipline of the Religious Society of Friends with Advices: Being Extracts from the Minutes and Epistles of their Yearly Meetings, Held in London, from Its First Institution.* 3rd ed. (London: Darton and Harvey, 1834), Printed Epistle (1767), 210-11; Printed Epistle (1812), 212.

14. *Rules*, Printed Epistle (1809), 212; Printed Epistle (1691), 206.

15. 'Quakerism', *The Westminster and Foreign Quarterly Review* (July & October, 1875): 320; Howard H. Brinton, *Friends for 300 Years* (Wallingford, PA: Pendle Hill Publications, 1994), 121.

16. *Rules*, Printed Epistle (1691), 206; *Extracts*, Printed Epistle (1692), 107; Brinton, *Friends*, 137.

17. Obituary, 'Death of Mr. Lewis F. Day: A Famous Decorative Artist', *Glasgow Herald* (April 19, 1910): 8; Obituary, *Manchester Guardian* (April 19, 1910): 8.

18. Crane and Day, *Moot Points*, 54; Dorothy M. Ross, 'Lewis Foreman Day, Designer and Writer on Stained Glass', *Journal of the British Society of Master Glass Painters* (April 1929); reprint (Cambridge: W. Heffer & Sons, 1929): 5. Ross was a close friend of the Day family.

19. Barclay Day, in a letter to Joseph Green after Day's death, quoted in Green, 'Late Lewis Day', 329. Barclay Lewis Day (1839-1913), first a wine merchant, became a painter of flowers and domestic subjects in the 1870s and exhibited at venues including the Royal Academy and Suffolk Street Gallery. See Christopher Wood, *Victorian Painters, Vol. 1, Text* (Woodbridge, Suffolk: Antique Collectors' Club, 1995), 133. He wrote several articles for the *Magazine of Art* in the early 1880s and in the early 1900s edited two books on intellectual history. Barclay and Lewis Day remained close in later years.

20. Crane and Day, *Moot Points*, 54.

21. Richard Tames, *Dulwich and Camberwell Past: with Peckham* (London: Historical Publications, 1997), 110.

22. 'Lewis Foreman Day', *Journal of Decorative Art*, 891.

23. 'Lewis Foreman Day', *Journal of Decorative Art*, 891; Ross, 'Lewis Foreman Day', 5; Green, 'Late Lewis Day', 329.

24. Guildhall Library, microfilm 360/3, Merchant Taylors' School Admissions and Admitted Register 1853-76.

25. Howard Staunton, *The Great Schools of England: An Account of the Foundation, Endowments, and Discipline of the Chief Seminaries of Learning in England* (London: Sampson Low, Son & Marston, 1865), 240; Thomas Edward Kebbel, *The Battle of Life* (London: T. Fisher Unwin, 1912), 67.

26. Ross, 'Lewis Foreman Day', 5; James Augustus Hessey, *Merchant Taylors' School* (London, Founders and Governors of Merchant Taylors' Corporation, c. 1861), 68; Staunton, *Great Schools*, 241.

27. F.W.M. Draper, *Four Centuries of Merchant Taylors' School: 1561-1961* (London: Oxford University Press, 1962), 134, 154; Merchant Taylors' School Archaeological Society, *Merchant Taylors' School: Its Origin, History and Present Surroundings* (Oxford: Basil Blackwell, 1929), 64.

28. Merchant Taylors' School Archaeological Society, *Merchant*, 67; Staunton, *Great Schools*, 240.

29. Staunton, *Great Schools*, 240, 260; Hessey, *Merchant*, 68-9.

30. Staunton, *Great Schools*, 253.

31. Lewis F. Day, 'The Ornament of the Period', *Architect* 29 (1883): 60.

32. Guildhall Library, microfilm 359(64), Merchant Taylors' School Probations, vol. 8, 1848-1859.

33. Obituary, *Manchester Guardian* (19 April, 1910): 8.

34. Lewis F. Day, 'Decorative Art 6', *British Architect* 10 (1878): 2.

35. Obituary, *Manchester Guardian* (19 April, 1910): 8.

36. Lewis F. Day, 'Design in Lettering', *Journal of the Society of Arts* 45 (1896-7): 1110.

37. 'Lewis Foreman Day', *Journal of Decorative Art*, 891; Ross, 'Lewis Foreman Day', 5; Henry Trueman Wood, 'Lewis Foreman Day', *The Dictionary of National Biography*, Supplement, Jan. 1901-Dec. 1911 (Oxford: Oxford University Press, 1976), 483. Wood was a fellow-member of the Society of Arts and became a life-long friend of Day.

38. 'Lewis Foreman Day', *Journal of Decorative Art*, 891; Obituary, *Glasgow Herald* (19 April, 1910): 8; Ross, 'Lewis Foreman Day', 5-6.

39. Ross, 'Lewis Foreman Day', 5.

40. 'Lewis Foreman Day', *Journal of Decorative Art*, 891; Wood, 'Lewis Foreman Day', 483; Ross, 'Lewis Foreman Day', 5.

41. 'Lewis Foreman Day', *Journal of Decorative Art*, 891.

42. 'Lewis Foreman Day', *Journal of Decorative Art*, 891.

43. Lewis F. Day, 'William Morris and His Art', Easter Art Annual, *Art Journal* (1899): 2.

44. 'Lewis Foreman Day', *Journal of Decorative Art*, 891.

45. Ross, 'Lewis Foreman Day', 5-6; 'Obituary', *Glasgow Herald* (19 April, 1910): 8.

46. Lewis F. Day, 'How to Make the Most of a Museum', *Journal of the Society of Arts* 56 (1907-8): 149.

47. *Builder* 26 (1868): 825; 'Lewis Foreman Day', *Journal of Decorative Art*, 891. This essay does not appear to have been published.

48. 'Lewis Foreman Day', *Journal of Decorative Art*, 891; Wood, 'Lewis Foreman Day', 483.

49. 'Lewis Foreman Day', *Journal of Decorative Art*, 891.

50. Lewis F. Day, 'Stained Glass: Its Application to

Domestic Architecture', *Architect* 7 (1872): 59-60.

51. Donald J. Olsen, *Town Planning in London: The Eighteenth and Nineteenth Centuries* (London: Yale University Press, 1964), 80, 91-2.

52. 'Obituary, Mrs. Day', *The Times* (25 May, 1929).

53. Wood, 'Lewis Foreman Day', 483; Ross, 'Lewis Foreman Day', 8. In her MA dissertation 'Lewis Foreman Day' (Royal College of Art, 1980), Elizabeth Rycroft refers to information in the family Bible belonging to a relative of Day that Lewis and Temma Day had a stillborn son in 1875. No records from public or private sources have been located to independently verify this.

54. Full citations for Day's articles and books are given in the Appendix: Selected Bibliography.

55. Walter Crane, *An Artist's Reminiscences* (London: Methuen & Co., 1907; reissued Detroit: Singing Tree Press, 1968), 223-4.

56. Obituary, *Glasgow Herald* (19 April, 1910): 8.

57. Lewis F. Day, 'Art and Life', *Macmillan's Magazine* 85 (1901-2): 429.

58. Day, 'Art and Life', 430-1.

59. Lewis F. Day, 'Principles and Practice of Ornamental Design', *Journal of the Society of Arts* 35 (1886-7):724; Lewis F. Day, 'Some Masters of Ornament', *Journal of the Society of Arts* 41 (1892-3): 803; London correspondence to *Manchester Guardian*, quoted in Green, "Late Lewis Day," 329.

60. Lewis F. Day, 'Stained Glass Windows: As They Were, Are, and Should Be', *Journal of the Society of Arts* 30 (1881-2): 299. A number of times Day described designers as being impatient; see also *Journal of the Society of Arts* 35 (1886-7): 724; *Journal of the Society of Arts* 41 (1892-3): 803.

61. 'Lewis Foreman Day', *Who Was Who 1897-1916* (London: Adam & Charles Black, 1966), 187.

62. Lewis F. Day, *Windows: A Book about Stained and Painted Glass*, 3rd ed. (London: B.T. Batsford, 1909): vii; 'Lewis Foreman Day', *Journal of Decorative Art*, 894; Obituary, *Glasgow Herald* (19 April, 1910): 8.

63. In 1884 the firm changed from a partnership to a limited liability company, occasioned by the retirement of Thomas Buxton Morrish, who was a partner in the business.

64. Council of the Society for the Encouragement of Arts, Manufactures, and Commerce, *Reports on the London International Exhibition of 1872* (London: Bell & Daldy, 1872), 27; *Art Journal Supplement, London International Exhibition 1872*, 5.

65. *Art Journal* (1873): 182, 188. Henry Day was probably a relative.

66. 'The Exhibition of Paintings on China', *Magazine of Art* 1 (1878): 177-9.

67. 'Lewis Foreman Day', *Journal of Decorative Art*, 891.

68. *Architect* 30 (1883): 69, near 69; Metford Warner, 'Some Victorian Designers', manuscript read at the Design Club (Nov. 24, 1909): 20; Victoria and Albert Museum, National Art Library, 86.H.H.13.

69. 'Lewis Foreman Day', *Journal of Decorative Art*, 891; Ross, 'Lewis Foreman Day', 6.

70. 'Lewis Foreman Day', *Journal of Decorative Art*, 891; Ross, 'Lewis Foreman Day', 6.

71. *Art Journal Illustrated Catalogue of the Paris Exhibition 1878*, 106.

72. Lewis F. Day, 'Notes on English Decorative Art in Paris 3', *British Architect* 10 (1878): near 16; *Furniture Gazette* 10 (1878): 159; *Furniture Gazette* 11 (1879): 8-9.

73. *Art Journal Illustrated Catalogue of the Paris Exhibition 1878*, 46; George Augustus Sala, *Paris Herself Again* (London: Remington & Co., 1879), 320.

74. Lewis F. Day, 'Some Conclusions', *Art Journal* (1909): 199.

75. Lewis F. Day, 'Decorative Art 2', *British Architect* 9 (1878): 65.

76. Lewis F. Day, *Nature in Ornament* (London: B.T. Batsford, 1892): 8.

77. Day, *Nature*, 178; Lewis F. Day, *Ornament and Its Application* (London: B.T. Batsford, 1904), 133.

78. Day, *Nature*, 205.

79. Lewis F. Day, 'Decorative Art 3', *British Architect* 9 (1878): 109-110.

80. Day, 'Some Conclusions', 200.

81. Day, *Nature*, 147.

82. Lewis F. Day, 'Originality and Tradition in Design', *Builder* 94 (1908): 422.

83. Lewis F. Day, 'Ornament of the Period', *Architect* 29 (1883): 80.

84. Lewis F. Day, 'Decorative Art 11', *British Architect* 10 (1878): 252; see also Day, 'Ornament of the Period', 60.

85. 'Lewis Foreman Day', *Journal of Decorative Art*, 891.

86. Ross, 'Lewis Foreman Day', 8; Herbert Batsford, 'The Late Mr. Lewis F. Day', *British Architect* 73 (1910): 273.

87. A.F.P., 'The Work of Beatrice Waldram', *Arts and Crafts* (1905): 75.

88. Lewis F. Day, *Pattern Design* (London: B.T. Batsford, 1903), 202, 253.

89. Day, *Pattern Design*, 263-4.

90. For further discussion of this, see Chapter 2: The Designer for Industry.

91. Day, *Pattern Design*, 131,136.

92. Day, *Ornament*, 37, 301.

93. Day, *Ornament*, 312; Day, *Pattern Design*, 262.

94. Day, *Pattern Design*, 55.

95. Day, 'Decorative Art 12', 253.

96. National Archives, BT 50/5, #2487, reg. 26 Feb. 1884; *Furniture Gazette* (1 Nov., 1884): near 356.

97. *Jubilee 1881-1931* (Ramsbottom, Lancashire: Turnbull & Stockdale Ltd., 1931), 19.

98. Anthony J. Cross, *Pilkington's Royal Lancastrian Pottery and Tiles* (London: Richard Dennis, 1980), 53.

99. Batsford also marketed Day's later books as *Textbooks of Ornamental* Design and a few were released through Scribner's Sons in New York for the American market.

100. Crane, *Artist's Reminiscences*, 223-4.

101. H.J.L.J. Masse, *The Art Workers' Guild 1884-1934* (Oxford: Art Workers' Guild, 1935), 7, 22.

102. Masse, *Art Workers'*, 25-7.

103. Minutes of the general committee of the Arts and Crafts Exhibition Society, 13 Nov., 1896, Victoria and Albert Museum, Archive of Art and Design, AAD 1/43-1980. Hereafter this source will be referred to as V&A, AAD.

104. Day, 'William Morris and His Art', 7.

105. See Chapter 2: The Designer for Industry.

106. 'Lewis Foreman Day', *Journal of Decorative Art*, 894.

107. Obituary, *Glasgow Herald* (19 April, 1910): 8; Obituary, 'The Late Mr. Lewis F. Day', *British Architect* 73 (1910): 272-3; Obituary, *Royal Society of Arts Journal* 58 (1909-10): 560.

108. Obituary, *Manchester Guardian* (19 April, 1910): 8; Obituary, *Glasgow Herald* (10 April, 1910): 8; *Journal of the Royal Society of Arts* 58 (1909-10): 267; A. F. P., 'Work', 75; George T. B. Davis, 'The Future of House Decoration', *House Beautiful* 5 (1899): 264.

109. William Burton, 'Note', *Catalogue. Paris Exhibition 1900* (Clifton Junction, Manchester: Pilkington's Tile and Pottery Co., 1900): 12.

110. Burton, 'Note', 12.

111. Lewis F. Day, 'The New Lancastrian Pottery', *Art* Journal (1904), 201.

112. Day, 'New Lancastrian', 203.

113. Day, 'New Lancastrian', 202.

114. Day, 'New Lancastrian', 202-4.

115. Day, 'New Lancastrian', 201-2; Lewis F. Day, 'Favrile Glass', *Magazine of Art* (1901): 544.

116. Lewis F. Day, 'Wall Coverings and Hangings at the Paris Exhibition', *Art Journal Supplement, Paris Exhibition 1900*, 163; *Paris Exhibition 1900: Official British Catalogue* (London: Royal Commission, 1900), 120.

117. Warner, 'Some Victorian Designers', 20-4.

118. *Journal of Decorative Art* 30 (1910): 50.

119. Day, *Ornament*, fig. 42; Jeffrey & Co., presscuttings, Victoria and Albert Museum (V&A), E.42B (2)-1945: 181; *Paris Exhibition 1900: Official British Catalogue*, 116.

120. Jeffrey & Co., presscuttings, V&A, E.42B(2)-1945: 97-8.

121. Lewis F. Day, 'Decorative Art at the Paris Exhibition 3', *Manchester Guardian* (June 26, 1900): 12.

122. 'Wall Coverings and Hangings', 161-5.

123. Lewis F. Day, *Every-day Art* (London: B.T. Batsford, 1882), 207-8.

124. Lewis F. Day, 'L'Art Nouveau', *Art Journal* (1900): 294; Day, 'Decorative Art at the Paris Exhibition 3', 12; Lewis F. Day, 'The New Art', *Macmillan's Magazine* 85 (1901-2): 22.

125. Day, 'L'Art Nouveau', 294-6; *Magazine of Art* (1904): 211-12; Walter Crane, *William Morris to Whistler* (London: G. Bell & Sons, 1911), 232.

126. Day, 'New Art', 19.

127. Day, 'L'Art Nouveau', 294, 295-6.

128. Lewis F. Day, 'Decorative and Industrial Art at the Glasgow Exhibition 2', *Art Journal* (1901): 240-1. While Day made a passing reference to Mackintosh's innovative design for the School of Art, he did not discuss him in any length in any of his journalism.

129. Day, 'Decorative Art at the Paris Exhibition 3', 12.

130. Crane and Day, *Moot Points*, 29.

131. Crane and Day, *Moot Points*, 30; Day, *Ornament*, 137.

132. Day, *Ornament*, 262, 312.

133. Crane and Day, *Moot Points*, 24, 34.

134. Crane and Day, *Moot Points*, 11.

135. Crane and Day, *Moot Points*, 25, 62.

136. Crane and Day, *Moot Points*, 31, 34.

137. *Art Chronicle* (April 2, 1910).

138. Lewis F. Day, 'Machine-Made Art', *Art Journal* (1885): 108.

139. Day, *Ornament*, 137-8.

140. Lindsay Butterfield, *Autobiography* (unpublished manuscript, undated) 85; *Commencement Programs* (Philadelphia: Philadelphia School of Design, 1900-5; Barbara Morris, *Inspiration for Design* (London: Victoria and Albert Museum, 1986), 77-8.

141. Butterfield, *Autobiography*, 85; Morris, *Inspiration*, 77.

142. By 1914 (four years after Day's death), William Turnbull's second son (also named William) had assumed the artistic directorship. *Jubilee*, 27.

143. Lewis F. Day, 'Art Teaching in Relation to Industrial Design', *Third International Art Congress for the Development of Drawing and Art Teaching and Their Application to Industries. Transaction.* (London: Office of the Congress, 1908), 191.

144. Lewis F. Day, 'Design', *Reports of a Conference on the Teaching of Drawing in Elementary and Secondary Schools* (London: London County Council, 1912), 66.

145. Board of Education: *Victoria and Albert Museum: Report of the Committee of Re-arrangement* (London: HMSO, 1908), 17.

146. Lewis F. Day, 'The Making of a Stained Glass Window', *Journal of the Society of Arts* 46 (1897-8): 421-8; Lewis F. Day, 'How to Make the Most of a Museum', *Journal of the Society of Arts* 56 (1907-8): 146-55.

147. Obituary, *Manchester Guardian* (19 April, 1910): 8; *Royal Society of Arts Journal* 58 (1909-10): 454; V&A AAD, Lewis F. Day nominal file, SF934, letter from A. Richmond to Day, 24 September, 1909.

148. Day, 'Originality and Tradition', 43.

149. Obituary, *Glasgow Herald* (19 April, 1910): 8.

150. Day, *Pattern Design*, 264.

151. Obituary, 'Ruth Morrish Day', *Royal Society of Arts Journal* 66 (1917-8): 188.

Chapter 2: Designing for Industry

1. Lewis F. Day, 'Decorative Art at the Paris Exhibition 3', *Manchester Guardian* (26 June, 1900): 12.

2. Lewis F. Day, 'Decorative Art 12', *British Architect* 10 (1878): 253.

3. Lewis F. Day, 'Victorian Progress in Applied Design', *Art Journal* (1887): 185-202; this reference 185. In this article Day assessed major developments in design and manufacture between the Great Exhibition in 1851 and the Royal Jubilee Exhibition in 1887.

4. In 'Victorian Progress in Applied Design', Day discussed the contributions of Owen Jones in some detail, but did not mention the activities of Henry Cole and his exhibition on 'False Principles of Design' in 1852. In referring to the Department of Science and Art, which administered the design education system, Day commented that "it is rather strange how little direct influence the Department has had upon British manufacture generally"(191). Day had plenty to say about the shortcomings of the design education system regarding its mission of training designers for industry. For further discussion of this, see Chapter 10: Colleagues and Students.

5. Lewis F. Day, 'Some Conclusions', *Art Journal* (1909): 199.

6. Day, 'Some Conclusions', 199.

7. Day, 'Some Conclusions', 200.

8. Day, 'Decorative Art 12', 253; Lewis F. Day, 'Mere Ornament', *Art Journal* (1901): 18.

9. Day, 'Decorative Art 12', 253.

10. Day, 'Some Conclusions', 200.

11. Lewis F. Day, *Ornament and Its Application* (London: B.T. Batsford, 1904), 1.

12. Lewis F. Day, 'Decorative Art 2', *British Architect* 9 (1878): 64.

13. Lewis F. Day, 'Decorative Art 1', *British Architect* 9 (1878): 18; Day, 'Some Conclusions', 199; Lewis F. Day, 'Meaning in Ornament', *Art Journal* (1887): 237.

14. Lewis F. Day, 'Decorative Art 9', *British Architect* 10 (1878): 229.

15. Day, *Ornament*, 15.

16. Day, 'Decorative Art 9', 228; Day, *Ornament*, 1.

17. Day, *Ornament*, 18, 267, 260.

18. Day, *Ornament*, 232.

19. Day, *Ornament*, 87; Day, 'Decorative Art 2', 65.

20. Lewis F. Day, 'Mere Ornament', 51; *Art Journal* (1901): 51; Lewis F. Day, *Nature in Ornament* (London: B.T. Batsford, 1892), 236.

21. Day, 'Mere Ornament', 19.

22. Day, *Nature*, 244-6.

23. Walter Crane and Lewis F. Day, *Moot Points: Friendly Disputes on Art & Industry* (London: B.T. Batsford, 1903), 78; Day, 'Meaning', 239.

24. Day, 'Mere Ornament', 20-1.

25. Day, 'Some Conclusions', 199.

26. Day, 'Decorative Art 1', 18; Day, *Nature*, 12.

27. Day, 'Decorative Art 2', 65; Day, 'Some Conclusions', 200.

28. Day, 'Decorative Art 1', 18.

29. Day, 'Some Conclusions', 199.

30. Day, 'Decorative Art 1', 18.

31. Day, *Ornament*, 7-8.

32. Day, *Ornament*, 10.

33. Day, *Nature*, 84.

34. Day, 'Decorative Art 1', 18; Day, *Nature*, 6; Day, *Ornament*, 13.

35. Day, *Nature*, 27.

36. Lewis F. Day, *Pattern Design* (London: B.T. Batsford, 1903), 263; Day, *Nature*, 85.

37. Day, *Pattern Design*, 261.

38. Day, 'Some Conclusions', 200.

39. Lewis F. Day, 'Fortnightly Notes on Ornament 21', *British Architect* 12 (1879): 162.

40. Day, 'Some Conclusions', 200.

41. Day, *Nature*, 8.

42. Day, *Nature*, 8; Day, 'Some Conclusions', 200.

43. Day, *Nature*, 52-3.

44. Lewis F. Day, 'An Artist in Floral Design', *Art Journal* (1901): 369.

45. Day, *Nature*, 102; pl. 48.

46. Day, *Nature*, 98-9.

47. Day, *Nature*, 83.

48. Day, *Nature*, 80.

49. Day, *Nature*, 79; pl. 38.

50. Day, 'Victorian Progress', 193.

51. Day, 'Artist in Floral Design', 370; Crane and Day, *Moot Points*, 20; Day, 'Mere Ornament', 50.

52. Lewis F. Day, 'Decorative Art 3', *British Architect* 9 (1878): 109-10.

53. Lewis F. Day, 'The Ornament of the Period', *Architect* 29 (1883): 78.

54. Day, 'Ornament of the Period', 78; Day, *Nature*, 175.

55. Day, 'Decorative Art 3', 109; Day, *Nature*, 175.

56. Day, *Nature*, 7; Day, 'Ornament of the Period', 60.

57. Day, 'Some Conclusions', 200.

58. Day, *Nature*, 104-5.

59. Day, 'Fortnightly Notes on Ornament 2', *British Architect* 11 (1879): 25; Day, *Nature*, 44.

60. Day, *Nature*, 70.

61. Day, 'Some Conclusions', 199; Day, 'Ornament of the Period', 78.

62. Day, 'Victorian Progress', 191.

63. Day, 'Victorian Progress', 191-2.

64. Day, 'Victorian Progress', 190.

65. Day, 'Victorian Progress', 194.

66. Day, 'Victorian Progress', 194. For further discussion of Day's views on Talbert and his influence, see Chapter 7: Clocks and Furniture.

67. Day, *Nature*, 147.

68. Day, 'Fortnightly Notes 2', 25.

69. Day, 'Victorian Progress', 195.

70. Day, 'Victorian Progress', 195.

71. Lewis F. Day, 'Decorative Art 6', *British Architect* 10 (1878): 53.

72. Day, 'Victorian Progress', 197.

73. Day, 'Victorian Progress', 197.

74. Day, 'Decorative Art 6', 52-3.

75. Lewis Foreman Day, *Windows: A Book About Stained and Painted Glass*, 3rd ed. (London: B.T. Batsford, 1909), vii; 'Lewis Foreman Day', *Journal of Decorative Art 6* (1886): 894; Obituary, *Glasgow Herald* (19 April, 1910): 8.

76. Dorothy M. Ross, 'Lewis Foreman Day. Designer and writer on Stained Glass', *Journal of the British Society of Master Glass Painters* (April 1929); reprint (Cambridge: W. Heffer & Sons, 1929): 5-6; 'Obituary', *Glasgow Herald* (19 April, 1910): 8. See also Chapter 10: Colleagues and Students.

77. Lewis F. Day, *Every-day Art* (B.T. Batsford, 1882), 259-60; Day, 'Victorian Progress', 187; Ralph N. Wornum, *Analysis of Ornament: The Characteristics of Styles*, 7th ed. (London: Chapman & Hall, 1882); Owen Jones, *The Grammar of Ornament* (London: Messrs. Day & Son, 1856). Wornum's book was first published in 1855. Both books went through many editions.

78. Day, 'Victorian Progress', 187-8.

79. Day, 'Victorian Progress', 188.

80. Day, 'Victorian Progress', 188.

81. Lewis F. Day, 'Originality and Tradition in Design', *Builder* 94 (1908): 422.

82. Lewis F. Day, 'Eclecticism', *British Architect* 17 (1882): 146; Day, 'Originality and Tradition', 422.

83. Lewis F. Day, 'Eclecticism, or Choice', *British Architect* 17 (1882): 170.

84. Day, 'Originality and Tradition', 422.

85. Day, 'Originality and Tradition', 422.

86. Day, 'Ornament of the Period', 80; Day, 'Originality and Tradition', 422.

87. Day, 'Originality and Tradition', 422; Day, 'Ornament of the Period', 80.

88. Day, *Ornament*, 72-3.

89. Day, *Ornament*, 26.

90. Day, 'Some Conclusions', 199.

91. Day, *Ornament*, 125.

92. Day, 'Decorative Art 12', 253.

93. Day, 'Eclecticism', 146.

94. Day, 'Originality and Tradition', 422.

95. Lewis F. Day, 'Some Conclusions', 199.

96. Day, 'Some Conclusions, 199; Day, *Ornament*, 260.

97. Day, 'Decorative Art 1', 18.

98. Lewis F. Day, 'Design Applied to Woodcarving', *Journal of the Society of Arts* 38 (1889-90): 810.

99. Lewis F. Day, 'Machine-Made Art', *Art Journal* (1885): 110.

100. Day, *Pattern Design*, 2-3.

101. Day, *Pattern Design*, 8.

102. Day, *Pattern Design*, 4.

103. Day, *Pattern Design*, 168.

104. Day, *Ornament*, 261.

105. Day, *Pattern Design*, 191-2.

106. Day, *Pattern Design*, 252-3.

107. Day, *Ornament*, 52.

108. Day, *Pattern Design*, 2-3.

109. Day, *Ornament*, 260.

110. Day, *Pattern Design*, 164.

111. Day, *Pattern Design*, 8.

112. Day, *Pattern Design*, 8.

113. Day, *Pattern Design*, 168.

114. Day, *Pattern Design*, 168.

115. Day, *Pattern Design*, 163; 166, illus. 182.

116. Day, *Pattern Design*, 197.

117. Day, *Pattern Design*, 70.

118. Day, *Pattern Design*, 182.

119. Day, *Ornament*, 285.

120. Day, *Ornament*, 266.

121. Day, *Pattern Design*, 201.

122. Day, *Pattern Design*, 253.

123. Day, *Pattern Design*, 211.

124. Day, *Pattern Design*, 204-6; illus. 213.

125. Crane and Day, *Moot Points*, 93-4, 89.

126. Day, 'Mere Ornament', 51.

127. Crane and Day, *Moot Points*, 80.

128. Crane and Day, *Moot Points*, 87; Day, *Ornament*, 286.

129. Day, *Nature*, 178; Lewis F. Day, 'Animals in Decoration: A Rejoinder', *Magazine of Art* 9 (1886): 494.

130. Crane and Day, *Moot Points*, 88.

131. Day, *Ornament*, 133.

132. Day, *Nature*, 180.

133. Crane and Day, *Moot Points*, 92, 87-9; Day, *Ornament*, 290.

134. Crane and Day, *Moot Points*, 89.

135. Crane and Day, *Moot Points*, 93, 86.

136. Day, *Nature*, 193.

137. Lewis F. Day, 'An Artist in Design', *Magazine of Art* 10 (1887): 95-100.

138. Day, 'An Artist', 98.

139. Day, 'An Artist', 98.

140. Day, *Pattern Design*, 191.

141. Day, *Pattern Design*, 193, illus. 206. The 'Grotesque' wallpaper was substituted by his fabric of the same name in later editions of the book.

142. Day, *Nature*, pl. 106.

143. Day, *Nature*, 205.

144. Day, *Nature*, 211.

145. Day, *Nature*, 196-7.

146. Day, *Nature*, 195-6.

147. Day, *Pattern Design*, 263-4.

148. Day, *Pattern Design*, 59.

149. Day, *Ornament*, 238.

150. Day, *Pattern Design*, 55.

151. Day, *Pattern Design*, 131.

152. Day, *Pattern Design*, 136, 49.

153. Day, *Pattern Design*, 132.

154. Day, *Pattern Design*, 132.

155. Day, *Pattern Design*, 264.

156. Day, *Pattern Design*, 264.

157. Day, *Nature*, 166.

158. Day, *Ornament*, 295-6.

159. Day, *Pattern Design*, 202, 253.

160. Day, *Nature*, 166; Lewis F. Day, 'Cotton Printing': *Catalogue of Works Exhibited by Members of the Northern Art Workers' Guild of the City of Manchester September 26 to October 22 1898* (Manchester: Chorlton & Knowles, 1989), 11.

161. Day, *Ornament*, 295.

162. Day, *Ornament*, 37.

163. Day, *Ornament*, 301.

164. Day, *Ornament*, 300.

165. Letter from Lawrence Pilkington and William Burton to Lewis F. Day, 23 Jan., 1896; I am grateful to Lawrence D. Burton for sharing this letter. Letter from William Burton to Lewis F. Day, 8 Nov., 1895, reprinted in Lawrence D. Burton, 'William Burton and Pilkington's Tiles Limited', *Journal of the Tiles and Architectural Ceramics Society* 4 (1992): 36; Metford Warner, 'Some Victorian Designers', manuscript read at the Design Club (24 Nov., 1909): 21, Victoria and Albert Museum, National Art Library, 86.HH.13. As Art Director of Turnbull & Stockdale from c.1888-89 and member of the Board of Directors from 1892 to the early 1900s, he would have made many visits to the firm's production facilities in Bury, Lancashire.

166. Day, *Pattern Design*, 262; Day, 'Machine-Made Art', 110; Crane and Day, *Moot Points*, 30.

167. Day, 'Ornament of the Period', 80.

168. Day, 'Machine-Made Art', 110; Lewis F. Day, 'Letter to the Editor', *Journal of the Society of Arts* 46 (1897-8): 495.

169. Lewis F. Day, 'Some Masters of Ornament', *Journal of the Society of Arts* 41 (1892-3): 825; Lewis F. Day, 'Decorative and Industrial Art at the Glasgow Exhibition 2', *Art Journal* (1901): 243.

170. Day, 'Machine-Made Art', 108.

171. Day, *Pattern Design*, 56; Day, *Ornament*, 240.

172. Day, 'Decorative Art 12', 253.

173. Day, 'Machine-Made Art', 108-10; Day, *Ornament*, 181.

174. Day, 'Machine-Made Art', 108; Crane and Day, *Moot Points*, 41-4.

175. Day, 'Machine-Made Art', 108.

176. Day, 'Machine-Made Art', 110.

177. Day, 'Machine-Made Art', 109.

178. Day, 'Machine-Made Art', 109; Crane and Day, *Moot Points*, 16.

179. Crane and Day, *Moot Points*, 20.

180. Day, 'Machine-Made Art', 110.

181. Crane and Day, *Moot Points*, 41.

182. Lewis F. Day, 'A Kensington Interior', *Art Journal* (1893): 144.

183. Day, 'Victorian Progress', 202.

184. Lewis F. Day, 'William Morris and His Art', *Art Journal* (1899, Easter Art Annual): 7; Crane and Day, *Moot Points*, 41.

185. In a letter to Quaker relative Joseph Green after Day's death, Barclay Day referred to his younger brother Lewis as "an uncompromising Liberal", but whether that represented a political affiliation or was simply his brother's interpretation of Lewis Day's views, is unknown; quoted in Joseph J. Green, 'The Late Lewis Forman [sic] Day', *The Friend* 50 (May 20, 1910): 329.

186. Crane and Day, *Moot Points*, 31.

187. Day, *Ornament*, 137.

188. Day, *Moot Points*, 29.

189. Day, *Ornament*, 312.

190. Crane and Day, *Moot Points*, 31-3, 35.

191. Day, *Pattern Design*, 262.

192. Crane and Day, *Moot Points*, 78.

193. Crane and Day, *Moot Points*, 78.

194. Crane and Day, *Moot Points*, 80, 84.

195. Crane and Day, *Moot Points*, 85.

196. Day, 'Decorative Art 12', 252.

197. Crane and Day, *Moot Points*, 11

198. Crane and Day, *Moot Points*, 49.

199. Crane and Day, *Moot Points*, 5, 12.

200. Day, *Ornament*, 132; Day, 'Decorative Art 12', 253.

201. Crane and Day, *Moot Points*, 74, 52.

202. Day, *Ornament*, 138.

203. Day, *Ornament*, 137.

204. Day, 'Machine-Made Art', 108.

205. Day, 'Decorative Art 12', 253.

206. Crane and Day, *Moot Points*, 11; Day, 'Decorative Art 12', 253.

207. Crane and Day, *Moot Points*, 46.

208. Crane and Day, *Moot Points*, 25.

209. Crane and Day, *Moot Points*, 46.

210. Crane and Day, *Moot Points*, 62.

211. Crane and Day, *Moot Points*, 58.

212. Crane and Day, *Moot Points*, 67.

213. Crane and Day, *Moot Points*, 68.

214. Crane and Day, *Moot Points*, 64.

215. Crane and Day, *Moot Points*, 52.

216. Crane and Day, *Moot Points*, 34.

217. Crane and Day, *Moot Points*, 8-9.

218. Crane and Day, *Moot Points*, 8, 53.

219. Crane and Day, *Moot Points*, 31.

220. Crane and Day, *Moot Points*, 34.

221. Crane and Day, *Moot Points*, 32.

222. Day, *Ornament*, 267.

223. Day, 'Decorative Art 12', 253.

224. Crane and Day, *Moot Points*, 46-7.

225. Lewis F. Day, 'Decorative Art 8', *British Architect* 10 (1878): 189.

226. Day, *Pattern Design*, 198-9.

227. Day, 'Decorative Art 8', 189; Day, 'Decorative Art 9', 229.

228. Crane and Day, *Moot Points*, 24, 34.

229. Lewis F. Day, 'Principles and Practice of Ornamental Design', *Journal of the Society of Arts* 35 (1886-7): 101.

Chapter 3: The Writer and Critic

1. *Builder* 26 (1868): 825; *Builder* 27 (1869): 20; *Builder* 28 (1870): 900. Apparently the essay was not published.

2. Lewis F. Day, 'Decorative Art 1', *British Architect* 9 (1878): 18.

3. Lewis F. Day, 'To the Reader', *Every-day Art* (London: B.T. Batsford, 1882), n.p.

4. Lewis F. Day, 'Another Moot Point: An Imaginary Debate, Lewis F. Day v. Hansard', *Art Journal* (1904): 160.

5. Lewis F. Day, 'Machine-Made Art', *Art Journal* (1885): 109.

6. Day, 'Another Moot Point', 160-1.

7. Day, 'Another Moot Point', 160-1.

8. Full citations for Day's articles and books are given in the Appendix: Selected Bibliography.

9. *British Architect* 14 (1880): 279.

10. 'The Magazine of Art' – Its Majority: A Retrospect', *Magazine of Art* 23 (1899): 317.

11. 'Retrospect', 319.

12. 'Retrospect', 317.

13. 'Retrospect', 318.

14. *Artist* (1883): 94.

15. *Architect* 29 (1883): 203; *Journal of Decorative Art* 2 (1882): 277.

16. *British Architect* 72 (1909): 489.

17. Obituary, 'The Late Mr. Lewis F. Day', *British Architect* 73 (1910): 272-3.

18. Batsford published all of Day's books, with these exceptions: *Tapestry Painting and Its Application* (London: Howell & James, 1880); *The Nodding Mandarin: A Tragedy in China* (London: Simpkin, Marshall & Co., 1883); and *Stained Glass* (London: Chapman & Hall, 1903), one of the Art Handbooks of the Victoria and Albert Museum.

19. Lewis F. Day, 'The Principles and Practice of Ornamental Design', *Journal of the Society of Arts* 35 (1886-7): 91-101, 105-15, 118-28, 132-44.

20. Dorothy M. Ross, 'Lewis Foreman Day, Designer and Writer on Stained Glass', *Journal of the British Society of Master Glass Painters* (April 1929); reprint (Cambridge: W. Heffer & Sons, 1929): 5. Ross was a friend of the Day family.

21. Lewis F. Day, *The Application of Ornament* (London: B.T. Batsford, 1888): v.

22. *British Architect* 34 (1890): 418.

23. *Magazine of Art* 14 (1891): xv-xvi; *Builder* 54 (1888): 96; *Magazine of Art* 11 (1888): xxxv; *Builder* 55 (1888): 443; *British Architect* 31 (1889): 3; *Magazine of Art* 18 (1895): 399.

24. *Studio* 3 (1894): vii.

25. *Studio* 3 (1894): vii.

26. Day, 'Decorative Art 1', 18; Lewis F. Day, *Nature in Ornament* (London: B.T. Batsford, 1892), 6. For a full discussion of naturalistic and conventional treatment of nature and use of animals and human figures in ornament, see Chapter 2: The Designer for Industry.

27. *British Architect* 37 (1892): 61-2.

28. *Art Journal* (1892): 96.

29. *Magazine of Art* 15 (1892): xxviii.

30. *Studio* 3 (1894): vii.

31. Lewis F. Day, *Windows: A Book About Stained and Painted Glass* (London: B.T. Batsford, 1897), v.

32. Lewis F. Day, *Windows: A Book About Stained and Painted Glass*, 3rd ed. (London: B.T. Batsford, 1909), vii.

33. Day, *Windows*, 3rd ed., vii.

34. Day, *Windows*, 3rd ed., n.p.

35. *Art Journal* (1898): 26; *Architect & Contract Reporter* 58 (1898): 388.

36. Lewis F. Day, *Alphabets Old and New* (London: B.T. Batsford, 1898), v.

37. Day, *Alphabets*, v.

38. Lewis F. Day, 'Victorian Progress in Applied Design', *Art Journal* (1887): 185-202.

39. Anthony Burton, 'Nineteenth Century Periodicals', in Trevor Fawcett and Clive Phillpot, eds., *The Art Press: Two Centuries of Art Magazines* (London: Art Book Company, 1976), 6.

40. Lewis F. Day, 'The Criticism of Decorative Art', *Art Journal* (1893): 64.

41. Lewis F. Day, 'William Morris and His Art', *Art Journal, Easter Art Annual* (1899).

42. Lewis F. Day, 'The New Lancastrian Pottery', *Art Journal* (1904): 201-2; Lewis F. Day, 'Favrile Glass', *Magazine of Art* (1901): 544.

43. Day, 'New Lancastrian', 202-4.

44. Lewis F. Day, 'L'Art Nouveau', *Art Journal* (1900): 293-7.

45. William Haslam Mills, *The Manchester Guardian: A Century of History* (London: Chatto & Windus, 1921), 122-6; J.L. Hammond, *C.P. Scott of the Manchester Guardian* (London: G. Bell & Sons, 1934), 52-3.

46. Lewis F. Day, 'The "New Art" at South Kensington', *Manchester Guardian* (27 June, 1901): 4.

47. Lewis F. Day, 'William Morris and His Decorative Art', *Contemporary Review* (1903): 787.

48. *British Architect* 60 (1903): 436. For further discussion, see Chapter 2: The Designer for Industry.

49. *Architect & Contract Reporter* 70 (1903): 293.

50. *Architect & Contract Reporter* 70 (1903): 292.

51. *Magazine of Art* 2, New Series (1904): 454.

52. Lewis F. Day, *Ornament and Its Application* (B.T. Batsford, 1904), vii.

53. *Studio* 35 (1905): 269.

54. *Decorator* (1904): 173.

55. The 4th and 5th editions were released in 1914 and 1927 respectively, and contained additional material by Mary Buckle Hogarth.

56. Lewis F. Day, *Lettering in Ornament* (London: B.T. Batsford, 1902), v.

57. *Journal of Decorative Art* 23 (1903): 184.

58. *Magazine of Art* 2, New Series (1904): 454; *Builder* 87 (1904): 181.

59. Lewis F. Day, 'Some Conclusions', *Art Journal* (1909): 199-200.

60. *Builder* 97 (1909): 2.

61. *Journal of Decorative Art* 29 (1909):120.

62. Ross, 'Lewis Foreman Day', 6.

63. Lewis F. Day, *Enamelling* (B.T. Batsford, 1907): v.

64. Day, *Enamelling*, v-vi.

65. *Builder* 95 (1908): 2.

66. 'Note by Miss Day', in Lewis F. Day, *Penmanship of the XVIth, XVIIth, & VIIIth Centuries* (London: B.T. Batsford, n.d.), n. p.

67. Lewis F. Day, 'Decorative Art 6', *British Architect* 10 (1878): 52-3.

68. Obituary, *Manchester Guardian* (19 April, 1910): 8; *Royal Society of Arts Journal* 58 (1909-10): 454; Victoria and Albert Museum, Archive of Art and Design, Lewis F. Day nominal file, SF934, letter from A. Richmond to Day, 24 September, 1909.

Chapter 4: Stained Glass

1. Lewis F. Day, 'Decorative Art 6', *British Architect* 10 (1878): 53.

2. Lewis F. Day, *Windows: A Book About Stained and Painted Glass* (London: B.T. Batsford, 1897), v.

3. Charles Harvey and Jon Press, *William Morris: Design and Enterprise in Victorian Britain* (Manchester: Manchester University Press, 1991), 57.

4. Martin Harrison, *Victorian Stained Glass* (London: Barrie & Jenkins, 1980), 10.

5. Will Low, *Scribner's* (4 Dec., 1888): 675.

6. Harrison, *Victorian Stained Glass*, 9.

7. 'Lewis Foreman Day', *Journal of Decorative Art* 6 (1886): 891; Dorothy M. Ross, 'Lewis Foreman Day, Designer and Writer on Stained Glass', *Journal of the British Society of Master Glass Painters* (April 1929); reprint (Cambridge: W. Heffer & Sons, 1929): 5.

8. 'Lewis Foreman Day', *Journal of Decorative Art*, 891.

9. 'Lewis Foreman Day', *Journal of Decorative Art*, 891.

10. Harvey and Press, *William Morris*, 59.

11. 'Lewis Foreman Day', *Journal of Decorative Art*, 891.

12. Harrison, *Victorian Stained Glass*, 10, 76; Harvey and Press, *William Morris*, 61.

13. Harrison, *Victorian Stained Glass*, 32.

14. Ross, *'Lewis Foreman Day'*, 5.

15. *Builder* 28 (1870): 900.

16. *Builder* 26 (1868): 825; *Builder* 27 (1869): 20; 'Lewis Foreman Day', *Journal of Decorative Art*, 891. Day, who was still employed at Clayton & Bell, reportedly read the essay to the Architectural Association in January 1869, though the text does not appear to have been published.

17. Ross, 'Lewis Foreman Day', 6.

18. Lewis F. Day, 'Notes on English Decorative Art in Paris 2', *British Architect* 10 (1878): 4; Lewis F. Day, 'Victorian Progress in Applied Design', *Art Journal* (1887): 187.

19. Jeremy Cooper, *Victorian and Edwardian Décor: From the Gothic Revival to Art Nouveau* (New York: Abbeville Press, 1987), 93.

20. 'Lewis Foreman Day', *Journal of Decorative Art*, 891; Ross, 'Lewis Foreman Day', 6-7.

21. 'Lewis Foreman Day', *Journal of Decorative Art*, 891.

22. 'Lewis Foreman Day', *Journal of Decorative Art*, 891; Stan Valler, former managing director, W.B. Simpson & Sons, interview 13 March, 2002.

23. 'Lewis Foreman Day', *Journal of Decorative Art*, 891; *Architect* 17 (1877), Supplement: 7.

24. Valler, interview 13 March, 2002.

25. Day, 'Notes 2', 4; Ross, 'Lewis Foreman Day', 6.

26. About two dozen original designs for stained glass, mostly for domestic windows, have survived and are held by the Victoria and Albert Museum. As is the case with most of the domestic windows illustrated in Day's books and articles, it is not known whether they were produced or, if so, then by whom.

27. Lewis F. Day, *Every-day Art* (London: B.T. Batsford, 1882), 130; Lewis F. Day, *Some Principles of Every-day Art* (London: B.T. Batsford, 1890), 26.

28. Lewis Foreman Day, 'Stained Glass: Its Application to Domestic Architecture', *Architect* 7 (1872): 59-60.

29. Day, 'Stained Glass: Its Application', 59.

30. Day, 'Stained Glass: Its Application', 59.

31. Day, 'Stained Glass: Its Application', 59.

32. Day, 'Stained Glass: Its Application', 59.

33. Day, 'Stained Glass: Its Application', 59.

34. Day, 'Stained Glass, Its Application', 59.

35. Day, 'Stained Glass: Its Application', 59.

36. Day, 'Stained Glass: Its Application', 59.

37. Victoria and Albert Museum (V&A), E.13-1976.

38. V&A, E.939-940-1911; E.942-1911.

39. Three original designs for these windows are: V&A, E. 943-1911; 944-1911; 945-1911.

40. Joan Payne and Brenda Hargreaves, *Christ Church, Streatham: A History and Guide*, 3rd ed. rev. Christopher Ivory (Streatham: Parochial Church Council of Christ Church, 2000), 20.

41. *The Parish Church of St. Mary the Virgin, Great Dunmow: A Brief History and Guide* (Ramsgate: The Church Publishers, 2003), 11-17.

42. Ross, 'Lewis Foreman Day', 6-7.

43. *Dunmow Parish Magazine* (March 1906).

44. John 15:5.

45. 'Arts and Crafts', *Art Journal* (1909): 378-9.

46. Lewis F. Day, 'Stained Glass Windows: As They Were, Are, and Should Be', *Journal of the Society of Arts* 30 (1882): 302.

47. *Church Diary: Works Connected with the Church* (Great Dunmow: Church and Parochial Records, nd.). Though this account is neither dated nor signed, it was possibly an entry made by a churchwarden during the time of John Evans, Vicar 1905-1914.

48. *Church Diary*, nd.

49. Day, 'Stained Glass Windows', 303.

50. Lewis F. Day, 'The Making of a Stained Glass Window', *Journal of the Society of Arts* 46 (1898): 423-4.

51. Day, 'Making', 423-4.

52. Harrison, *Victorian Stained Glass*, 31-2, 63; Sarah Brown, *Stained Glass: An Illustrated History* (London: Bracken Books, 1992), 24-8; Harvey and Press, *William Morris*, 53.

53. Harrison, *Victorian Stained Glass*, 13, 45, 54.

54. Day, 'Stained Glass Windows', 304.

55. Lewis F. Day, 'Glass, Stained', *Encyclopaedia Britannica* 12 (Cambridge: University Press, 1911): 110; Day, 'Stained Glass Windows', 302.

56. Day, 'Stained Glass Windows', 303.

57. Day, 'Stained Glass Windows', 303.

58. Lewis F. Day, 'From Gothic Glass to Renaissance', *Magazine of Art* 8 (1885): 286.

59. *Royal Society of Arts Journal* 58 (1910): 470.

60. *Royal Society of Arts Journal* 58 (1910): 469-70.

61. Day, 'Making', 428.

62. Day, 'Making', 427.

63. Day, 'Making', 427; Lewis F. Day, 'Cinque-Cento Picture Windows', *Magazine of Art* 8 (1885): 342.

64. Day, 'Gothic Glass to Renaissance', 286.

65. Lewis F. Day, 'Glass-Painting: The Beginning of the End', *Magazine of Art* 8 (1885): 381.

66. Day, 'Glass, Stained', 111.

67. Day, 'Stained Glass Windows', 303.

68. Day, 'Stained Glass Windows', 303.

69. Day, 'Stained Glass Windows', 303.

70. Lewis F. Day, 'Old Glass at Munich', *British Architect* 15 (1881): 153-4, 165-6; Lewis F.

Day, 'Glass-Painting in the Fourteenth Century', *Magazine of Art* 5 (1882): 289-94.

71. *Builder* 26 (1868): 825; *Builder* 27 (1869): 20.

72. Day, 'Stained Glass: Its Application', 59-60.

73. Day, 'Notes 2', 4-5.

74. Day, 'Stained Glass Windows', 292-306.

75. *Builder* 50 (1886): 156-8, 194-6.

76. Lewis F. Day, 'The Earliest Cathedral Windows', *Magazine of Art* 5 (1882): 19-23; Lewis F. Day, 'Glass Painting in the Fourteenth Century', *Magazine of Art* 5 (1882): 289-94; Lewis F. Day, 'Later Gothic Glass in England', *Magazine of Art* 6 (1883): 420-4.

77. Day, 'Gothic Glass to Renaissance', 282-6; Lewis F. Day, 'Cinque-Cento Picture Windows', *Magazine of Art* 8 (1885): 341-6; Day, 'Glass Painting: Beginning of the End', 377-81.

78. Lewis F. Day, 'Modern Mosaic in England', *Architectural Record* 2 (1892): 79-88; Lewis F. Day, 'The Windows of a New Church', *Art Journal* (1896): 197-200; Lewis F. Day, 'A Missing Link', *Art Journal* (1905): 282-4.

79. Lewis F. Day, *Windows: A Book About Stained and Painted Glass* (London: B.T. Batsford, 1897).

80. Day, *Windows*, v.

81. Lewis Foreman Day, *Windows: A Book About Stained and Painted Glass*, 3rd ed. (London: B.T. Batsford, 1909): vii.

82. Day, *Windows*, 3rd ed., vii.

83. Walter Crane, 'Obituary', *Manchester Guardian* (19 April, 1910): 8.

84. *Art Journal* (1898): 26; *Architect and Contract Reporter* 58 (1898): 388.

85. *Journal of the Society of Arts* 46 (1898): 429.

86. Day, 'Making', 421-30.

87. Day, 'Making', 428.

88. Day, 'Making', 428-9.

89. Day, 'Stained Glass Windows', 292.

90. Day, 'Cinque-Cento', 341.

91. Day, 'Making', 426.

92. Lewis F. Day, 'Stained Glass', *Architect* 35 (1886): 51.

93. Day, 'Stained Glass', 51.

94. Day, 'Cinque-Cento', 341; Day, 'Later Gothic Glass', 424.

95. Day, 'Stained Glass Windows', 300; Day, 'Glass, Stained', 107.

96. Day, 'Stained Glass', 51.

97. Day, 'Notes 2', 4; Day, 'Stained Glass Windows', 303.

98. Day, 'Stained Glass Windows', 303.

99. Day, 'Stained Glass: Its Application', 59-60.

100. Lewis F. Day, *Stained Glass* (London: Chapman and Hall, 1903).

101. *Magazine of Art* (1904): 454; *Builder* 87 (1904): 181.

102. 'Glass, Stained', 105-12.

103. Ross, 'Lewis Foreman Day', 7.

104. Ross, 'Lewis Foreman Day', 6.

105. Noel Heaton, 'The Foundations of Stained Glass Work', *Royal Society of Arts Journal* 58 (1910): 454-69.

Chapter 5: Wallpaper

1. Alan V. Sugden and John L. Edmondson, *A History of English Wallpaper 1500-1914* (London: B.T. Batsford, 1926), 139.

2. *Furniture Gazette* 5 (1876): 383.

3. Lewis F. Day, 'Wall-Paper Decoration', *Magazine of Art* 15 (1892): 190-91; Lewis F. Day, 'The Choice of Wall-Papers', *Magazine of Art* 15 (1892): 168.

4. Day, 'Choice of Wall-Papers', 168.

5. Day, 'Choice of Wall-Papers', 168.

6. Lewis F. Day, 'Decorative Art 12', *British Architect* 10 (1878): 253; Lewis F. Day, 'Mere Ornament', *Art Journal* (1901): 18; Lewis F. Day, 'Some Conclusions', *Art Journal* (1909): 200.

7. Day, 'Decorative Art 12', 253.

8. 'Lewis Foreman Day', *Journal of Decorative Art* 6 (1886): 891; Metford Warner, 'Some Victorian Designers', manuscript read at the Design Club (24 Nov., 1909), 20-24. Victoria and Albert Museum, National Art Library, 86.HH.13.

9. Stan Valler, former managing director, W.B. Simpson & Sons, interview, 13 March 2002.

10. Lewis F. Day, 'Fortnightly Notes on Ornament 2', *British Architect* 11 (1879): 25.

11. Charles Locke Eastlake, *Hints on Household Taste* (New York: Dover, 1969; reprint of 1878 ed.), 115-16.

12. Lewis F. Day, 'Decorative Art 1', *British Architect* 9 (1878): 18.

13. Day, 'Decorative Art 1', 18.

14. *Art Journal* (1909), 200. For a full discussion of Day's views on treatment of natural forms, see Chapter 2: The Designer for Industry.

15. Lewis F. Day, *Every-day Art* (London: B.T. Batsford, 1882), 124-5.

16. Lewis F. Day, 'Notes on English Decorative Art in Paris 1', *British Architect* 9 (1878): 302.

17. Lewis F. Day, *Pattern Design* (London: B.T. Batsford, 1903), 201.

18. Day, *Pattern Design*, 253.

19. *Architect* 30 (1883): 69, near 69.

20. Day, *Pattern Design*, 121-4, pl. 149.

21. Day, *Pattern Design*, 123.

22. Day, *Pattern Design*, 123.

23. Warner, 'Some Victorian Designers', 20.

24. Day, *Every-day Art*, 207-8.

25. Day, 'Choice of Wall-Papers', 165.

26. Eastlake, *Hints*, 123.

27. Day, *Every-day Art*, 207.

28. Day, 'Wall-Paper Decoration', 191.

29. Day, *Every-day Art*, 207.

30. Day, 'Wall-Paper Decoration', 191-2.

31. Day, 'Wall-Paper Decoration', 189.

32. Walter Crane and Lewis F. Day, *Moot Points: Friendly Disputes on Art & Industry* (London: B.T. Batsford, 1903), 80.

33. Day, *Every-day Art*, 208.

34. Day, *Every-day Art*, 208.

35. Day, *Every-day Art*, 208-9.

36. Day, 'Wall-Paper Decoration', 192.

37. Day, 'Wall-Paper Decoration', 192.

38. Day, *Every-day Art*, 209.

39. Day, 'Wall-Paper Decoration', 193.

40. Day, 'Wall-Paper Decoration', 193.

41. *Journal of Decorative Art* 6 (1886): 891-2.

42. *Journal of Decorative Art* 23 (1903): 236; Sugden and Edmundson, 251.

43. *Journal of Decorative Art* 1 (1881): 29.

44. *Journal of Decorative Art* 18 (1898): 311; prior to decimalisation in February 1971, British currency comprised pounds (£), shillings (s.) and pence (d.), where £1 = 12s. = 240d. For a detailed discussion see Judith Flanders, *Consuming Passions: Leisure and Pleasure in Victorian Britain* (London: Harper Press, 2006).

45. *Journal of Decorative Art* 17 (1897): 136-9; *Journal of Decorative Art* 4 (1884): 472.

46. *Journal of Decorative Art* 17 (1897): 136-9.

47. Day, *Ornament and Its Application* (London: B.T. Batsford, 1904), 312.

48. *Architect* 33 (1885): 195, near 195.

49. Crane and Day, *Moot Points*, 87.

50. Lewis F. Day, *Ornament*, 288.

51. Day, *Pattern Design*, 262.

52. *Journal of Decorative* Art 16 (1896): 187.

53. *Journal of Decorative Art* 1 (1881): 30.

54. *Journal of Decorative Art* 16 (1896): 186.

55. Lewis F. Day, *The Planning of Ornament* (London: B.T. Batsford, 3rd ed., 1893), pl. 23.

56. *Journal of Decorative Art* 16 (1896): 314.

57. *Builder* 72 (1897): iv; *Architect, Contract Reporter Supplement* 57 (1897): 6.

58. *Architect, Contract Reporter Supplement* 57(1897): 9.

59. *Architect, Contract Reporter Supplement* 57(1897): 6; *Builder* 72 (1897): iv.

60. Day, 'Wall-Paper Decoration', 191.

61. *Journal of Decorative Art* 13 (1893): 50-1.

62. Day, 'Wall-Paper Decoration', 191-2.

63. Day, 'Wall-Paper Decoration', 192.

64. *Journal of Decorative Art* 19 (1899): 133.

65. Warner, 'Some Victorian Designers', 20-4.

66. *Journal of Decorative Art* 30 (1910): 50.

67. Warner, 'Some Victorian Designers', 20-1.

68. For a full discussion of Day's views, see Chapter 2: The Designer for Industry.

69. Jeffrey & Co. press cuttings, Victoria and Albert Museum (V&A), E.42A(1)-1945:56-57; Jeffrey & Co.,

Patent Hygienic Wall Papers, 1885, Archive, Arthur Sanderson Ltd.

70. *British Architect* 25 (1886): 574, 595.

71. Crane and Day, *Moot Points*, 87; Day, *Ornament*, 286.

72. *Building News* (1889): 198; *Furniture Gazette* 20 (1889): 95-6.

73. *British Architect* 31 (1889): 89.

74. *Magazine of Art* 12 (1889): xxxii.

75. *Magazine of Art* 12 (1889): xxxii.

76. *Illustrations of the Victorian Series, and other Wall-Papers*. Jeffrey & Co., c. 1889. Manchester Metropolitan University, Special Collections. Pages in the catalogue are not numbered.

77. *Victorian Series*.

78. *Building News* (Feb. 8, 1889): 198.

79. Jeffrey & Co. press cuttings, V&A: E.42A(1)-1945:69.

80. V&A, 19.A.16-20.

81. *Victorian Series*.

82. *British Architect* 31 (1889): 89.

83. Day, 'Wall-Paper Decoration', 192.

84. *Victorian Series*.

85. Jeffrey & Co. press cuttings, V&A, E.42B(2)-1945: 46, 48, 52.

86. Sugden and Edmundson, 229.

87. Jeffrey & Co. press cuttings, V&A, E.42A(1)-1945: 69; *Architect, Contract Reporter Supplement* 41 (1889): 11.

88. Jeffrey & Co. press cuttings, V&A, E.42B(2)-1945:180.

89. Jeffrey & Co. logbook (Vol. II, no. 1: 62), Archive, Arthur Sanderson Ltd.; Jeffrey & Co. press cuttings, V&A, E.42A(1)-1945: 69.

90. *Art Journal Supplement, Paris Exhibition 1889*, illus. ii; xvi; Day, *Pattern Design*, pl. 182.

91. Jeffrey & Co. press cuttings, V&A, E.42A(1)-1945: 69, 89-90; *Architect, Contract Reporter Supplement* 41 (1889): 11.

92. Metford Warner, 'Progress of Design in Paperhangings', *Journal of Decorative Art* 30 (1910): 49.

93. Day, *Pattern Design*, 78.

94. Jeffrey & Co. logbook (Vol. II, no. 1: 69), Archive, Arthur Sanderson Ltd.

95. *Journal of Decorative Art* 13 (1893): 95.

96. *Journal of Decorative Art* 13 (1893): 95.

97. *Journal of Decorative Art* 13 (1893): 95.

98. Lewis F. Day, 'Wall Coverings and Hangings at the Paris Exhibition', *Art Journal Supplement, Paris Exhibition 1900*, 161-5, 164.

99. V&A, E.1067-1911; Jeffrey & Co. logbook (Vol. II, no. 3: 234), Archive, Arthur Sanderson Ltd.

100. Day, *Ornament*, 49, fig. 42, 52.

101. *Art Journal* (1898): 59.

102. Jeffrey & Co., presscuttings, V&A, E.42B (2)-1945:181; *Paris Exhibition 1900: Official British Catalogue* (London: Royal Commission, 1900), 116.

103. Jeffrey & Co. press-cuttings, V&A, E. 42B(2): 157.

104. Day, 'Wall-Paper Decoration', 190.

105. Day, 'Wall-Paper Decoration', 190.

106. Jeffrey & Co. press cuttings, V&A, E.42B (2): 225.

107. *Decorator* (1904): 359; *Art Journal* (1904): 60.

108. Lewis F. Day, 'Decorative Art at the Paris Exhibition', *Manchester Guardian* (June 26, 1900): 12.

109. Day, 'Decorative Art at the Paris Exhibition', 12.

110. Day, 'Wall Coverings and Hangings', 165.

111. Day, 'Wall Coverings and Hangings', 165.

Chapter 6: Tiles and Art Pottery

1. Lewis F. Day, 'Tiles', *Art Journal* (1895): 343.

2. Terence Lockett, *Collecting Victorian Tiles* (Woodbridge, Suffolk: Antique Collectors' Club, 1987), 20-1.

3. Hans van Lemmen, 'Tiles and Interior Furnishings', *Fired Earth: 1000 Years of Tiles in Europe* (Shepton Beauchamp, Somerset: Richard Dennis and Tiles & Architectural Ceramics Society, 1991), 52.

4. Charles Locke Eastlake, *Hints on Household Taste: In Furniture, Upholstery, and Other Details* (London: Longmans, Green, 1868; reprint of 1878 ed., New York: Dover, 1969), 50; Robert W. Edis, *Decoration and Furniture of Town Houses* (London: C. Kegan Paul, 1881), 154.

5. 'Lewis Foreman Day', *Journal of Decorative Art* 6 (1886): 891.

6. 'Lewis Foreman Day', *Journal of Decorative Art*, 891.

7. Shropshire Records and Research Centre, *First Minute Book of Maw & Co. 1860-1870*, 1420/1, Letter No. 938, Oct. 13, 1868.

8. Stan Valler, former managing director, W.B. Simpson & Sons, interview March 13, 2002.

9. Victoria Bergeson, *Encyclopedia of British Art Pottery* (London: Barrie & Jenkins, 1992), 147; Nancy E. Owen, *Rookwood and the Industry of Art* (Athens, Ohio: Ohio University Press, 2001), 104.

10. See Chapter 7: Clocks and Furniture.

11. Lewis F. Day, *Nature in Ornament* (London: B.T. Batsford, 1892), 205.

12. Lewis F. Day, 'Fortnightly Notes on Ornament 22', *British Architect* 12 (1879): 181.

13. 'Howell and James (Limited)', *Pall Mall Gazette* 39 (1884): 16.

14. Lewis F. Day, 'Notes on English Decorative Art in Paris 11', *British Architect* 10 (1878): 126, illus. near 126-7.

15. Day, 'Notes 11', illus. near 126-7.

16. *Pottery and Glass Trades Journal* (1878): 75.

17. *Art Journal Illustrated Catalogue of the Paris International Exhibition 1878* (London: Virtue & Co., 1878), 106.

18. *Pottery and Glass Trades Journal* (1878): 75.

19. *Pottery and Glass Trades Journal* (1878): 75.

20. *Art Journal Catalogue 1878*, 106.

21. *The Queen* (June 9, 1883): 537.

22. Day, 'Notes 11', 126.

23. 'Art Notes', *Magazine of Art* 2 (1879): xxx.

24. 'The Exhibition of Paintings on China', *Magazine of Art* 1 (1878): 177-9.

25. *Art Journal Catalogue 1878*, 97; 'Exhibition of Paintings' 177; *British Architect* 19 (1883): 252.

26. Day, 'Notes 11', 126; Day, 'Fortnightly Notes 22', 181.

27. Lewis F. Day, 'Fortnightly Notes on Ornament 23', *British Architect* 12 (1879): 201.

28. Day, 'Fortnightly Notes 22', 181.

29. Day, 'Fortnightly Notes 22', 181.

30. 'Lewis Foreman Day', *Journal of Decorative Art*, 891.

31. *Journal of Decorative Art* 3 (1883): 356.

32. *Builder*, Supplement, 44 (1883): 486.

33. *Architect* 31 (1884): 229.

34. Day, 'Tiles', 344.

35. *British Architect* 15 (1881): 286; *Journal of Decorative Art* 2 (1882): 272-3; 3 (1883): 356.

36. *British Architect* 16 (1881): viii.

37. *British Architect* 17 (1881): near 414, 448, 450-1, 461, 472, 474, 478, 485, 497, 511.

38. Eastlake, *Hints*, 115-6.

39. Day, 'Decorative Art 1', *British Architect* 9 (1878): 18; Lewis F. Day, 'Some Conclusions', *Art Journal* (1909), 200.

40. *Architect* 17 (1877): 196, near 196.

41. Lewis F. Day, *Nature in Ornament* (London: B.T. Batsford, 1892), 34-5. For a full discussion of Day's views on treatment of natural forms, see Chapter 2: The Designer for Industry.

42. *Architect* 17 (1877): 196.

43. *Architect* 25 (1881): 435, illus. near 435; *Architect* 26 (1881): 159, illus. near 159.

44. Lewis F. Day, 'Fortnightly Notes on Ornament 2', *British Architect* 11 (1879): 25.

45. *Architect* 17 (1877): 196, illus. near 196.

46. Lewis F. Day, *Ornament and Its Application* (London: B.T. Batsford, 1904), 312.

47. *Architect* 25 (1881): 435, illus. near 435.

48. *British Architect* 17 (1881): 414.

49. Robin Reilly, *Wedgwood: The New Illustrated Dictionary* (Woodbridge, Suffolk: Antique Collectors' Club, 1995), 274-5; J. and B. Austwick, *The Decorated Tile* (London: Pitman House, 1980), 76.

50. Bergeson, *Encyclopedia*, 171; Elizabeth Cameron, *Encyclopaedia of Pottery & Porcelain: The 19th & 20th Centuries* (London: Faber & Faber, 1986), 35.

51. Reilly, *Wedgwood*, 131, 275; Maureen Batkin, *Wedgwood Ceramics 1846-1940* (London: Richard Dennis, 1982), 110.

52. Batkin, *Wedgwood Ceramics*, 110-6; Reilly, *Wedgwood*, 131.

53. Cameron, *Encyclopaedia*, 207.

54. Shropshire Records and Research Centre, *First Minute Book of Maw & Co. 1860-1870*, 1420/1, Letter No. 938, Oct. 13, 1868.

55. Julian Barnard, *Victorian Ceramic Tiles* (London: Studio Vista, 1972), 15; Hans van Lemmen, *Victorian Tiles* (Princes Risborough, Buckinghamshire: Shire Publications, 1981), 12-4.

56. *Journal of Decorative Art* 7 (1887): 140.

57. A red lustre tile c. 1890, featuring a dragon-like beast with raised tail and breathing fire and manufactured by Maw neighbour and competitor Craven Dunnill, has been attributed to Day (Victoria and Albert Museum, Circ. 215-1976). Day made no reference in his writings to having designed for the firm.

58. *Journal of Decorative Art* 7 (1887): 136-7, 142. For a full discussion of Day's use of these trade figures, see Chapter 7: Clocks and Furniture.

59. For a discussion of Day's sources of inspiration, see Chapter 2: The Designer for Industry.

60. *Journal of Decorative Art* 7 (1887): 136-7, 142.

61. *Journal of Decorative Art* 7 (1887): 136-7, 142; *Architect* 39 (1888): near 9.

62. Walter Crane and Lewis F. Day, *Moot Points: Friendly Disputes on Art & Industry* (London: B.T. Batsford, 1903), 92; Day, *Nature*, 205.

63. Victoria and Albert Museum (V&A), E.984-1911; E.1005-1911.

64. 'Tiles and Tiling', *Art Journal* (1889): 7-8.

65. 'Tiles and Tiling', 7.

66. Day, 'Tiles', 345.

67. 'Tiles and Tiling', 7.

68. Day, 'Tiles', 346.

69. Day, 'Tiles', 346.

70. *Architect* 39 (1888): 13; V&A: E.1058-1911.

71. *Journal of Decorative Art* (1890): 15.

72. Shropshire Records and Research Centre, 6001/6012.

73. Ironbridge Gorge Museum Trust, *Catalogue*, Maw & Co., undated, c. 1907, D/Maw/7/30, Pl 2a, Nos. 1, 2; Lockett, *Collecting*, 40.

74. At the Arts and Crafts Exhibition in 1889, Maw & Co. also exhibited a tile panel that was a joint effort by Day and Walter Crane. Painted in ruby d'oro lustre, the panel featured a central figure of the Goddess of Plenty, with labourers and reapers above and below. The figures were designed by Walter Crane and the border of scrollwork and lilies designed by Day. See *Journal of Decorative Art* (1890): 13-4; Day, *Nature*, pl. 39.

75. *Journal of Decorative Art* 7 (1887): 141.

76. Lewis F. Day, 'Modern Mosaic in England', *Architectural Record* 2 (1892): 85.

77. Day, 'Modern Mosaic', 85, illus. 86.

78. Bergeson, *Encyclopedia*, 179, 182.

79. Lewis F. Day, 'The New Lancastrian Pottery', *Art Journal* (1904): 202.

80. I am grateful to Tony Cross for pointing out this connection.

81. 'Famous Manchester Works: A Visit to Messrs. Pilkington's Tile Works, Clifton Junction', *Journal of Decorative Art* 14 (1904): 219.

82. 'Famous Manchester Works', 219.

83. Day, 'New Lancastrian', 202.

84. Lawrence Burton, 'William Burton and Pilkington's Tiles Limited', *Journal of the Tiles and Architectural Ceramics Society* 4 (1992): 31; Anthony J. Cross, *Pilkington's Royal Lancastrian Pottery and Tiles* (London: Richard Dennis, 1980), 12.

85. Cross, *Pilkington's*, 89.

86. Cross, *Pilkington's*, pl. XI, 13; 89, reg. 253079; Lockett, *Collecting*, 94.

87. Day, 'Tiles', 348.

88. Lomax, *Royal Lancastrian*, 40; Cross, *Pilkington's*, 75-7.

89. Letter from Lawrence Pilkington and William Burton to Lewis F. Day, Jan. 23, 1896; I am grateful to Lawrence Burton for sharing this letter.

90. Pilkington's Tile & Pottery Co., *First Minute Book*, extracts, Feb. 6, 1899, cited in Richard Gray, 'The Pilkington Tile and Pottery Company: Some Early Designs', *English Ceramic Circle Transactions* 2, Part 3 (1983), 175.

91. Cross, *Pilkington's*, 53.

92. Cross, *Pilkington's*, 53.

93. 'Famous Manchester Works', 219; *Journal of Decorative Art* 21 (1901): 180.

94. Julian Barnard, *Victorian Ceramic Tiles* (London: Studio Vista, 1972), 77.

95. 'Famous Manchester Works', 219; *Journal of Decorative Art* 21 (1901): 180.

96. Day, 'Tiles', 348.

97. 'The Use and Abuse of Tiles', *The Artist and Journal of Home Culture* 2 (1881): 242.

98. Day, 'Tiles', 348.

99. William Burton, 'Note', *Catalogue. Paris Exhibition 1900* (Clifton Junction, Manchester: Pilkington's Tile and Pottery Company, 1900): 12.

100. William Burton, 'Note', 12.

101. William Burton, 'Note', 13.

102. Lewis F. Day, 'Decorative Art at the Paris Exhibition', *Manchester Guardian* (June 26, 1900): 12.

103. *Catalogue 1900*, 24-6.

104. Day, 'Tiles', 348.

105. Aymer Vallance, 'Building Trades Exhibition', *Magazine of Art* 21 (1897): 99.

106. *Catalogue 1900*, 27; *Catalogue 1901* (Clifton Junction, Manchester: Pilkington's Tile & Pottery Company, 1901): 29.

107. Day, 'Tiles', 348; Lewis F. Day, *Pattern Design* (London: B.T. Batsford, 1903), 70, illus. 90.

108. Day, 'Tiles', 345; *Studio Yearbook* (1906): 222, 226.

109. *Catalogue 1900*, 19, 31; *Catalogue 1901*, 23.

110. See Chapter 5: Wallpaper.

111. *Catalogue 1900*, 20.

112. *Art Journal Supplement, Paris Exhibition 1900*, 100.

113. *Catalogue 1900*, 32, 20.

114. *Catalogue 1900*, 20.

115. *Catalogue 1900*, 17.

116. *Catalogue 1900*, 28.

117. *Catalogue. Wolverhampton Exhibition 1902* (Clifton Junction, Manchester: Pilkington's Tile and Pottery Company, 1902): 36-7.

118. *Catalogue 1900*: 28; Gray, 'Some Early Designs', 175; Judy Rudoe, *Decorative Arts 1850-1950* (London: British Museum Press, 1991), 25-6.

119. Walter Armstrong, *Alfred Stevens: Architectural Sculptor, Painter and Designer* (London: Constable, 1939), pl. 18, 259, 270; *Architect* 18 (1877): 19.

120. Lewis F. Day, 'Victorian Progress in Applied Design', *Art Journal* (1887): 190; also *Architect*, 32 (1884): 382.

121. Lewis F. Day, 'Decorative and Industrial Art at the Glasgow Exhibition', *Art Journal* (1901): 274-5.

122. *Catalogue 1902*, 6-7.

123. H.C. Marillier, 'Pilkington's Tiles & Pottery', *Franco-British Illustrated Review* (London: Chatto & Windus, 1908), pl. 18; Cross, *Pilkington's*, 21-2, 25, pl.18, 66.

124. Lewis F. Day, 'The Arts and Crafts Exhibition', *Art Journal* (1903): 91; Arts and Crafts Exhibition Society, *Catalogue of the 7th Exhibition* (London: The Society, 1903), 128-9; *Studio* 29 (1903): 23.

125. *Studio* 28 (1903): 183.

126. Day, 'Arts and Crafts Exhibition', *Art Journal* (1903): 92.

127. *Art Workers' Quarterly* 2 (1903): 60.

128. *Notes Descriptive of the First Exhibition of the New Lancastrian Pottery: Shown at the Galleries of Henry Graves & Co., Ltd., 6 Pall Mall, London, S.W., June 1st to June 25, 1904* (Manchester: Pilkington's Tile and Pottery Company, 1904), 8.

129. *Notes Descriptive*, 8.

130. Gray, 'Some Early designs', 176, pl. 98a, 98b; Lewis F. Day, *Ornament*, 146.

131. Abraham Lomax, *Royal Lancastrian Pottery* (printed privately, 1957), 39-41; Victoria and Albert Museum, Archive of Art and Design (V&A, ADD), nominal file, D. M. Ross: letter from P. Floud, Sept. 13, 1952.

132. Day, 'New Lancastrian', 204; Lomax, *Royal Lancastrian*, 40-1.

133. 'Famous Manchester Works', 219.

134. Day, 'New Lancastrian', 203; *Notes Descriptive*, 7.

135. Day, 'New Lancastrian', 204.

136. Day, 'New Lancastrian', 203-4.

137. Day, 'New Lancastrian', 204.

138. Day, 'Tiles', 347.

139. John A. Bartlett, *British Ceramic Art 1870-1940* (Atglen, PA: Schiffer, 1993), 180; Bergeson, *Encyclopedia*, 223.

140. Lawrence Burton, 'William Burton', 30.

141. 'Famous Manchester Works', 219.

142. See Chapter 1: Life.

143. *British Architect* 66 (1906): 339; *British Architect* 69 (1908): 53.

144. Lawrence Burton, 'William Burton', 30; *Catalogue 1902*, 14-5.

145. Marillier, 'Pilkington's Tiles & Pottery', 210.

146. *British Architect* 70 (1908): 146.

147. Lawrence Burton, 'William Burton', 30-1.

148. Board of Education, *Victoria and Albert Museum: Report of the Committee of Re-arrangement* (London: HMSO, 1908), 36; Lawrence Burton, 'William Burton', 31.

149. Day, 'New Lancastrian', 202.

150. Day, 'New Lancastrian', 202; Day, 'Tiles', 347.

151. Day, 'New Lancastrian', 203.

152. Day, 'New Lancastrian', 202.

153. Day, 'New Lancastrian', 201.

154. Day, 'New Lancastrian', 201.

155. Day, 'New Lancastrian', 201-2.

156. Day, 'Tiles', 346.

157. Day, 'New Lancastrian', 204.

Chapter 7: Clocks and Furniture

1. Lewis F. Day, *Every-day Art* (London: B.T. Batsford: 1882), 226.

2. *Art Journal Illustrated Catalogue of the Paris International Exhibition 1878* (London:Virtue & Co., 1978), 98.

3. Lewis F. Day, 'Notes on English Decorative Art in Paris 11', *British Architect* 10 (1878): 127.

4. Day, 'Notes 11', 127.

5. *Art Journal* (1873), 182, 188.

6. *Art Journal Catalogue 1878*, 106.

7. Day, 'Notes 11', 126-7.

8. Day, 'Notes 11', 127, illus. near 127.

9. Day, 'Notes 11', 127, illus. near 127.

10. Day, 'Notes 11', 127.

11. *Architect* 17 (1877): 230, illus. near 230.

12. *Journal of Decorative Art* 7 (1887): 137; see Chapter 6: Tiles and Art Pottery.

13. *Architect* 17 (1877): 230, illus. near 230.

14. *Art Journal Catalogue 1878*, 106.

15. *Art Journal Catalogue 1878*, 98.

16. Lewis F. Day, 'Notes on English Decorative Art in Paris 13', *British Architect* 10 (1878): 179.

17. Lewis F. Day, 'Notes on English Decorative Art in Paris 3', *British Architect* 10 (1878): 16.

18. Day, 'Notes 3', 16.

19. *Furniture Gazette* 10 (1878): 159; *Furniture Gazette* 11 (1879): 8-9.

20. *Furniture Gazette* 10 (1878): 159; Day, 'Notes 3', 16.

21. *Magazine of Art* 1 (1878): 116; *Art Journal Catalogue 1878*, 46.

22. George Augustus Sala, *Paris Herself Again* (London: Remington & Co., 1879), 320.

23. Lewis F. Day, 'Notes on English Decorative Art in Paris 4', *British Architect* 10 (1878): 28.

24. Lewis F. Day, 'Notes on English Decorative Art in Paris 9', *British Architect* 10 (1878): 95; Day, 'Notes 13', 179.

25. *Architect* 17 (1877): near 196, 230.

26. Lewis F. Day, 'Fortnightly Notes on Ornament 26', *British Architect* 12 (1879): near 254. See also Lewis F. Day, *Instances of Accessory Art* (London; B.T. Batsford, 1880).

27. Lewis F. Day, *Nature in Ornament* (London: B.T. Batsford, 1892), illus. 70, 93.

28. Whitworth Art Gallery, T.112.1985. See Chapter 8: Textiles.

29. Victoria and Albert Museum, Archive of Art and Design, MAA, Nominal File, Edith Strode. Edith Strode was Lewis F. Day's niece.

30. Day, 'Fortnightly Notes 26', near 254.

31. I am grateful to Simon Carter for bringing this to my attention.

32. Day, *Every-day Art*, 216.

33. Lewis F. Day, *Every-day Art* (London: B.T. Batsford, 1882).

34. For a full discussion of this, see Chapter 2: The Designer for Industry.

35. Lewis F. Day, 'The Arts and Crafts Exhibition', *Art Journal* (1903): 90.

36. Day, *Every-day Art*, 194, 196.

37. Day, *Every-day Art*, 171-2.

38. Day, *Every-day Art*, 213-4.

39. Day, *Every-day Art*, 174; Lewis F. Day, 'Decorative Art', *Magazine of Art 3* (1880): 274.

40. Day, *Every-day Art*, 214.

41. Day, *Every-day Art*, 214.

42. Day, *Every-day Art*, 214.

43. Day, *Every-day Art*, 214.

44. Day, 'Decorative Art', 274; also Day, *Every-day Art*, 176.

45. Lewis F. Day, 'Decorative Art', *British Architect* 9 (1878): 18.

46. Lewis F. Day, 'Victorian Progress in Applied Design', *Art Journal* (1887): 185-202; this 199.

47. Day, 'Victorian Progress', 195.

48. Day, 'Victorian Progress', 196.

49. Christopher Dresser, *Japan: Its Architecture, Art, and Art Manufactures* (London: Longmans, Green & Co., 1882); Walter Crane, *Line and Form* (London: George Bell & Sons, 1900), 186-98.

50. Day, 'Victorian Progress', 195.

51. Day, 'Victorian Progress', 195.

52. Day, 'Notes 3', 16.

53. Day, 'Notes 3', 16.

54. Susan Weber Soros, 'The Furniture of E.W. Godwin', in *E. W. Godwin: Aesthetic Movement Architect and Designer*, ed. Susan Weber Soros (New York and London: The Bard Graduate Center for Studies in the Decorative Arts and Yale University Press, 1999), 257; see also Deanna Marohm Bendix, *Diabolical Designs: Paintings, Interiors, and Exhibitions of James McNeill Whistler* (Washington: Smithsonian Institution Press, 1995), 164-5.

55. Day, 'Victorian Progress', 192.

56. Day, 'Victorian Progress', 192.

57. Day, 'Victorian Progress', 192.

58. Day, 'Victorian Progress', 192.

59. Day, 'Victorian Progress', 192.

60. Day, 'Victorian Progress', 192.

61. Day, 'Victorian Progress', 194.

62. Day, 'Victorian Progress', 194.

63. Day, 'Victorian Progress', 194.

64. Lewis F. Day, 'Notes on English Decorative Art in Paris 5', *British Architect* 10 (1878): 40; Day, 'Victorian Progress', 199.

65. Lewis F. Day, 'Notes on English Decorative Art in Paris 8', *British Architect* 10 (1878): 87.

66. Day, 'Victorian Progress', 194.

67. Day, 'Notes 8', 87.

68. Day, 'Notes 8', 87.

69. Day, 'Victorian Progress', 194.

70. Day, 'Notes 9', 95; Day, 'Notes 4', 28.

71. Day, 'Victorian Progress', 194.

72. Day, 'Notes 13', 179.

73. Day, 'Notes 5', 40.

74. Day, 'Notes 5', 40.

75. Day, 'Notes 8', 87.

76. Day, 'Notes 8', 87.

77. See Chapter 10: Colleagues and Students. For further discussion on participation by professionals and amateurs, see Alan Crawford, 'United Kingdom: Origins and First Flowering', in *The Arts and Crafts Movement in Europe and America: Design for the Modern World*, ed. Wendy Kaplan (Los Angeles: Thames & Hudson and Los Angeles County Museum of Art, 2004), 20-67.

78. Victoria and Albert Museum (V&A), Circ. 349-1955, 349:2-1955.

79. V&A, Circ. 350-1955.

80. *Arts & Crafts* 2 (April 1905): 246.

81. Lewis F. Day, *Nature in Ornament* (London: B.T. Batsford, 1892), pl. 9, pl. 90; *Arts & Crafts* 2 (February 1905): 138, 140.

82. Lewis F. Day, 'Design Applied to Wood-Carving', *Journal of the Society of Arts* 38 (1889-1890): 786.

83. *Builder* 96 (1909): 433.

84. *Arts and Crafts*, 3 (1905): 118-20. Day's daughter Ruth was involved with the School along with her father. After his death in 1910, she succeeded him as a member of the

Committee and continued to take an active part in its programmes. 'Obituary, Ruth Morrish Day', Jan. 25, 1918, *Journal of the Royal Society of Arts* 66 (1917-18): 188.

85. Lewis F. Day, 'Design Applied to Wood-Carving', *Journal of the Society of Arts* 38 (1889-1890): 781-90, 793-802, 805-14.

86. Lewis F. Day, 'Design in Furniture', *Art Journal* (1893): 304.

87. Walter Crane, *Line and Form* (London: George Bell & Sons, 1900), 184-98.

88. Lewis F. Day, 'Arts and Crafts', *Art Journal* (1893): 332.

89. Lewis F. Day, 'Design in Furniture', *Art Journal* (1893): 302.

90. Day, 'Design in Furniture', 302.

91. Day, 'Design in Furniture', 302-3.

92. Day, 'Design in Furniture', 303.

93. Day, 'Design in Furniture', 303.

94. Day, 'Design in Furniture', 304.

95. Day, 'Design in Furniture', 303-4.

96. Day, 'Design in Furniture', 304.

97. Day, 'Design in Furniture', 304.

98. Day, 'Design in Furniture', 302.

99. Lewis F. Day, 'The Arts and Crafts Exhibition', *Magazine of Art* 20 (1896-1897): 33.

100. Day, 'Arts and Crafts Exhibition', 63.

101. Day, 'Arts and Crafts Exhibition', 32-4.

102. Day, 'Arts and Crafts Exhibition', 65-7; Lewis F. Day, 'Fifth Exhibition of the Arts and Crafts', *Art Journal* (1896): 330.

103. Day, 'Arts and Crafts Exhibition', 35-6.

104. Day, 'Arts and Crafts Exhibition', 63.

105. Lewis F. Day, 'L'Art Nouveau', *Art Journal* (1900): 293.

106. Lewis F. Day, 'Decorative Art at the Paris Exhibition', *Manchester Guardian* (June 26, 1900): 12.

107. Lewis F. Day, 'The "New Art" at South Kensington', *Manchester Guardian* (June 27, 1901): 4.

108. Day, 'L'Art Nouveau', 294.

109. Day, '"New Art" at South Kensington', 4.

110. Day, 'Decorative Art at the Paris Exhibition', 12.

111. Day, '"New Art" at South Kensington', 4.

112. Lewis F. Day, 'The New Art', *Macmillan's Magazine* 85 (1901-1902): 22.

113. Day, '"New Art" at South Kensington', 4.

114. Day, 'The New Art', 22; Day, '"New Art" at South Kensington', 4.

115. Anthony Burton, *Vision & Accident: The Story of the Victoria and Albert Museum* (London: V&A Publications, 1999), 169.

116. Day, 'L'Art Nouveau', 296.

117. Lewis F. Day, 'The Arts and Crafts Exhibition', *Art Journal* (1903): 93.

118. Day, 'Arts and Crafts Exhibition' (1903), 93.

119. Day, 'Arts and Crafts Exhibition', (1903), 94.

120. Day, 'Arts and Crafts Exhibition' (1903), 90.

121. Day, 'Arts and Crafts Exhibition' (1903), 89.

122. Day, 'Arts and Crafts Exhibition' (1903), 89.

123. Day, 'Arts and Crafts Exhibition' (1903), 89.

124. Day, 'Arts and Crafts Exhibition' (1903), 87.

125. Day, 'Arts and Exhibition' (1903), 90.

126. Day, 'Arts and Crafts Exhibition' (1903), 88.

127. Lewis F. Day, 'Decorative and Industrial Art at the Glasgow Exhibition', *Art Journal* (1901): 243.

128. Day, 'Arts and Crafts Exhibition' (1903), 90; Day, 'Decorative and Industrial Art," 301.

129. Day, 'Decorative and Industrial Art', 299.

130. Day, 'Decorative and Industrial Art', 240.

131. Day, 'Decorative and Industrial Art', 241.

132. Day, 'Decorative and Industrial Art', 240.

133. Day, 'Arts and Crafts Exhibition' (1903), 88.

134. Day, "New Art' at South Kensington', 4; Day, 'Decorative Art at the Paris Exhibition', 12.

135. Day, 'Arts and Crafts Exhibition' (1903), 89.

136. Day, 'Decorative Art at the Paris Exhibition 3', 12.

137. Day, 'Arts and Crafts Exhibition' (1903), 90.

138. Day, 'Arts and Crafts Exhibition' (1903), 89.

Chapter 8: Textiles

1. E.J. Hobsbawm, *Industry and Empire: From 1750 to the Present* Day (London: Penguin Books, 1969), 143.

2. Pamela Clabburn, *The National Trust Book of Furnishing Textiles* (London: Penguin, 1989), 56.

3. Mary Schoeser and Celia Rufey, *English and American Textiles: 1790 to the Present* (London: Thames & Hudson, 1989), 106.

4. Gordon G. Cullingham, *The Royal Windsor Tapestry Manufactory 1878-1890* (Maidenhead, Berkshire: Royal Borough of Windsor and Maidenhead, 1979), 4. Royal patronage was bestowed on the firm in 1880.

5. W.G. Thomson, 'Tapestry Weaving in England - VIII', *Art Journal* (1912): 81.

6. Victoria and Albert Museum (V&A), E.1034-1925.

7. Cullingham, 4-7, 15-6.

8. V&A, E.1033-1925, E. 1033a-1925.

9. Lewis F. Day, 'Notes on English Decorative Art in Paris 6', *British Architect* 10 (1878): 62-3.

10. Day, 'Notes 6', 62-3.

11. *A List of Tapestries in Stock at the Royal Tapestry Works Windsor* (Windsor: Royal Windsor Tapestry Manufactory, 1888).

12. Day, 'Notes 6', 62-3.

13. Day, 'Notes 6', 62-3.

14. Berkshire Record Office, D/EX788/4/58; D/EX788/4/67.

15. 'Lewis Foreman Day', *Journal of Decorative Art* 6 (1886): 891.

16. Lewis F. Day, 'Notes on English Decorative Art in Paris 15', *British Architect* 10 (1878): 239.

17. Day, 'Notes 15', 239.

18. *House Furnisher & Decorator* 1 (1871): 148.

19. *House Furnisher & Decorator* 1 (1871): 114-5.

20. *House Furnisher & Decorator* 1 (1871): 114-5.

21. *House Furnisher & Decorator* 1 (1871): 114-5.

22. *Architect* 23 (1880): 117.

23. *Architect* 23 (1880): 117.

24. Lewis F. Day, *Ornament and Its Application* (London: B.T. Batsford, 1904), 46; Lewis F. Day, *Every-day Art* (London: B.T. Batsford, 1882), 140.

25. *Architect* 23 (1880): 117.

26. 'Lewis Foreman Day', *Journal of Decorative Art*, 891.

27. Linda Parry, *Textiles of the Arts and Crafts Movement* (London: Thames and Hudson, 1988), 138.

28. James Caw, 'The Mortons of Darvel', *Art Journal* (1900): 10; Jocelyn Morton, *Three Generations in a Family Textile Firm* (London: Routledge & Kegan Paul, 1971): 111-3.

29. Victoria and Albert Museum, Archive of Art and Design (V&A, AAD): Morton Sundour Fabrics Ltd., VAA, 1948-52(2).

30. Caw, 'The Mortons', 10.

31. Morton, *Three Generations*, 2; pl. II.

32. Morton, *Three Generations*, 2.

33. Morton, *Three Generations of Textile Creation*. Exhibition Catalogue. (London: Victoria and Albert Museum, 1973), #50.

34. Schoeser and Rufey, *English and American Textiles*, 116.

35. *Cabinet Maker & Art Furnisher* 8 (1887-1888): 2; Parry, *Textiles*, 132.

36. *The Studio* 2 (1893): 24.

37. V&A: E.1314-1970; T.423-1970.

38. Mabel Cox, 'Sir Thomas Wardle and the Art of Dyeing and Printing', *The Artist* 19 (1897): 211.

39. *The Artist* 19 (1897): 215.

40. Parry, *Textiles*, 152.

41. *The Artist* 19 (1897): 214.

42. *Builder* 77 (1899): 531.

43. The V&A has about a half-dozen printed cottons and velveteens with floral and palmette patterns designed by Day that may have been produced by Wardle & Co.

44. David Thompson (former archivist) and Susan T. Swannell (archivist), Brinton's Carpets, Ltd., interview 28 Nov., 2001.

45. Thompson and Swannell, 28 Nov., 2001.

46. Thompson and Swannell, 28 Nov., 2001. For additional designs by Day held by Brinton's, see Chapter 2: The Designer for Industry.

47. J. Neville Bartlett, *Carpeting the Millions: The Growth of Britain's Carpet Industry* (Edinburgh: John Donald, 1978), 12.

48. Walter Crane and Lewis F. Day, *Moot Points: Friendly Disputes on Art & Industry* (London: B.T. Batsford, 1903), 88. He also stressed that large surfaces in a room should form a relaxing backdrop for the eye.

49. Lewis F. Day, *Pattern Design* (London: B.T. Batsford, 1903), 104, 109.

50. Day, *Pattern Design*, 104, illus. 131.

51. Temma Day continued to add to the embroidery collection after her husband's death and bequeathed over 300 items to the Corporation of Manchester. The collection is now held by the Manchester City Galleries, Gallery of Costume, Platt Hall, Rusholme. *Catalogue of the Lewis F. Day Collection of Embroideries* (Manchester: Manchester City Art Galleries, 1930).

52. *Art Workers' Quarterly* 2 (1903): 154.

53. Day, 'Notes 15', 239.

54. Lewis F. Day, *Nature in Ornament* (London: B.T. Batsford, 1892), 93, illus. 70.

55. Day, 'Fortnightly Notes on Ornament 26', *British Architect* 12 (1879), near 254.

56. Lewis F. Day and Mary Buckle, *Art in Needlework* (London: B.T. Batsford, 1900).

57. *Magazine of Art* 25 (1901): 94. Two of Day's students became noted embroider-esses: Beatrice Waldram and Louisa Pesel (A.F.P., 'The Work of Beatrice Waldram', *Arts and Crafts* 4 (1905-06): 75; Parry, *Textiles*, 141.

58. *Art Journal* (1906): 91.

59. Lewis F. Day, *Nature and Ornament II: Ornament the Finished Product of Design* (London: B.T. Batsford, 1909): 8, 11.

60. Lewis F. Day, 'Some Conclusions', *Art Journal* (1909), 200.

61. *St. Louis International Exhibition 1904. The British Section*. (London: Royal Commission, 1906), 315-6.

62. V&A: T.82-1946.

63. Lewis F. Day, 'Victorian Progress in Applied Design', *Art Journal* (1887): 200.

64. Lewis F. Day, 'A Tour-de-Force in Damask', *Art Journal* (1895): 286.

65. George Trobridge, 'Design in Linen Damask', *Magazine of Art* 24 (1900): 11.

66. Trobridge, 'Design', 11; Day, 'Tour-de-Force', 286.

67. Day, 'Victorian Progress', 200; Trobridge, 'Design', 11.

68. 'Art Handiwork and Manufacture', *Art Journal* (1905): 187.

69. Rosa Crandon Gill, 'Damask, Napery, and Needlework', *Art Journal* (1891): 179.

70. Trobridge, 'Design', 11.

71. Day, 'Victorian Progress', 200.

72. Gill, 'Damask', 179; *Art Journal* (1905): 187; *Arts and Crafts* 4 (1905-6): 105; Trobridge, 'Design', 11-12.

73. 'Tour-de-Force', 287.

74. Trobridge, 'Design', 11.

75. Trobridge, 'Design', 11; Schoeser and Rufey, *English and American Textiles*, 66.

76. *Art Journal* (1905): 187-8.

77. I am grateful to Linda Parry for her insights on textile retailing, interview, 5 Dec., 2003.

78. *Art Journal* (1899), inside front cover.

79. Gill, 'Damask', 182.

80. Day, 'Tour-de-Force', 286.

81. *Art Journal* (1905): 187-9.

82. Day, *Nature*, 134, 174.

83. *Art Journal* (1905): 187.

84. Day, 'Tour-de-Force', 286.

85. Day, *Ornament*, 48; Trobridge, 'Design', 12.

86. Trobridge, 10-2.

87. Gill, 'Damask', 180.

88. Gill, *'Damask'*, 180; *Art Journal* (1899), inside front cover.

89. Gill, 'Damask', 180

90. Day, *Nature*, 172. For a full discussion of Day's sources of inspiration and his views on adapting nature to purpose and materials, see Chapter 2: The Designer for Industry.

91. An example of one of these is at the Geffrye Museum, 0441-6, Box 38, tag temp.0421.

92. Gill, 'Damask', 179.

93. Gill, 'Damask', 179-80.

94. 'Note on a Table Cloth Designed by Walter Crane for John Wilson & Sons', Cheltenham Museum and Art Gallery.

95. Gill, 'Damask', 180; Trobridge, 'Design', 10-12; *Art Journal* (1905): 187.

96. Lewis F. Day, 'Decorative Art 8', *British Architect* 10 (1878): 189.

97. Day, 'Tour-de-Force', 287.

98. Day, *Ornament*, 301.

99. Day, 'Tour-de-Force', 287.

100. Lewis F. Day, *Pattern Design* (London: B.T. Batsford, 1903), 263-4.

101. Trobridge, 'Design', 12.

102. Day, 'Tour-de-Force', 287.

103. Day, 'Tour-de-Force', 287.

104. Trobridge, 'Design', 12.

105. *Magazine of Art* 24 (1900): 12.

106. *Jubilee 1881-1931* (Ramsbottom, Lancashire: Turnbull & Stockdale Ltd., 1931, 13; Lewis F. Day, 'Progress in Cotton Printing', *Art Journal* (1895): 50. *Jubilee 1881-1931* was privately published by the firm and given as a gift to supportive customers. I am grateful to Edward M. Turnbull for this information.

107. Lewis F. Day, 'Decorative Art 12', *British Architect* 10 (1878): 253.

108. *Jubilee*, 13.

109. *Jubilee*, 12-3.

110. *Jubilee*, 15-7.

111. *Jubilee*, 17, 19.

112. *Jubilee*, 13, 19, 27-9, 33, 45.

113. National Archives: BT 50/5, #2487, reg. 26 February 1884.

114. *Jubilee*, 23.

115. *Jubilee*, 19; *The Furnisher* (1899-1900), inside front cover.

116. Day, 'Victorian Progress', 201.

117. *Jubilee*, 19.

118. Parry, *Textiles*, 149.

119. *Jubilee*, 19; V&A AAD, Turnbull & Stockdale, Nominal File 54/163.

120. Crane and Day, *Moot Points*, 52.

121. *Jubilee*, 25.

122. *Jubilee*, 25.

123. *Jubilee*, 21.

124. Parry, *Textiles*, 149.

125. *Art Journal* (1891): 108-13, 230-6; *Art Journal* (1895): 50-3.

126. Lewis F. Day, 'Wall Coverings and Hangings at the Paris Exhibition', *Art Journal Supplement, Paris Exhibition 1900*, 161-5; 163; *Paris Exhibition 1900. British Official Catalogue* (London: Royal Commission, 1900), 120; B. Bernard, ed., *Anglo-Saxon Guide to the Paris Exhibition 1900* (London: Boot & Son, 1900), 7.

127. *Art Workers' Quarterly* 3 (1904): 62.

128. *Jubilee*, 27.

129. *Jubilee*, 19.

130. Lewis F. Day, 'Fortnightly Notes on Ornament 2', *British Architect* 11 (1879): 25.

131. *Art Journal Supplement, Paris Exhibition 1900*, 346.

132. Day, *Nature*, 83.

133. Day, *Pattern Design*, 163.

134. Day, *Nature*, 205.

135. Lucie H. Armstrong, 'Chintzes and Cretonnes', *Art Journal* (1891): 113.

136. Day, *Nature*, 80-3; 79.

137. Aymer Vallance, 'Velvets, Velveteens, and Plushes', *Art Journal* (1891): 234.

138. *Art Journal Supplement, Paris Exhibition 1900*, 346.

139. Lewis F. Day, 'Cotton Printing', *Catalogue of Works Exhibited by Members of the Northern Art Workers Guild of the City of Manchester September 26 to October 22 1898* (Manchester: Chorlton & Knowles, 1898), 12.

140. Day, *Ornament*, 37.

141. *Art Journal Supplement, Paris Exhibition 1900*, 346.

142. Walter Crane, *William Morris to Whistler: Papers and Addresses on Art and Craft and the Commonweal* (London: G. Bell & Sons, 1911), 232; Lewis F. Day, 'L'Art Nouveau', *Art Journal* (1900): 294.

143. See Chapter 6: Tiles and Art Pottery.

144. Vallance, 'Velvets', 234; Elizabeth Aslin, *The Aesthetic Movement: Prelude to Art Nouveau* (Frederick A. Praeger, 1969), 177, 189, citing Julius Hoffmann, Jr., ed., *Fur das Kuntsgewerbe*, Stuttgart Bilderschatz, 1892.

145. *St. Louis International Exhibition 1904: The British Section* (London: Royal Commission, 1906), 255, 257, 327; *Art Journal* (1906): 993-4.

146. Heal order books, V&A, AAD/1978/2/193/1, 1904-09.

147. *Art Journal* (1895): 50-3; *Catalogue of Works Exhibited by*

Members of the Northern Art Workers' Guild of the City of Manchester September 26 to October 22 1898 (Manchester: Chorlton & Knowles, 1898), 8-13.

148. *House Beautiful* 5 (1899): 164-8.

149. Cox, 'Sir Thomas Wardle', 212.

150. Day, 'Cotton Printing', 9.

151. Day, 'Cotton Printing', 11.

152. Day, 'Cotton Printing', 9-11.

153. I am grateful to Linda Parry for her insights on textile printing methods.

154. Day, 'Progress', 53.

155. Day, 'Progress', 53.

156. Day, 'Progress', 50.

157. Day, 'Cotton Printing', 11.

158. Day, 'Cotton Printing', 11.

159. Day, 'Progress', 50.

160. Day, 'Cotton Printing', 8-9.

Chapter 9: The Domestic Interior

1. c.1904 Day moved to 15 Taviton Street, Gordon Square, where he lived until his death in 1910.

2. Lewis F. Day, 'How to Make the Most of a Museum', *Journal of the Royal Society of Arts* 56 (1907-8): 152.

3. 'Obituary', *Manchester Guardian* (Apr. 19, 1910): 8.

4. *Journal of Decorative Art, Supplement* 7 (1887): x; 'Lewis Foreman Day', *Journal of Decorative Art* 6 (1886): 892; Lewis F. Day, 'The Place of Pictures in the Decoration of a Room', *Magazine of Art* 4 (1881): 323. In 1880-1 Day directed the redecoration of the Town Hall at Hull, and an original drawing for the ceiling of the Council Chamber, signed and dated 1880, has survived. Victoria and Albert Museum (V&A), E.995-1911. The *Journal of Decorative Art* (1886) referred to Day's work on the decoration of Barnwood House, near Gloucester, but this has not been independently verified.

5. 'Lewis Foreman Day', *Journal of Decorative Art*, 892.

6. No original drawings of full or significant portions of interiors appear to have survived.

7. Lewis F. Day, 'Another Moot Point: An Imaginary Debate, Lewis F. Day v. Hansard', *Art Journal* (1904): 160.

8. W. Hamish Fraser, *The Coming of the Mass Market, 1850-1914* (London: Macmillan, 1981), 54-6.

9. Charles Locke Eastlake, *Hints on Household Taste: In Furniture, Upholstery, and Other Details* (London: Longmans, Green, 1868); Robert W. Edis, *Decoration and Furniture of Town Houses* (London: C. Kegan Paul, 1881); Clarence Chatham Cook, *The House Beautiful: Essays on Beds and Tables, Stools and Candlesticks* (New York: Scribner, Armstrong, 1878); William John Loftie, *A Plea for Art in the House; with a Special Reference to the Economy of Collecting Works of Art, and the Importance of Taste in Education and Morals*. Art at Home Series, edited by William Loftie (London: Macmillan, 1876); Mary Eliza Haweis, *The Art of Decoration* (London: Chatto & Windus, 1881); J.E. (Jane Ellen Frith) Panton, *Nooks and Corners* (London: Warn & Downer, 1889); Mrs. C.S. (Dorothy Constance) Peel, *The New Home: Treating of the Arrangement, Decoration and Furnishing of a House of Medium Size to be Maintained by a Moderate Income* (London: Archibald Constable, 1898).

10. Fraser, *Mass Market*, 25; K. Theodore Hoppen, *The Mid-Victorian Generation 1846-1886* (Oxford: Oxford University Press, 1998), 35.

11. Mrs. C.S. (Dorothy Constance) Peel, *How to Keep House* (London: Archibald Constable, 1902), 32-5.

12. *Pall Mall Gazette* (Dec. 29, 1892): 4.

13. Full citations for Day's articles and books are given in the Appendix: Selected Bibliography.

14. Day, *Every-day Art*, 165.

15. Lewis F. Day, 'How to Hang Pictures', *Magazine of Art* 5 (1882): 58.

16. Day, *Every-day Art*, 163.

17. Day, *Every-day Art*, 163.

18. Day, *Every-day Art*, 187.

19. Day, *Every-day Art*, 178.

20. Day, *Every-day Art*, 178.

21. Day, 'How to Hang Pictures', 58; John D. Crace, 'Household Taste', *Builder* 42 (1882): 244; Day, *Every-day Art*, 179.

22. Day, *Every-day Art*, 161-2; Day, 'Decorative Art 4', 355.

23. Lewis F. Day, 'The Arts About Us', lecture to the Institute of British Decorators, *Journal of Decorative Art* 23 (1903): 7; Day, *Every-day Art*, 153; Lewis F. Day, 'The Art and Trade of House Decoration', *Journal of Decorative Art* 22 (1902): 323.

24. Day, *Every-day Art*, 258.

25. Day, *Every-day Art*, 180; Day, 'Arts About Us', 6-7; Day, *Every-day Art*, 219.

26. Day, *Every-day Art*, 220, 202; Day, 'Arts About Us', 6-7.

27. Day, *Every-day Art*, 259-60; Ralph N. Wornum, *Analysis of Ornament: The Characteristics of Styles* (London: Chapman & Hall, 1882, 7th ed.) Wornum's book was originally published in 1855, with numerous subsequent editions.

28. Day, *Every-day Art*, 35-6; 259.

29. Crace, 'Household Taste', 243; Day, 'Arts About Us', 6.

30. Crace, 'Household Taste', 244-5; Lewis F. Day, 'The Woman's Part in Domestic Decoration', *Magazine of Art* 4 (1881): 459.

31. Day, *Every-day Art*, 180; Lewis F. Day, 'Decorative Art 4', *Magazine of Art* 3 (1880): 355.

32. Day, *Every-day Art*, 71, 194.

33. Day, *Every-day Art*, 187-8.

34. Day, *Every-day Art*, 205.

35. Lewis F. Day, 'Fortnightly Notes on Ornament 6', *British Architect* 11 (1879): 112.

36. Day, *Every-day* Art, 205; Day, 'Arts About Us', 6-7.

37. Day, 'Fortnightly Notes 6', 113; Day, 'Art and Trade', 324; Lewis F. Day, 'Modernity in Decoration', *Journal of Decorative Art* 24 (1904): 127; Day, 'Arts About Us', 7.

38. Day, *Every-day Art*, 162; Day, 'Arts About Us', 7.

39. Day, *Every-day* Art, 71-2.

40. Day, *Every-day Art*, 202-3.

41. Day, 'A Kensington Interior', *Art Journal* (1893): 142.

42. Day, *Every-day Art*, 226; Day, 'Woman's Part', 459; Day, *Every-day Art*, 7.

43. Lewis F. Day, 'How to Decorate a Room', *Magazine of Art* 4 (1881): 186; Day, *Every-day Art*, 191-4.

44. Day, *Every-day Art*, 191.

45. Day, *Every-day Art*, 191-3.

46. Day, *Every-day Art*, 191.

47. Day, *Every-day Art*, 193-4.

48. Day, *Every-day Art*, 194.

49. Day, *Every-day Art*, 192-3.

50. Day, *Every-day Art*, 205-6.

51. Day, *Every-day Art*, 207-8.

52. Day, *Every-day Art*, 207.

53. Day, *Every-day Art*, 207-8, 210.

54. Day, *Every-day Art*, 208; Day, 'Art and Trade', 323.

55. Day, *Every-day Art*, 208.

56. Day, *Every-day Art*, 208-9. For a more detailed discussion of wall treatments, see Chapter 5: Wallpaper.

57. Day, *Every-day Art*, 114-5.

58. Day, *Every-day Art*, 116-7.

59. Day, *Every-day Art*, 210.

60. Day, *Every-day Art*, 115-6.

61. Day, *Every-day Art*, 209-10.

62. Day, *Every-day Art*, 212.

63. Day, *Every-day Art*, 212, 254; 'Decorative Do's and Don't's', *Journal of Decorative Art* 18 (1898): 199.

64. Day, 'Woman's Part', 458.

65. Day, *Every-day Art*, 257.

66. Day, *Every-day Art*, 210-1.

67. Day, *Every-day Art*, 210.

68. Day, *Every-day Art*, 210-1.

69. Day, *Every-day Art*, 213.

70. Day, *Every-day Art*, 196.

71. Day, *Every-day Art*, 178, 211.

72. Day, *Every-day Art*, 213-4.

73. Edis, *Decoration and Furniture*, 16.

74. Edis, *Decoration and Furniture*, 16; Loftie, *Plea for Art*, 30-1; Day, *Every-day Art*, 214, 176. For a full discussion of Day's views, see Chapter 7: Clocks and Furniture.

75. Day, *Every-day Art*, 188.

76. Day, *Every-day Art*, 189; Crace, 'Household Taste', 245.

77. Day, *Every-day Art*, 198.

78. Day, *Every-day Art*, 189.

79. Day, *Every-day Art*, 189.

80. Day, *Every-day Art*, 200.

81. Day, *Every-day Art*, 201.

82. Day, *Every-day Art*, 201; Day, 'Art and Trade', 324.

83. Day, *Every-day Art*, 198.

84. Day, *Every-day Art*, 212.

85. Day, *Every-day Art*, 212.

86. Day, *Every-day Art*, 200-6.

87. Day, *Every-day-Art*, 217.

88. Day, *Every-day Art*, 211.

89. Day, *Every-day Art*, 217.

90. Day, *Every-day Art*, 215.

91. Day, *Every-day Art*, 212-3.

92. Day, *Every-day Art*, 213.

93. Day, *Every-day Art*, 214.

94. Day, *Every-day Art*, 177; Day, 'Decorative Art 4', 358.

95. Day, *Every-day Art*, 214-5.

96. Day, 'Art and Trade' 320-5; 'Mr. Lewis F. Day on House Decoration', *House Beautiful* 13 (1903): 273-4.

97. Day, *Every-day Art*, 180.

98. Day, *Every-day Art*, 179-80.

99. Day, *Every-day Art*, 179-80.

100. Day, *Every-day Art*, 176.

101. Day, 'Arts About Us', 6.

102. Day, 'Kensington Interior', 144.

103. Day, *Every-day Art*, 166.

104. Day, 'Art and Trade', 322-3.

105. Day, 'Art and Trade', 324.

106. Day, *Every-day Art*, 172.

107. Day, *Every-day Art*, 182.

108. Day, *Every-day Art*, 181.

109. Day, 'Fortnightly Notes 6', 112.

110. Day, 'Art and Trade', 325.

111. Day, 'Fortnightly Notes 6', 112.

112. Day, *Every-day Art*, 172.

113. Day, *Every-day Art*, 173-4.

114. Day, *Every-day Art*, 174.

115. Day, 'Arts About Us', 6.

116. Day, *Every-day Art*, 172.

117. Day, 'Arts About Us', 6.

118. Day, 'Decorative Art 4', 355-9.

119. Crace, 'Household Taste', 244.

120. Day, 'Art and Trade', 323.

121. Day, 'Art and Trade', 323.

122. Day, 'Art and Trade', 323.

123. Day, 'Art and Trade', 323.

124. Day, *Every-day Art*, 166; Day, 'Art and Trade', 321.

125. Day, *Every-day Art*, 169.

126. Day, *Every-day Art*, 170-1.

127. Day, 'Art and Trade', 323.

128. Day, 'Art and Trade', 322.

129. Day, 'Art and Trade', 320.

130. Day, 'Art and Trade', 321.

131. Day, 'Art and Trade', 322.

Chapter 10: Colleagues and Students

1. 'Obituary', *Glasgow Herald* (April 19, 1910): 8; 'Obituary', *Journal of Decorative Art* 30 (1910): 161.

2. Martin Nadaud, *Histoire des Classes Ouvrieres en Angleterre* (Paris, 1872), referenced in Jose Harris, *Private Lives, Public Spirit: Britain 1870-1914* (London: Penguin Books, 1994), 220.

3. *Builder* 28 (1870): 900.

4. *Architect* 5 (1871): 305; *Architect* 5 (1871): 37-8; Lewis F. Day, 'Art and Life', *Macmillan's Magazine* 85 (1901-2): 433.

5. *Builder* 26 (1868): 825; *Builder* 27 (1869): 20. The text does not appear to have been published.

6. Lewis F. Day, 'Stained Glass: Its Application to Domestic Architecture', *Architect* 7 (1872): 59-60; Lewis F. Day, 'Some Lessons From Old Glass', *Architect* 35 (1886): 47-8, 50-3, 68-70.

7. 'Lewis Foreman Day', *Journal of Decorative Art* 6 (1886): 891; Walter Crane, *An Artist's Reminiscences* (London: Methuen & Co., 1907; reissued Detroit: Singing Tree Press, 1968), 223.

8. *Architect* 1 (1869): 80; 'Lewis Foreman Day', *Journal of Decorative Art*, 891; *Architect* 4 (1870): 261-2.

9. *Architect* 4 (1870): 262; *Builder* 27 (1869): 894.

10. Society of Arts, *Royal Charter*, 1847.

11. *Journal of the Society of Arts* 38 (1889-90): 3; 'Obituary', *Journal of the Royal Society of Arts* 58 (1910): 560.

12. For a full discussion of Day's views on the rôle of the designer, see Chapter 2: The Designer for Industry.

13. 'Obituary', *Journal of the Royal Society of Arts*, 560.

14. Lewis F. Day, 'Stained Glass Windows: As They Were, Are, and Should Be' *Journal of the Society Arts* 30 (1882): 292-306.

15. Lewis F. Day, 'The Principles and Practice of Ornamental Design 1-4', *Journal of the Society of Arts* 35 (1886-7): 91-101, 105-15, 118-28, 132-44.

16. Lewis F. Day, 'Craftsman and Manufacturer', *Journal of the Society of Arts* 36 (1887-8): 635-43.

17. Lewis F. Day, 'Design Applied to Wood-Carving 1-3', *Journal of the Society of Arts* 38 (1889-90): 738, 781-90, 793-802, 805-14.

18. Lewis F. Day, 'Some Masters of Ornament 1-4', *Journal of the Society of Arts* 41 (1892-3): 793-803, 805-15, 817-26, 830-40; Lewis F. Day, 'Design in Lettering 1-4', *Journal of the Society of Arts* 45 (1896-7): 1103-6, 1106-12, 1115-20, 1120-5.

19. Lewis F. Day, 'The Making of a Stained Glass Window', *Journal of the Society of Arts* 46 (1897-8): 421-30; Lewis F. Day, 'How to Make the Most of a Museum', *Journal of the Society of Arts* 56 (1907-8): 146-55; 782.

20. *Journal of the Society of Arts* 41 (1892-3): 826-7.

21. *Journal of the Society of Arts* 53 (1904-5): 6; Elizabeth Rycroft, 'Lewis Foreman Day, 1845-1910, and the Society of Arts', *Journal of the Royal Society of Arts* (1992): 334-5.

22. *Journal of the Royal Society of Arts* 58 (1910): 454.

23. Crane, *Artist's Reminiscences*, 223-4.

24. Crane, *Artist's Reminiscences*, p. 224; also Walter Crane, 'The English Revival of Decorative Art', *Fortnightly Review* 58 (1892): 815-6.

25. Crane, *Artist's Reminiscences*, 223; Peter Stansky, *Redesigning the World: William Morris, the 1880s, and the Arts and Crafts* (Princeton, New Jersey: Princeton University Press, 1985), 142.

26. Crane, *Artist's Reminiscences*, 224.

27. E.S. Prior, 'The Origins of the Guild', in H.J.L.J Masse, *The Art-Workers' Guild 1884-1934* (Oxford: Art-Workers' Guild, 1935), 9; Crane, *Artist's Reminiscences*, 224.

28. Prior, 'Origins', 7; Masse, *Art-Workers' Guild*, 22.

29. Masse, *Art-Workers' Guild*, 133-4; Prior, 'Origins', 6-13.

30. Prior, 'Origins', 7.

31. Masse, *Art-Workers' Guild*, 47-50, 81.

32. Masse, *Art*-Workers' *Guild*, 3.

33. Masse, *Art-Workers' Guild*, 80.

34. William Burton, Preface, *Catalogue of Works Exhibited by Members of the Northern Art Workers' Guild Exhibition at the City Art Gallery Manchester, September 26 to October 22, 1898* (Manchester: Chorlton & Knowles, 1898); Crane, *Artist's Reminiscences*, 480.

35. Lewis F. Day, 'Cotton Printing', *Catalogue of Works Exhibited by Members of the Northern Art Workers' Guild Exhibition at the City Art Gallery Manchester, September 26 to October 22, 1898* (Manchester: Chorlton & Knowles, 1898), 8-13.

36. Lewis F. Day, 'Design and Handicraft', *Catalogue of Works Exhibited by Members of the Northern Art Workers' Guild* (Manchester: Municipal School of Technology, 1903), 16-21.

37. Stansky, *Redesigning*, 178.

38. Masse, *Art Workers' Guild*, 25-7; Crane, *Artist's Reminiscences*, 298.

39. Crane, *Artist's Reminiscences*, 298.

40. Papers Concerning the Founding of the Arts and Crafts Exhibition Society, Victoria and Albert Museum, Archive of Art and Design (V&A, AAD), 1/15-1980; Minutes of the General Committee of the Arts and Crafts Exhibition Society, May 25, 1887, V&A, AAD, 1/40-1980.

41. Minutes of the General Committee of the Arts and Crafts Exhibition Society, Apr. 6, 1888, V&A, AAD 1/20-1980.

42. Minutes of the General Committee of the Arts and Crafts Exhibition Society, Jan. 5, 1889, V&A, AAD 1/42-1980; Crane, *Artist's Reminiscences*, 299-301.

43. Minutes of the General Committee of the Arts and Crafts Exhibition Society, Mar. 5, 1888, V&A, AAD, 1/40-1980.

44. Crane, *Artist's Reminiscences*, 298.

45. Masse, *Art-Workers Guild*, 85.

46. Lewis F. Day, 'Of Designs and Working Drawings', *Arts and Crafts Exhibition Society. Catalogue of the 2nd Exhibition*. (London: The Society, 1889), 16, 93-102.

47. *Arts and Crafts Exhibition Society. Catalogue of the 4th Exhibition*. (London: The Society, 1893, n.p.

48. Minutes of the General Committee of the Arts and Crafts Exhibition Society, 13 Nov., 1896, V&A, AAD 1/43-1980.

49. Walter Crane, 'Preface', *Arts and Crafts Exhibition Society. Catalogue of the 10th Exhibition*. (London: The Society, 1912), 6-17.

50. For further discussion, see Gillian Naylor, *The Arts and Crafts Movement* (London: Trefoil, 1990), 7-10.

51. Lewis F. Day, 'William Morris and His Art', Easter Art Annual, *Art Journal* (1899): 7.

52. *Year's Art* (1895-1901).

53. Society of Antiquaries,

Certificates of Candidates for Election, July 1, 1904; *Proceedings of the Society of Antiquaries of London* 23 (nd): 174-5.

54. Quentin Bell, *The Schools of Design* (London: Routledge, 1963). See Chapter 7, 'The Branch Schools.'

55. *Year's Art* (1898), 53-4.

56. *Year's Art* (1900), 59.

57. National Archives: ED 23/29: *Report of Committee of Inquiry on National Art Training School* (London: Lords of the Committee of Council of Education, 1889), 1-12; Lewis F. Day, 'Looking Back Upon South Kensington', *Art Journal* (1896): 315-8; Lewis F. Day, 'What South Kensington Is Doing', *Art Journal* (1896): 472-5; Stuart Macdonald, *The History and Philosophy of Art Education* (London: University of London Press, 1970), 294.

58. National Archives: ED 23/61, ED 23/62; Crane, *Artist's Reminiscences*, 417.

59. *Year's Art* (1898), 53; Day, 'Looking Back', *Art Journal* (1896): 318.

60. Simon Jervis, *Dictionary of Design and Designers* (London: Penguin, 1984), 438.

61. *Year's Art* (1896-1900); *Minutes Relating to the Royal College of Art for 1899*, National Archives, ED 23/39; 'Obituary', *Journal of the Royal Society of Arts*, 560; 'Obituary', *Times* (April 19, 1910):13; 'Obituary', *Journal of Decorative Art* 30 (1910): 161.

62. 'Obituary', *Journal of the Royal Society of Arts*, 560.

63. Victoria and Albert Museum, National Art Library, 97.PP.85: *Directory (Revised to June 1892) with Regulations for Establishing and Conducting Science and Art Schools and Classes* (London: Department of Science and Art of the Committee of Council on Education, 1892), v, 266-9 and *Directory (Revised to June 1893) with Regulations for Establishing and Conducting Science and Art Schools and Classes* (London: Department of Science and Art of the Committee of Council on Education, 1893), vi, 272-4; Elizabeth Rycroft, 'Lewis Foreman Day, 1845-1910', *Journal of the Society of Decorative Arts* (1989): 21.

64. *Year's Art* (1891-1909).

65. Day, 'What South Kensington Is Doing', 472-3.

66. Lewis F. Day, 'National Competition in Design – 1899', *Art Journal* (1899): 281.

67. Day, 'Looking Back', 316.

68. Lewis F. Day, 'National Competition Awards', *Art Journal* (1894): 350.

69. Day, 'National Competition in Design', 281.

70. Day, 'National Competition Awards', 350.

71. Day, 'Looking Back', 318.

72. Day, 'National Competition in Design', 281; Day, 'Looking Back', 317.

73. *Third International Art Congress for the Development of Drawing and Art Teaching and Their Application to Industries. Transactions* (London: Offices of the Congress, 1908), 190.

74. *Journal of Decorative Art* (1896): 216.

75. 'Obituary, '*Glasgow Herald*, 8.

76. 'Obituary', *Journal of the Royal Society of Arts*, 560.

77. 'Obituary', *British Architect* 73 (1910):273; George T.B. Davis, 'The Future of House Decoration', *House Beautiful* 5 (1899): 264.

78. *Journal of the Royal Society of Arts* 58 (1909-10): 267.

79. A.F.P., 'The Work of Beatrice Waldram', *Arts and Crafts* 4 (1905): 75-80.

80. Linda Parry, *Textiles of the Arts and Crafts Movement* (London: Thames & Hudson, 1988), 141.

81. Davis, 'Future of House Decoration', 264.

82. Ellen Paul Denker, 'The Grammar of Nature: Arts and Crafts China Painting', in Bert Denker, ed. *The Substance of Style: Perspectives on the American Arts and Crafts Movement* (Winterthur, Delaware: Henry Francis du Pont Winterthur Museum, 1996), 284.

83. Barbara Morris, *Inspiration for Design* (London: Victoria and Albert Museum, 1986), 77.

84. Morris, *Inspiration*, 77-8; *Commencement Programs* (Philadelphia: Philadelphia School of Design, 1900-05). I am grateful to Page Talbott for providing additional information.

85. Lindsay Butterfield, *Autobiography* (unpublished manuscript, undated), 85; Morris, *Inspiration*, 78.

86. Board of Education, *Victoria and Albert Museum: Report of the Committee of Re-arrangement* (London: HMSO, 1908), 19.

87. *Committee of Re-arrangement*, 4.

88. *Committee of Re-arrangement*, 36.

89. *Committee of Re-arrangement*, 4-5.

90. Anthony Burton, *Vision & Accident: The Story of the Victoria & Albert Museum* (London: V&A Publications, 1999), 158.

91. Burton, *Vision*, 158.

92. *Committee of Re-arrangement*, 6.

93. *Committee of Re-arrangement*, 17.

94. *Committee of Re-arrangement*, 18-9.

95. Burton, *Vision*, 163.

96. Henry Trueman Wood, 'Lewis Foreman Day', *Dictionary of National Biography*, Supplement 1901-11 (Oxford: Oxford University Press, 1912), 483.

97. Day, 'How to Make', 146-55, 782.

98. Day, 'How to Make', 149.

99. Day, 'How to Make', 149-50.

100. Day, 'How to Make', 148-9.

101. *Journal of the Royal Society of Arts* 56 (1907-8): 782.

102. Lewis F. Day, 'Manchester's Ideal Art Gallery', *Manchester Guardian* (March 19, 1907): 14.

103. *Third International Art Congress*, 486-7.

104. *Third International Art Congress*, 486-7.

105. *Builder* 96 (1909): 235-6.

106. *Daily Graphic* (Feb. 17, 1909).

107. *Art Chronicle* (Apr. 2, 1910).

108. Butterfield, *Autobiography*, 50.

109. Lewis F. Day, 'Design', *Reports of a Conference on the Teaching of Drawing in Elementary and Secondary Schools* (London: London County Council, 1912), 62-7.

110. Lewis F. Day, 'Art Teaching in Relation to Industrial Design', *Third International Art Congress for the Development of Drawing and Art Teaching and Their Application to Industries. Transaction.* (London: Office of the Congress, 1908), 188-97.

111. Christopher Frayling, *Royal College of Art: One Hundred Years of Art & Design* (London: Barrie & Jenkins, 1987), 71; Council of Art, *Memorandum Upon the Royal College of Art Submitted to the Board of Education*, June 1900, National Archives, ED 23/43; Jervis, *Dictionary*, 438.

112. Day, 'Art Teaching', 191.

113. Day, 'Art Teaching', 191.

114. Frayling, *Royal College*, 78-9.

115. When Day died in April 1910, the Board of Education had not yet considered his report. Frayling, *Royal College*, 78-9.

116. Day, 'Art Teaching', 188-97.

117. Day, 'Art Teaching', 193.

118. Day, 'Art Teaching', 195-6.

119. Day, 'Art Teaching', 195.

120. Day, 'Art Teaching', 194.

121. Day, 'Art Teaching', 190-1.

122. Day, 'Design', 63.

123. Day, 'Design', 66.

124. Day, 'Design', 66.

125. Day, 'Art Teaching', 193.

126. Day, 'Art Teaching', 192.

127. Day, 'Art Teaching', 196.

128. Day, 'Art Teaching', 188-97.

129. Day, 'Art Teaching', 193.

130. Day, 'Design', 65-6.

131. Day, 'Design', 66.

SELECTED BIBLIOGRAPHY OF LEWIS F. DAY'S BOOKS AND ARTICLES

This Selected Bibliography includes Lewis F. Day's books, journal and magazine articles, essays contributed to exhibition catalogues, and published lectures. As is evident from this list, Day was a prolific writer. While this bibliography does not include every piece he wrote, it does represent the majority of his published writings, and in particular, those that pertain to the content of this book. References in the text to the writings of other authors are cited in full in the Endnotes.

A few clarifications may prove helpful in navigating this list and locating specific entries. Writings are listed by year of publication, and within a given year they are listed alphabetically. The original date and place of publication is given for books and articles.

Although Day's books went through many subsequent editions and reprintings, and his articles were often reprinted or paraphrased in other periodicals, these are not listed.

As researchers are painfully aware, bibliographic data for many 19th- and early 20th-century periodicals is incomplete. For the sake of consistency, this order has been followed: title of the article; periodical in which the article was first published; volume number (whenever available); year of publication, and relevant pages. For daily newspapers, the title of the article, newspaper, date of publication, and pages are given. Some daily newspapers had more than one edition, and consequently pagination may vary between editions.

Day reviewed books authored by others, and these are listed towards the end of entries for a given year. He also co-authored several works, and these appear as the final entry for that year. In the relatively few cases of undated or unpaginated publications, these are indicated by n.d. or n.p., respectively.

1872

'Stained Glass: Its Application to Domestic Architecture'. *Architect* 7 (1872): 59-60.

1877

'An Apology for the Conventional'. *Art Journal* (1877): 5-7.

1878

'Decorative Art 1-5'. *British Architect* 9 (1878): 18, 64-5, 109-10, 181-2, 276-7.

'Decorative Art 6-12'. *British Architect* 10 (1878): 52-3, 79-80, 189-90, 228-30, 241-2, 252-3, 253.

'Notes on English Decorative Art in Paris 1'. *British Architect* 9 (1878): 301-2.

'Notes on English Decorative Art in Paris 2-15'. *British Architect* 10 (1878): 4-5, 15-6, 28, 40, 62-3, 70-1, 87, 95-6, 104, 126-7, 170-1, 179-80, 199-200, 239.

1879

'Fortnightly Notes on Ornament 1-13'. *British Architect* 11 (1879): 4, 24-5, 44, 68-9, 93, 112, 132, 152, 172, 203-4, 224, 232, 244, 262-3.

'Fortnightly Notes on Ornament 14-26'. *British Architect* 12 (1879): 15, 35, 51, 70-1, 101, 121-2, 141, 162, 181, 201, 220-1, 240, 250-1.

1880

'Decorative Art 1-4'. *Magazine of Art* 3 (1880): 103-7, 191-8, 270-5, 355-9.

'Dragons'. *Magazine of Art* 3 (1880): 375-9.

Instances of Accessory Art. London: B.T. Batsford, 1880.

Tapestry Painting and Its Application. London: Howell & James, 1880.

1881

'Copyright in Design'. *British Architect* 15 (1881): 13-4.

'The Decoration of the Home'. *Magazine of Art* 4 (1881): 98-101.

'How to Decorate a Room'. *Magazine of Art* 4 (1881): 182-6.

'Neutral Ground'. *Art Journal* (1881): 360-1.

'Old Glass at Munich'. *British Architect* 15 (1881): 153-4, 165-6.

'The Place of Pictures in the Decoration of a Room'. *Magazine of Art* 4 (1881): 319-23.

'The Woman's Part in Domestic Decoration'. *Magazine of Art* 4 (1881): 457-63.

1882

'Can Work Be Too Well Done?' *British Architect* 17 (1882): 61.

'The Earliest Cathedral Windows'. *Magazine of Art* 5 (1882): 19-23.

'Eclecticism'. *British Architect* 17 (1882): 146.

'Eclecticism, or Choice'. *British Architect* 17 (1882): 170.

Every-day Art. London: B.T. Batsford, 1882.

'Glass-Painting in the Fourteenth Century'. *Magazine of Art* 5 (1882): 289-94.

'How to Hang Pictures'. *Magazine of Art* 5 (1882): 58-60.

'The Lowly Arts'. *Art Journal* (1882): 341-4.

'Reproduction and Copyism'. *British Architect* 17 (1882): 195.

'The Obsolete Teachings of Owen Jones'. *Decorator and Furnisher* 1 (1882-3): 10.

'On Some Characteristics of Renaissance Ornament'. *Art Journal* (1882): 89-92.

'On Stained Glass Windows'. *British Architect* 17 (1882): 76-8.

'Stained Glass Windows: As They Were, Are, and Should Be'. *Journal of the Society of Arts* 30 (1881-2): 292-303.

1883

'The Art of the Future'. *British Architect* 19 (1883): 18-9.

'Contradictory Decoration'. *British Architect* 19 (1883): 13.

'Door Decoration'. *Decorator and Furnisher* 1 (1882-3): 106, 108.

'Later Gothic Glass in England'. *Magazine of Art* 6 (1883) 420-4.

The Nodding Mandarin: A Tragedy in China. London: Simpkin & Marshall, 1883.

'The Ornament of the Period'. *Architect* *29* (1883): 60-1, 78-80.

'The Relation of the Architect to the Decorator'. *British Architect* 19 (1883): 125-6.

'The Trade Element in Professional Practice'. *British Architect* 20 (1883): 203.

1884

'Alas, Poor Stevens!' *Architect* 32 (1884): 382-3.

'First Impressions of Glass Mosaic'. *Architect* 32 (1884): 2-3.

'Geometric Ornament'. *Architect* 32 (1884): 80-1.

'Is It Desirable that an Architect Should Limit the Character or Extent of His Work?' *British Architect* 21 (1884): 145.

1885

'Chartered Wrong'. *Architect* 33 (1885): 157-8.

'Cinque-Cento Picture Windows'. *Magazine of Art* 8 (1885): 341-6.

'From Gothic Glass to Renaissance'. *Magazine of Art* 8 (1885): 282-6.

'Glass-Painting: The Beginning of the End'. *Magazine of Art* 8 (1885): 377-81.

'Grotesques'. *Art Journal* (1885): 45-8.

'Hildescheim'. *Art Journal* (1885): 209-13.

'Machine-Made Art'. *Art Journal* (1885): 107-10.

'Wings'. *Art Journal* (1885): 165-8.

1886

'Animals in Decoration: a Rejoinder'. *Magazine of Art* 9 (1886): 494-5.

'Art in Metalwork'. *Magazine of Art* 9 (1886): 241-4.

'Artist and Artisan'. *Magazine of Art* 9 (1886): 294-5.

'Principles and Practice of Ornamental Design 1-4'. *Journal of the Society of Arts* 35 (1886-7): 91-101, 105-15, 118-28, 132-44.

'The Profession of Art'. *Magazine of Art* 9 (1886): 122-3.

'Some East Indian Wood Carving'. *Magazine of Art* 9 (1886): 328-32.

'Some Lessons from Old Glass'. *Architect* 35 (1886): 47-8, 50-3, 68-70.

1887

'An Artist in Design'. *Magazine of Art* 10 (1887): 95-100.

The Anatomy of Pattern. London: B.T. Batsford, 1887.

'Meaning in Ornament'. *Art Journal* (1887): 237-40.

'New Coins for Old'. *Magazine of Art* 10 (1887): 416-20.

The Planning of Ornament. London: B.T. Batsford, 1887.

'Victorian Progress in Applied Design'. *Art Journal* (1887): 185-202.

'Unavailable Art'. *Art Journal* (1887): 366-8.

1888

The Application of Ornament. London: B.T. Batsford, 1888.

'Art and Handicraft'. *Magazine of Art* 11 (1888): 410-11.

'Craftsman and Manufacturer'. *Journal of the Society of Arts* 36 (1887-8): 635-43.

'The Crown: Its Growth and Development'. *Magazine of Art* 11 (1888): 277-83.

'Fashion and Manufacture'. *Transactions of the National Association for the Advancement of Art and Its Application to Industry, Liverpool Meeting, 1888.* London: National Association for the Advancement of Art and Its Application to Industry, 1888: 218-28.

'The Relationship of Architecture to the Arts and Crafts'. *British Architect* 30 (1888): 452-3.

'The Stopping Point in Ornament'. *Magazine of Art* 11 (1888): 372-7.

1889

'Insignia of Mayoralty'. *Magazine of Art* 12 (1889): 27-31.

'Of Designs and Working Drawings'. *Arts and Crafts Exhibition Society. Catalogue of the 2nd Exhibition.* London: The Society, 1889: 93-102.

1890

'Design Applied to Wood-Carving 1-3'. *Journal of the Society of Arts* 38 (1889-90): 781-90, 793-802, 805-14.

'A Lesson in Ornament: The Vine and its Modifications 1-2'. *Magazine of Art* 13 (1890): 127-32, 151-6.

Some Principles of Every-day Art. London: B.T. Batsford, 1890.

'The Work of Morel-Ladeuil'. *Magazine of Art* 13 (1890): 271-5.

1892

'Artistic Homes: The Choice of Wall-papers'. *Magazine of Art* 15 (1892): 165-71.

'Artistic Homes: Wall-paper Decoration'. *Magazine of Art* 15 (1892): 189-95.

'Modern Mosaic in England'. *Architectural Record* 2 (1892): 79-88.

Nature in Ornament. London; B.T. Batsford, 1892.

1893

'Arts and Crafts'. *Art Journal* (1893): 330-3.

'The Criticism of Decorative Art: An Editorial Statement'. *Art Journal* (1893): 64.

'Decoration by Correspondence'. *Art Journal* (1893): 85-8.

'Design in Furniture'. *Art Journal* (1893): 302-4.

'A Kensington Interior'. *Art Journal* (1893): 139-44.

'Some British Industries at Chicago'. Chicago Exhibition Supplement, *Art Journal* (1893): v-viii.

'Some Masters of Ornament 1-4'. *Journal of the Society of Arts* 41 (1892-3): 793-803, 805-15, 817-26, 830-40.

1894

'Art in the Shop Windows'. *Art Journal* (1894): 52-4.

'Early Italian Art'. *Art Journal* (1894): 120-1.

'French Decorative Art in London'. *Art Journal* (1894): 5-6.

'National Competition Awards, 1894'. *Art Journal* (1894): 350.

'The Wonder of Siena 1-2'. *Magazine of Art* 17 (1894): 368-71, 410-13.

1895

'Carving at Carpenters' Hall, in 'Notes on Recent Decorative Work.' *Art Journal* (1895): 252.

Commentary, in *Note on a Table Cloth Designed by Walter Crane for John Wilson & Sons.* London: John Wilson & Sons, n.d.: 3-10.

'Progress in Cotton Printing'. *Art Journal* (1895): 50-3.

'Some New National Acquisitions'. *Art Journal* (1895): 279-80.

'Tiles'. *Art Journal* (1895): 343-8.

'A Tour-de-Force in Damask'. *Art Journal* (1895): 286-7.

1896

'The Arts and Crafts Exhibition 1-2'. *Magazine of Art* 20 (1896-7): 32-40, 63-8.

'The Coin of the Realm'. *Magazine of Art* 19 (1896): 275-9.

'Decorative Art at the Winter Exhibitions'. *Art Journal* (1896): 92-4.

'Fifth Exhibition of the Arts and Crafts'. *Art Journal* (1896): 329-32.

'Looking Back Upon South Kensington'. *Art Journal* (1896): 315-8.

'Needle-Craft'. *Art Journal* (1896): 20.

'Notes on Decorative Art'. *Art Journal* (1896): 254-6.

'Stencilled Stuffs'. *Magazine of Art* 20 (1896-7): 40-1.

'There Is Nothing Like Leather'. *Magazine of Art* 19 (1896): 88-91.

'What South Kensington Is Doing'. *Magazine of Art* 19 (1896): 472-5.

'The Windows of a New Church'. *Art Journal* (1896): 197-200.

Book Review: *Cartoons for the Cause*, by Walter Crane. *Art Journal* (1896): 320.

1897

'Aids to Design'. *Art Journal* (1897): 319.

Alphabets Old and New. London: B.T. Batsford, 1897.

'Art in Advertising'. *Art Journal* (1897): 49-53

'Design in Lettering 1-4'. *Journal of the Society of Arts* 45 (1896-7): 1103-6, 1106-12, 1115-20, 1120-25.

'European Enamels'. *Art Journal* (1897): 284-5.

'Fans, Ancient and Modern'. *Art Journal* (1897): 253.

'Turning and Throwing'. *Art Journal* (1897): 380-1.

Windows: A Book about Stained and Painted Glass. London: B.T. Batsford, 1897.

Book Review: *Plants and Their Application to Ornament*, Eugene Grasset, ed. *Art Journal* (1897): 255-6.

[with E. R. Pennell] 'Le Puy en Velay, France: The Most Picturesque Place in the World'. *Architectural Review* 3 (1897-8):1-7, 61-8.

1898

'Art for Winter Evenings'. *Art Journal* (1898): 49-52.

'Cotton Printing'. *Catalogue of Works Exhibited by Members of the Northern Art Workers' Guild Exhibition at the City Art Gallery, Manchester, September 26 to October 22, 1898.* Manchester: Chorlton & Knowles, 1898: 8-13.

'French Wood-Carvings'. *Magazine of Art* 22 (1898): 104-6.

'Home Arts at the Albert Hall'. *Art Journal* (1898): 223-4.

'The Making of a Stained Glass Window'. *Journal of the Society of Arts* 46 (1897-8): 421-8.

'Modernity in Bookbinding'. *Art Journal* (1898): 218-20.

1899

'Home Arts and Industries'. *Art Journal* (1899): 218-9.

'Introduction'. In Anton Seder, *Sketch Designs for Artistic Objects in Pottery and Glass, Metalwork, Etc.* London: B.T. Batsford, 1899: n.p.

'The National Competition in Design 1899'. *Art Journal* (1899): 281-2.

'William Morris and His Art'. Easter Art Annual, *Art Journal* (1899).

Book Review: *The Bases of Design*, by Walter Crane. *Magazine of Art* 23 (1899): 168-9.

Book Review: *William Morris and His Art*, by Aymer Vallance. *Magazine of Art* 23 (1899): 29-32.

1900

'L'Art Nouveau'. *Art Journal* (1900): 293-7.

'Decorative Art at the Paris Exhibition 1-4'. *Manchester Guardian* (11 June, 20 June, 26 June, 27 July, 1900): 3, 4, 12, 10.

'The Glass at Paris'. *Art Journal Supplement, Paris Exhibition 1900* (1900): 265-70.

'Iron and Steel Work at the Burlington Fine Arts Club'. *Magazine of Art* 24 (1900): 317-8.

'Modern Pottery at the Paris Exhibition'. *Art Journal Supplement, Paris Exhibition 1900* (1900): 97-102.

'Old Decorative Work at the Paris Exhibition'. *Manchester Guardian* (11 September, 1900): 7.

'Wall Coverings and Hangings at the Paris Exhibition'. *Art Journal Supplement, Paris Exhibition 1900* (1900): 161-5.

[with Mary Buckle] *Art in Needlework*. London: B.T. Batsford, 1900.

1901

'Animals in Design: A Friendly Dispute Between Walter Crane and Lewis F. Day'. *Art Journal* (1901): 212-4.

'Art and Life'. *Macmillan's Magazine* (1901-2): 429-38.

'The Artist and His Trade'. *Art Journal* (1901): 118-9.

'An Artist in Floral Design'. *Art Journal* (1901): 369-73.

'Cloth Bookbindings'. *Art Journal* (1901): 113-7.

'The Decoration of the Page: A Friendly Dispute Between Painter and Decorator'. *Art Journal* (1901): 377-8.

'Decorative and Industrial Art at the Glasgow Exhibition 1-5'. *Art Journal* (1901): 215-6, 237-43, 273-7, 299-302, 327-30.

'Favrile Glass'. *Magazine of Art* 25 (1901): 541-4.

'Mere Ornament 1-2'. *Art Journal* (1901): 18-22, 49-52.

'Modern Stencilling'. *Art Journal* (1901): 143-9.

'The New Art'. *Macmillan's Magazine* 85 (1901-2): 19-23.

'The "New Art" at South Kensington'. *Manchester Guardian* (June 27, 1901): 4.

'Walter Crane: A Hungarian Appreciation'. *Art Journal* (1901): 79-82.

1902

'The Art and Trade of House Decoration'. *Journal of Decorative Art* 22 (1902): 320-6.

'Book Illustration: A Friendly Dispute Between Edward F. Brewtnall, R.W.S., and Lewis F. Day'. *Art Journal* (1902): 315-6.

'Cosmopolitan Art: A Friendly Dispute Between Mr. Selwyn Image and Mr. Lewis F. Day'. *Art Journal* (1902): 374-5.

'An Heraldic Artist of Today'. *Art Journal* (1902): 49-54.

Lettering in Ornament. London: B.T. Batsford, 1902.

'Poetic Ornament: A Friendly Dispute Between Walter Crane and Lewis F. Day'. *Art Journal* (1902): 270-2.

'Tooled Bookbindings'. *Art Journal* (1902): 317-20.

1903

'The Arts About Us'. *Journal of Decorative Art* 23 (1903): 6-8.

'The Arts and Crafts Exhibition'. *Art Journal* (1903): 87-94.

'Design and Handicraft'. *Catalogue of Works Exhibited by Members of the Northern Art Workers' Guild, Municipal School of Technology, Manchester*. Manchester: The Guild, 1903: 16-21.

Pattern Design. London: B.T. Batsford, 1903.

Stained Glass. Victoria and Albert Museum Art Handbook. London: Chapman & Hall, 1903.

'A Twentieth-Century Herbal'. *Art Journal* (1903): 246-8.

'William Morris and His Decorative Art.' *Contemporary Review* (1903): 787-96.

[with Walter Crane] *Moot Points: Friendly Disputes on Art & Industry Between Walter Crane and Lewis F. Day*. London: B.T. Batsford, 1903.

1904

'Another Moot Point: An Imaginary Debate, Lewis F. Day v. Hansard'. *Art Journal* (1904): 160-1.

'Modernity in Decoration'. *Decorator* (22 May, 22 June, 22 July, 1904): 317-9, 345-7, 1-2.

'The New Lancastrian Pottery'. *Art Journal* (1904): 201-4.

Ornament and Its Application. London: B.T. Batsford, 1904.

'The Profession of Art'. *Macmillan's Magazine* 91 (1904-5): 342-9.

1905

'A Disciple of William Morris'. *Art Journal* (1905): 84-9.

'The Eighth Exhibition of the Arts and Crafts Society'. *Magazine of Fine Arts* 1 (1905-6): 353-63.

'English Gothic Needlework at the Burlington Fine Arts Club'. *Art Journal* (1905): 222-3.

'A Missing Link'. *Art Journal* (1905): 282-4.

1906

'English Poster Design'. *Art Journal* (1906): 97-116.

'A New Thing in Metal Inlay'. *Art Journal* (1906): 40-2.

1907

Enamelling. London: B.T. Batsford, 1907.

'Manchester's Ideal Art Gallery'. *Manchester Guardian* (19 March, 1907): 14.

'Old German Ironwork in London'. *Manchester Guardian* (23 April, 1907): 5.

1908

'Art Teaching in Relation to Industrial Design'. *Third International Art Congress for the Development of Drawing and Art Teaching and Their Application to Industries. Transaction*. London: Office of the Congress, 1908: 188-97.

'Design'. *Reports of a Conference on the Teaching of Drawing in Elementary and Secondary Schools*. London: London County Council, 1912: 62-7.

'How to Make the Most of a Museum'. *Journal of the Royal Society of Arts* (1907-8): 146-55.

Nature and Ornament 1: Nature the Raw Material of Design. London: B.T. Batsford, 1908.

'Originality and Tradition in Design'. *Builder* 94 (1908): 421-4.

1909

Nature and Ornament 2: Ornament the Finished Product of Design. London: B.T. Batsford, 1909.

'Some Conclusions'. *Art Journal* (1909): 199-200.

1910

'Glass, Stained'. *Encyclopaedia Britannica*, Vol. 12. 11th ed. Cambridge: University Press, 1910: 105-12.

1911

Penmanship of the XVI, XVII and XVIII Centuries. London: B.T. Batsford, 1911.

INDEX

Page numbers in **bold** refer to images and/or captions